THE WORLD'S
Your Oyster!

The life and times
of a *lady* baby boomer

Shirley McLaughlin

Published 2017

Copyright © Shirley McLaughlin

All Rights Reserved. No part of this publication may be reproduced or transitted in any form by any means, electronic or mechanical, including photocopy, recording or any other information storage and retrieval system, without prior permission in writing from the publisher.

ISBN: 978-0-6482064-0-8

Typeset in 12.5pt Adobe Garamond Pro Regular
Printed on Bulky News 80gsm
Printed by Foot & Playsted, Launceston, Tasmania 7250

This is a work of non-fiction and includes many true stories involving friends, foes and associates, living or dead. Some names, places and incidents have been changed by the author to protect their privacy, innocence and/or guilt.

Also by Shirley McLaughlin

SELF HELP

Appointing People (Staff Recruitment in the 1990s) 1990
Minding your Own Business (101 Great Ways to Make Money) 1991 Reprinted 1992
Making a Living (The Job Seeker's Manual) 1992 Reprinted 1992
Give Yourself a Job (A Guide to Starting Your Own Business) 1993
  WRIGHTBOOKS
Money for Life   (The Complete Guide to Australian Home Budgeting) 1997
  ALLEN & UNWIN

BIOGRAPHY

The Driving Force (200 Years of Australian Success Stories) 1995 Reprinted 1995
  ANGUS & ROBERTSON

FICTION

A Good Reputation (UK) 1995
    Released in Australia and New Zealand as: *Billy Batchelor* - 1996
    Translated in The Netherlands as: *Dromen die Nooit Vervagen* - 1997

Acknowledgments

Special thanks to
Editor, Katherine Drew: katherine.drew@icloud.com
Foot and Playsted:
    Director, Ross Martin - www.footandplaysted.com.au
    Artwork, cover and formatting: Cathy Chapman
    Proof reading: Cecilia Chiu
Project consultant, Lesley Williams, Major Street Publishing

For Bev and Rob, Steven, Dale and Jeff

In memory of

Margery and Alan, Craig, Gareth and Beris

With apologies here and hereafter

to William Shakespeare...

You're talented, young, healthy and wealthy – the world's your oyster!
(The Merry Wives of Windsor)

S/he that filches from me my good name
Robs me of that which not enriches me
And makes me poor indeed.
(Othello)

Much virtue in "if"
(As You Like It)

There's daggers in wo/men's smiles
(Macbeth)

Just one rose, By any other name would smell as sweet
(Romeo and Juliet)

**All the world's a stage,
And all the men and women merely players;
They have their exits and their entrances,
And one woman in her time plays many parts,
Her acts being seven ages...**

CURTAIN UP...

PROLOGUE ix

AGE ONE (1947 – 1963)
At first the infant 1

The chance of it all 3
A country upbringing..10
Growing up takes forever for some 16
Learning the hard facts of life 18
The changing times 29
New beginnings 35

1st Intermission..37

AGE TWO (1964 – 1969)
And then the lover 39

The rocky road to adulthood 40
Prelude to freedom..48
Sex, guns, friends and refugees 50
Family secrets unravelling..62
Moving out, moving back, moving on...66
Husband No. 1 76
In at the deaths – whack, whack, whack! 80

2nd Intermission..91

AGE THREE (1970 – 1973)
Then the lady soldier 93

The American Dream 96
Deportation, fate and *If it's Tuesday, it's Belgium!* 117
Television productions, personalities and persecutors 128
Husband No. 2 153
In search of a dentist on the streets of London.....................164
A tragic homecoming 167

3rd Intermission 169

AGE FOUR (1974 – 1986)
And then the justice..171

The changing times 172
24/7 Flesh-to-Flesh enterprises 175
Déjà vu…close to home in the underworld 201
Burying icons, placing executives, dismissing lovers...........210
There's money in oysters 231
Jason Bourne, eat your heart out! 239
Life happens when you're looking the other way................252

4th Intermission 257

AGE FIVE (1987 – 2000)
Full of wise saws and modern instances...........................261

In the real world now 262
The fabulous forties 265
Full circle 284
Becoming an author 288
You could write a book about it!..294

The shifting times 304
Life ends, and life begins again 311

5th *Intermission* 315

AGE SIX (2001 – 2016)
The sixth age shifts into lean and sensible slacks 317

The chance of it all 318
Lucky 13, and a bedsit in Chelsea 322
When the going gets tough 328
The *real* third time lucky 332
Old Adelaide boy offers cougar bride new start...................337
The Apple Isle 341
The changing times 344
A handful of friends 346
Looking forward – with love 354

6th *Intermission* 360

AGE SEVEN (2017 –   )
Last scene of all..367

EPILOGUE..369

PROLOGUE

The plays and poems of William Shakespeare continue to be read and studied as passionately today as they were hundreds of years ago. Ironically, the reasons why this is so are largely unacknowledged by students and book lovers of the four generations born in the 20th century.

The Bard was born at a time when men's view of life was considered superior. This ancient conceit had emerged thousands of years before when the gods of all religions instructed ardent believers to, effectively, take dictation and disseminate their words far and wide. These holy books have been translated and re-translated innumerably since the invention of the printing press. And nothing has changed.

Yet Shakespeare's words, which describe the human preoccupations of power, corruption, double standards, thwarted freedom, brutality and vulnerability, were translated from English into hundreds of languages and remain universal and timeless.

His characterisations of the male and female of the human species were perceptive for a young man, at any time in history. He wrote without prejudice about the good, bad and ugly traits of both sexes, his prose time and again demonstrating that women were the more gifted performers and stage managers and that they could sometimes be even more ruthless than their male counterparts. Shakespeare depicted women as being more resourceful in overcoming the myriad challenges of life because of the primary role they were born to play.

The path I've followed during my 70 years on this mortal coil hasn't ever been traditional. Born a free spirit, I have broken most of the rules that my parents, in particular my independent, thespian, headstrong mother tirelessly taught me. I was brought up at a time in history when it was the norm for daughters to leave the familial home to marry and have children.

But I was different, dramatically different, and to me the prospect of conquering the world beyond the four walls of my stable family home was exciting! Mum used to say that you can do anything you want to, as long as you want it badly enough – and want it I did! On receiving the key to the door several years before I turned 21, I embarked on a journey that has been adventurous, hazardous, quixotic, passionate, adrenaline-charged and forever changing. Along the way I've been much loved and even enjoyed several heady tilts at my own 15 minutes' of fame.

I have also survived a few near-death experiences and more than one woman's fair share of 'knives in the back', bullying and abuse. I've crossed paths with loneliness and regret too, but only momentarily: having always been easily bored, I fast became adept at altering course. The show, or a new show, must go on!

The life I've led has shown me time and time again that truth is stranger than fiction and that everyone I've ever met has a story worth the telling, but the idea of writing a memoir had no appeal.

Long ago I'd sworn off producing one, being of the opinion that the format was nothing more than a thinly veiled pursuit of eminence, driven by vanity and informed by selective and fading memories. Plus, since I had no children of my own and most of the McLaughlin family were dead and gone, it would be only my beloved nephews Steven and Dale who'd read the thing – and then probably out of obligation! As far as I was concerned: 'When this strange eventful history is over', just bid me good riddance and send me packing.

In my 50s, whilst basking in the glow of a long-coveted literary career, I stumbled upon an idea, the research of which would require an authentic chronological review of my life. Essentially a self-help tome, it was inevitably part-autobiographical. Its working title was *The Facts of Life* and I sent the draft to an erstwhile publisher Geoff Wright and his daughter Lesley for their professional opinions. Their response was prompt and insightful, and included the recommendation that I should re-think my approach. Apparently, *The Facts of Life* had the makings of a memoir!

My response to their advice had been just as prompt. I'd stashed the manuscript in a bottom drawer and moved on.

But a book I chanced to read more recently started my reticence unravelling. I'd read that the English language boasted one million more words than the other 2,700 languages in use today. To learn that the average English-speaking adult's vocabulary comprised 3,000 words was certainly interesting, but when I read that 10 year-olds have a lexicon of about 7,000 words, and that they use about 700 every hour, I started to sweat. I was sure I'd be hard pressed to manage 700 words a day anymore!

I've always loved a challenge and told myself that writing my life story would deliver many benefits. Not only would it help to revitalise my vocabulary, but it might also delay the onset of any dementia lurking secretly in the wings. With justifications like these, perhaps it would be downright negligent not to write a memoir?

But I was still unconvinced. The heart of the matter had to be confronted. I didn't believe I could write an honest memoir. Warts and all? The highs and lows, and my part in them? I didn't want to horn-blow either, and the thought of telling the bad stuff was distressing.

Since childhood I've loved writing from the perspective of a fictional character and telling their stories as if they were my own – and it's still the best fun! Yet, ironically, I've been paid to write non-fiction (in first-person) for a large slice of my life.

I wondered if it would be possible to combine both approaches. Could I produce work that would faithfully convey the events of my life whilst also telling an entertaining story? And, an even more horrifying prospect, would I be the one to write and tell stories about me? I've always been fascinated with bridges – driving over them and wondering what was on the other side – but I suspected this was one too far.

I'd been sitting, staring at a blank screen for what seemed like hours when the solution occurred to me: 'I need a muse!'

Not a muse like Epicurus's inspiring goddesses, or Somerset Maugham's *Ashendon*. I needed to be able to tell my story from someone else's point of view (POV). It would free me from self-consciousness, and allow me to adopt a voice that was candid and contemporary, raunchy and emotive, and imbued with plenty of humour. And, as Shakespeare himself would say: 'The truth will out.'

I realised that I already knew the men for the job. Back when they were both still in short pants, my sister Bev had told her two sons that I was the only 'Auntie Mame' they were ever going to get so they might as well relax and enjoy me. Steven and Dale are the children I never had. We've always been close and they know me all too well.

Steven summed up my subsequent and rather long-winded proposition to him thus: 'Sort of an unauthorised autobiography, then?'

He'd been bemused that their Aunty Shirl could seriously believe that he and Dale would deliver an unbiased, uncensored account of her life and times (especially her life!) but warmed to the idea when I reiterated that it would be me putting the pen to paper, albeit through his and his brother's eyes.

Well, thanks a lot Bev for always being right, and hugs and kisses to Steve and Dale for helping me find a way to cross the Rubicon.

'The die is cast.'

AGE ONE (1947 – 1963)

At first the infant
Howling and puking in his nurse's arms;
And then, the whining school-girl, with her satchel
And shining morning face, creeping like snail,
Unwillingly to school.

13th May 1947

It was a dark and stormy night when the four-pound baby girl came into the world. She didn't scream. She didn't cry. In fact, she didn't perform like a 'normal' newborn at all and wasn't expected to live through the night.

Silent and deathly still, the infant lay swathed in a moth-eaten Army-issue blanket at one end of a large, chipped enamel bath in a make-shift hospital in country Victoria. Despite the traumatic birth, her pixie face was strangely wan and wrinkle free. This, along with the voluminous grey wrappings, gave her the look of her sister Beverley's neglected porcelain doll.

Four days later and the baby still hadn't cried. She'd sneezed, twice, and sucked fitfully on the teats of old glass bottles of fresh cow's milk that was delivered daily by a nearby farmer's lackey.

The Infirmary was a condemned house in Healesville. It had been loaned to the town in 1937 when its original owner joined the navy and left to see the world, never to return. The old bath had served as a basinet for premature babies throughout the long, still haunting war and two others just like it had recently been added to the unplumbed wash-room grandly titled 'The Nursery' in order to meet the growing demand of post-war births.

The Matron, Sister Mary, a resolute, practical woman with the physical strength of a man, was the only trained nurse in town and her daily routine demanded everything she had to give. She would kneel on the hard concrete floor, leaning over a fixed trough to wash the babies and dry them in her arms, a bucket nearby for the regular vomiters. During the war her duties had been less predictable. Mainly she'd tended to servicemen sent home early because of their wounds, physical and mental. That job had certainly required tough love and she'd felt a kind of pious comfort that the Diggers who couldn't be saved were generally ready to meet their Maker.

Caring for the sudden influx of babies, with and without fathers, was another matter altogether, especially under circumstances like this. Her best efforts were not going to save this infinitesimal life unless God-The-Father-Of-All-Creation could be persuaded to intervene.

Mary prayed as she'd never prayed before, not only for the nameless, motionless little soul who appeared for all the world to have no interest in being, but also for her mother, Margery, who was still fighting intermittently for her life. The baby's parents were neighbours and friends of Sister Mary's. She'd delivered their first daughter Beverley on Victory Day 1945 and although her arrival hadn't exactly been smooth sailing, it now seemed a snap compared to this.

On the sixth day, when Margery's heart and the baby's pulse had all but given up and the local priest dropped by to give Mary communion in her broom-cupboard office, she campaigned to get the baby christened and blessed immediately.

'I know its irregular, Father,' she pressured him in her tight lipped way, 'but it's not the child's fault the parents are only Presbyterians.'

The priest wavered, looking up at the ceiling whilst thoughtfully stroking his non-existent hair. Mary took this to be a good sign.

'Allowing my dear friends' child to go to Purgatory would be sinful for a devout Roman Catholic, Father. Surely God would agree?'

'Have you thought of a name?' he replied with exaggerated resignation and more than a hint of human pride.

'She's got a lovely round face and black curly hair, just like Shirley Temple,' Mary responded joyfully. 'Given Margery's performance background – did you know that before she was married she was famous in the theatre and had the first women's program on the wireless? – I'm sure she would agree that Shirley is just right.'

Mary couldn't have known that Margery's own birth 35 years earlier had been identical (give or take a pound or two) to that of her second daughter, yet somehow the matron was convinced that if this poor little thing had managed to cling to life this long she was destined to be her mother's daughter – and then some. Yes, 'Shirley' would definitely 'fit the bill'.

'Shirley it is then,' the priest responded with appropriate gravity, following the matron into the second bedroom where Margery and her baby lay unconscious.

Suddenly Shirley proceeded to scream at the top of her lungs, as if declaring she'd moved past the worst of it and was at last ready to join the land of the living. Likewise, in that moment Margery withdrew her foot from the grave, propped herself up and opened her arms expectantly.

Mary swiftly obeyed the call, insisting the priest immediately perform the christening – as well as both patients' Last Rites, just in case. God was performing a miracle but, she warned severely, 'he sometimes changes his mind when his disciples don't keep their promises.'

The chance of it all

Mary was adamant that it was no accident Margery and Shirley had both survived. God was in charge. It was the beginning of a revolutionary time in modern history and He needed good people to have lots of babies who would one day return His Kingdom to a happy, safe and God-fearing place.

Most of the locals embraced the matron's reasoning as gospel. Although the world at the time was changing, it was mostly those in the big cities who felt the impact of progress. For people in the bush, life remained the same. Shirley's parents saw things differently.

'Mary's reasoning is skewed by Catholicism and country bumpkin nonsense!' Margery declared to Alan shortly after she came home with the baby. 'It's 1947, dear! We've just survived the biggest war in history and if there is a God and man was created in His image, he's got little to shout about. "His Will" is seriously beginning to grate on me. Surely it's time we took responsibility for our own actions without having to pass our successes or failure onto our supposed Maker!'

Her husband of seven years nodded but said nothing. Alan and Margery McLaughlin were, unusually for the time, of one accord – as yet unresolved.

Back before WW1, about 90 per cent of Australia's population were practising Christians and only 10 per cent lived in urban areas. In 1915 the world population was 1.8 billion. Today there are about 7.2 billion people on the planet, and half of Australia's population comprises city-dwelling, non-practising Christians. By the time Generation Z have offspring of their own, this statistic is expected to have surpassed 70 per cent!

Considering that in 1947 even established scientific facts were unimaginable to most country folk, long-term predictions didn't stand a chance. But Margery and Alan were aware. They may have been unique people who'd come from different backgrounds, but they shared much common ground. Raised in hard-working families in country Victoria and brought up in the Christian tradition, both were well-educated, avid readers; passionate explorers of history, philosophy and the English language. From early childhood, they'd also developed a deep love of nature.

Chance and circumstance and just a few degrees of separation would see them meet in a St Kilda pub in 1939, and right from the start they were unstoppable when one or the other initiated a pet conversational topic. Between curious minds there are rarely subjects that are off limits.

They'd agreed immediately that the odds of our conception, birth and genetic makeup were a matter of chance, but what we do with our lives is a matter of choice. To them, being born white, into a loving family environment on a continent with no borders was a question of luck, as was the chance of being born on planet earth at a time in history when there were no wars or natural disasters. Of all the promises (and threats) made by the gods of various religions, none had never eventuated and never would. That they might, or could, was simply down to a flight of the imagination made possible only by the unique, unexplainable gift of having a brain.

Many years later, when their daughters' minds began to ripen, their questions took an inevitable turn toward the existential. *Who am I? What's it all about? Why am I here? What is the purpose of my life? How will I know I'm in love? Is there a supreme being who made and cares about me? What should I believe?* Margery summed up thus: 'First our brain dreams, then it searches for answers to the big questions, from which we make our choices.'

Alan, who'd long connected the words 'chance' and 'choice' to scientific certainties and religious ambiguities, was enthralled to learn that Margery was not only well informed on the subjects, she was also prepared to risk being wrong rather than accept simply didactic, outmoded dogma from men of politics or the cloth. She loved the gamble of life, the sheer chance of it all.

In his wildest dreams, Alan had never imagined he could be so lucky; what a beautiful, intelligent, confident and beguiling woman she was!

Margery and Alan were part of what became known as the Great generation. The men and women of this cohort were too young to absorb much of the First World War and grew up during the Great Depression which gave way to the second. Theirs was an unsophisticated era. News of the rest of the world was minimal, late and hard to get; ill health was difficult to diagnose and treat; life was short and still in Almighty God's hands.

Bizarrely, some discoveries seemed to strengthen religious beliefs amongst the devout. Copernicus' model of the universe, which ultimately saw him put to death for heresy and blasphemy, dared to suggest that the earth was not the centre of the universe and so, by implication, neither was God. Though long verified by cosmologists and astronomers, and effectively confirmed by the respective theories of Darwin and Einstein, Copernicus' model still wasn't taught in schools. Modern discoveries about human life and the fact that the universe was continuously expanding were widely published in scientific journals and newspapers, but read and accepted by few.

Margery and Alan were two of the few. That the human being was but one of many millions of living species evolved from common ancestors, sharing 99 per cent of their DNA with chimpanzees and 33 per cent with mushrooms, had taken time for them to swallow. That 99.9 per cent of their genes were identical and 0.1 per cent contained all the differences between the shortest and tallest, blackest and whitest of the human race was a resounding leveller in their lives. In his usual economic way, Alan summarised that they were just a tiny drop in the ocean. Characteristically, Margery responded brightly. 'If there are more cells in our bodies than stars in a thousand Milky Ways, and every day our bodies create 300 billion new cells like every other living organism, we can't afford to take ourselves too seriously, Alan. We're never going to get out of here alive.'

If as somebody once said 'the brain boggles the mind,' no wonder most members of the Great and Pre boomer generations preferred not to know the facts. And little wonder God was so popular!

Alan's father, John McLaughlin, was born in Donagheady, Northern Ireland in 1858 and came to Australia with his family in the sailing ship *Thunderbolt* in 1865. He married his first wife Annie in 1883, they had five children, he purchased his first farming property in Victoria in the 1890s and Annie died in 1900. He married Harriet Marshall Potter in Melbourne in 1910 and proceeded to have another seven children. According to legend, it was years later before Harriet learned of John's previous life.

Alan was their first born and spent the first 10 years of his life on the family's farm in Mansfield, helping his father maintain the property and learning woodwork from him in the evenings. In 1920 John's ailing health prompted him to sell the farm and move the family to Auburn in Melbourne. When he died two years later, 12-year-old Alan assumed the role of 'man of the house', a responsibility he took seriously as evidenced when he sponsored the trade apprenticeships of two of his brothers 10 years later.

Alan attended Melbourne High School and a visiting lecturer sold the job of teaching for its security, knowledge, access to sport and good hours and holidays. The youngest lad in form six, Alan matriculated dux of Melbourne High with a scholarship to set him on his way.

In the early days he was just a *lowly* teacher, a term used to indicate very poor wages. Teaching wasn't considered a profession until many years later. On the job at 15 years of age, he would sometimes be left alone with classes of 40 or 50 children covering six grades in one room, 'The strap' was very much in disciplinary vogue and it was widely agreed that without it generations of children would never have learned the Three Rs – reading, 'riting and 'rithmetic.

Alan spent his 20s honing his classroom management skills, playing and teaching cricket, tennis and football, as well as developing competence in carpentry and useful men's faculties that had been cut short when his father died. Whilst he took girls to the pictures and accompanied them to functions, family weddings and the like, he was extremely self-conscious of the poorly matched, greenish glass eye he'd acquired following an accident with a screwdriver the year his father died. He may have had 20/20 vision in his one blue eye, but he hesitated to approach women, tending instead to wait for them to ask him out.

By the time he was 30 he'd been recruited as a lay preacher for the Presbyterian Church of Australia. The clergy of the day travelled hundreds of miles a week across dirt roads in unreliable old cars to spread 'the word' and tend their flocks, hence competent volunteer speakers were essential to help out on Sundays. Alan was always in demand and Bev and Shirley tagged along, dressed in their best and behaving in a manner befitting their fathers' role. Notwithstanding, the girls often nodded off during the sermon. They'd already heard it at home.

Margery McLaughlin came from Welsh stock and was born in 1912. Christened Florence Maude Julia Jones, she was called Maude for the first 24 years of her life. Her parents were free-settling immigrants and her father, Stanley Jones, was a railway worker who moved from town to town to get promotions. Her mother, Emma, was a striking, articulate woman and a firm disciplinarian with superior domestic and gardening skills.

Margery had one older brother, Stan Junior, who eventually became a successful, self-employed financial broker in Collins Street, Melbourne until the 1960 credit squeeze bankrupted him. He subsequently became the general manager of a large publishing company in Maryborough, Victoria.

By the time the Jones' children were attending secondary school, their father had been appointed station master of the Ballarat Railway Station in south-west Victoria. In the last century, during the gold-rush years, a third of the world's gold was found in the isolated settlement of Ballarat. In the first half of the 20th century, when Ballarat had become a sizeable country town, Stan's job was an important one. Most goods were transported by rail.

Margery, or 'Maude' as she was known then, was a classically beautiful young woman, and a gifted elocutionist by the time she was crowned Queen of Commerce in her final year at Ballarat High School. As was the lot of women in the '20s and '30s, she was not expected to utilise her training and talents in commercial employment. Whilst still single, living at home and assisting her mother in all things domestic, it was acceptable for her to continue her recitations at church services and functions, and to perform as a star member of the local theatre group.

Mainly to oblige her parents, she was courted by a handsome young man called Michael from a highly regarded family who took her on a 'dangerous' flight to Melbourne in his father's airplane. When they landed, he helped her out and on bended knee proposed to her. She accepted the dazzling ring but the engagement didn't last long. Michael had attained his pilot's license during their courtship without telling her and that was okay because he was a suitable husband and she was a born risk taker. When he joined the Masonic Lodge without her knowledge a few months later she could not forgive him, gave back the ring and as politely as possible asked her parents to please forgive her.

Her first steps into independent womanhood came when she started to search for a job. It was 1936 and the directors of local radio station 3BA Ballarat had agreed that the huge audience of women listening to their station, particularly on isolated farms and in small towns around the country, deserved a daily program especially for women. Margery was perfect for the job and formed the 3BA 'Friendship Circle' program with the motto: 'To have a friend – Be a friend'. In doing so she became the first woman in country Australia to host her own woman's radio program.

She'd always hated being called Maude and seized the moment to change her name to Margery Daw. She'd dreamed of changing her name as a child, and when Shirley was about the same age and wanted to know 'Why Margery Daw?' she did her best to explain.

'I rejigged a couple of nursery rhymes…' she began hesitantly.

'"Mary, Mary, quite contrary, how does your garden grow…" was my very favourite because I was bold and pretty, just like Mary, and I loved helping my mother in the garden, but the name Mary was as old-fashioned as Maude so I used to sing, "Seesaw, Margery Daw, how does your garden grow, With silver bells and cockle shells, and pretty maids all in a row." It's a bit silly really, but I never tire of the name. That's why.' Shirley thought it was wonderful.

Old timers' children's children around rural Australia still remember Margery Daw of 3BA's Friendship Circle because of the Charity she began, and the extraordinary funds she'd managed to raise for underprivileged children.

But it was to be a career cut short.

In 1938, two years after she'd begun, Margery blacked out during a live broadcast for no apparent reason and was forced to consult a specialist in Collins Street, Melbourne. He had no idea what was wrong with her and suggestions she might be working too hard and in need of rest were familiar, and ridiculous.

The on-air incident was a sign; she couldn't go back. Within weeks she turned the uncertainty of her future into an opportunity to leave the bush and move to the big smoke, quickly securing a position as a consultant in one of Melbourne's first personnel agencies.

'It was a considered choice to make my life mean something before the scientists discovered some embryonic incurable disease from one of my childhood illnesses,' she told Shirley two decades later. 'Looking back, I think I was sicker of mind than body,' she said. 'I loved the job but bailed out because I was a successful woman in a man's world and the boss was the only man I can remember who treated me with respect.'

This was a time in history when a new generation was being born into a world where women as well as men were going to be educated and free to do and be whatever they liked, but gender equality was still not yet discussed in polite company, any more than misogyny, or racism, or prejudice.

Chance may have drawn Margery and Alan together, but it was choice – theirs alone – that saw them marry.

It was a simple ceremony at Scott's Church, Ballarat, in 1940, just six months after they met. Margery was 28 and Alan was 29. There was no reception to follow. It was war time. The bride dressed in a tailored mauve skirt and jacket she made herself and they drove to Geelong in the groom's old Holden for a short honeymoon.

On day three Alan called a local doctor to their hotel. Margery had fainted and was clearly unwell. She was hospitalised immediately and recovered two days later. There was no diagnosis other than the doctor's suggestion that the episode was caused by the stress in the lead-up to the wedding.

They moved to the tiny town of Healesville, 60 miles and a long drive then from Melbourne, where Alan took up his first primary school 'head teacher' position at the local primary school.

Three months after Shirley was born, Margery fell ill with a mix of old and new symptoms and was referred to her original Collins Street specialist, Mr Graham Robertson, for tests. She was finding it difficult to walk, suffering periods of blindness, tingling fingers, tiredness, tremors, loss of balance…

finally the signs were unmistakeable. Multiple sclerosis. 'MS' for short, although there was nothing short about it.

MS is a disease of the brain and spinal cord, and back then all that was known about it was that it was an unidentified virus that interfered with the brain's ability to control the body. As a child Margery had had rheumatic fever, an inflammation of the heart valves following a bacterial infection and Mr Robertson thought this might be responsible. Antibiotics were not readily available until the 1950s, too late for her to benefit, and the early rheumatic fever now complicated the situation because of the permanent damage it had inflicted on her heart.

The prognosis wasn't good. On Margery's insistence, Mr Robertson acknowledged she was unlikely to see her daughters to primary school.

'I'll prove you wrong, doctor,' she countered decisively. Against his better knowledge, he was inclined to think she might.

Alan had sole responsibility for the primary school in Healesville, Bev was full of life and running around like any two and a half year old, and Shirley needed a nurse. Grandma Jones, widowed five months earlier, caught the first train from Mornington to Healesville and took over everything. She stayed three months until Margery was walking unaided. It would be the first of many similar journeys she would make to every 'God-forsaken' town in country Victoria where Alan was posted. The regular moves were the direct result of him needing more promotions in order to meet the costs of a young family, and to cover the medical bills ahead.

A country upbringing

Bev and Shirley were at primary school in Yarrawonga when they first overheard their parents and neighbours talking about them and their peers as a group. Their names weren't mentioned; they were simply 'Baby Boomers' – all of them! 'Goodness knows what they'll do with their lives when they grow up, if they ever do?' was a frequent utterance in their direction.

Eventually they picked up from these conversations that Bev was born too soon to be a 'boomer'.

'It's not fair,' Shirley sighed heavily. 'I'm so sorry you've missed out,' she said.

'I'm not!' Bev promptly replied, ''cos I'll always be the older sister.'

Age One

Despite 1946 being the first official year of this 'new generation', in the McLaughlin household it was 1947 that was the beginning. It's hard to fathom how two sisters branded with different titles but with only two and a half years between them could turn out so characteristically matched to their generational identities.

Shortly after the 1940s 'batch was hatched', the generation through to 1965 was carelessly saddled with a name reflecting their parents' fecundity, the term evolving in the Western world because of the increase in births when our respective nations' servicemen returned home from World War 2. First generation white Australians were pushed along by the government's national campaign to 'populate or perish,' and New Australians from Europe responded in their millions to the international advertising campaign. They arrived in ships with nothing but the promise of a fresh start. Many were alone: young, single adults who'd suffered more than most Australians would ever know.

The parents of baby boomers had yet to deal with, get over and move on from the Korean War, the Suez Canal crisis, The Cold War, the loss of loved ones in Vietnam, rampant inflation, the Berlin Wall and the threat of nuclear war. Whilst some of their baby boomer sons and daughters would serve and die in Vietnam, throughout these tumultuous years all Australians benefitted from an exceptional time of political stability and increasing prosperity. Sir Robert Menzies was prime minister from 1949 to 1966 and his conservative, pro-British nationalism suited the mores of the day. Whilst it was not an era of innovation or modernism, it was as if the wars had somehow restored Australia to one big happy Commonwealth family and the post-war boom brought low unemployment, the expansion of private enterprise, home ownership and increased living standards.

In February 1950, Alan was promoted to the role of head teacher of a small school in the northern Victorian town of Chiltern, with joint teaching and lay-preaching responsibilities in the nearby towns of Barnawatha and Springhurst. He'd commenced studying by correspondence for a Bachelor of Arts degree shortly after the honeymoon, and was in the final throes of completing his Bachelor of Education in like manner. The Victorian Education Department had already acknowledged he was going to pass with flying colours; his future was set and he figured life was as good as it was going to get.

The day after Alan and Bev's first day at the Chiltern Primary School, Shirley's imaginary new friend Wendy Barr turned up. Shirley was lonely and needed a friend.

Margery considered Wendy's arrival providential and made it her mission, whilst she still could, to teach her younger daughter everything she knew about becoming a good friend. Wendy was invited to play dress-ups, climb trees and help make and eat mud pies in the garden. She shared the responsibilities of organising 'parties', pouring the tea and handing out the sandwiches, and also learned to listen attentively to ABC music and news on the wireless, with Shirley and Mummy. On the rare occasions she was permitted to 'stay over', Wendy chose the bedtime stories. Margery talked to both girls as if they were adults and it became patently obvious that it was very handy to have a friend like Wendy Barr; she asked a lot of questions Shirley badly wanted answered. *Wendy wants to know how we got born Mummy? Why don't we have any Grandpa's? Are they all in heaven? Wendy doesn't want to go to heaven but she'd still like to know how we got born, please Mummy?*

By 1951 Bev was happily settled at school and Shirley was 'full on' and determined to catch up with her sister. Margery was enjoying a lengthy remission from her MS and grabbed the opportunity to throw a party for Shirley's fourth birthday. Recently burdened with boots and leg irons to correct flat feet and knock knees, Shirley was feeling unattractive and restricted and was allowed to leave them off for the whole day.

Half the town turned up, including the local minister and friends of Bev's, accompanied by their parents. Wendy and her parents couldn't make it because Wendy's mother was often sick too, but Shirley joined the older children in the back yard and they played unsupervised for hours, helping themselves to bread and butter smothered in hundreds and thousands, home-raised and cooked chicken legs and wings, and a large sponge birthday cake made strictly for the children.

When everyone had gone home and the ABC announcer delivered the shocking news that The Reverend John Flynn had died on duty in outback Australia, Margery began to cry. Shirley had never seen her mother cry before and asked what she desperately needed to know in one long sentence.

Margery blew her nose, wiped her eyes, took a deep breath and managed to answer in a few short sentences. 'He's gone to heaven with Grandpa Jones and Grandpa McLaughlin. The Reverend Flynn was a missionary and began the Royal Flying Doctor Service. They fly planes to help sick people in the outback of Australia. The Aboriginal people call it Country.'

Shirley absorbed the information thoughtfully then unexpectedly yawned. Margery and Alan dared to hope that that was that. It was nearly bedtime.

'Do white grandpas ever go to Hell?' she asked. 'When I grow up I don't want to be a teacher because it would be terribly boring talking to children all day. I want to become an air hostess and work for the Flying Doctors. And get paid too. Do you get paid to look after us, Mummy? When I'm flying in the sky, will I be able to see the people in the stars having their birthday parties?'

'If there are people in the stars, I'm sure you will, darling. Where did you put your boots? We need to have them ready with the irons for the morning so you'll have arches and lovely straight legs, and no more knock knees when you grow up and go flying.'

'I'm not wearing irons tomorrow Mummy,' she sighed. 'Wendy doesn't have to and I like bare feet. How much longer do I have to wear them? There's a man in the moon so there must be people in the stars!'

'There probably are, darling, but right now I want you to go to the toilet and brush your teeth, and I'll help you put your boots and irons on in the morning.'

Shirley started school in 1952. Alan was reticent because she was only four and a half and still wearing irons, but Margery insisted. 'She wrote her first story on your foolscap pad on my kitchen floor when she was three, Alan. She's ready. And so am I!'

On her second school day, Wendy Barr's mother's health worsened and the family had to move to Sydney. Shirley missed her terribly because she hated school from day one and declared she always would.

It transpired that after she'd 'borrowed' a stick of red chalk from a boy who had lots of chalk (while she 'only had a yellow one!'), Miss Hargreave had hit her on the knuckles with a ruler. She cried and cried because she was only four and a half and 'it wasn't fair.' When instructed to leave the room until she stopped crying, she ran down the passage to Alan's office. He instructed her firmly to return to class, apologise and give the chalk back. She did as she was told but she wasn't happy. She hated boys thereafter too. It wasn't an encouraging start.

There was no birthday party for Shirley in 1952. Margery was sick, Grandma Jones was struggling to maintain her commercial flower garden and a bit under the weather herself, and every spare minute Alan had was spent applying for Victorian Education Department advertisements worthy of his two bachelor degrees.

At the end of the year they moved from Chiltern to Yarrawonga, a prosperous and pretty Victorian town with a large primary school. The Murray River ran through it and its twin town of Mulwala, New South Wales. Grandma Jones' horticultural efforts were finally supplementing her pension and she'd found a part-time gardener so she caught the train from Mornington to assist throughout the move and remained for the first three months of 1953.

Margery's health had been up and down but she was now improving dramatically. She was walking without aid and became involved in tutoring and producing school plays. She'd recognised a familiar, natural talent in her younger daughter and had already begun to teach Shirley how to recite poems to convey meaning and style, using her hands and facial expressions and careful delivery of the words. 'Don't put your daughter on the stage, Mrs Worthington' was well known to her, but she'd had her moment in the sun and was determined to be a teacher, not an ego-driven stage mother. Bev showed little interest in the dramatic side of theatre but had an ear for music and a promising singing voice. She was also displaying a talent for drawing and painting.

Openly, Margery was delighted by her girls' artistic talents. Quietly, however, she worried, her fear of time running out forever nigh. 'Our girls need to acquire some survival skills whilst I can still applaud, commiserate, shepherd…don't you think?' she asked Alan. Saving money was an essential habit that 'has to be taught' and was near the top of the survival list; they both had their own little Commonwealth bank books now so that was in place. Swimming and learning to take risks 'flying through the air' from the diving board were easily accommodated; the Murray River running through town had long ensured nobody died young from drowning. Handling bullies was right up there too, but how to broach the subject? 'How can they know what to do when it starts? Unless we talk to them about it, how will they have the confidence to let us know when it happens and they need help?'

Yarrawonga was a wake-up call, on many fronts.

Age One

Margery and Alan knew better than most that prejudice, and jealousy and fear infiltrated school yards every day of the week, encouraging bullies of all denominations, races and creeds to target the ones they believed they could crush.

'Regardless of the presence of well trained, vigilant teachers, Alan, we have to grow up fast now to ensure our girls can happily take their time,' Margery warned unnecessarily.

In the 1950s bullies often focused on whether your father had gone to the war. A significant number of youngsters were living with disturbed, 'returned' fathers, many of whom were wittingly or unwittingly mentoring their sons, and sometimes daughters, to follow their angry and/or abusive lead in order to win and be in control. Those whose fathers didn't go to the war were easy targets. 'Your father's a coward!' the bullies would shout and point and slap and throw stones when the yard teacher wasn't looking. Parents were loath to discuss the past and the McLaughlin girls did not escape this trauma. Indeed, Shirley's inquisitive nature and somewhat precocious personality saw her cop the worst of it.

Alan had volunteered to go to war but had been knocked back, primarily because he only had one eye. It had never been mentioned until Shirley started asking questions following unspeakable bullying.

'Why has Dad got one blue eye and one green one?' she finally asked from the back seat of the little Ford Prefect on the long drive to Grandma's for the Christmas holidays. Although she'd left unsaid the horrid things the boys at school had said about her father, Margery twigged immediately. She apologised profusely, explained why Dad had only one eye and hadn't been permitted to participate in the war, and added that as a head teacher, he was providing 'essential services' at home.

From personal experience she knew the most common form of bullying was verbal abuse. She also knew the only way to stop a bully in his or her tracks is to take action at the very start. That, or it will continue – and worsen.

'I'm very sorry you've been treated badly,' she murmured soulfully. 'If anyone begins to bully you again, tell them you're not interested, walk away and come home and tell us immediately.'

'If I'd told you about this when it was happening Mummy,' Shirley responded benignly before Alan could get a word in, 'you'd have told Daddy and he would have punished them and then everyone would think I'd told him and it would have been much worse.'

'She's got a point, Lovely,' Alan spoke in 'teacher' voice, strong and clear. 'It might be a good idea if I get her teacher to give her a few detentions. Take the pressure off a bit, show she isn't getting any favouritism?'

'Good idea,' Margery agreed (equally as loudly) in response. 'I'm trying to think of our younger daughter as a challenge, rather than a handful. But they're both street smart!' she smiled broadly and the girls in the back seat giggled.

'They're exceptional, especially for ones so young, Lovely,' Alan replied.

He'd been calling her Lovely for years but it was the first time it had resonated with Shirley. 'You are lovely and I love you and Dad very much, Mum,' she said as she leaned forward, wrapping her arms around her mother in the front seat, managing to plant a kiss on her right ear.

Margery welled up, Alan and Bev smiled broadly and, whether consciously deciding at the time or not, Shirley never called her mother 'Mummy' again.

Growing up takes forever for some

The years rushed by. The younger daughter wished they would go faster and the older wondered why her sister was in such a hurry.

Despite or because of the special circumstances governing their upbringing, Bev and Shirley were relatively self-reliant from an early age. They knew they did much more around the house than their peers yet never felt hardly done by or restricted in their activities. Santa Claus had given them their first bicycles when they started school so they walked or rode everywhere, took themselves to sporting pursuits, music and dance lessons, and played unsupervised in their or their friends' back yards every day of the week.

Most Australian-born children could pretty much do as they liked between the hours of 3.00pm when school finished, and 5.30pm when 'tea' was served. Breaking the rules earned a firm smack (although Shirley usually avoided the hit because she was a very fast runner) and generally some extra chores, but they had countless hours of freedom throughout their growing years and often 'played up' without anyone seeming to notice. Puberty brought with it certain caveats on the rules, but it didn't bother them much. The world was their oyster.

Age One

Notwithstanding, 1953 was a turbulent, stressful year for the McLaughlin family, collectively and individually. It began with another MS relapse for Margery, King Edward's death and news that Princess Elizabeth was going to be crowned Queen of England. Alan's plans to buy a television set on which to watch the Coronation, however, had to be postponed until the Melbourne Olympic Games the following year; there was no spare cash to buy one.

To ease her disappointment, Shirley's parents threw her a birthday party but half way through serving the sausage rolls and pies, Margery started vomiting in the kitchen. Alan took over the cleaning up whilst quickly hustling the parents and children out of the house and on to the road to play, calling them back for birthday cake minus candles and song. The guests got the message and hastily left, but half an hour later a torrential storm ruined Alan's tomatoes, potatoes and peas in the garden, and Debbie the family cocker-spaniel named after Debbie Reynolds was hurt whilst sniffing out a rabbit and had to have surgery the next day. It was 'all Alan's fault' because Margery's cigarette had started a fire in the bedroom during the storm and Alan was too busy saving the house when he should have been outside saving Debbie from breaking her leg.

When the fire was out (not before it had ruined the side table and left a large black hole in the carpet) and Bev was sound asleep and Shirley was pretending to be, Alan made a pot of tea and joined Margery in the living room. She embarked on a strange diatribe about how Mother Nature was in control and there was nothing they could do about it so they just had to learn to go with Her and adjust. Alan replied that Mother Nature would lose some of her power if only his Lovely would give up smoking, to which Margery quoted a recent study from England that showed there was no proof that smoking caused lung cancer.

Shirley began listening more earnestly to their conversations after that. She had so much to learn and there wasn't a moment to lose.

Bev began piano lessons and started singing in the school choir and Margery taught Shirley some Henry Lawson and C.J. Dennis poems to recite at two major functions later in the year. She'd also cast her as the Fairy Godmother in *Soot and The Fairies*, a part she carried off remarkably well given it was her first singing/acting role.

Margery had cast the wrong daughter for a musical, a mistake she wouldn't make again. Whilst not tone deaf, Shirley was incapable of staying in tune, which came as a terrible disappointment that often brought tears before bedtime. She'd dreamed of becoming a singer the first day she heard Bev singing in the bath.

Perhaps to compensate for this, she fell in love with Enid Blyton and started 'The Secret Seven Club'. Alan built her a cubby house in the big oak tree in the backyard so that she and her friends could be 'very secret'. By early 1954 Jane and Annie were sick of it so they left and she re-named the group 'The Famous Five'. Amanda and Lucy turned up for six months until they decided the cubby house was dangerous, Shirley was too bossy and they didn't want to be famous anymore. Janet and Alice agreed to stay and become 'The Terrible Three', a name Shirley made up on the spot. She told her sister that if there were further desertions she could always become Miss Blyton's 'Naughtiest Girl'. They both knew it was only a matter of time.

Shirley was getting bored with the club anyway and had cast herself as an independent 'Wicked Gal'. She was enjoying her own company in the cubby house when Alan was given an important promotion to Warracknabeal in central Victoria, an hour's drive from Horsham and about six from Melbourne. Alan was elated. It was a definite indication that his next promotion would be to the big city! The girls, equally excited, were ready for a new adventure.

But Margery was devastated. The MS was progressing at a frightening pace, she may have outlived the specialist's prognosis but the remissions were shortening and becoming less frequent.

She wanted to make the final move to Melbourne now whilst she could cope, and she desperately wanted to be close to Grandma Jones when the next attack struck. Famous last words.

Learning the hard facts of life

Just before Christmas 1955, the family moved to Warracknabeal. The chooks went with them, travelling in the boot of the Prefect, the expedition stopping every 50 miles to water down their feathered travel companions. The day after they arrived, Alan cut off one of the birds' heads so they could have roast chicken for lunch on Christmas Day.

Age One

With a population in excess of 5,000, including the farmers in the district around 'Warrack', Alan's primary school had 500 enrolled students plus a full complement of staff and he was quietly exhilarated by the challenges ahead. Shirley was going be in grade five and was dreading her first week, wishing she was starting high school with her sister. There'd be even more students at the high school and Bev was excited to be commencing form one. Margery was miserable and Christmas Day didn't help. Bev had an asthma attack and Grandma should have been on the train two days earlier but didn't arrive and her telephone was out of order. The oven was terrible and the chicken was black so she didn't miss much. The chickens who'd survived the journey (and lunch) got out of Alan's makeshift wire fence and the neighbours were cross because they had to leave their Christmas lunches to help him round them up and fix the fence.

'We should never have come to this God-forsaken town!' Margery cried quietly. She lit a cigarette and asked Alan if there was any beer or wine in the boxes they hadn't yet unpacked.

'I'm so sorry, Lovely,' Alan wrapped his arms around her as tears streamed down his face. The girls were also teary by then. They'd never seen their father cry before but Shirley's tears stopped before Bev's. 'How come both Dad's eyes are weeping when he only has one?'

Both girls knew their parents were not happy but couldn't fathom why. It was a big promotion for their father and there'd been lots of bad days before, without tears. They wondered if it was their mother's health, or just the mosquitoes and the heat.

The arguments after dinner began when the girls had gone to bed. Before long Shirley would tiptoe into the lounge when she'd hear Alan leave for a toilet break, and beg her mother to stop 'going on' at him. Margery's anger would dissipate as the guilt swept over her and the next day she'd teach her protégé a new poem. Alan didn't say much but Shirley had been joining him in the chook house for years when he was cutting off a head, or cleaning up the aftermath, and sometimes he'd mutter 'bloody', 'bugger' or 'damn'. She liked 'bugger' best; that's what he always said after a bad night in the lounge - bugger, bugger, bugger!

'Mum doesn't mean it,' Shirley would say.

'I know, Shirley,' he'd reply with a sad nod. 'I know.'

On the Thursday afternoon of her first week at Warracknabeal Primary School, Shirley stormed into the house, changed her shoes, pulled up a chair at the kitchen table where Margery was bottling jam and got straight to the point.

'I'm leaving home, Mum.'

'Where are you going, darling?' Margery replied as if she was asking her daughter if she'd like a cup of tea. 'I'm going to join The Circus,' she replied rather loudly. 'I'm going to become a trapeze artist.'

'Well, the circus is only here until tomorrow so I suppose you'll need to pack?'

'Yes, thank you, Mum. I will,' she replied in her usual ladylike manner.

'I'll help you,' Margery smiled and took her into the bedroom to sort some clothes, leaving her briefly to find a small suitcase and three crisp one pound notes from a gold box in her dressing table. Shirley had two pounds and fifteen shillings in her own savings passbook, and quite a lot of pennies, threepenny bits and single shillings in her tin piggy-bank, but savings must be kept and there wasn't time to cycle into town to the bank.

'I'll take your money as a loan, thank you Mum. I'll just have to make it last until I'm good enough to earn a proper living flying around the roof of the big top.'

They got to the front gate with the suitcase and the three pound notes neatly tucked in a little purse, but Shirley was hungry.

'Might as well stay home for tea, darling,' Margery smiled. 'Your new circus family will be eating now.'

By the time Alan and Bev arrived home Margery had roast lamb with all the trimmings cooking away, nearly ready to serve.

'Shirley's joining the circus,' she informed them brightly as Alan stirred the gravy. They didn't seem in the least surprised. When the apple pie with ice-cream and chocolate sauce was eaten, Margery used her and Alan's 'private aside' tactic to convey her hope that Shirley would realise how rude it would be to arrive at the big top so late. All the animals would be waiting to be fed and the staff would be working. He concurred it would be much better manners to go tomorrow.

In the morning Margery turned the wireless on after breakfast and Bill Haley and The Comets were singing *Rock Around The Clock*. It was a lucky break. They were one of Shirley's current favourites and Margery seized her lightened mood.

Age One

'I'll begin to teach you *The Women of the West* the moment you get home from school this afternoon, darling. And if you're very good,' she added a bonus that surprised even her, 'I'll introduce you to Shakespeare. You're a bit young, but it might slow you down for a spell.'

Alan was washing the breakfast dishes and muttered under his breath, 'Thank God she's her mother's daughter, Lovely. How else would we know how to handle her?'

Raised voices in the lounge after bedtime ceased without notice, for a while. The night they began again seemed to explain everything.

Bev was asleep and Shirley lay very still so as to not miss a word. She could hardly wait to tell her sister in the morning that she knew why Mum and Dad were so unhappy. 'There are hundreds of Aborigines enrolled in the Warracknabeal Primary School…well, at least a few dozen, and Mum said it was a wonderful opportunity but Dad said he'd learned at Melbourne High School that you can't teach them, they just go walkabout so you might as well not try. Mum argued colour doesn't matter, everyone is equal until they prove otherwise and Dad sort of agreed, but all the indigenous students in Yarrawonga had gone walkabout and were never seen again. "They're the facts, Lovely," he said.'

Apparently Margery responded as her mother would have done (at least that's what Alan said later).

'Well, what are you going to do about it?' she asked and he said he didn't know.

'Isn't it your job to find ways to make them want to come to school?' she persisted. 'You're a gifted, inspiring teacher! Just because you're the Head doesn't mean you should avoid the classrooms! Get in there and give them all an hour a week of instruction about important things like this, dear. Make them excited to learn – white and black, Alan! Talk to your staff, get them to invite their indigenous students' parents to a welcome at the school, make them feel part of it all. Show them how important it is. And please do it soon whilst I'm still walking so I can host a morning tea.'

Apparently Alan laughed. Shirley asked her sister why he'd laughed and Bev deftly replied that Mum's throw-away lines always work.

And then there was the news on the ABC that six Aborigines in Queensland were ordered to dig a hole on a farm and the white men shot them in the back and they fell dead in the hole they'd just dug. A politician was interviewed and he said it was a lie.

They were all in the kitchen at the time, completing their respective tasks for dinner. 'Is it true, Mum? Dad?' Shirley had to know.

They replied that it was true, told the girls about the stolen generation and tried to explain white attitudes to black people since Australia was colonised by our English ancestors. Margery said they'd heard similar stories to the likes of the 'shootings' in every country town they'd lived in and Alan shook his head and mumbled as if to himself that there was 'an incident' just out of Yarrawonga not long before they left.

Shirley spontaneously dissolved into tears. How could white men, men she might even know, do this? Her never-to-be-repeated experience of camping, stuck for three days with the Girl Guides in tents on a paddock outside Yarrawonga was when the reality of the Aborigines' life in the bush first registered. And now, when white men are so well off, they're still shooting them and leaving them to rot in holes in the ground they had to dig themselves!

'They're still doing it! Still getting away with it!' She was sobbing now. 'Somebody has to do something, Dad?' she spluttered and shivered, attempting to blow her nose on her apron.

Bev, amazingly mature at just 12 years of age, broke the disquieting void that followed, wrapping her arms around her little sister and leading her outside. In the aftermath of countless traumas that occurred in her presence, Bev consoled her sister (with no parenthesis required).

'Mum is sick and battling to get up every day. Dad is a caring man with a big job and he works very hard, but he can't change the world, Shirl.'

At the turn of the 20th century, boys reached puberty in their mid to late teens and the average age for a girl to get her period was 14 or 15. Of course, most parents didn't discuss such matters in those days.

In a bold, if nervous departure from their own upbringings, Great generation parents took their young sons and daughters to segregated sex education presentations. Inadvertently, these vague and unsatisfying lectures about the birds and bees and 'the wonders of nature' provided baby boomers with proof they'd have to find out for themselves all the important things.

In 1928, Margery was 16 when her period arrived, but she'd been expecting blood to pour out of her since she was 12 after overhearing two women talking about it over the back fence as she picked peas and potatoes for her mother. By the second half of the century boys were reaching puberty around the age of 14, while the average for girls had dropped to 12 and a half years. Anticipating this generational shift, Margery told her girls when Bev turned nine and the inquisitive younger daughter was included to save her eaves-dropping.

Continuing to be early for everything, Shirley's period arrived two weeks after her 10th birthday. Instantly she became the only girl in the school excused from sport once a month. Surely everyone had to know why - they'd all been to the 'Facts of Life' instructions!

The reality was that most of her peers still knew nothing specific about menstruation, or sex for that matter, and many interpreted Shirley's sick days as yet another special privilege for the headmaster's daughter. Compounding the situation, she suffered cramps from the start and couldn't stand straight for assembly, compelling Margery to keep her home for a day or two. This added complication prompted Margery to beg Alan to shorten his addresses at assembly.

On account of her flat feet, the boys were in the habit of placing threepenny bets with each other that Shirley would be first to faint at Monday's assembly. Her period came on a Sunday night and tended to be regular, so once a month the boys were doubly miffed because she was the most reliable fainter in the school and didn't turn up to give them a win. Margery encouraged her sad little girl to laugh about it. 'Look on the bright side, darling. You've finally beaten them!'

The year got worse when Shirley became the fastest female runner in the school and won all the swimming races in her age group, and the diving competition too. A few girls ganged up and said her races were rigged. She wished she'd lost.

Two days after her last win for the year, she went to the toilet at school and heard a big girl called Hope speaking in the cubicle next door. There was someone with her who started crying, then suddenly yelling, 'Please stop it stop it stop it, take your finger out of me and let me go, please?'

Shirley was afraid but pushed her door ajar and a saw a little girl run out. Another girl was walking in, Hope grabbed her as she was passing, slammed and locked the door and instantly the cries for help began again. Unable to bear it any longer, Shirley ran from her cubicle to her bike and peddled home to Mum as fast as her legs would take her.

Alan made some discrete phone calls to back up his daughter's evidence, called Hope's parents into his office, advised he'd reported their daughter to the authorities and dismissed her from the school. Before rumours had time to circulate that Shirley had 'dobbed' on Hope, Alan addressed each class and closed the case with Hope's dismissal. It saved another onslaught of atrocious harassment, but didn't ease the ever-empathetic Shirley's pain.

'How will those girls ever get over it, Mum? Life isn't fair, is it,' she sighed as she climbed into bed.

'No darling, sometimes it isn't. Don't forget to say your prayers.'

'I'm not praying tonight, Mum,' she said. 'I don't like God anymore, and if he knew what I was thinking he wouldn't like me either.'

Shirley's grade six teacher Bill Hunt was Alan's deputy head and favourite staff member. She'd overheard her father say Bill could be outrageous at times so she knew she was going to like him. By the end of the first day he had the entire classroom of 50 students in the palm of his hand. He finished that class with the memorable idiom: 'Horses sweat, men perspire and ladies glow.' Shirley could hardly wait to get home to tell her mother.

'Isn't it wonderful, almost like poetry!' she gushed.

Nothing happened by accident in Mr Hunt's classroom. Every day was a regaling, yet genuinely scholarly affair that would conclude with a scintillating hint of tomorrow's theme or subjects. He was passionate about children and the English language, and he believed that if he could instil in his students a love of history and poetry, they would navigate puberty without losing their way, grow up with respect for others and appreciate their own good fortune.

In one particularly memorable example of Mr Hunt's classroom charisma, he began by explaining why everyone in his class was a 'post-war baby boomer'. Pre-pubescent youngsters in the '50s took predictably prurient delight in learning about the government's 'procreate or perish' campaign, but the class' excitement ebbed swiftly when they were instructed to write down three reasons why Australia needed more people.

Mr Hunt followed up with a sobering explanation for the influx of immigrants from Greece and Italy. 'Their homes and livelihoods were destroyed during the second world war. They needed to come to a welcoming country where they could find work, like the Snowy Mountain Hydro Electricity Scheme, for example.' Then, in his calm, dignified way, he added that from this day forward he would strap six times on the backside any student he heard using the words 'wog' or 'dago' in any circumstance! The crux of Mr Hunt's lesson may not have been what his students were expecting, but it was certainly clear. 'The welcome to our New Australians starts here, boys and girls. Today! Got that?'

There are few secrets in country towns. The war had been over for more than a decade but had left a resounding, painful impression on many families. Predictably, word had got around Warracknabeal that the primary school headmaster didn't go to the war.

It was in one of Mr Hunt's classes that a boy put his hand up and announced that Mr McLaughlin didn't fight so he must be a coward. Shirley's previous experience of being bullied in Yarrawonga inspired her to stand and respond in her practised thespian voice she had never used before in a real-life situation: 'You are a bully and my father is not a coward.'

The classroom exploded into a rabble, everyone talking and shouting to one another around the room. In raised voice, Mr Hunt ordered his students to 'shut up, sit down and listen to me!' or they'd face certain expulsion before lunch. He told them to pick up their pens and open a fresh page in their exercise books.

'There are three facts about wars that it's high time you understood. I will speak slowly and you will write down, and *memorise* every word I say.

'Number one; most of our young men volunteered to go to the last war, but that doesn't mean they were all accepted. It wasn't about personal choice.

'Number two; the government chose who went based on age, health and the needs of the nation. Who was going to keep business going, sow our fields and teach our children if everyone who volunteered was accepted? You wouldn't have been born and Australia might no longer exist!

'Number three; it is ignorant and insulting to suggest that men who don't fight in wars are cowards. Some of your families went overseas to help save our country, but it took just as much courage and strength to stay behind and keep the home fires burning.

'Now, write this down in block letters please. *I will never again make judgements about anyone until I know all the facts.*'

He always seemed a little surprised when his handling of controversial situations like these worked a treat, swallowing hard before moving onto the next lesson. (Forty years later Shirley met a couple of Mr Hunt's old students who'd also retained this lesson, almost verbatim.)

When Shirley got home she asked Margery if Dad had been bullied because he didn't go to war. 'Yes, darling,' Margery nodded gravely, 'it went on for years and he still feels guilty. Sometimes what looks like bad luck turns out to be a blessing in disguise,' she added obliquely.

'Was getting multiple sclerosis a blessing in disguise?' Shirley jumped from her father's misfortune to her mother's, regretting it immediately.

'No, darling,' Margery replied directly. 'That was simply bad luck. But I desperately wanted to go to the war,' she surprised. 'Would have got there too, working on radio in Cairo if it hadn't been for the telegraphic reference check they made to 3BA. Blacking out on air killed my chances, just as only having one eye killed Dad's. All wars are about power and money so perhaps it *was* a blessing in disguise,' she sighed. 'Otherwise we would never have met!'

The arguments between her parents increased in 1957 and continued until late 1959 when Alan was finally promoted to a Melbourne posting. Whilst the promise of 1960 gave the family something positive to look forward to, it still seemed a long way away.

By the late '50s Bev and Shirley had gained a wealth of practical and philosophical insights into their capabilities and future possibilities, different as they were. They still shared a bedroom, but as they started to chase their individual dreams, early conflicts fizzled out. Bev, active in sport, music and singing, was also being recognised for her artistic talent, in and outside the art classroom. There was also a hint of romantic interest from a couple of boys in her form.

Shirley had finally, thankfully arrived at secondary school. Her nights and weekends remained focused on learning new material for recitation and dramatic performances all over town, and Margery had also agreed to her undertaking piano lessons from the nuns at the local convent, along with gymnastics at school. The relief of no longer being the headmaster's daughter, coupled with the very fact of being at high school, helped her settle. To her mind, it brought her closer to the time when she could leave school altogether, travel the world and realise her gargantuan ambitions to do a thousand things most girls would never even think to try.

During their last couple of years in Warracknabeal there were many highlights that allowed the family to forget their troubles. A stand-out was the centennial 'Back to Warracknabeal' anniversary concert. Alan was on the organising committee; Margery was producing segments, supervising rehearsals and making dresses; Bev was singing in the choir with a solo part; and Shirley was reciting *The Man from Snowy River* and *The Women of the West*. The concert took place on a portable stage at the showgrounds with an audience of over 2,000 ex-students and their families.

It was Shirley's first solo performance in front of so many people. The crowd loved her and she brought her mother to tears reliving the experience the following day. 'The last time I thought about the showgrounds, I was leaving home to join the circus!' she shrieked. 'Thank goodness you stopped me. I wouldn't have lasted a day! But I'll remember last night and the words of the poems all the days of my life, Mum, especially the women who left everything behind in England to come and settle in outback Australia…"For love, they faced the wilderness: The Women of the West." We're so lucky, Mum. We have you and Dad, and running hot water and flushing loos, and we'll never be alone and poor like the Aborigines are and the women of the West were. I'd like to live my life for love,' she beamed. 'You and Dad do everything for love. Even when you're arguing…and you always make up before you go to bed. If you didn't, I'd never get to sleep.'

Christmas holidays at Grandma's in Mornington continued to be much anticipated and a lot more fun because Alan had bought a big 'new' car (actually a second hand Vauxhall). With the Mornington peninsula's close proximity to Melbourne, Margery had decided they would spend a week of their holidays this year and next 'house-sitting' in the city in order to see plays, musicals and comedies at the Princess Theatre and vaudeville at the Tivoli.

The selection criteria was Margery's alone. Shakespeare featured every year so the girls experienced murder scenes and all manner of adult mayhem as only The Bard could write. Many of the vaudeville shows featured near-naked men and women, the comedies were often risqué but rarely went over their heads, and a few known and unknown musicals and workshop plays performed by small repertory groups exceeded Margery's expectations, and sometimes even shocked!

Consistently the only children in the audience, the girls felt very special and grown up. Bev was inspired to become a musical comedy star and Shirley renewed her plans, for a while, to become a professional actress. Every new year on the long drive home Margery would remind them that they could be anything they wanted to be, as long as they wanted it badly enough, 'but you must never, never, never reduce your standards to suit the people you're with!'

They both listened attentively and although Shirley sometimes muddled her mother's endless quotes and philosophical advice, the guts of them were indelibly embedded into both girls' characters: *Always tell the truth. Take risks and don't be afraid of failure; have another go or try something else. Luck is a poor man's estimate of a worker's success. Don't take yourselves too seriously. Live and let live. The days that make us happy, make us wise.*

'Behave at all times like a lady' was persistent advice and already habitual for both girls, but Shirley was quietly beginning to wonder if it was always going to be possible to obey all the rules, behave like a lady and have fun at the same time.

Somewhat circuitously she got to thinking about the concept of 'working hard to get lucky' and this led her to the realisation that when it came to gambling it didn't seem to matter if one was 'only a girl'. Before her mother had met her father, she'd won £100 on the fabulous Phar Lap, running on the day at 100 to one. It was a lot of money and the odds were the same for men and women! The cost of the bet was the same, as were the winnings. That Margery had lost some male friends who were with her that day was not surprising. They'd accused her of being tipped off and not telling them. They'd never been beaten by a woman before. When she denied their accusations and explained that he was a fine looking horse, his gate number was good and she liked the jockey, they dropped her completely.

The lessons from this were crystal clear – don't gamble with friends or colleagues, and learn how to win – and her mother would be the best teacher in the world! Margery had long been an astonishingly accurate palm reader, loved the risks of striking an outspoken spirit at a séance, and predicting events based on numerology. She'd already begun to teach Shirley palmistry and the time was right for rules on 'wagering' and 'choosing horses.'

Margery insisted that betting on the neddies was very high risk and best left alone for a while, but it was definitely time her younger daughter learned how to play Black Jack.

'It will teach you some handy gambling skills for life,' she promised.

The changing times

The isolation and sanctuary of country town living in Australia was no longer impervious to the winds of change. Television and the international news media had infiltrated the great majority of homes and even illiterate country yokels were beginning to yield to the influences of the wider world. It wasn't all for the better; responsible parents feared for their children's futures.

Margery and Alan had worked hard to keep the girls' vocabularies free of derogatory name-calling, but nicknames like 'micks' for Catholics, 'heathens' for Protestants and unmentionable names for Masons, Aborigines and migrants from all over the world had become firmly entrenched in the Aussie lingo. Despite most Australians and New Australians attending their respective churches regularly, religious and racial prejudice had been an Australian tradition since the British landed a couple of centuries earlier.

The pubs closed at 6pm to appease the 'wowsers' and temperance societies but much gossip, rumour and grog were shared before the patrons ordered their last beers and the inaccurately named 'six o'clock swill' occurred. As long as they'd ordered before six, men could stay another half an hour before being shown the door.

Tradesmen and leaders of commercial enterprise drank freely with ministers of religion and government, farmers, local shopkeepers and members of the Italian mafia without necessarily knowing it. A beer was a beer and blokes didn't have to introduce themselves when dropping in for a pint. Local police on duty, and 'after hours' cops in plain clothes dropped in too, along with criminals who often as not had financial interests in the inner city clubs and pubs. Some carried guns but the goodies and the baddies were not there to cause trouble. Certainly the goodies were often there to keep an eye on the baddies, but rough scenes in pubs were not encouraged and the mafia fellows were rarely arrested for anything anyway because they paid off the publicans…and anyone else who could be bought.

The constabulary at large were forever busy with the cut and thrust of everyday urban life, plus Australia's and the wider world's newsworthy events used to give journalists sufficient news to please their editors and meet their deadlines. But times were changing. The subtle, increasingly intemperate exaggerations and alleged 'facts' from the idiot box and national and local rags were new forces to be reckoned with.

Australia is a big continent with a small population and has never had much bad news. To fill the rapidly expanding media outlets, the news gatherers began to invent headlines and stories. What was transpiring under the radar of some of the long established, highly regarded organisations, churches and government bodies were the big stories that journalists and/or their bosses were not prepared to publish.

As a head teacher in half a dozen Victorian country towns, and a lay preacher for nearby protestant churches, Alan was privy to many secrets the kind of which have only really surfaced in recent years. He knew several paedophile priests, including the notorious Father John Michael Joseph Day who, as Shirley overheard Margery fuming, was moved on from Horsham in order to 'destroy the lives of another town's children!'

Bev slept whilst Shirley listened. She already knew that the Methodist wowser who taught religious instruction at her father's school was under investigation for interfering with boys, and girls. Alan called a colleague in the education department in Melbourne to ask why he was 'on leave' during the investigation and got no answer. A couple of nights later Shirley learned that a local policeman reported two cases of rape in a private catholic school, and named the rapist. Apparently his superior conferred with his boss in Melbourne and the decision was taken that the priest had to be 'moved on', and so did the cop who was forced to accept a new posting interstate.

'They're all in it!' Alan told Margery with a sense of despair Shirley recognised; it was exactly how he spoke when Margery had had a turn and he was phoning the doctor or the hospital. 'The top men in the church are destroying children's lives and stealing money from their parents, supposedly raising funds for the poor that goes straight into their own pockets! At least two top dogs in the police force are accomplices - probably reckon they'll go to heaven if they keep their mouths shut, and the chiefs of petty sessions in half the towns we've lived in are bribed into silence. So many of God's disciples, cops and lawyers are bloody crooked, Lovely! They're *all* in it!' he repeated again and again. 'Where the hell is God?'

When Shirley recited yet another poem at a normal service in Warracknabeal's Presbyterian Church a few weeks later, she did not know it was going to be the last. The poem was Rudyard Kipling's *'If'*. The traditionally silent, sombre congregation knew the poem well but had never heard it delivered so strongly by one so young. There was a breathless pause following the last verse:

'…If you can talk with crowds and keep your virtue,
Or walk with Kings – nor lose the common touch,
If neither foes nor loving friends can hurt you,
If all men count with you, but none too much;
If you can fill the unforgiving minute
With sixty seconds' worth of distance run,
Yours is the Earth and everything that's in it,
And – which is more – you'll be a Man, my son!'

Shirley stepped down from the pulpit for the last time to unbridled applause and some months later Alan stopped lay preaching and both parents stopped going to church regularly. Friends and the local minister put it down to Margery's deteriorating health. The girls were still encouraged to attend church and Sunday school and could make their own decisions when they were older.

Bev and Shirley acquired their first boyfriends in the same year and their memories of Warracknabeal would always be connected to the change of life romance begets.

A farmer in his early 20s called Peter Anderson was courting Bev. Margery and Alan liked him very much and the courtship continued for some time, although Bev eventually decided she liked the head prefect, Keith Livingston more and took up with him until Alan's promotion to Melbourne.

At the same time, a boy in Bev's form called David Streeter had fallen for Shirley when he saw her recite a poem at the town hall. *Girl in Hammock* was a funny, saucy elegy with hand and body movements for every line. 'Shady tree, babbling brook, girl in hammock, reading book…' A man goes by with a 'big moustache' and the girl quickly 'makes a mash'. The man and the maiden marry and have babies, but the man can't cope with burnt food and screaming in the night so he shoots his head off and the wife returns to her hammock. 'Shady tree, babbling brook, pretty widow, reading book…' and there will be 'no more mash!'

David pursued her on his bicycle (resplendent with its stunning rabbit tail hitched to the back) and soon became her first boyfriend. He taught her how to kiss, for which she's been forever grateful.

Of course Margery and Alan knew their little girl often rode home with him and lingered in the lane (the old night-cart driveway) that backed onto the McLaughlin's fence. The lessons were 'allowed to continue' but sometimes Alan would pace the veranda calling 'Shirley, it's time for tea!' At this the kissing would stop immediately, David would ride home and Shirley would land breathlessly at the front door as if she'd just completed the two mile cycle from school. Even one unforgettable accident did not stop the two of them.

One afternoon Alan's pacing yielded no response from the laneway and Margery had insisted he leave them be. David was a respectful boy, Shirley was nearly 14 and knew the rules and would come home when she was hungry.

After their younger daughter had stayed too long, she decided to climb through the front window and enter the kitchen just in time for tea. She'd always been clumsy because of her terrible feet and it's impossible to know specifically how it happened, but instead of sauntering nonchalantly into the house as she'd planned, Shirley fell straight through the wire screen and half-closed window, making a shocking racket and an awful mess of shattered glass, blood and tears.

Alan drove everyone to the hospital where a handsome doctor told Shirley her injured right leg would heal without stitches but that – thrillingly - she'd have the scar forever! She told Grandma Jones later that it had all been so exciting: Mum made the doctor laugh and Dad didn't even say bugger once!

Margery was adamant that punishment, sympathy or focus on the injury Shirley had brought upon herself would diminish the lesson she had surely learned, so not a word was spoken about the accident. Fortunately, the kissing in the lane lessons were only limited by her sore leg for a week or two, but soon resumed with renewed vigour and continued until the family left Warrack.

When Margery was ill and confined to bed she was comfortable that her older daughter's common sense, quiet confidence and growing maturity would protect her in difficult situations. Shirley, however, was a different kettle of fish. Her little girl lived in a world of her own, dreaming, questioning, always wondering 'if', all the while imagining a beautiful big world out there just waiting to be conquered. Margery couldn't help but ruminate in the quiet of her bedroom. *Have I given her too much confidence, too much identity too soon? Is she heading for a fall?*

When her next remission kicked in, she'd remember Shakespeare and ultimately decided to adopt one heartening line from *As You Like It* as a mantra to ease her fears: 'Much virtue in "if"'. After all, hadn't she set the example, dragging herself out of bed to take her first faltering steps along the passage, only to fall then get up and try again? She'd learned how to fall, never broke a bone and must have walked a million miles more than the doctors foretold.

When her world caved in again and the terrors returned, she'd remind Shirley of the dangers out there. 'Don't speak to strangers. Never accept a lift from any man, including and especially if you know him! Get on your bike and peddle straight home. If you're walking alone, go into the first house with a car in the drive and knock loudly on the door!'

One Sunday afternoon Shirley was propped up on the end of Margery's bed, about to read her the news from Melbourne's *The Age*, when she matter-of-factly reported, 'Yesterday when I was at Beckworth's farm with David and Ted, there was a man wearing a minister's collar sitting on the river bank.'

Margery held her breath as her body involuntarily trembled.

'I was getting a bucket of water for the boys,' Shirley continued unperturbed. 'They were having a race on their bikes in the dam and were absolutely filthy. The man asked me to sit down for a minute with the bucket because there was a fish nearby and he'd catch it for me. I said only for a minute because I had to take the water to the boys. "What have you got in your panties?" he asked when I sat down. Then he opened his fly and pulled out his penis. It was the biggest, ugliest thing I've ever seen, Mum.'

'Oh my God! What did you do?'

'I told him he was a dirty old man and ran back to tell David and Ted that we had to leave straight away, so we did.'

Margery struggled to commend her for her excellent handling of the situation, instead preoccupied with how on earth Shirley had come to know the term 'dirty old man'. She must have read it somewhere…yet she'd recently learned the word 'fuck' and that certainly wasn't printed anywhere!

It struck Margery then, with a painful, heart-stabbing sense of loss that her extrovert daughter had begun to keep some things to herself. These days Shirley rarely read her mother the 'bad news' stories, like the ones about cyclones, murders or political intrigues, and Margery began, for the umpteenth time that felt like the first, to accept that she was running out of time.

Shirley picked up *The Age* and sorted the sections. The business pages and anything to do with baby boomers were always dealt with first, in order to get onto the interesting stuff. 'Did you know that one-fifth of the 2.1 million babies born between 1946 and 1956 have at least one migrant parent, Mum? They say Australia's baby bonus is one of Menzies' best initiatives.

'And listen to this! "Thousands of Greek men are rioting in Melbourne because the bridal ship, *Castel Felice*, is nine hours late!"' she read with melodramatic aplomb. 'I'll travel on a Sitmar ship one day, Mum, but not that one. Imagine being on a ship full of Greek brides!'

Margery shook her head, mystified as to how she'd failed her daughter so badly, but moments later was laughing at her foolishness. '"The Memphis Draft Board has enlisted Elvis Presley for a two-year stint in the armed services." People in the streets of New York and Texas were sobbing on the telly last night, Mum. He's sold 40 million records and his monthly salary, according to this, will drop from $100,000 a week to $83.20. What will rock and roll fans in America do without him? Why do they call him Elvis the Pelvis, Mum?'

'You're old enough to have noticed, darling,' was the best Margery could manage.

'"Graham Kennedy will chalk up his 300th nightly appearance on *In Melbourne Tonight* tomorrow. Can I please stay up to watch it, Mum? Please let me? I know it's a school night but I've got so much to learn if I'm going to finish up in television - he's the very best we've got. Oh, and how about this! "In October the first women peers will take their seats in the House of Lords in London." About time too. What have they been doing all these centuries?'

Margery was up and down for the remainder of the year and learned first from Shirley that Prime Minister Bob Menzies had been swept back into power.

'Who says the times are changing, Mum? It's Menzies' fifth successive election "with a majority of 26 seats in the House of Reps" and he's gained control of the Senate! Have you and Dad always voted Liberal?'

'Of course, although we don't discuss it.'

'But you're married!'

'It's not the done thing to discuss politics, Shirley. And it saves arguments.'

'I'm going to be a swinging voter because it's ridiculous one party can stay in power for so long. How can anyone be sure they haven't become corrupt or lazy or are just building a bureaucracy like the hierarchy in the churches, and the mafia gangs in the inner suburbs – and the gangs at school…I guess that's where it all starts, right Mum?'

Margery's face opened up with a mix of maternal pride and curiosity, and she felt an unexpected eagerness to welcome the New Year fast approaching.

'This is our last year in country towns, Shirley. We're going to the city and I can't wait!' she laughed heartily, perhaps to silence the small voice warning her she was tempting fate.

'Are you afraid of dying, Mum?'

'That's a question I wasn't exp… Why do you ask?'

'I've read that people often laugh loudly when they're scared. Did you know that seven people are born every second compared with five who die at the same rate? I can't argue with your science heroes who've always said our existence is a matter of chance and we've got to die some time so we need to live in the present, but sometimes it can be damned hard to do that, don't you think?'

'Yes darling, yes I do. Come over here and give me a big hug,' she urged, throwing back the quilt to open her arms as one large tear trickled down her cheek.

'It feels like the sixth day after you were born,' she cried.

New beginnings

Alan commenced as head teacher of the special, first class Ashwood Primary School in Melbourne in late January 1960. Being in charge of a teacher-training school with over 1,000 students from grades one to six, his days were destined to be long.

The family packed up in Warracknabeal, sent their furnishings by truck to a self-storage unit near the school and drove to Grandma Jones' for the Christmas holidays. The plan was to find a house to rent in the New Year until they had time to look for one to buy.

As if she knew she wasn't up to the move, Debbie, the family's beloved cocker-spaniel and Margery's constant companion, lay down and died the afternoon before they left. She was buried in the rose garden. Everyone cried, Alan quickly shovelled soil over the body, and Margery and the girls scattered petals over the mound.

A couple of days after they'd arrived at Grandma's, just before Christmas, Alan rolled over in bed and his heart momentarily stopped. The right side of Margery's face had dropped. Though she was already awake and realising the remission leading up to the move was over, she had no knowledge she'd suffered a stroke. She refused to believe it until Alan helped her to the toilet and she saw herself in the bathroom mirror.

For the next few days everyone except Margery was in a state of shock, but it was her resilience and extraordinary courage that brought them back to earth. Her beautiful face was no more but her smile returned quickly – even though it was just a half 'Lovely' smile now, which broke Alan's heart. Instinctively she knew that she was going to be bedridden for months. She cursed her anger and the cruel, pointless niggling she'd inflicted on her husband for four long years because she needed to be close to her mother when this happened. The irony was bitter but she counted her blessings and immediately took control of her family's future: Alan and the girls must proceed with their commitments!

'I have a plan,' she advised firmly.

Alan could drive to the city each day, drop the girls off at their respective schools, go to his school, finish around 4pm whenever possible, pick up the girls who could read in the shelter shed or play sport whilst they were waiting, and return to Mornington in plenty of time for tea. 'This will work,' she nodded with endorsement of her plan. 'The schools are in three suburbs relatively close to each other and you're still a fit and very able man, dear,' she continued brightly to Alan, knowing he would be happier with this arrangement than any other, not that she could think of any alternatives.

'You can count on me to be up and about in three months,' she added in her most assertive voice. 'All you have to do is be positive and supportive of each other, do well at your schools and tell me all about it when you get home. I'll be looking forward to that every day.'

'So will I,' murmured Grandma Jones. She was a tough old girl and didn't mince words.

1st Intermission

There are many great ships —
but the greatest is Friendship

Souvenir of
3BA
FRIENDSHIP
CIRCLE

If you call yourself my friend,
   I ask this much of you—
An equal footing in the game—
   And truth the whole way through.

I want you please to understand
   You take me as I am—
Whatever else I claim to be
   Devoid of Lie or Shame!

I ask no favours in the game—
   I too can take a chance—
And lose as well as any man
   In gamble or romance!

I ask a kind encouragement—
   A Ready sympathy—
An understanding friendliness—
   And an equality—

A high and noble comradeship
   A fairness to the end—
I ask this much of any one
   Who calls herself my friend!

David Streeter

AGE TWO (1964 – 1969)

And then the lover
Sighing like furnace, with a woeful ballad
Made to her master's eyebrow.

Bev met her third boyfriend, Robert Gosbell, at the Canterbury Methodist Church in Melbourne. Twelve months later, on the 28th August, 1965, they married there. Bev was 20 years of age and Rob was 23.

The wedding was a typical Australian baby boomer event, despite the bride and groom being born near the end of the pre boomer era. Alan gave Bev away, Shirley was one of the bridesmaids, and Rob's two brothers were best men. Most of the extensive Gosbell family were present, along with the few remaining McLaughlins, plus 50 friends of the bride and groom.

Bev was beautiful in a tight fitting, white linen gown, chicly trimmed around the neckline with fur. The long flowing veil and equally streaming white bouquet was a sight to behold. The bridesmaids also looked stunning in blue and mauve checked, long satin gowns with short puffy sleeves and sphere-shaped bouquets to match.

Margery was serene and stylish in a woollen two piece suit, the stroke-affected right side of her face more obvious than usual because she couldn't stop smiling. She hadn't expected to be alive for this day and the possibility of an early grandchild was energising.

In his dark grey suit, white shirt and red tie, Alan was as proud as a father of the bride could be. Rob and his brothers made a handsome group and the father and mother of the groom, Gordon and Val, were elegantly dressed and clearly delighted with their son's choice of wife.

The speeches at the reception were short, funny and well received. Many of the 100 guests danced until 11, then formed the obligatory guard of honour for the farewell and subsequent throwing of the bouquet. Everyone agreed that the handsome couple were a perfect match, and they were right. Mr and Mrs Robert Gosbell departed for their honeymoon with a degree of excitement and apprehension. As was customary at the time, their union was yet to be consummated.

Shirley had turned 18 that May, and Margery and Alan managed a private aside when the other bridesmaid caught the bouquet, ever so grateful it wasn't their younger daughter. But Shirley was already contemplating the idea of finding a husband for herself and the magic of such a wonderful day, full of love and music and high hopes for the future, had made it compelling.

When Bev and Rob dropped in for tea after returning from their honeymoon, Shirley cornered her sister in the bathroom. 'Well, how did it go?' she giggled.

Bev smiled, wrinkled her nose and proceeded to wash her hands.

'You know what I mean,' Shirley persisted. 'You've got to tell me what it's like! Making love…did it hurt?'

Bev's silence was deafening. 'It must have been awful!' her sister deduced.

'It wasn't that bad, Shirl! It was quite funny washing the sheets. We had to stifle our laughter in case we woke the people next door. It's been good ever since.'

Shirley decided there and then that she was not going to be a virgin on her honeymoon. The where, when and with whom was not yet known, but she had a plan!

The rocky road to adulthood

It was many months after Margery's stroke that the family departed Grandma Jones's house in Mornington.

Thanks to Margery's brother Stan, they were able to purchase their very own home without having to borrow at 23 Compton Street, Canterbury. The 1960 credit squeeze had bankrupted Stan, but he managed to return Alan and Margery's life-long savings moments before the liquidators took over.

Age Two

They settled into their charming new home with a mixture of delight and relief. It was walking distance to Shirley's high school and the Canterbury Methodist Church, a tram ride for Bev to Swinburne Technical College, and an easy drive for Alan to the Ashwood Primary School.

In mid-1961, Shirley shocked everyone and seriously underestimated her father's reaction to her tenacious decision to leave Camberwell High and attend Stott's Business College. Determined to gain a Diploma of Commercial that would 'set her up for life,' she eventually won the day. Not only was Alan deeply disappointed that his younger daughter, the one most needing a university education was leaving school early, but was also embarrassed when she explained why.

'I have to learn Pitman shorthand or I'll never be able to write faster than 90 words a minute, Dad!' she exclaimed.

Margery pointed out that this was an inadequate argument from a girl voted form captain by 30 girls 10 days after she'd started at Camberwell High School, so Shirley did some homework and tried again.

'The state schools in Victoria have been teaching second-rate Dacomb shorthand since 1943 because one of the Dacomb sisters had an affair with the minister for education,' she explained pragmatically. 'Both sisters were strong women just like you in the 1930s, Mum. Beatrice was big and forbidding and Clara was small and a vivacious good mixer. The education department knew Dacomb shorthand wasn't a patch on Pitman's, but it wouldn't take long for teachers to learn. The minister for education had his way, so to speak.'

'Dear God,' Margery wiped her lopsided eye with a white handkerchief. 'Where on earth did you learn this? You can't have read it in the library!'

'Well I did, mostly. Then I told Miss Denison what I'd read and asked her why the education department made such an amoral, unjust decision. She told me it was the minister's fault because he was having an illicit affair with Clara…everyone knows now,' she added categorically.

Alan acknowledged it was true, and quietly agreed with Margery's sound arguments in the lounge room later that night.

The youngest student at Stott's by three years, Shirley worked hard day and night, desperate for her father to be proud of her. On 'even' week nights she topped up her lessons with two hours typing on Alan's Underwood typewriter, clicking away at long passages from books to ensure a good pass. 'Odd' week nights and weekends, she practised her Pitman shorthand, taking down the ABC news bulletins on her lap in front of the TV and typing them back. She was dux of her year, able to type at 85 words per minute, take shorthand at 120 wpm shorthand and scoring 98 per cent on her 'English' and 'Commercial Principles and Practice' exams.

Shirley's successful completion of her diploma in late November, 1961, was a source of pride and relief! Alan had taken up teaching English to Spanish immigrants in the city three nights a week in order to pay Bev's second year of a three-year Diploma of Art at Swinburne Tech (she left to work in a photo laboratory prior to marrying Rob) and Shirley's one-year diploma.

At the beginning of 1962, aged 15½, Shirley began her first junior secretarial position at her beloved Australian Broadcasting Commission (ABC) radio stations 3LR and 3LO. This quickly laid plan to follow in her mother's footsteps proved to be a very fast track into the adult world, and also led to her decision nine months later to get the hell out of there before things got worse!

Her first boss, known as 'BJB' (Black Jack Boozer), was the program manager at the station. Upon returning from his daily four-hour lunches, he would lean over her whilst 'checking her typing' and run his hands over her ears, arms and breasts. That was bad enough, but his breath was worse. On top of this, she was getting bored!

Within weeks of her appointment she'd finished typing the week's radio programs by Wednesday lunchtime and gladly accepted the part-time position of secretary to the station manager, whose long-time secretary was on extended sick leave. She loved using her shorthand, the big boss was a gentleman and the work infinitely more interesting, but in this position she was at anybody's and everybody's mercy.

One of the national ABC newsreaders would regularly pressure her into massaging his back whilst reading the news live-to-air, and take every opportunity to jump out of his studio seat to kiss her passionately, pushing her into the airlock between the two doors that separated his studio from the passage during music breaks.

Likewise, after securing weekend work re-writing radio race calls for evening TV news bulletins, she soon learned to sprint from the sports news desk as the last race was still running to escape the attentions of the sports editor.

When the station manager's secretary returned two months later, Shirley quietly advised her boss that she couldn't continue to work for Mr BJB and his roving hands. She was moved to the position of APRA (Australian Performing Rights Association) Clerk, where she was responsible for recording all copyright royalties owed to creative producers of words and music played on the ABC.

She hadn't been in the role long when an older woman who'd befriended her when she first started began to make her days a nightmare. She had no idea why this woman considered her a threat but remembered her mother's stories of the jealousies she'd encountered during her radio days. Margery subsequently provided her with an explanation as concise as it was conclusive. 'Some people are so insecure that they're afraid of nearly everyone. You've handled three jobs and one weekend job inside a year and still finish them all before sign-off time. This woman must be terrified her job will be next. Resign and move on, darling,' she advised.

Shirley was still two years shy of the minimum age required to work in television at the ABC so she took her mother's advice and did temporary work whilst looking for something permanent.

She gave that away on her fourth day as relief secretary to the state manager of the Victorian Employers' Federation in Melbourne. During a coffee break, the boss crushed her against a wall in his office, grasping her cheeks and sticking his tongue down her throat. She was powerless to move as he simultaneously thrust his 'tool box' hard against her groin. When he thought he had her pinned, he used one hand to pull up her skirt. It was then that she kicked him slightly left of his penis, but chanced to get his testicles. She broke loose, grabbed her handbag and ran for her life.

The moment Shirley arrived home she informed the temp agency who'd arranged the gig, but also wanted to call the police…or someone? Margery counselled against it. 'It's their responsibility to report his unquestionable attempt to overpower and rape you.'

Shirley was not paid for her three and a bit days' work and the fact that she'd quit gave the agency a perfect out, as if it had never happened. That was the way it was then. Margery knew it and was angry, but decided to take the chance to give her daughter some tough advice. She was pretty sure now that she wouldn't be around the next time something bad happened so the lesson had to encompass far more than sexual abuse.

'Unless you've got plenty of witnesses, don't even consider suing people who do you wrong, Shirley. The pain and angst isn't worth it and the lawyers are the only ones who win. Learn from your loss or trauma, put it behind you and move on. And never forget that no amount of money can compensate for heartache and loss.'

The gamble worked in a roundabout way and Shirley acknowledged she'd have to become a lot more discerning and much tougher before she'd be able to make any difference to women's lot.

'Get yourself right first, girl!' came her mother's rapid retort. 'You won't be right for anyone else until you do.'

In 1963 she went from beautifully spoken bullying and sexual harassments at the ABC and The Employers' Federation to none in the real theatre of life - Melbourne's Alfred Hospital. She became one of five clinical stenographers assigned to a long list of specialists who consulted at 40 outpatient clinics per week.

Like BJB, her next boss also had terrible body odour, but she was a kind and liberal teacher. (At that time Shirley didn't know that she too had body odour and was later grateful that this generous woman wouldn't have noticed. Margery had every right to pride herself in overlooking nothing of importance in her girls' upbringings, but unfortunately deodorant had been one.) As to the big picture, The Alfred Hospital was a lucky break on many fronts. The timing, and the training, the intelligent, caring people and the sheer theatre of it all restored Shirley's faith in humankind.

On Friday 22nd November 1963 President Kennedy was assassinated. It was Saturday in Australia and Shirley was catching up on a backlog of work. She was walking through the emergency department when she heard the news from a patient reading *The Melbourne Sun* as he lay flat on his back in the receiving corridor. She turned white, began to sway and dropped the folder of patients' treatment plans she was carrying. Two staff members came to her aid and caught her as she fainted.

It was a family affair at The Alfred and that day the family clung tightly together whilst carrying on. Nobody molested, attacked or bullied her at The Alfred, and when she fainted in the women's clinic the honorary gynaecologist dictating the letters called in a nurse and instructed Shirley to undress and lie on the table. He examined her and decided she needed to go on the new contraceptive pill to stop the cramps she endured each month and make her working life happier and more reliable.

'It's not just your flat feet after all,' he smiled encouragingly.

That was another lucky break and the same man gave her a wonderful reference when she was leaving to take up a position in private practice.

Money is exactly like sex: if you don't have any, you think of nothing else, and you think of other things if you do.

Shirley was 17, still a virgin and thinking a lot about sex and money in that order when she applied for a job with two highly respected doctors who ran a specialist practice in Collins Street and a pathology clinic in Camberwell.

During her successful interview with doctors Bate and Dorevitch, she disclosed her mother's condition and advised she might have to cut back to part-time hours in the near future. They juggled some staff and put her on the front desk in Camberwell, which was a short tram trip from home.

Her medical terminology was excellent and her knowledge and interest in the scintillating, dangerous and sometimes fatal sexual activities of men and women stepped up a pace when she joined the clinic. In the business of pathology, the 'stuff' that comes across the front desk and the subsequent results of tests and letters written back to referring doctors can be confronting. But Shirley loved the work, the people and the insights she was gaining about blood and guts and the human condition. It didn't take long to grasp that test results seemed to come down to diagnoses of good or bad luck, or dire dilemmas for the self-inflicted with known diseases, uncertain prognoses and limited pharmacological cures.

As expected, several months later Margery was confined to bed and Shirley became her day-carer for the next six months. As soon as Alan arrived home from Ashwood Primary, she'd head off by tram to work from late afternoon through to nine in the evenings.

The one night of the week she didn't work, Shirley took a tram to the city to finally learn to sing. By chance, Miss Colburn, her teacher was a rare soul who instantly recognised she had a high achiever on her hands. She was able to extract from Shirley that she'd been dreaming of becoming a professional singer, rather than actor, for most of her tender years.

It was a delicate situation. Her student loved music but had no ear or voice for it. The classes began with the rudiments of scales and didn't improve with practice so she decided to teach her enthusiastic pupil how to sing one song well. 'My Guy' was a pop song that required very little in the technical skills department.

Nothing you can say can take me away from my guy,
No handsome face will ever take the place of my guy.
I'm sticking to my guy like a stamp to a letter,
like birds of a feather we'll stick together,
I'm telling you from the start I can't be torn apart from my guy.

Shirley loved the song and the night she sang it straight-up from start to finish in the same key turned out to be the last lesson. The previous four concentrated sessions had made it possible and Miss Colburn was elated, but had to tell her pupil that her singing career was over.

'Well done, Shirley!' she exclaimed. 'I'm very proud of you. You love music and have an excellent understanding of the technicalities now. It isn't necessary to be able to sing to enjoy singing, or to appreciate those who can. With your personality and theatrical training and love of music, you could finish up helping others achieve their goals one day.'

When Shirley got off the tram at the top of her street that night, an hour earlier than usual, she was thinking about her lost singing career and wondering if marriage might be the best option. So deeply immersed in her philosophical state of mind, she didn't immediately notice that someone was following her. Now she quickened her pace, but then so did her follower.

The footsteps from behind were marching with hers, and getting closer. Just a few doors from home she straightened her shoulders and chin, stopped dead in her tracks on the footpath and turned around to face him. The street was well lit and the tall, dark man stumbled, and froze. She tipped her chin to the starlit sky, threw her head back in a theatrically arrogant way and quickly strode home.

Shirley's confidence and survival instincts were beginning to work on several levels. In the midst of her fear, it had crossed her mind that the man might have been waiting for her to get off the tram. But she dismissed that thought when she remembered she was an hour earlier than usual.

She reached the gate and ran to the back door so as not to disturb her mother who would by now have taken her sleeping pills, or her father who would be in the dining room editing his latest text book titled *Better Ways to Teach English*.

Take a deep breath and walk calmly into the laundry, she told herself. *No need to say anything. You gambled and won. You can always take Mum's advice next time and run into the nearest house with its lights on and a car in the drive.*

But the moment she opened the back door she was engulfed in smoke. She ran down the passage, past the closed dining room door and into her parents' bedroom screaming, 'Dad! Dad!'

In that split second the flames leapt from the quilt covering her mother's prone body to the curtains across the room. Alan was suddenly at Shirley's side; together they lifted Margery out of bed and onto the floor in the passage before turning their attention to putting out the fire. It was a close call.

'It's my fault, my fault!' Alan cried as they ripped the blankets off the bed to smother the flames. 'I always check her every few minutes but I got distracted…bugger, bugger, bugger! Thank God you came home early!'

Margery slept through it all. In the morning she had no memory of the incident.

'I was never going to die from smoking,' she said with her crooked smile when Alan explained why she'd woken to find herself on the couch in the lounge.

'I think I'm glad you left your singing lesson early, darling. How did it go?' she mused to Shirley after breakfast.

'Really well, Mum. My singing dreams are over, but perhaps it's a blessing in disguise? I can't be good at everything, but I've realised that poetry will always be my guide to the mind and heart and *will carry me beyond artifice, back to myself and what is actually so*. I'm free to be me now and I'll never be able to thank you enough, Mum.'

By the time Dr Maybourne arrived to check on his patient the sleeping pills had worn off, but it was his first visit in a long time when he didn't immediately say, 'Have a smoke, Mrs Mac.' Predictably Margery confronted him. 'Don't you go soft on me now, doc! You know smoking's about the only thing I can do for myself these days so I'm going to keep doing it.'

Nobody expected her to get up from this latest near-fatality, but get up she did.

Prelude to freedom

It was late 1964 when Shirley realised Australia was too small for her ambitions.

She'd been back three months, working full-time in Dr Dorevitch's CBD specialist practice, and had become friends with her immediate boss, a biochemist named Belinda.

Like a second mother or older sister, Belinda had cared and shared with Shirley since she'd begun the job in Collins Street. It was Belinda who told her she had body odour and purchased her first deodorant, to be applied daily. When word of the death of a patient Shirley knew well at the Camberwell clinic reached the city practice, it was Belinda who asked Shirley to drop her reception duties and come into her office immediately. And it was Belinda who rescued Shirley the first time she experienced a patient screaming in one of the surgeries during an invasive spinal test.

Shirley confided in her that her Mum sometimes screamed with pain but no sound came out so in a strange way it was a kind of relief to hear people screaming because they know the pain will stop. Belinda wrapped her arms around her and held her tight, the simple act bringing a flood of tears. She cried then as she hadn't done in all the months she'd nursed her mother.

Belinda had also awakened Shirley to the possibilities of overseas charity work. She'd committed to three month's voluntary service with an American organisation in Hong Kong, was departing in a couple of months and would enquire about future opportunities for her.

The impact Belinda made ran deep. She'd told her young protégé the truth from day one, and taught her not to bottle things up. 'Let them go,' she said. 'Let them go!'

When Shirley arrived to work on a Monday in August, Dr Dorevitch called all the staff into his office. Belinda had been killed in a car accident on Saturday night.

It took Shirley several weeks to tell Margery, by which time she'd done her homework and volunteered her services to Project Concern Inc. in Hong Kong.

A couple of weeks later she announced to both parents that she'd made her travel arrangements. Alan was cooking dinner at the time and suddenly began to cry, his tears streaming down into the white sauce he was stirring.

Margery slumped further into her chair, her eyes sending a clear message to her husband. She'd had another 'turn' a few nights earlier and Dr Maybourne had finally admitted there was nothing more he could do. Alan had promised his wife he'd keep the doctors' report of her deteriorating health from the girls.

'They've got their lives to live, dear, and the doctors haven't been right yet!' she'd insisted.

Alan kept his promise. He did however proceed to give Shirley a disturbing lecture on the risks of travelling to South East Asia during the Indonesian Confrontation with Malaysia, particularly in light of her inexperience with men, her inability to speak the local language, as well as her lack of knowledge and skills to work on sampans with Chinese refugees.

It wasn't as if it was the first time she was leaving home anyway. At only 16 she'd gone to Sydney on a working holiday with a couple of 20-year-old girlfriends. Margery and Alan had welled up a couple of times in the lead up to that excursion, but ultimately waved her off at Spencer Street Station with nervous resignation.

To her mind, all she'd done this time was tell her parents that she was going to visit friends in Malaysia for Christmas, then go to Hong Kong to work as a volunteer for a non-profit American organisation dedicated to relieving the plight of millions of dispossessed Chinese refugees living on sampans in Kowloon Bay. Project Concern Inc. employed volunteers to help provide medical and dental services, food and clothing to those in need. She hadn't exactly anticipated applause in response to her announcement…at least she hadn't thought she did, but was it unreasonable to expect a small show of parental pride and encouragement?

'You'd think I'd become a woman of ill repute and was leaving home to go to London and share a flat in Earls Court with loose, drug dependent yobbos,' she told a speechless Bev later, whilst continuing to patiently reassure her parents.

'Dr Dorevitch has given me three months' unpaid leave and it's high time I got some experience on ships and aeroplanes, exploring other countries and cultures. I've booked a cabin on Sitmar's *Castel Felice* to Singapore – and there'll be no Greek brides!' she laughed to ease their fears, serving only to validate and accelerate them. 'I've got an open dated return Qantas ticket home so please don't worry, Mum and Dad. I'll run out of money in three months anyway so I'll be back long before Bev's wedding. You won't even have time to miss me.'

Margery spoke passionately to Alan in the full flight of old.

'Belinda was due to leave next month, dear. Our daughter knows she can't fill her shoes but she wants to give something back. The only way she can see to do that is to offer her services. "Another pair of hands," she said. She'll only be in Hong Kong for a few weeks until her money runs out. She's saved every penny since she started work and has this desperate need to find her calling. We must send her off with our blessings.'

'She can't save the world, Lovely,' Alan murmured.

'That's not her goal, dear. She'll be with friends from the Alfred, Patricia and David Fam, in Kuala Lumpur for Christmas,' she continued, determined to get everything done and dusted right then. 'We can ask her to call us collect on Christmas Day. It might be the only way she'll manage to phone because she'll be at Trish's in-laws' home on Snob Hill.'

'Seems she's got the whole damn thing planned, Lovely. Why am I so concerned?'

'Perhaps because you've got more than a thousand young lives, dozens of staff and a constant stream of trainees to manage, dear! And me. What a hand full! But everything will turn out fine. Shirley needs to cultivate her street smarts and only experience will do that. The sooner the better, Alan. No point in worrying.'

'It's not Shirley I'm worried about,' he mumbled.

Sex, guns, friends and refugees

It was mid-November, 1965.

Margery and Alan waved her off, sending a little prayer to a God that no longer existed. 'Perhaps we should buy a lottery ticket, dear?'

The *Castel Felice* was the baby of the Sitmar Line fleet but Shirley figured the odds that she'd be a good sailor were better than even. It was the only available ship that would meet her timetable. She'd always been a water baby and was sure she'd cope if they struck rough seas. She'd had two bets on The Melbourne Cup a couple of weeks earlier and her horses came first and second so the luck was with her. (Of course she should have spent another quid and taken the Quinella, but never mind.)

They left the Melbourne wharf an hour before a storm struck and all other ships were detained in the harbour for 48 hours. The *Castel Felice* had no stabilisers and the Melbourne skyline disappeared as the passengers were advised by loud speaker to commence taking their sea-sickness pills.

Shirley hadn't thought to bring any but the chief purser, a handsome man named Andreas from northern Italy, seemed to single her out as she walked up the gang plank, proceeding to solve problems she didn't know she had. She was dressed in a light, tailored suit with a pretty raincoat hanging loose, a sparkling blue floral scarf over her black curly hair because it was raining heavily. Whilst escorting her to the main reception desk in order to change her cabin, he complimented her on the way her scarf highlighted her beautiful eyes, using a mix of English and Italian adjectives she'd never heard before. There was a better four-berth cabin available that would be less affected by turbulence and she wouldn't have to share with anyone either so she'd be much more comfortable.

Although younger than her father, this quietly spoken man had the manners and appearance of someone from the great generation. She felt safe, and flattered, and thanked him very much. He asked if she would accept a dance with him in the ballroom after dinner.

It was good to have a cabin to herself but when she'd unpacked she wandered up to the main deck in search of company. The bar was already busy and a group of men invited her to join them. She accepted a beer and was offering her cigarettes around when it struck her that nearly everyone was smoking already and that the smell was not common tobacco.

'My name's Cal,' a young man dressed in black winked as he offered her a rollie. 'Have a decent smoke.'

'I don't...err, thanks all the same. My name is Shirley,' she smiled, extending her hand. He responded firmly as another man grabbed the cigarette she'd refused, lit it and moved on.

'Are his manners always like that?' she asked.

'You don't do drugs and expect manners!' Cal replied in frank amazement.

'I'm sorry, Shirley,' he lowered his voice, looking furtively around as if he might be judged for his courtly behaviour. 'Clearly this isn't the group for you. The dining room is open, might be better luck there?'

She whispered thank you in return. In the dining room a waiter took her to a table of mature travellers who welcomed her warmly.

The moment the band started playing after dinner, Andreas approached.

'May I have this dance?'

He was dressed in a formal uniform, gold buttons and medals on his chest and ribbons around his sleeves, reminding her of an officer out of a British documentary about the Royal Family.

He danced divinely, holding her close whilst swirling her around the dancefloor, and suddenly began to recite, *'Shall I compare thee to a summer's day? Thou art more lovely and more temperate…'*

'Rough winds do shake the darling buds of May,' Shirley returned immediately, *'And summer's lease hath all too short a stay.'*

They were opening lines of her favourite Shakespearean sonnet and as soon as her response had left her mouth she regretted it. He was the first man ever to recite to her! If only she'd let him own the moment.

'Ah, you know Shakespeare and speak so beautifully, far better than my poor Italian English. Please forgive me?'

'That will…won't be difficult,' she stuttered as he turned her in the middle of the foxtrot, proceeding to keep the turn in play. She was giddy enough already.

The constant rocking up and down on the huge waves as they left Port Phillip Bay was a mere bagatelle compared to what was to come.

On entering Bass Strait, the ship began to roll in massive surges, from side to side between the ups and downs. It was bad enough to keep the ship's captain in his stateroom for the entire seven days to Singapore.

By the second day most of the passengers were sick, as well as half the crew. The overwhelming smell of vomit meant that staff were retching into sick bags as they attempted to clean the ever-present mess in the passageways and around the decks.

Shirley was one of a group of about 30 passengers and six members of the band who turned up nightly for dinner, and dancing in the ballroom afterwards. Andreas was always there and by night four had reserved a table for two. She was loving being courted in a deliciously romantic and gentlemanly way, albeit with considerable haste. She realised there wasn't much time, and wondered what should she do. She couldn't comprehend why a 40-year-old man would be interested in an 18-year-old girl. He knew her age because he'd personally checked her passport, but did he know she was a virgin? Could he tell, somehow?

That night he told her about his family in Italy. He talked about his parents, brothers and sisters, nieces and nephews. He did not mention a wife and Shirley didn't ask. He then made his first approach to take her to his cabin. Unable to think straight, she told him she had her period. Obviously aware that she'd made it up, Andreas shrugged his shoulders, poured her another wine then swept her back onto the dance floor. Finally he walked her back to her cabin, where he kissed her gently.

At the break of day six he presented at her cabin door, appealing to her to make the decision to join him in his cabin that evening. The ship's crew had made up time and would be docking in Singapore tomorrow morning.

Shirley always thought her first lover would be a man she'd known forever. Someone she planned to marry, perhaps. *Never mind,* she told the sun streaming through the porthole in her cabin. *You'll be the only girl you'll ever know to lose her virginity to a mature officer on the Castel Felice.*

Whilst dressing for the most thrilling night of her life, she counted her lucky stars that she was not one of those Greek brides heading blindly into marriage with an uneducated, immature Aussie bloke.

'Be still and let me make love to you. You don't have to do anything, beautiful lady.

"Who will believe my verse in time to come
If it were filled with your most high deserts?
Though yet, heaven knows, it is but as a tomb
Which hides your life, and shows not half your parts.
If I could write the beauty in your eyes
And in fresh numbers number all your graces…"'

He made love to her several times during the evening and she decided there and then that going to his cabin was the best decision she'd ever made. Some of the night she lay awake, her mind and body overflowing with gratitude and relief that she hadn't bled because he was so gentle. Later she remembered an accident she'd had as a child when she'd fallen on barbed wire climbing over a neighbour's fence. Seven or eight years of age at the time, she'd been in excruciating pain and had bled, but not for long. Margery had obviously played it down.

Thanks Mum, she thought and then recited a little soliloquy in her head whilst Andreas held her close.

> Every woman should lose her virginity to a handsome, intelligent, experienced Italian. No schoolboy fumbling and embarrassment in the back seat of a car, no fear of waking up pregnant and no heartache when I leave him because we've only just met! He will write to me and I will get on with my life and see what happens.

He woke her at six in the morning, gently told her she'd better go to her cabin, pack her suitcase and have some breakfast.

As they parted, he said, 'Come to Reception after we've docked. I'm taking you to the airport.'

'There is a problem, beautiful lady. I am sorry, the aeroplanes are on strike. Confrontation very tricky, much fighting in Indonesia, but we will go into the city to my travel friend, see what she can do for you.'

They were driven to a travel agency and Shirley felt dizzy at the speed and complexity of the arrangements being made, mostly without input from her. She would need to stay overnight in Singapore. A hotel was booked and paid for. One of the staff would wake her at five in the morning and take her to the airport. She would board a special businessman's flight to Bangkok, with a few stops en route including her destination, Kota Baharu.

Her commercial ticket was refunded, a seat on the private jet was booked and paid for and a new ticket issued. Andreas would have to go back to the ship but would drop her at the hotel; she could spend the day exploring the city and get an early night. She would also need to send a telegram to Trish and David Fam to alert them to her new arrival time.

Andreas held her hand in the back seat of the cab and they sat in silence most of the way to the hotel.

'How will I ever be able to thank you, Andreas?' she smiled as he took her to the front door.

'The thanks are mine. "Then happy I, that love and am beloved where I may not remove nor be removed."'

He gave her a quick hug and one last kiss, and then he was gone.

Age Two

The plane was full and she was the only woman on board.

They landed in towns she could not find on the map in her seat pocket. When the plane stopped, passengers got off and new passengers got on but everyone else was ordered to remain seated at all times. Two uniformed policemen checked everyone's tickets and passports whilst half a dozen men in army uniforms surrounded the plane for the duration of the stopovers, pointing rifles and handguns at the windows to ensure nobody moved.

The first time it happened was terrifying and Shirley was not alone with her fears. But after they'd endured several take offs and landings, most of the passengers had adjusted to the situation.

Shirley was sitting next to a Chinese American who enjoyed the sound of his own voice. Ironically, his running commentary helped normalise the situation for her. Malaya had signed a long forgotten Friendship Pact with Indonesia in 1959 and here they were, in late 1965, still fighting each other. 'But it'll be over soon,' he continued on in his cocksure way. 'They'll make a Peace Agreement next year and Malaya will formally become Malaysia, mark my words.' He was right, too.

While a male steward served the men lunch and Chinese tea on the flight, Shirley was given water but no food. Her new companion gave her his bowl of unfinished rice and two dim-sims, and though it wasn't much, it was good. She ate with her fingers like everyone else, and somehow felt safer once she had food in her stomach.

They'd been travelling for eight hours when she disembarked at Kota Baharu.

Predictably, the telegram she'd sent to Trish and David hadn't arrived so there was nobody at the one-shed, single-runway airport to meet her. A taxi eventually turned up and the driver, who spoke no English, was given instructions by the man in charge of the shed. For 20 minutes and in total silence he drove at break neck speed on winding, unmade roads surrounded by rice paddies. Finally they came to a small village.

'Sini!' he smiled at her through the rear vision mirror, pulling into the driveway of a relatively modern western-style building with a commercial sign on the front gate.

'Di-sini!' he pointed to the sign.

Shirley laughed out loud. The weight of the journey she'd taken to get to 'sini' spontaneously lifted with the point of a stranger's finger, and a single word whose meaning, under the circumstances, would have been clear in any language. She was *here*!

'Thank God you're here!' Trish rushed out of the house to greet her whilst the driver hauled her case off the back seat.

David was close behind, running out of the front office to repeat verbatim, 'Thank God you're here!'

'We'd nearly given up on you today,' Trish hugged her again, the physical contact alerting Shirley to her friend's pregnant state.

'Congratulations – your first child! How wonderful!' she exclaimed.

'I was about to call the Embassy in Singapore,' David added as he ushered them inside.

Briefly she told them about the past 24 hours, fighting back tears when admitting she'd been a bit scared.

'A bit? That's incredible!' Trish took control. 'Thankfully you're safe now, but you won't have time to unpack before dinner. A stiff drink might help? We're expecting our bank manager and a friend from Brunei any minute.'

By the time Shirley and her friends drove to Kuala Lumpur for Christmas three weeks later, she was feeling very grown up and ready for anything.

Four men had attacked her at the local market, then chased her after she'd taken a photo of a woman sitting cross-legged on her stall table. She'd been eaten alive by mosquitoes as she helped Trish cook dinner in a kitchen flooded with knee-deep water. She'd also been wined and dined by the town's bank manager, who had been gracious in defeat when she declined to stay over, and played poker with the locals (and won) at a club where everyone gambled on one game or another.

The friendship with Trish had begun when she was working in the Alfred Hospital library and dating David Fam, a Malaysian student attending Melbourne University. They married shortly after David attained his degree in architecture, and accepted a promising position in Kota Baharu. Trish was wearing the going-away dress Shirley had made her for the wedding when she waved them off to begin their new life a year ago.

David's family, and their luxurious home on Snob Hill, were everything that she'd expected – and some. His parents and siblings welcomed her warmly and made it clear she was not permitted to do anything for herself, or them; there was a servant for everything. It was her first experience with paid help and it affected her deeply. The servants performed all the menial tasks around the house with charm and a willingness that surprised her, notwithstanding some obvious jealousies and protective tactics between the kitchen and domestic staff. Given the holiday season, the mansion was rather crowded, which meant she had to share a large bedroom and bathroom with Trish and David. As intuitive as ever, Shirley went for walks in the afternoons so they could 'take a nap' in private.

On the 13th December, prior to departing Kota Baharu, she woke with a fever. Sweats and chills followed and then the illness quickly subsided, only for the symptoms to return a few days later. Trish took her to a doctor.

'I am very sorry,' he said as he wrote her a script for malaria pills.

'Not as much as we are,' Trish groaned. 'Must have been those damn Anopheles mosquitoes in our kitchen.'

Perhaps her friend's translation of the prognosis ('*Sometimes it's quick but can take years*') had been wrong, or maybe the pills had simply worked in miracle time, but the Plasmodium parasite did not progress to more serious symptoms. Shirley ascribed it to her lucky number 13.

On Christmas Day the servants cooked pretty ordinary steak and chips for Patricia and Shirley 'to make you feel at home' whilst serving course after course of fabulous Chinese dishes to the extended family around the 20-seat dining table. The children present could speak several languages and were immediately cast in the role of interpreters.

During the celebrations Shirley attempted to make good on her promise to call Melbourne collect, but it didn't happen until Boxing Day. Although it was common during the Confrontation for local technical difficulties to sabotage communication with the outside world, Shirley was visibly distressed at the thought of letting her parents down. Would they think she'd forgotten? Guessing correctly that she was homesick, Trish and the servants did their best to cheer her up.

A few days later she wrote in an airmail letter home that for reasons she didn't yet understand, or question, she'd decided to conquer her itchy feet and be settled in her own business, with a permanent cleaning lady, by the time she turned 25. She couldn't know then that this was just the first of several reinventions of herself she would make during the next seven years before doing exactly that.

Every day with Trish and David was a new experience. To the relief of her friends, she attributed her persistent sweats and chills to acclimatisation and before she left the three of them made a commitment to never lose touch. And they never have.

Landing at the old international Kai Tak airport in Hong Kong was a death-defying experience.

Its single runway jutted out into the harbour at a hair-raising angle to Lion Rock. With nail-biting proximity that challenged pilots with a lifetime of experience, they flew the planes in between the mountains and Kowloon's crowded apartment blocks. When air traffic was heavy and the weather wild, circling prior to landing was inevitable. Even seasoned travellers steeled themselves to cope with the bumpy landing that followed. Overhead lockers sprung open and spilled their contents into the aisles, adults were violently ill and every child on board screamed.

Shirley, in the grip of recurrent malaria symptoms, found an airport bar when they finally landed, washing two pills down with a straight Scotch. She collected her suitcase before queuing for a cab. She'd planned to get the hospitality bus to her hotel but decided against it whilst they were circling. What if the streets were as congested as the sky?

The hotel manager, Peter Yeung, greeted her warmly with a firm handshake. Appearing not to notice her flushed cheeks and sweaty palms, he checked her in and escorted her to her room. It was a comfortably furnished hotel and her bedroom contained a single bed, dressing table, radio, desk and chair. The share-bathroom was nearby.

'One of Project Concern's staff will be here soon to take you out to meet everyone on the American launches in the centre of Kowloon Bay,' Peter said, one hand lingering on the centre of her back. 'Pay attention to where you are going; you may have to return on your own. I will take you to dinner tonight, yes?'

She studied him closely then. He was Eurasian and stood tall in a lightweight grey suit, white shirt and black bow tie. His English was excellent and he smiled continuously. He had to be 30 but was not wearing a wedding ring. Neither did Andreas for that matter, and he was 40.

Age Two

Shirley quickly caught herself. *Wake up, girl! Great and pre boomer generations don't wear rings. Only their women do…so what are you going to do this time?*

'Thank you, I'd be happy to dine with you,' she returned his smile. A girl has to eat.

'I've never seen so many happy children,' she mused to the boy steering the sampan through the maze of sampans en route to the two donated American Navy launches. Smiling faces and waving hands, thousands upon thousands of them, were so close they could reach out to grab the hand of the pretty lady passing by.

'We happy in Eternal City, lady. Harbour for us. Lots better than home.'

It was 1964 and the influx of refugees forced out of China was still constant; it was hard to comprehend how this teeming harbour could accommodate any more. Shirley had spent her first day on a tour of the city and her sense of astonishment would remain throughout her stay in Hong Kong.

Her tour had begun in the incense-choked Man Mo Temple which pre-dated the Brit's arrival in 1841. Here the people still burned bank notes, in denominations large and small, for one's deceased kin to use in the after-life. It presented a stark contrast to the countless surrounding stores, which sold everything from alternative medicine and credit cards to children's and adults' toys, clothes, food, fridges and tour guides. In the commercial high-rise buildings close by, indistinguishable from flats housing millions of permanent residents, Chinese businessmen took refuge for survival reasons too, but with dramatically different outcomes. Squeezed off the mainland as a result of the Communist Party's deep suspicion of its rivals, they had proceeded to make their fortunes in the comfort and security of the English colony.

Traditional medicine, religion, primitive cuisine and ancient art were peddled peacefully here in the bay, alongside contemporary commerce conducted by multi-millionaires, rogues and international operators in every field imaginable. It was a lot to absorb in one day.

After 20 minutes of moving at a snail's pace, they reached the Navy launches. Shirley's observations of life in the city yesterday had surprised her, but every aspect of the refugees' lives in Kowloon Bay was a revelation and she was glad of the time. Children and adults waved happily, dogs barked and jumped overboard in search of anything edible, and birds whistled and sang as they flew overhead. Babies laughed and cried and screamed, water and sewerage and left-over chicken bones and noodles and soiled nappies clung to the edges of anything fixed. Young and old men in sampans overloaded with vegetables, fruit and unidentifiable goods skilfully manoeuvred to shore to set up stalls at the market. The sky was blue and the sun shone on a world of people who had virtually nothing, all living happily in one horrendously crowded bay.

It was hard to think. What could you think? You could only feel. It was bigger than anything she'd ever seen or known before.

'Welcome Miss Shirley,' Dr Turpin's permanent guide, Miss Celina, greeted her. 'We are glad you are here. Thank you for caring. This morning you will observe, this afternoon you will feed the children. Sometimes it is hard for Western people to adjust. If you are not ready, we wait. Now I will introduce you to new friends.'

First she met the medical and dental staff and the introductions to their work took the morning. When her guide led her up to the top deck where a couple of chefs were serving lunch, the smorgasbord of freshly made Chinese dishes and huge bowls of rice was confronting; she couldn't possibly eat anything today. She didn't feel sick exactly, but her stomach was churning. She was going to help feed 500 children soon, which entailed pushing food packages through a porthole into the outstretched hands of children and parents on sampans, queued in long, zigzagging formations. Her hands were shaking at the thought of it.

'Tomorrow you help the land team take food and donated clothing to the people who live in the tents on the hills. Third day you do menial tasks for surgeons on the medical launch. Weekend off I think, then day after you will do the same for dental clinic. Fifth day usually you help nurses visit very sick people on the sampans, unable to get to us. This is your job, every week about the same,' Miss Celina informed her.

A few days later one of the leaders took Shirley aside, regarding her with concern. 'Many of the staff have drinks and supper at The Ritz on Fridays but do you think you'll be eating lunch by tomorrow? You haven't eaten since you got here and we are worried.'

'I'm so sorry,' she apologised, 'but I have been eating. Peter at the hotel has been shouting me dinner. I'm hungry by the end of the day.'

'Well! Lucky you!' the woman snapped sarcastically. 'Thank you for telling us and putting our minds at rest. Very thoughtful of you!'

Not surprisingly Shirley was fighting tears when she got back to her hotel but Peter cheered her up, reminding her of her mother.

'You are different, Shirley. Mainstream get jealous of people who are different. Chin up. I'm taking you to see The Flying Circus tonight.'

Doctor Jim Turpin, the medical practitioner, businessman and philanthropist who founded and ran Project Concern Inc. from his home in America, arrived for a brief visit two weeks later. He invited Shirley to accompany him to a sponsorship lunch and added obliquely that he'd had some interesting feedback about her.

They were joined by five men: two Caucasian financiers and three Chinese businessmen. Dr Turpin managed to speak to them all individually before moving around the table to speak quietly to Shirley.

'I've decided I want you to start taking some of my entrepreneurial acquaintances to lunch. I'll take you to one more tomorrow before I fly out, although you've already got the hang of it. We just picked up US$50,000. Well done!'

Trish and David had taught her to eat with chopsticks, a staff member was appointed to extend and monitor the invitations and accompany her and pay the bills, and the first three lunches she hosted were immediately successful with generous donations committed. It was the kind of steep learning curve Shirley loved and would almost certainly have led to a salaried, public relations position locally, or via Dr Turpin's diverse interests in the States.

Yet despite the promise of such opportunities, she left Hong Kong two weeks later without fully explaining why. She told her colleagues that her mother needed her. This was true, of course, and she was certainly homesick, but her money was holding up and would have lasted the three months she'd committed.

However, it wouldn't have taken a genius to surmise the kind of salacious incidents that had occurred at the five lunches she'd hosted that compelled her to quickly depart.

She travelled home via Bangkok, and stayed over in KL for a week with Trish and David, who'd returned briefly on business. She was lucky to get through Malaysian customs without being arrested, given she was found to have in her possession a contraband book of poetry she'd picked up second hand. Detained by four uniformed men, she was questioned for two hours, during which she recited several of the 'illegal' poems. One such rendition brought tears to the chief interrogator's eyes. Eventually they gave up and allowed her to join her friends who had been waiting patiently on the other side of the arrivals gate. The red-eyed chief kept the book.

Shirley arrived home on St Valentine's Day, 1966, the day Australia changed from using pounds, shillings and pence to decimal currency. She changed her Hong Kong currency into Australian dollars at the Melbourne airport and soon returned to Dr Dorevitch's practice.

On her first day back on the job in Collins Street, she realised that it was not going to be permanent. She'd been away nearly three months and changed much more than her money by the time her feet hit the 20th floor of 18 Collins Street.

'Never go back!' her mother had counselled. 'History repeats itself because the only thing we learn from it is that we don't learn!'

Sorry Mum. I'll never go back again, she resolved.

Family secrets unravelling

Shirley arrived home to find Margery in a brief remission, Alan serving as president of the Melbourne chapter of the Multiple Sclerosis Association, and Bev still working in the photographic studio but busy planning her August wedding.

As for herself, Shirley struggled to settle on anything.

During her absence Grandma Jones had followed in Margery's footsteps and suffered a stroke. But hers was severe and Alan had secured a room for her in a nursing home a short taxi ride from Canterbury.

Everyone was very sad. Shirley visited Grandma Jones once a week with her mother until she finally slipped away in her sleep. Margery noted bitterly, 'It doesn't seem fair that she's gone before me.'

There had been a letter from Andreas waiting for Shirley upon her homecoming, posted in England with a return post office box address in Rome. She sent a reply, applied to several job advertisements in *The Age* and decided to move into a flat with her Camberwell High School friend,

Lyn Armstrong, as soon as she secured a new position. At the same time she arranged a large fundraising party in the backyard in Canterbury for Project Concern. Bev sang, as did one of her artist friends, Jeff Carter, and they raised nearly AU$200 to send to Hong Kong. It was a good effort for those days.

Shirley hadn't been kissed for what seemed like forever, but received one uninvited at the end of that evening. A former classmate from Stott's lured her to her car to listen to the latest Presley album in her new cassette player. In a sudden and aggressive move, the woman grabbed Shirley's elbows and kissed her fervently on the lips. Shirley struggled, managed to free one arm and used it to slap her face.

'I've never been so disinclined to listen to Elvis!' she sputtered with a glare as she jumped out of the car and bolted back to the house.

Alan was devastated that Shirley was planning to move out, but spoke only of his disappointment that his younger daughter hadn't gone to university. Margery, refusing to differentiate between the girls, reminded him yet again that they had minds of their own and would make successes of their lives regardless.

'Most of their friends aren't going to uni either, Alan. It takes more than one generation to change a culture!' she added recklessly. Alan let it go and kept the source of his angst to himself. Bev was getting married and that was as it should be, but if only Shirley had gone to uni she'd be there now, and boarding at home for at least another two or three years.

Whenever Margery got agitated these days, Alan went out to the shed on one pretext or another. She was tame now, rarely passionate for long anymore, and he'd finally begun to acknowledge to himself that it depressed him. He had reason to worry about depression and was harbouring the fact that they'd kept his sister, Phyllis, and brother Jack's suicides from the girls, along with his brother Arthur's mysterious death. Margery had agreed to tell them, but kept putting it off, still quoting Wordsworth from a lifetime ago:

A simple child that lightly draws its breath.
And feels its life in every limb.
What should it know of death?

The phone calls came regularly when they were in Yarrawonga and Warracknabeal. The beautiful Phyllis, a true lady with a big heart and sharp sense of humour finally managed to kill herself on her third attempt. The first time she threw herself into the Yarra River, but a man on the foreshore had dived in to rescue her. Her depression escalated and the second time she overdosed, but not enough. She finally succeeded via the gas oven in the kitchen; she couldn't bear living with her drunken, abusive husband any longer.

Brother Jack had been visiting and entertaining the girls with his lovely nature and down-to-earth repartee only weeks before his wife and young son found him asphyxiated in his car in the garage.

Arthur's death followed and was less dramatic, but closure was impossible – there was no diagnosable cause. He also suffered depression and died under mysterious circumstances in a nursing home.

Alan's mother, Harriet Potter McLaughlin had died recently in her home in Melbourne where she'd lived alone and virtually penniless since husband John died 40 years earlier.

He was a successful farmer who'd made a small fortune, and even sponsored Douglas Mawson's first Antarctic Expedition. Mawson became Australia's greatest polar explorer but John died too soon to receive accolades or benefits, and his personal affairs were left in a terrible mess.

Harriet was a woman who knew how to spend money, not manage it. Every time Alan thought about his father's previous family, and his siblings' depressive natures, his own depression deepened. He wondered if he'd passed the gene onto his girls, and how many other secrets his father had taken to the grave.

Until Harriet's death, Margery agreed that Alan could take Bev and Shirley to visit his mother once a year, but refused to go with them. Since the girls were out of nappies he'd dutifully driven them to 'Nana's' house in Auburn for afternoon tea during the Christmas holidays and they always arrived back (to Grandma's home in Mornington) bursting with tell-tale stories, unconsciously set-up by Margery's tendency towards snobbery that she'd learned from her own mother.

'The floors are filthy,' Shirley would begin, 'the house is dark, the biscuits are soft and crumbly and there's always a terrible smell in the house, Mum, as if someone's died and been buried in the walls.'

Margery replied circuitously. 'Reading Agatha Christie at your age is probably not a good idea for a girl like you. You only have to visit Nana once a year so please don't complain again.'

The succession of departed family members had prompted a few of the remaining relatives to surreptitiously conjecture that there'd soon be a spot of money coming their way. This was depressing Alan as much as anything.

Grandma Jones' property in Mornington was finally on the market. Following his bankruptcy in 1960, Margery's brother, Stan was doing well as CEO of the publishing business in Maryborough but had just been diagnosed with lung cancer. Given the likelihood that his affairs would be in order, there was little chance there, yet his wife and grown children had heard the rumblings and were troubled. Stan must have made a will! Perhaps he hadn't told them?

Alan's greatest fear was that if something happened to him in the midst of all this, who would take charge? There was a wedding fast approaching and the girls needed to be in full possession of the facts.

He'd been carrying the world on his shoulders without falter or complaint for a quarter of a century. In the last decade he'd lost half his siblings, his own mother and mother-in-law were gone, he was losing the love of his life and now his beloved girls were leaving home.

Most days he managed to shake himself free of depressive thoughts about his own lot because there wasn't time to wallow. In the process he'd inevitably switch focus to his 'Lovely' and wonder if she was depressed too. How could she not be? The doctor's news was dire yet she continued to 'live through the night' and battle along the passage until she could walk with the aid of a stick again. Notwithstanding, there were subtle changes in her disposition, as if she had a secret. She was a rare woman who could keep secrets.

Any aspirations for herself had gone, lost in the constancy of pain and her close proximity to death. The girls' futures still worried her – it seemed more or less that the lot of mainstream women in the 1960s was the same as it had been forever; first childhood, then puberty blossoming into adulthood, then a short stint on paltry wages in the work force, followed by a long life of domestic slavery in a hopefully happy marriage producing hopefully healthy children. Should they chance to find a career they loved, they'd have to give it up when they married anyway, or go into business for themselves. And one still required the endorsement of a male guarantor to borrow money from the bank in order to compete in a market place where women 'do not belong!' The only upside her troubled mind could grasp was that at least nowadays they didn't have to remain spinsters to look after their aging parents.

In a saner state of mind, she took the girls aside and told them the whole sad story of the aunt and uncles they'd lost to suicide, the current covetous gossip in the family and the likely financial outcome. She apologised for not telling them how their uncles and aunty died, and even divulged she'd put aside a small inheritance for them to receive when she left this mortal coil.

'Make the most of everything,' she instructed for the umpteenth time.

These moments of clarity still saw her daring to hope that Shirley would find her calling and become successful and happy.

As she kissed Shirley goodnight, she would whisper, 'Whatever happens, you'll never be mainstream, darling!' A few days later, when she overheard Bev repeating those words to her sister, her joy was overwhelming.

Moving out, moving back, moving on

In the lead up to Bev's wedding, Shirley played the part of Diamondi in the Box Hill Repertory Company's season of *The Gardens of Adonis*. Though her performance had been a great success, the role was challenging and at times distressing.

Diamondi cried a lot and didn't speak English so Shirley said 'fuck' a lot when learning her lines by heart and sound, the latter requiring countless rehearsals. Her character's provocative actions with her male co-actors was difficult to sustain and on the final night she became a genuine damsel in distress when the curtain failed to drop at the end of Act Two. Alone, centre stage, she cried and sobbed for the next 35 seconds without needing to act and received her first standing ovation on her hands and knees with mascara pouring down her face.

'It's hard to explain, but it was a bit of an anti-climax when the curtain finally fell,' she told Margery and Alan when she got home.

None of the family saw this first performance in an adult play. Margery was too sick, Alan was her carer and Bev was too busy. The only evidence of her week on stage was the local rag's rave review complete with headline 'Young Actress', accompanied by her photo.

After Bev's wedding, Shirley moved into Lyn's flat in Hawthorn. She had to do something, anything, to kick-start her life again. Lyn needed someone to share the rent, and whilst their friendship had been strained during their time at Camberwell High, both girls were determined it would never break again.

Lyn's father would drive her and her sisters to Australian Football League matches every week. Late that year, when their team 'The Cats' were playing a semi-final in Geelong, Shirley was invited to join them. Mr Armstrong had insisted his girls sit in the back of his old Holden for the hour's drive from Melbourne so that Shirley could sit in the front 'to enjoy the view'. As they were driving, his hand reached across to fondle her breasts and legs before groping under her skirt. She'd push it away but back it would come.

Of course Shirley insisted on sitting in the back on the way home, but the following day she told Lyn she was changing teams and wouldn't be coming anymore.

Lyn later discovered the truth from her youngest sister who'd been sexually abused by her father for years. Mrs Armstrong finally kicked him out, but not before Lyn had left home and was now struggling to pay the rent.

Margery and Alan let Shirley move out without objection. Alan was sure she'd come home as soon as she got it out of her system, or when her mother needed her – whatever came first. Margery sensed her daughter was suffering from loneliness and a lack of purpose; she'd been there once herself.

'She's looking for love, Alan. Her experiences in Asia sated her dreams, for a while, but her heart craves nourishment now. A like-minded girlfriend is a good start, until someone turns up she can call her own.'

When Shirley was appointed secretary to Gertrude Johnson, Founding Director of the Australian National Theatre in 1966, it would forever be cast in her mind as an enigmatic, life-changing experience. Miss Johnson, an internationally renowned opera singer who'd performed in London's West End and Convent Garden, was the current Lessor of the Princess Theatre in Melbourne.

So much happened during the next 12 months, with so many dramatic, unexpected events taking place one after another that it was impossible to guess where this employment would lead, or what choices Shirley would make to fulfil her dreams.

Whilst loving her role as Miss Johnson's secretary, her enduring passion for the stage prompted her to audition for the Princess Theatre. She turned out for their ensemble cast and returned for a second audition. This led to her first professional offer of a small part in a forthcoming play, but she was strangely undecided. She'd recently met a young man by the name of Allan Uebergang, and Margery decided he was the reason for her hesitancy.

The greatest impact at the start was Gertrude Johnson herself, an authoritarian woman of dynamic presence and purpose who mentored her new protégé with passion and humour. Her iron fist was reserved for others. Of course Shirley asked a lot of questions and quickly discovered Miss Johnson loved being questioned. Her answer to why she'd gone from singing opera to directing plays was delivered with usual aplomb.

'Sir Laurence Olivier started the National Theatre in London, where I performed to many standing ovations, my dear. When I was growing tired, and missing family and friends, I decided to do the same thing in my own home town. Several luminaries you'd know by name, if I were to divulge confidences which I won't, say I'm doing it better than Laurence, but they might be biased.'

Every day was busy and the potential for distraction constant. Shirley spent lunch hours and breaks watching actors rehearsing, gradually slipping into character. There was no immediate indication she missed learning lines and performing herself, seeming to take it all in her stride.

When Ray Milland flew in from London to take the lead role in *Dial M for Murder*, it was Shirley who presented him with an opening night bouquet at the reception for Melbourne's elite in the dress circle foyer. Yet it was her good manners that inspired her to thank Gertrude for the opportunity, rather than any star-struck gratitude.

It was a hot and steamy night but the audience was unreserved in its applause. Mr Milland took the flowers, kissed Shirley on the cheek, handed back the flowers and proceeded to address his adoring public for 15 minutes in glorious English tones. He wound up with an overview of the history of the Princess Theatre, and the joy of being in Melbourne, then turned brusquely to Miss Johnson.

'If *you* don't get the fucking air conditioning working in this bloody theatre by tomorrow night, Gertrude, you can put my understudy on because I'll be leaving on the next plane home!'

That said, he planted another kiss on Shirley's cheek, took the bouquet, stormed down the stairs, strode out of the theatre and jumped into a waiting cab.

In the thick of these theatrical days and social nights, Shirley's passion for the news of the world was largely abandoned due to lack of time.

Apart from headlines, like Australia's conscripts landing in Vietnam and Prince Charles settling into his new school at Timbertop in Victoria's high country, Allan Uebergang and his family and their Lutheran Church were taking up a large part of her spare time. She was also endeavouring to support Bev with the adjustments involved in living with the in-laws whilst waiting for their house to be built.

Like most young marrieds Bev was working all day, starting again when she got home and beginning to wish she could start a family. If she gave up her day job, she'd stop feeling used and exhausted. Shirley quoted a recent article in *The Australian* that men were currently paid 35 per cent more than women in the same job and Bev's decision to start a family crystallised… *'as soon as we move into our new home.'*

The death of one of Margery's favourite authors, Evelyn Waugh, brought Shirley back to the wider world. Author of *Midnight Orgies at No. 10* and *Vile Bodies*, which satirised the life and times of the bright young things of London society, Waugh was a man who refused to have radio or television in his home yet wrote savage, modern satire and, upon his death, received an extraordinary outpouring from fans around the world.

Simultaneously Mao's Cultural Revolution was happening, Australia's PM Harold Holt was going 'all the way with LBJ' (Lyndon B. Johnson) and London was becoming the swinging capital of the world with its embrace of the contraception pill, pot and freedom. Perhaps as an encouraging note to her younger daughter, Margery mused to Alan in Shirley's presence that she always thought her girl would go to London to find her calling. 'Of course, she's got plenty of time,' she smiled.

Margery's heart, body and mind were overwhelmed by the multiple sclerosis now. A commode chair was permanently installed on her side of the bed, her sleeping pill dosage had doubled and with it the number of Alpine cigarettes she lit every day, although she only managed to smoke half before they went out. Between work and social commitments Shirley continued to help her father with nursing duties but her extracurricular activities had increased because Allan Uebergang had proposed, and she had accepted.

Flatting with Lyn lasted fewer than six months but they were strong friends by the time Shirley left and she did so with Lyn's blessings.

A week after her arrival home she received a personal letter from Ian Mair, CEO of Angus and Robertson publishers, congratulating her on some poems she'd written. 'Most earnestly I urge you to keep on writing,' he concluded by hand, 'reading, writing and keeping your eyes open!' She'd been writing creatively for years but had stopped when she met Allan and was briefly unsettled by Mair's encouragement. Was she cutting herself off from the 20th century like Evelyn Waugh, before she'd written her masterpiece?

'Allan is a kind and genuine man, Mum,' she reassured herself and her mother.

'You said he's in the Royal Australian Navy?' Margery asked happily, beginning to take this new boyfriend seriously.

'Yes, and it's a very skilful job. He has one younger brother and one sister who's a nurse. His father is a publican and his mother is lovely – but not "Lovely" like you!'

'He's a sailor?' her mother surmised shrewdly.

'Radio operators are highly trained, Mum.'

'Does he intend to stay in the Navy – for life?'

'I don't know. He had to sign on for nine years. Can I bring him home for dinner one night? I'll cook. You'll like him.'

Margery and Alan were confident Bev had chosen the right man to marry but they were seriously concerned about Shirley's choice. Her secretarial and theatrical skills had landed her in an auspicious place for a girl with talent and big dreams, so why had she lost sight of the harbour she was heading for?

As strange as it seemed, her sister's unwitting influence appeared to be leading her towards a life befitting most young women of the time – a suburban life built on 'normal' expectations. Bev had married a man from the Methodist 'wowser' Church and Shirley had followed by joining the Wattle Park Presbyterian Church, immediately becoming a Sunday school teacher. Bev was still singing, playing piano and working for a photographic studio whereas Shirley had stopped writing, left the repertory group that had given her a promising start and reneged on an offer at the Princess Theatre that almost certainly would have landed her the career she'd long coveted. Or had she? Was that Margery's dream?

Age Two

Alan surprised himself when pressing his wife for answers. 'What's happened to her, Lovely? She's always been different, but it looks like she's running away to safety. What happened overseas? What's she running from?'

Margery sighed heavily whilst repositioning her aching legs. It was a fair question she couldn't have answered until recently, but apologised for not telling Alan earlier and proceeded to summarise what had transpired. Their girl had lost her virginity to Andreas, the Head Purser on the *Castel Felice*, he'd been very good to her in Singapore when she needed to get to Kota Baharu, they'd exchanged letters, he came back a few months ago and she'd joined him on board at the Melbourne docks. He then left her in his cabin for a short time to check on his crew and two hours later she heard the first call for all visitors to leave the ship. She tried to get out but the door was locked. Could it be…was he kidnapping her? It didn't make sense. He was a kind, gentle man who recited Shakespeare to her. She was trapped and it was terrifying.

Alan was deeply involved now and demanded a blow by blow description of how she got off the ship. 'Ten minutes after the last call, the cleaning lady let herself in!' Margery stepped up a pace. 'Shirley grabbed her bag and ran. The only gangplank still down was the crew's, and it began to draw back seconds after she was on it and running for her life. She literally jumped three feet onto the pier. She didn't look back, collapsed into the front seat of the first cab waiting on the wharf and told the driver "Go! Just go!" She smiled, dear, when she said that. Obviously in shock, she then began to wonder if she could trust the taxi driver!'

'This experience could have put her off trusting men for life, Lovely! I don't get it. Why wouldn't she go for a career instead of settling for the first man to propose marriage?'

'We don't know that she's settled on Allan yet, although I suspect she will. She received a letter from Andreas several weeks after the kidnap attempt. He apologised profusely, said he'd sent the cleaner in to give her a chance to leave the ship, or stay. "I'm not much good at judging men, Mum," she said, "and I don't like my chances of succeeding in a man's world until I get smarter."'

'What? She's going to try the traditional path until she gets more experience of men, and the world we run?'

'Well! You said it, Alan. May I suggest you don't sit in judgment of your younger daughter until the world you run changes, dear?'

'I guess I deserved that, but I always thought she was going to take over where you left off and help make change happen.'

Margery recrossed her legs and wiped her brow again. It was a sign and Alan relaxed a little.

'Let's not give up on her yet, dear. Let's approach this with belief and disbelief suspended. No thanks to us, she'd moved house seven times before she left home of her own accord. She's changed jobs at least that many too, won and lost dozens of friends and been used and abused by more men (and women) than she's disclosed to me. Her imagination and natural acting ability will rescue her when boredom sets in, which it probably will for as long as she lives. It's her biggest flaw and greatest asset. She just doesn't know it yet.

'This last journey failed to live up to her vivid imagination of what life should be. A new start is essential and she's dreaming it up as she goes. She has to learn the hard way, but she'll always be a paradox, Alan. Creative yet practical; mentally and physically tough and determined yet emotionally vulnerable, passionate and gregarious by nature but a loner by choice; always interested but quickly bored!'

'Well,' Alan grimaced, 'with belief and disbelief suspended? I think I've got it.'

The excitement of the engagement, and some delicate issues with the Uebergang family were briefly put aside when Shirley personally rubbed shoulders with the ghost of the Princess Theatre. It was the afternoon of the dress rehearsal of *As You Like It,* and Shirley had overheard members of the cast discussing what sounded to her like superstitious urban legend.

The old and beautiful theatre had long been said to have a resident ghost, witnessed during the last century by countless actors from around the globe. The cast of this Shakespearean production were professionals, well known to Australian and UK audiences and daring to hope the ghost would appear. It was an established fact that when it did appear at a dress rehearsal of a Shakespearean play, the season would be long and successful and the cast would receive a standing ovation on opening night.

That afternoon Shirley had a folder of typed letters for Gertrude to sign. She knew her boss would be sitting in the aisle seat, front row, right side of the dress circle, watching the rehearsal. The upstairs doors were open. She walked through and stood for a moment to watch the actors on stage.

'Jealous in honour, sudden and quick in quarrel;
Seeking the bubble reputation
Even in the cannon's mouth…'

Suddenly she was lightly pushed from behind by a man in a long, heavy coat. Spontaneously she turned and looked around. A number of cries and squeals from the stage below made her look back and an actor stopped mid-sentence to stare upstairs. Not *at* her but *near* her. And there was the ghost, minus a face, walking down the stairs of the dress circle. It was definitely the in-house spectre – his supernatural height, the flowing cape, the faceless head…

He turned from the aisle and walked along the row of seats behind Gertrude. She heard him, felt the presence of his heavily clothed body and stood up sharply. He walked across two aisles and 'floated' back up the far right stairway until he disappeared through the exit door.

Shirley watched the ghost until he'd left the dress circle, his gown billowing behind him as if blown by a wind.

One of the cast called up to Gertrude: 'We have a hit on our hands, ma'am! The ghost has appeared! Did you see him?'

'I didn't,' she called to the actor playing Orlando, 'but I felt him.'

'I saw him!' Shirley cried as she ran down the stairs to Miss Johnson, the folder of letters still glued to her fingers.

'You're a good girl,' Gertrude replied, grabbing the folder with both hands. 'Do you believe what you saw, Shirley?'

'I've never believed in ghosts but I felt him behind me, saw him come down the stairs, walk behind you and stride back to the exit. I think I need time to understand it.'

'You never will, Shirley. You just need time to accept it. Look up at the evening sky and you might find the answer to believing in poltergeists. The spirit lives, my dear!'

The following night she went out to look up at the sky. It was a stormy night with flashes of lightning, but a half-moon was strobing the blustery clouds with streaks of white, grey and fading pink. It was stunning and surreal and brought to mind a line from a poem, 'The moon was a ghostly galleon, tossed upon stormy seas' which she'd never understood before. 'So when the clouds pass over the moon, it's like a boat sailing through a storm!' she smiled happily to the sky and went off to bed, only to sleep fitfully and wake the next morning from a nightmare.

At the beginning of the dream she was at school. Mr Hunt was teaching the class that a galleon was a cargo or slave boat, merchant, container or Navy ship…this then became a foreboding of Allan on a Royal Australian Navy (RAN) ship two or three years into the future. It was a moonlit night when the ship sank and many sailors sank with it. She saw her future husband standing on the deck, but his face was gone. It was an omen or an illusion and she hoped she could forget it; he was due to be posted overseas in a couple of years and her dream had been all too encoded and bizarre to mention to anyone.

Following Shirley's acceptance of the marriage proposal, an engagement ring was chosen and the wedding date set 10 months hence on 25th November, 1967, the 25th anniversary of Allan's parents' wedding.

Several months later Shirley declined to attend further Lutheran instructions on the grounds that conversion to Allan's church was a waste of her time, and entirely unnecessary. After all, they were both protestants and even as she personally questioned the existence of God, concluded with conviction that there could surely only be one!

The Uebergang family graciously accepted the decision that the wedding would be Presbyterian. All they wanted for their son and daughter-in-law-to-be was that they have a long and happy marriage just like they'd enjoyed for the last 25 years.

Mrs Ueby warmed to Shirley immediately and was always delighted to have her help in the kitchen, and her company in the lounge with the rest of the family. The only problem was that Mrs Ueby's 'great, handyman' husband liked to fondle Shirley's thighs, breasts…whatever was easiest, whenever he felt like it. On most occasions his behaviour was quite plain to see yet the fondling seemed to be an acceptable practice within the family. Mr Ueby was usually on his third or fourth beer following a long day at his hotel when he insisted she sit next to him in the lounge settee. The only way to stop his wandering hands was to kick him under the coffee table with her right foot whilst simultaneously laughing or coughing loudly, or excusing herself to go to the bathroom or help Mrs Ueby or Allan's sister Marianne in the kitchen.

On one occasion Mrs Ueby approached her discreetly to ask a personal question, if she didn't mind. Shirley held her breath, wondering how she'd respond, but the question had nothing to do with Allan's father's gross behaviour. Surprisingly, her own mother had asked the same question a few weeks earlier.

'You've been on the stage since you were in primary school, Shirley,' she began whilst busily drying the dishes her soon-to-be daughter-in-law was washing. 'You've had some success already and I'm just wondering how you can be sure you're not going to regret giving up the chance of having a professional acting career?'

Shirley responded unequivocally. 'In many ways an actor is helpless and dependent,' she replied, 'forever caught between instant fame and total obscurity. You're just a role-player, moving and morphing your character's performance into a mould that fits in with the story and the rest of the cast. No matter how talented you are there's always a writer, producer, director, editor, lighting person, etcetera, in charge and calling the shots. There's no security and ultimately it's less about talent than just being in the right place at the right time, with the right contacts. An actor's job is indivisible from the person, yet the person is always pretending to be somebody else.

'I want to be my own person, make my own decisions, plot my own course, finish what I start, produce successful outcomes! And I will never be dependent. Never! But I'm grateful I've learned to act because it's an essential skill in life, especially for women,' she concluded potently with a rapidly beating heart, but the inference was missed.

'Gertrude Johnson helped me understand all this,' she added superfluously.

'Thank you, dear,' Mrs Ueby smiled happily. 'My Allan is a very lucky man.'

Shirley caught up with her ex-flatmate in the city the following day and filled Lyn in on the situation with her future mother and father-in-law. 'Is it possible that Mrs Ueby and the family think Mr Ueby's shameless behaviour is okay? Normal?' she asked of her worldly friend who had recently borrowed some money to have an abortion.

'Don't ask me!' Lyn retorted. 'My mother had five children and didn't know what her husband was capable of until my sister told her when she turned 20!'

'I'm 20 now,' Shirley muttered obliquely.

'Yeah. How lucky are we that it didn't happen to us when we were youngsters?'

Husband No. 1

Bev gave birth to Steven, the first born son on the 5th September 1967. He was a joy to behold and would bring great happiness to one and all, but it was also excellent timing on Bev and Rob's part because nothing else important happened in the family that September. If he'd been conceived a bit later it would have clashed with Shirley's wedding.

As it was, Margery spilt a saucepan of boiling water onto both her feet nine days prior to the wedding and two teachers on Alan's staff were on sick leave so he was teaching grades four and six when he wasn't looking after Margery, or visiting Steven, his first grandchild.

Wrapped in bandages and in terrible pain, Margery was unable to walk for the next seven days, necessitating the last-minute purchase of a pair of sandals close enough to beige to match her bag for the wedding. Resolutely she recovered in time to present as the mother-of-the-bride, her bandaged feet and logic-defying crooked smile attesting to her inimitable courage and determination.

Alan was quietly in awe of his Lovely and the fact that they'd managed to stay together 27 years, let alone have two daughters who were now off their hands. He wasn't convinced this marriage was a good thing, and didn't want to think about how long it might last. If Mr and Mrs Uebergang were surprised to be celebrating their own 25th anniversary they didn't show it, and none of the family commented on the significance of the date. As with many marriages of the era, the wife was compliant or ignorant of her husband's little indiscretions and since the topic of Mr Ueby's behaviour was never broached with Shirley, it simply didn't exist. He behaved extremely well at the reception but the bride had arranged the seating to ensure there would be no chance of wandering hands on any of the female guests.

They were married at the Wattle Park Presbyterian Church in a simple ceremony conducted by the Reverend T.B. Howells, who'd welcomed Shirley into the fold a couple of years earlier. He also attended the reception and Margery later commented that she might have remained a Presbyterian if she'd met him before she 'gave up on God and His Wowsers'. Shirley made her own gown, a mix of satin and lace with a headpiece she'd selected to hold the veil she designed and sewed. She was a svelte, smiling bride and the groom was visibly moved throughout the service.

Age Two

The reception went without a hitch and the happy couple left for their honeymoon on the resplendent property of Allan's favourite uncle and aunt in western Victoria, otherwise known as 'Lutheran country'. Their first few days of marriage were spent shooting rabbits at ungodly hours of the morning, followed by brunch and a leisurely day and evening in the homestead.

By day four Shirley was done with shooting. She didn't mind the killing in principle because rabbits had to be culled, but watching the little chaps dying was too much. She kissed her husband goodbye each morning and rolled over in the guest bedroom as the men departed with a truckload of guns, knives, an Esky of beer and ice blocks for the carcasses.

Her new aunty was concerned this might be a bad omen but Shirley quickly set her mind to rest. 'I've had enough of blood and guts and early mornings,' she declared. 'I'd rather be your company anyway.'

On return from their honeymoon, Mr and Mrs Allan Uebergang moved to Frankston, an outer seaside suburb of Melbourne known not for its class but rather its large government housing development occupied mainly by Navy personnel and their families. Whilst Frankston was the last major suburb en route to the Mornington Peninsula, so beloved in Shirley's youth, the location was chosen for its practicality. Allan had been posted to the Victorian Barracks of HMAS *Cerberus*, a short commuting distance by car.

They'd taken a month by month lease of a flat in central Frankston: Allan was due for a posting to Sydney to take up additional training on a Navy patrol boat and Shirley had resigned from the Princess Theatre to sign on with a temporary secretarial agency in Melbourne's CBD, an hour's travel each way by train.

The work was varied and mainly stimulating, the hours were nine to five and the money was good, but it came as a shock to Shirley that she'd become a replica of her sister. She was effectively working longer hours than her husband whilst also doing all the domestic duties. Of course Allan's future, and therefore hers was destined to change soon, and it did, several times during the next couple of years.

The Sydney posting was full of fun and surprises. After sharing a flat for a couple of weeks with another sailor posted to Allan's ship, Ted Sands as it happened, best friend of Shirley's first boyfriend David Streeter from

Warracknabeal, Shirley managed to secure them a double room in the Salvation Army Hostel in the CBD.

On the 13th May 1968 she turned 21 and took the day off from her temp job so Allan could give her a guided tour of the aircraft carrier, HMAS *Melbourne*, docked in Sydney Harbour, followed by dinner at a waterfront pub.

It was late when they returned, virtually legless to the hostel and Shirley removed her shoes in order to tiptoe upstairs and avoid waking the Salvo's night watchman, a 50 or 60-year-old Army man who was a little bit in love with her, but he had been waiting patiently to give her a gift-wrapped box of chocolates and sing *Happy Birthday* at the top of his beautiful tenor voice. She was wobbling but managed to give him a hug and alcoholic kisses on both cheeks, for which he thanked her profusely, adding that he wouldn't wash his face for a week. The only thing she could think to say in return was 'What have you been drinking?'

Some months later Allan was posted back to HMAS *Cerberus* and Shirley secured a short-term apartment in Frankston and returned to the temporary agency. Her third assignment put her back in the medical world as a private secretary to a world-renowned psychiatrist named John Diamond. He churned out a great deal of work, dictated everything and was very appreciative of Shirley's work ethic, particularly her ability to get through dozens of letters and reports every day whilst also attending to patients on the front desk. When he learned she and her new hubby were on the waiting list for a Navy house in Frankston, he made two phone calls and secured one for them the same day.

On the down side, while he was brilliant he was also quite mad. His volatile temper made him impossible to predict and no day passed without incident. He'd be greeting a patient in reception late afternoon and object to the staff trying to finish their lunch. 'What's all this eating?' he'd yell. 'I'm not paying you to eat!'

Staff turnover was high and Shirley was tired of the pressure and the long journey to the city and back each day. She gave him notice, planning to find a permanent job in Frankston. Five hours later his wife came into the practice to beg her to stay. 'Please don't go, please Shirley! He's been so much easier to live with since you came.'

Some years later, following highly successful publications of his psychiatric texts, Dr Diamond closed his practice, moved to New York and became more famous, no doubt continuing to save many lives in the process.

Living on a housing commission estate was a challenging experience. Allan was on duty for several days at a time and Shirley had some frightening experiences from knocks on the front door in the middle of the night and regular bashings in the street to piercing screams from the next door neighbour.

On the positive side she met and became lifelong friends with Alan and Jackie Brecht. Alan, an officer in the RAN, lived nearby and the friendship that developed was exclusively with Shirley. Officers and sailors didn't mix socially.

She'd secured a local position as private secretary to John McCoy, General Manager Sales at H.J. Heinz Co Australia Ltd. While working with this highly successful food processing manufacturer and marketer of branded grocery products, she discovered a good deal about herself. She hadn't worked in a dedicated sales and marketing environment before and quickly realised she'd landed in the people business. The staff were selected for their intelligence, personality and ability to create, package, market and sell a large range of products. The upbeat nature of the business and the focus on good relationships stimulated her imagination whilst stirring up old dreams of conquering the world.

It was early days in her marriage to Allan and they were as happy as young lovers should be. Allan was an honest, industrious, likeable young man with a secure job and the additional gift of being in a loving relationship with a girl he adored. Shirley thrived on new beginnings, was a competent cook and housekeeper, and loved the independence of making a house their home. Like Allan, she was also grateful to finally be able to have regular, 'respectable' sex.

Despite Allan's irregular hours, they spent most of their free time together. The friends they socialised with were mainly sailors and their girlfriends or wives. Shirley struggled to connect with them but ignored deeper concerns because her work, and co-workers stimulated her days and all of her waking hours were full.

They'd been married nine months when Allan was told he'd be taking up his first overseas posting in March 1969 and Shirley started vomiting in the mornings. The pregnancy confirmed, she was happy but felt insecure. Allan would be gone and how was she going to handle living on her own in the Frankston housing estate with a new baby?

'Don't worry about it yet,' Allan reassured her. 'You can always move back to Melbourne and stay with your parents, or mine.'

This was an unrealistic solution on either front and Shirley was stunned, but kept her thoughts to herself. Thankfully the morning sickness stopped as quickly as it arrived and she was also able to keep her pregnancy quiet. She needed her job, they needed her income even more now and pregnant women were usually given notice to quit. Jackie and Alan Brecht were her only confidants and offered empathy and helpful suggestions.

As Christmas was coming and Allan had some leave, they planned a second honeymoon in western Victoria with his aunt and uncle. Shirley was blossoming now, wearing loose shirts to conceal her condition, having set to work at the sewing machine to make a couple of smocks. Not only was pregnancy unwelcome in the workforce in those days, but it was also considered unbecoming to show off your baby bump.

On a daily basis she scrutinised herself in the mirror to see if she looked pregnant, answered yes and wondered why she was so concerned about it. She'd have to leave her job in the New Year anyway.

What's happened to me? Where have I gone? she asked her reflection.

In at the deaths – whack, whack, whack!

A few days before Christmas, Jackie Brecht dropped in unexpectedly without her young children. Shirley's Allan was at work, as was Jackie's.

Shirley's first reaction was, 'Where are the children? Is there something wrong?'

Jackie reassured her on that score, but said she had some unfortunate news and asked if they could they sit down and have a coffee? Shirley poured two glasses of wine, turned off the television and adjourned to the lounge. 'Have you ever had chickenpox?' Jackie asked.

'No, I don't think so. Measles, mumps, everything kids get, but not chickenpox.'

Jackie cut to the chase, as best she could. 'It's caused by a virus called herpes zoster. Our littlest has just been diagnosed and you were with her when she was highly contagious. Complications can occur when an adult catches the disease and our doctor wanted to be sure I wasn't pregnant again. I told him about you and he wants to see you immediately. They don't have a vaccination for it but he's had success with another herpes vaccination in cases where there's a chance of foetal abnormality. I'm so sorry.'

Shirley made an appointment and was given two very painful, slow injections in both thighs. She was 17 weeks' pregnant when the doctor explained that if her baby was abnormal the injections would cause a miscarriage within seven to ten days. She thought about all the misdiagnoses her mother had been given over the years and wondered if this man knew what he was doing, but what choice did she have?

At six o'clock on the morning of the 5th January 1969, Shirley was woken by contractions to discover she was lying in a pool of blood. Half an hour later she lost the baby in the toilet. Allan drove to the nearest phone booth to call the doctor but discovered he'd just left town with his family on a caravan trip. His answering machine message directed him to the hospital.

When they arrived a young intern and younger nurse quickly wheeled Shirley on a stretcher into a screened cubicle in Emergency. For the next hour and a half the contractions continued. According to the nurse, they were 'uncoordinated contractions' causing significant discomfort and not much progress. Whilst she was convinced Shirley was in the third stage of labour, the young intern continued to apply instruments and urge her to push and help expel the placenta. Finally she delivered another tiny foetus, followed by the afterbirth.

'I'm very sorry,' the young doctor said with tears in his eyes. 'I didn't know you were carrying twins.'

Allan sat alone in a chair not 10 yards from the curtained cubicle, unable to help, unable to comfort her. Throughout the ordeal Shirley cried, sobbed, coughed, gasped and cried some more whilst periodically begging the intern to stop and give her a chance to breathe. When it was over, Allan was allowed to sit with her and she knew from his tearful face and unsteady hands that his shock and distress ran as deep as hers.

Many hours later, whilst being prepared for surgery, she learned that her GP had called the hospital at nine that morning regarding another patient and was advised by a senior nurse that Shirley was being attacked with forceps whilst clearly still in labour. Aghast, he decided to leave his family in their first caravan park, turn the van around and come back to perform the curette.

When he arrived he pulled up a chair beside the operating table and talked Shirley through what had happened. He didn't say she'd have no trouble giving birth in the future after the hammering her womb had endured and the missing words loomed large in her heart, but she remained silent. He gave her a script for the pill to ensure she gave her body a six month break and reassured her she'd be able to fall pregnant again. He'd gone way beyond his duty of care and she was deeply affected by the personal effort he'd made.

'I'm very sorry I wasn't here for you this morning,' he said as the anaesthetist began.

'You're here now and I'll never forget your kindness,' Shirley whispered as she faded out.

The patient slept for a couple of hours, had a sandwich and coffee and was sitting up in bed when Allan returned to the hospital for visiting hour. He gave her a kiss and a hug, turned back towards the door and beckoned with his hand. Maggie, their next door neighbour rushed in with her six-month-old babe in arms and a bunch of flowers in her free hand, handing the baby to Allan whilst she embraced Shirley.

Any sign of shock or incredulity on Shirley's part was missed as Maggie and Allan talked over one another, eager to explain that Maggie had wanted to visit to reassure her that there would be plenty more chances and everything would be just fine next time. With sincere intentions they quoted that at least 25 per cent of all pregnancies end in miscarriage but most women go on to have as many babies as…

And so it went on and on, an unwittingly mindless, insulting hour unlike any she'd been subjected to before. Following the day's events, she didn't have the strength or courage left to stop it so she switched off and went into acting mode; a smile here, a nod there, an occasional question where good manners demanded, another smile until finally the visiting hour was over.

Allan picked her up next morning and they arrived home to a large bouquet of roses on the veranda, and a card with the inscription 'Much love from Mum and Dad'. For the first time since the morning before, Shirley burst into tears.

'What's all this crying?' Allan asked lightly, picking up the bouquet, opening the door and escorting her inside. 'They're beautiful flowers!'

Yes they are, she smiled through her tears.

She took two sick-leave days but finished the week at work as though nothing untoward had happened. Allan arranged a social evening, inviting Maggie and Jim to dinner for takeaway pizzas on Friday night. They came, with baby and toddler, and a feisty conversation developed about the bringing up of children. Shirley contributed little but made one passing comment to broaden the discussion and was howled down, again with no malice intended.

'How could you possibly know?' Maggie reminded her. 'You don't have any children.'

Shirley excused herself, turned on the kettle, went to the toilet and cried, blew her nose, touched up her lipstick and served coffee with homemade cake.

Sleep wouldn't come so she lay awake half the night feeling desperately sorry for her husband. He'd known her intimately for two years yet didn't seem to know her at all.

Allan had joined the Navy to see the world but his first overseas posting looked like all he was going to see was the sea.

He and Shirley had a tearful farewell and committed to writing to each other once a week, but their parting felt eerily final. He departed Sydney in early March on the HMAS *Stuart* to partake in a lengthy period of SEATO exercises in the South China Sea.

Shirley felt isolated in an empty house in the housing commission estate but was grateful that her boss at Heinz had employed a temp in her absence. It was good to be back in a job she enjoyed, and she had the car full-time now. It made a difference.

Margery was deteriorating rapidly, still walking with the aid of a stick but unable to do anything much. The only good thing about it was that she'd come to appreciate her Alan again, just like the old days. He was her rock and he gathered strength because of her renewed love and respect for his unwavering loyalty and care.

In April Bev announced she was pregnant again, due in late September or October (Dale was on the way, at last!) and everyone lightened up. It was happy news and Margery and Alan were the first to be told. Shirley was genuinely thrilled and displayed no lingering distress from her own recent loss, although Bev noted she was quieter than usual.

'She's lost a lot in the space of three months,' she reflected to Rob. 'When you think about it, the two most important things in her life at this moment in time have suddenly gone.'

Shirley drove to Ashwood most weekends and Alan drove Margery to Frankston fairly regularly. Late afternoon on the first Sunday in May, Margery and Alan arrived for an early dinner. They had a great chat during the main course and adjourned to the lounge for cake and a glass of port. Margery took herself to the toilet, quite ably with her stick, and Shirley grabbed the moment to quiz Alan about her current health.

A few minutes into the discussion one or the other of them suddenly realised she'd been gone too long. They rushed to the toilet and found her in a small crumpled mess on the floor, between the toilet and door. Alan carried her to the settee in the lounge, by which time she'd woken from what they could only surmise was a dizzy spell or faint and proceeded to eat the cake and drink the port before departing.

'I love you very much, Mum,' Shirley said as she hugged her parents goodbye, 'and love you heaps, Dad!'

Alan waved as he reversed out of the driveway and Margery returned, 'I love you very much too, darling,' just as they'd been doing for years when farewelling each other.

'See you next weekend for my birthday celebrations!' Shirley called as they drove away.

Two days later she was woken at two o'clock in the morning by a persistent knocking on the door. She'd staggered out of bed, thrown on a dressing gown, grabbed a copper poker from the fireplace and cautiously opened the door to confront a very drunk man looking for a match to light his cigarette.

'Wait here!' she'd ordered instinctively, shut and locked the door, retrieved a box of matches and the poker before reopening the door. 'Here's your matches. I won't forget your face. Never come here again or I'll call the police.' He was just a drunk, but bugger him!

Two days later, at 7.30 in the morning, she was heading to the shower when there was a loud knock on the front door. Who on earth could it be this time?

It was Bev's husband, Robert Gosbell. He'd driven from Melbourne on very little sleep to ensure he caught her before she left for work.

Shirley's face contorted, her large sparkling eyes cowered and her bottom lip fell. She stood perfectly still as her face turned white. Rob immediately put his arms around her.

'I'm so sorry, Shirl. Your mum died last night. She had a heart attack.'

'How did she die, Rob?' she asked after she'd showered, phoned her boss at Heinz and packed a bag.

'I need to know.' She'd managed to control her tears or perhaps it was shock, but she respected Rob deeply for taking responsibility to deliver such news.

'She had a heart attack, Shirl.'

'Yes. But *how* did she die?'

'Perhaps you'd prefer to ask Dad about that.'

'I can't wait that long, Rob. Just tell me what happened, please. I'm so grateful you came to tell me and take me home, but I need time to absorb this or I'll be no help to Dad.'

'Your father had a multiple sclerosis association meeting last night. Mum wasn't too good before he left but she promised to wait up and watch telly until he got home. He only stayed at the meeting for an hour and when… when he got home he found her in the bath. She had the heart attack getting into it.'

'Oh, Rob! Dad found her drowned in the bath?'

'Yeah. He lifted her out and carried her to the couch. Then he rang Dr Paterson, who had to call the police. The doc arrived first and comforted Dad and by the time the police arrived he knew it was just a formality. When someone dies alone the police have to be called. The law says you must have two doctors' signatures on the death certificate – they have to agree as to how the person died. Dr Paterson's been looking after Mum for years and assured the police that she died of a heart attack following a long illness. They were glad to sign off on it and leave.'

'Thanks Rob. I guess we'd better go?'

On the advice of Dr Paterson, Alan went back to work two days later, and Shirley asked the Reverend Howells who'd officiated at her wedding just two years earlier to arrange the funeral for her mother.

Alan and Margery's propensity to discuss God and science and the whole damn thing since the day they'd met left no doubt as to their funeral preferences. Alas, with only one medical signature on the death certificate a post mortem was mandatory prior to cremation. Alan couldn't handle the thought of that so they decided instead to bury her. Thankfully Margery was an old Presbyterian gal who'd liked the Reverend very much. 'I think she'd approve,' Alan said.

On the second morning Shirley realised her father had not entered the bathroom since Dr Paterson and the police had left, instead washing himself down in the laundry, and cleaning his artificial eye, and upper and lower dentures, in the kitchen sink. Margery's dog, Penny, who'd been kept outside until then, started running in and out of the bathroom barking and yelping, leaving a trail of water behind her to bark at the fridge until Alan remembered it was time for the dog's daily heart tablet that Margery had kept alongside her own.

When all was quiet again, Shirley entered the bathroom with a bucket and mop. Pools of water remained on the floor and small pieces of beige/brownish material were widely scattered in and around the bath. She couldn't identify what it was but it looked a bit like her mother's nightie had been torn to shreds.

'What's the strange material in the bath, Dad?' she asked Alan because she simply had to know.

His eyes welled up immediately. 'Burnt skin, Shirley. She only managed to turn on the hot tap.'

Shirley wrapped her arms around him and they held each other close until their first tears together gradually subsided.

'Go to the kitchen, Dad, and put the lunch Bev brought into the oven,' she instructed gently. 'We have to eat.'

The funeral was held at Wattle Park five days later and Alan, Bev, Rob and Shirley, accompanied by the minister, followed directly behind the hearse to Springvale Cemetery. Reverend Tom made a wonderful contribution to the ceremony and when the coffin had been lowered and family and friends were returning for refreshments at the church, Shirley described the moment as her mother might have done.

'Standing in that huge cemetery surrounded by acres of tombstones, flowers and trees felt like we could have been in Gallilee 2,000 years ago. Death hasn't changed much, has it?'

Shirley's 22nd birthday, exactly one week after Margery's death, was a sombre affair. She returned to work the next day and began to make enquiries about vacating the Frankston house. Unperturbed by the lengthy commute to work, she'd decided her dad needed her as much as she needed him, and cut her way through the bureaucracy to finally learn that only her absent husband Allan could break the housing commission lease. So be it.

Jackie Brecht came by to help Shirley pack up on her last day in Frankston and was stunned by her equanimity. 'You're strangely composed, as if it hasn't hit you yet?' she enquired tenderly. 'Your mother has been your…'

'Everything. I can't let her go yet, Jackie. No loss will ever be as great but there's more to come and I have to live up to her expectations. How I handle whatever's ahead has to make, not break me! Or anyone else for that matter.'

Allan was on the HMAS *Stuart* in the South China Sea when he received his wife's heartbreaking letter calling the marriage off.

On receipt of the letter, Allan instantly lodged a request for compassionate leave that was quickly approved when he explained that his wife lost babies in January, her husband in March and her mother in May. He earnestly believed he could rescue the marriage, if only he could get home.

When Shirley received his reply detailing his plans, she'd moved back to be with her dad in Ashwood, leaving all the furnishings and 'joint' personal effects in situ. She'd formally advised Allan she was leaving the marriage so it was up to him now. Since he paid the nominal rent via direct debit, it was his task to terminate the tenancy, or not. He could keep the chattels, if he wanted them.

Shirley's letter had arrived a week prior to the second collision of the ill-fated Australian flagship, aircraft carrier HMAS *Melbourne*, when it cut the USS *Frank E. Evans* American destroyer in half in the South China Sea pre-dawn on the 3rd of June 1969. Allan's return to Australia was going to have to wait.

He arrived by taxi from Tullamarine Airport to Ashwood mid-afternoon on the 1st of October 1969. The RAN had finally managed to send him home via five commercial and government aircrafts. During the previous four months he'd played his part in the horrific retrieval of decapitated heads and countless body parts of at least 56 American sailors who lost their lives.

Shirley had taken the day off to be at home whenever he arrived and had nearly finished her mother's gold-bound hardback version of *Marie Antoinette* when the doorbell rang. She had continued to write to him with words of support and genuine care for his sanity in the midst of the nightmares he and his colleagues were experiencing, at the same time failing to find appropriate words to explain why their marriage would never work. It was not easy because he loved her truly and hadn't intentionally done anything wrong.

Marie was being marched to the gallows when he landed, and there was something about that long-awaited moment that triggered clarity for Shirley. She opened the door with renewed hope because she finally knew how she could restore Allan's self-worth and end his guilt. It might take time, but he'd have closure.

On the very same afternoon Alan left his primary school in Ashwood to go to the hospital where Bev was in labour. He phoned Shirley precisely 10 minutes after Allan arrived with the news that Dale had just been delivered and that mother and baby were doing well. The irony was lost on no-one; a new life for Alan's first daughter, and the death of the marriage of his second. All in the same hour!

Shirley took full responsibility for her decision. She had been vulnerable and lonely when they met, had cared for her mother for six months and then gone back to work without a goal. She'd volunteered to save the world in Hong Kong and in the process 'find herself', but finished up escaping sexually deviant businessmen by the skin of her teeth. She'd moved into a flat with Lyn, whose father was tarred with the same brush ('as was Mr Ueby' she thought to herself).

'Most of the men I've met since I left school have been offensive, Allan, but not you. You're kind and normal, about my age and you wanted to marry me. I badly needed "kind" and "normal". But we were brought up differently and I've realised we're chalk and cheese. That might work if we had similar interests, beliefs, friends and aspirations but we don't.

'Sooner or later I would become a dominating, dissatisfied woman and you'd finish up wanting to kill me. Let's part friends and be forever glad we didn't do that to each other.'

Two weeks later Allan's sister, Marianne, rang to arrange a friendly visit and wasted no time getting to the point. She and her mother had come to the conclusion that it was perfectly understandable Shirley had met someone whilst Allan was away. They appreciated her need for company! They were not making judgements, not at all. They understood and empathised with the losses she'd had to deal with before and since Allan's absence. Without drawing breath she concluded that there would be no recriminations, all had been forgiven, the past is past!

Shirley knew there was nothing she could do to change their belief and remembered her mother's words: *Always act like a lady, and never reduce your standards to suit the people you're with.*

'There's no other man, Marianne, and I'm sorry you've misread my character,' she spoke gently, kindly. 'Allan's been through a great deal too during the last few months and will need time to adjust. I've written and spoken at length to him and he knows, and I believe understands why our marriage won't work. With respect, I don't think it's my place to discuss the reasons with you. Perhaps he'll tell you himself one day.'

Quod erat demonstrandum (QED). It was truly over now and she was grateful.

A few weeks later, and six months after Margery's death, Alan was invited to go on a weekend geological 'dig' by Margery's last GP, Dr Jim Paterson. The Glen family and John and Jennet Sharp, all passionate rock and mineral collectors, would be in company too and all were aware that Alan had minored in geology during one of his bachelor degrees.

There had been sufficient time since Margery's passing to make his positive response likely and he'd all but accepted the good doctor's invitation when he suddenly remembered that somebody would have to feed little Penny.

He'd sold the Ashwood property – too many bad memories and purchased a brick home with a large shed at 15 Kiah Street, Glen Waverley, not far from the Gosbells and still a relatively short drive to his school. He'd been so busy with the move, he'd only met one of the neighbours and Bev and Rob, with the children in tow were spending the weekend in the Grampians. Shirley was tidying up loose ends before Christmas, having given notice to H.J. Heinz, and would be in Frankston for the weekend to sort the furnishings and empty the house with Allan. But the luck was finally with him and the neighbours over the back fence were happy to oblige.

He headed off on his first hunter gatherer expedition since his early 20s and it was the beginning of a passion that would stimulate and occupy him in a multitude of ways for the rest of his life. He didn't know it then, but he was on his way to forming the Waverley Gem Club which would ultimately become the biggest gem club in Australia.

Unfortunately, that first weekend came at a harrowing cost.

Late Sunday afternoon he arrived home with a car full of rocks, his heart pumping with renewed life and his brain soaring with a sense of purpose he thought had gone forever. The car was parked and washed, and everything but the rocks unpacked, before he realised Penny was missing.

He found her floating in the fish pond in the front garden, flat on her back with her legs straight up and her tiny feet just above the water. She must have had *her* heart attack, he mused without emotion, gently lifting her out to lie her on the lawn.

It was so familiar yet other-worldly that her actual death didn't register immediately. He figured he had to be dreaming, having another nightmare, so he just stood there looking at her, trying to work out what to do. But he couldn't think of anything. He wandered aimlessly around the garden until he realised he was cold and needed to go inside. By the time the fire was burning bright, he sank into his favourite chair and wept.

In the morning he buried Penny in the back yard, creating a small tombstone out of a piece of agate he'd collected before heading off to a new week at Ashwood Primary.

At long last 1969 was nearly over! The only good news had been the birth of Dale, although the whole family had high hopes that the New Year would bring Grandpa and Aunty Shirley a permanent change of luck.

2nd Intermission

SS Castel Felice

Embarking 15/11/65

Right: 25/11/1967
Mr & Mrs Allan Uebergang

AGE THREE (1970 – 1973)

Then the lady soldier
Full of sincere oaths, and dressed to kill,
Desirous of honour, measured yet sprightly in battle;
Seeking the dynamic reputation
Even in the cannon's mouth.

It was just a small ad in the classified section of *The Melbourne Age*. Shirley chanced to come across it whilst resting her sore feet in a coffee shop in Bourke Street.

> **Wanted for immediate overseas posting.**
> Exp. secretary with m/ment potential for
> international co. 12 months in USA learning
> the ropes, to manage businesses in Oz.
> Phone Mick on (Ph #) at ABC Dance Academy.

It was the beginning of a new decade and her spirits were high. She'd already attended three interviews in the city that day and been offered each position on the strength of her personality, resume and five outstanding references. The latter all referred to her secretarial excellence but also highlighted attributes of enthusiasm, cheerfulness, thoughtfulness, charm, humour, reliability and exceptional people skills.

She'd ruminated for days whether to include all the references, wishing her mother was there to advise her. With so many compliments from executives in diverse industries, she must have been full of herself! With so many jobs in such a short time, she must be easily bored and won't be a keeper! Yet if she didn't present them all, wouldn't she leave doubt in an employer's mind about the truth of her resume?

If she could only get her foot in the right door, she knew she could overcome the objections. Young women in their early 20s with the life and work experience she had were thin on the ground in 1970 and it would be much easier to sell herself at interview if there was no doubt about her history.

With three offers in one morning, she'd overcome the objections alright, but the doors were wrong and her feet were killing her. She ordered another coffee, pulled out her shorthand notebook and wrote herself a rabble-rousing, two-sentence memo.

> Dear Shirley,
>
> You were born bright and pretty, had a fabulous upbringing, make good friends and attract bullies and sexual deviants, have excellent skills, confidence and a contagious laugh despite being flat footed, tone deaf and left handed. You've already lived in 16 houses, had seven jobs, been through one marriage, lost twins, lost your mother and grandmother and given up on God, but your dream world still exists, the show must go on and it's up to you to find a new play that runs longer than One Act or you'll never become a professional at anything.
>
> Break a leg, Love Shirley xxx

She was thinking about her father's new lease of life and plans to sell the car and buy a Land Rover, her sister's gorgeous little boys and devoted husband, and her own newfound freedom when she spotted the advertisement: Wanted for immediate overseas posting. *Why not?* The coffee shop manager loaned her his phone and the ABC Dance Academy receptionist gave her directions to the office.

Shirley would spend four hours with the boss, one of two brothers who owned 100 diverse businesses around the world. 'Call me Mick,' he greeted her with hand extended.

Age Three

Following an interview where Mick artfully ascertained a good deal about her professional and marital status, he suddenly thrust a notebook and pencil into her hands and dictated the history of his massive company at about 120 words per minute. Finally he gave her a cash receipts and payments book, turned to the pages of the dance academy's current month's finances that clearly needed corrections.

Sitting on the other side of Mick's large desk, Shirley transcribed her shorthand on an Underwood typewriter and corrected the figures whilst he took some phone calls and enjoyed a glass of Lagavulin, 'an 18-year-old whisky' he'd replied when she asked.

When he'd checked her work and remarked on her speed, accuracy and commendable ability to concentrate amidst constant interruptions, he offered her the job. She would be based in their Oklahoma City (OKC) head office, working full-time for his brother Pete, who ran the American operation. She would provide private secretarial, bookkeeping and front-of-house duties whilst learning how to run various hospitality and recreational businesses. On top of her US$900 monthly pay packet, the company would cover return airfares and accommodation en route, plus all expenses including free lunches when on duty. There were also some throw-away mentions of casinos, stud farms and The Melbourne Cup that further ignited her imagination. It was hard not to accept on the spot.

Yet it was actually thanks to Mick that she remembered in the nick of time that she had to use her head!

At his bidding she'd divulged that although her legal surname was Uebergang, her current passport bore her maiden name. He promptly advised her to ignore the rules, namely that she had to seek permission from her estranged husband to travel overseas.

'The law is sexist and unjust. It would take months to get approval, even if your ex was prepared to co-operate,' he said before going on to state his plans decisively.

He was returning to the Bahamas in two weeks but would escort her to New Zealand first where he would obtain a visa for her to work in the States. He would then put her on a plane to Los Angeles (LA) where she would take an internal flight to OKC whilst he returned to Nassau where he lived and also ran the international operations.

She thanked him for the wonderful opportunity but advised she would need time to speak to her father before making her decision. She had to ensure he was happy and fully supportive before she could leave him so soon after losing his beloved wife. Mick was sympathetic but resolute: he needed to know by Friday in order to make arrangements and give his brother time to prepare for her arrival.

On the way home she realised that Friday would be the 13th. Lucky for some, but was this offer for real, or simply too good to be true?

The American Dream

If only Margery was there, she'd know what to do. When Shirley said as much to Alan, he asked if she knew anyone who could check out the multinational. It so happened that she did.

There wasn't much time. She briefed a private detective (the brother of one of her old friends at the Princess Theatre) with the information she had and proceeded to buy a new suitcase, clean through her wardrobe, get a haircut, sell the car, complete the paperwork for bank transfers and purchase some travellers' cheques. With no news from the D by mid-afternoon Friday 13th, she called Mick to accept his offer. Arrangements would be made for their departure one week hence.

Bev, Rob and Alan threw her a farewell get-together for family and close friends the very next day. The party was in full swing when the investigator's phone call came.

'Sorry to be late...' he began.

'Could you speak up a bit, please?' Shirley replied loudly, silencing the party.

'The Australian company names you gave me are squeaky clean, altogether too clean for your brief. They're registered as independent small businesses, not as part of a large corporation. I located three of the American companies that connect directly to Oklahoma City and the Bahamas so if they own 100 businesses internationally, 98 per cent of them must be registered off-shore, if at all. It's a mystery and requires thorough investigation. My best advice is Don't Go!'

Shirley put the phone down pensively, realising the room was hushed.

'Well, what did he say?' Bev implored.

'They're a big international company that minimises their tax in off-shore havens. I've probably already worked for companies who do the same.'

'No doubts then, Shirl?' Bev persisted.

'Mum would say the hardest thing to determine is which bridge to cross and which to burn, and probably remind me that some people do nothing because they're afraid of failure.'

'What do you say?' Alan surprised her by asking.

'I'm a lady soldier battling to make my life mean something. I've been called up to go to America, Dad, as if it was fated the day I ran away from Project Concern in Hong Kong. I remember you saying that we only regret the chances we didn't take, so that settles it! Can we get on with the party now?'

The chance of any of the Uebergang clan travelling to New Zealand on the same day would have to be millions-to-one odds, yet stranger things had happened in Shirley's life. She was overwhelmed with relief once she'd got through airport immigration without questions. The knowledge that she was breaking the law had certainly been troubling her.

Mick was an attractive, middle-aged man and a good conversationalist with a sense of humour. They arrived in Auckland following a sumptuous lunch in Qantas Business Class. He'd booked a motel out of town for two nights and whilst the location seemed an odd choice, Shirley settled into what she thought was 'her' room while Mick departed in the hire car to the CBD on business.

When he returned, he brought his suitcase in with him. Her ever-present sparkling blue eyes and disarming smile probably helped when Shirley calmly informed him that she was going to be the best employee he and his brother had ever had but she did not do sex with bosses, or any man she'd just met for that matter. She politely asked him to book his own room so they could get on with establishing a professional relationship and, to his credit, he thanked her for her honesty and duly arranged another room.

In the morning he moved into a hotel in town, but not before advising that he'd booked a taxi to take her to the airport the following morning and that he would see her soon in OKC where he'd pay her salary 'in cash'. Mysteriously, he was already in possession of her economy airline tickets through to Oklahoma City, but had not requested her Passport in order to get the required work visa.

She boarded the American Airlines flight to LA without undue concern. Burdened now with the knowledge she was breaking Australian and American laws, and tacitly aware that her employer was probably on the make, she was just 22 years of age. Whilst the risk of what she was doing had dramatically increased, she was excited. She'd passed the first test by sticking to her standards. *I can do this,* she said to herself over and over again as she walked through the international terminal in LA to be greeted by Pete, Mick's brother.

Pete Wallington Junior had flown in his private jet to welcome her, and took his new private secretary to a double room at the Hilton, naturally with a view. Of course it was a set-up – she was always meant to stop-over in LA. She simply hadn't absorbed the date on the domestic ticket from LA to OKC. 'Play close attention to details!' she heard her mother say. She'd rebuffed his not-so-subtle advances, repeating her reason with the practised flow of a poem she'd recited to his brother 60 hours earlier. According to Pete all the single rooms were booked out but he'd managed to secure a suite they could share.

During that day he drove her down Hollywood Boulevard and up into the hills to see the Hollywood sign. Later they dined at an exclusive restaurant with a major Hollywood star - let's say Dick Van Dyke. (*What's in a name?'* Shakespeare coined. *That which we call a rose, By any other name would smell as sweet.* However, it wasn't exactly a rose garden Shirley had entered into, by name or smell, hence the need for nom de guerres; she calls Mick and Pete's business Wallington Enterprises.)

When they returned to the suite, an exhausted Shirley adjourned to the bedroom and Pete slept on the couch in the lounge. In the morning Shirley dressed to get from the bedroom to the bathroom whilst Pete remained on the couch, surrounded by scores of scattered pages from the LA Times.

His driver picked them up and dropped her at American Airlines, en route to Pete's private jet. 'Looking forward to welcoming you on Monday,' he smiled and waved as they drove away.

The moment she arrived at OKC airport she checked herself into the nearest hotel. Pete had given her the name and phone number of his accountant who would pick her up, but no way was she calling anyone until she'd had 12 hours of undisturbed sleep.

Age Three

On the fifth morning since she'd left home she woke up alone and opened the curtains to the extraordinarily barren vista of Oklahoma. To this day she swears she saw a man on a horse, riding over the endless red hills of sand who morphed into Gordon McCrea of Rodgers and Hammerstein's musical, *Oklahoma*, singing her favourite song: *Oh what a beautiful morning, oh what a beautiful day, I've got a beautiful feeling, everything's going my way…ay…Oh what a beautiful day.*

'I'm here, I'm here!' she ended the song, remembering the moment she'd finally landed at Trish and David's in Kota Baharu.

She phoned Carl, the accountant, after she'd showered and dressed. He arrived at the door inside 30 minutes, full of concern that she hadn't called last night, but genuinely appreciative of the fact that she'd needed a good night's sleep.

He drove her in his Cadillac to an apartment block where he'd reserved a one-bedroom unit in her name. Chester, the landlord and owner of the building, greeted them and escorted them to the vacant apartment. Carl wrapped his right arm around Shirley's back as he advised Chester that the company would be paying, but Shirley dislodged his arm to unzip her handbag and open her wallet to give Chester US$200 deposit.

Carl had also found her a car. She thanked him for his generosity but declined his offer to pay for it. She would be happy to purchase it herself.

His relief at her gentle knockbacks and assertions of independence gave Shirley a valuable insight into the Wallington brothers, and him. He was also full-on about his admiration for Mick and Pete, fine Christian men who loved God, attended church weekly and lived by the Ten Commandments! Of course Carl was a church goer too, and obviously did what the brothers told him, but his discomfort reassured her that he had some morals, and eased her fears considerably.

She'd knocked all three bosses back now; the new job was looking good for a clean start.

There's only so much we can write about Aunty Shirl's employment with the Wallington brothers without re-exposing her to a world she managed to leave in one piece. Fortunately, over a period of nearly 10 months she wrote long letters home to Alan and Bev and Rob so we can record some of the facts, several close calls on her life, and most of the highlights.

As predicted, Day One at Wallington Enterprises was a snap.

Shirley was an instant hit on the reception desk. Clients, mainly Americans, loved her accent and no doubt her manner and contagious laugh. When she explained she came from Australia, they heard 'Austria' and decided she must be a German with excellent English. Once corrected, they called more often. Australia was the new 'thing' in the early 70s and every second American said 'I've always wanted to go there,' followed by 'but it's so far away!'

The French novelist Balzac wrote: *Behind every great fortune lies a crime.* Suffice to say, Shirley's employers were exceedingly rich. Having legitimised the great majority of their international enterprises during the 50s and 60s, most of their ill-gotten gains were buried and by 1970 almost forgotten.

Mick and Pete had grown up in an America that believed they were the world's first chosen people. God was on their side. Dealers of all types, from cocaine through to Wall Street, shared a love of ostentatious consumption. Both extremes may have been trading in human misery but they also shared the modus operandi of America's most successful entrepreneurs. They called it holding on to market share.

Whilst naïve to the truth behind 'The American Dream', it was the sense of endless possibilities without limits that excited Shirley. Most cultures were built on the belief that you could only be what you were born to be, but Americans believed you could be what you decided to be. Over the next 10 months Shirley would gather numerous insights that would serve her well for 40 years in business.

She settled quickly into the head office environment and was given a couple of months to familiarise herself with the core business before taking on management responsibilities 'in the field'. Every day was different from the last and the lessons came thick and fast.

It was a 10-minute drive from her apartment to the office, the hours were relatively long and initially the work was stimulating. The staff were friendly until they became jealous of the favourable treatment they saw her receiving from the bosses. The fact was she did more for the bosses directly. She dealt with difficult situations at the front desk and on the phone, handled a large portfolio of private secretarial and bookkeeping duties and made the men's afternoon bourbon on the rocks. This in itself was reason enough for gossip.

Age Three

Ten days after she arrived Mick flew in from the Bahamas. He took her to lunch in one of the company's dozens of restaurants and paid for her first two weeks, plus a month in advance to cover all the initial expenses she'd had. The perfect gentleman, he complimented her on the way she'd settled in and made Pete's days easier. The New Zealand incident was not mentioned and they parted with another date four weeks hence.

By the time he returned she'd developed a social life via Chester the landlord and a couple of nearby tenants, and was about to move into a two-bedroom apartment with Vickie Morris, a private secretary in a large legal firm in town. Vickie was a Southern gal and a unique individual; she was funny, intelligent, sometimes crazy and contradictory, five years older than Shirley and a born-again Christian. Despite their differences they shared values, common interests and a sense of humour. Their friendship was instantaneous and continued for several decades.

Another friendly neighbour, Bruce, was a pilot in his 30s. At the time he was completing the paperwork to commence his own charter airline, in partnership with another pilot from Texas. 'Golden Eagle Aviation' comprised two planes with 40 passenger seats apiece and was targeting the weekend and domestic short-charter market for government, commercial and social group events, conventions and sporting activities. Bruce had arranged a six week training course for airhostesses with classes twice weekly at the airport and invited Vickie and Shirley to sign on. The girls were excited. 'Count us in!'

Following their acceptance, Vickie suggested to Shirley that it would be smart not to mention it at Wallington Enterprises.

'Your weekends are your own,' she began. 'Your bosses don't like their staff working for anybody else, especially when it happens to be someone from their past. Back in the good old days Bruce used to fly drugs to Cuba and the Caribbean for them, lady!'

From that day forward, Vickie took it upon herself to educate Shirley on all matters American. It was essential if Shirley wanted to get out of here alive, she said. During the next nine months she covered just about everything: racism, sexism, political skulduggery, prejudice, guns, churches, sex, food, high rollers, the death penalty, taxes, drugs and men at large. Especially the Wallington men.

Shirley grabbed her shorthand notebook when Vickie began a 'rave' and finished up with three notebooks full of zany humour and life-saving advice.

> Keep a straight face and show no emotion when people use racist epithets like Eastern bastards, Southern gentlemen (that's a laugh), Damn Yankees, niggers, natives, Latinos, cowboys, mossybacks or expressions like 'There's a nigger in the wood pile somewhere'. If you have to say anything, try, 'There's a negro gentleman in the lumber yard'.
>
> Show no interest when your bosses reminisce about their friendship with the Kennedys, and get on with your work when they talk about the Rat Pack. Sinatra flies in now and then for a game of tennis with Pete, at a thousand bucks a set I'm reliably informed, so stay sharp when he comes in next. They've got form and will try to set you up. It's a game and they're masters at it. Stay sharp, lady!
>
> There's no such thing as a free lunch, especially at the Wallington Bros' Steak Houses. You'll have to accept, but remember there'll be a cost.
>
> Don't drive through OKC's colour town. It's not safe for whites.
>
> Don't stress about the fuzz wearing guns, batons, knives and reams of bullets on their belts. Most American men own guns, well, even boys have guns but you won't have to worry about them unless you're in the wrong part of town. The last guy I slept with kept a gun under his pillow and it was very uncomfortable. I should have stayed on my side of the bed, but he was a great lover.
>
> Before I forget, don't get involved in conversation with anyone about our current president. My mother went to school with Tricky Dicky's wife and even *she* knows he's a nasty piece of work. He hates Jews, hates blacks, loves power and doesn't care what he has to do to keep it. But they're onto him and he won't last

> his term. When he was vice-president he said that America is a political reading of the Bible and the devout promoted him! Did I mention he's a fake? God only knows what He thinks of him.
>
> Don't relax at next month's lunch with Mick. He's changing tactics, making you think he's a good guy homebody type. I'd like to know just *whose* home his body is in. You could ask Ginger, who befriended you at the start. She's locked in, they've got heaps on all the staff but Miss Sour Face knows at least one of them intimately and might be willing to share, if only to stop you being so bloody trusting and charming – and the one getting all the attention!

By the time the two girls were officially qualified air hostesses and booked for their first weekend charter to Chicago, so much had happened that were it not for Shirley's rapidly filling, second shorthand notebook, it would have been impossible to recount events.

The mood had darkened and with it Vickie's speed of delivery. Shirley was forced to interrupt at times to slow her friend down. 'I can cope with 130 wpm, Vickie. Not 200!'

> Now that you've driven to Dallas to register race horses being shipped to England for six months' quarantine prior to running in the Melbourne Cup, I hate to tell you but those horses will be in Australia next week and that makes you an accomplice. When you filled in for the restaurant manager who disappeared overnight and hasn't been seen since, you also became a person of interest if the police get involved. Then there's the black money you're moving around on paper from one country to another, as if you know where it came from, and where it's going. You're in deep, lady. The fact that your passport isn't technically legal and you're working here without a green card is paltry by comparison. They can only arrest and deport you for that.

I learned a couple of lessons recently from a case I can't discuss so take note: for God's sake don't type up your shorthand notebooks until you get home! My bosses have learned that some immigration officers understand Pitman and there's one in LA so be warned; post them home before you leave! Of immediate importance, don't talk about your troubles on the phone to anyone, especially your father or sister. It's bound to be bugged. Keep writing the letters, stop the chatty international calls at once.

Mick got you into this and the only way out will be through him. You know now his third marriage to the Sydney woman is rocky and when I saw you guys together the other day it was so damn obvious he's got plans for you. He didn't have to bring you all the way here because he's expanding in Australia! Most of their Oz business is legit so why didn't they train you up there? Mick looks pretty sharp but has to be 50 / might be having a mid-life crisis! You're probably the first woman in decades who's knocked him back so he's keener than ever. Maybe you're his fourth wife? Don't laugh! I'm serious.

Speaking of men, you and I need to find ourselves lovers. It's unnatural to be sex free. I'd prefer to find a husband but Yanks with values are thin on the ground. We put men on the moon, won the battle of the Coral Sea (thanks guys, without you the lady and I would never have met) and we make cool musicals and chilli dogs, but Uncle Sam doesn't believe in equality so I'm going to have to settle for less. Are Aussie blokes any better?

It's just occurred to me that you're more in control of your destiny than either of us have grasped! <u>*I* know you're stressed, but nobody else does.</u> Sure, they've got you cornered like the rest of the staff, but *they've* been bought. You haven't! You were imported with who knows what connections at home (they won't want an international 'incident') and you're performing wonderfully well whilst maintaining your independence and principles in the process. You're different and Mick knows it.

Age Three

> What he doesn't know, and must never know is that you're acting, lady! God bless your mother. You're playing your first unscripted role on an American stage and the plot's thickening. There's a few more acts to go but you know your part off by heart now. When the denouement comes you just have to stay in character, at all cost. Give a believable final performance – there'll be no encores. And then get the hell of here!

For her first Golden Eagle charter flight, Shirley asked Pete if she could work through lunch and leave at 5.00pm Friday. He agreed without questions. He had something to ask of her.

His youngest nephew, newly qualified with a psych degree from a New York university, needed practise performing tests on the new 'in thing' Polygraph machine being used extensively in American corporations to check the honesty of staff. Pete simply 'couldn't refuse' him and asked Shirley to take the test.

For a second, or maybe two, she hesitated. Vickie's words thankfully resounded in her brain: *Stay in character!*

'Sure Pete,' she smiled. 'Might be fun.'

Nephew Jackson was a personable young man in his early 20s and made her laugh. Good sign. He explained he would be recording her breathing through the electronic cord he was tying around her chest, the reaction of her sweat glands through a cord around the right palm of her hand, and her heart beat by the blood pressure reading from a cord around her arm. By the time she was firmly strapped in she'd forgotten the explanation and was morphing into character.

The first half-dozen questions were random and of no consequence.

Do you like America? Yes.

Do you have a sister or brother? Yes.

One of each, both, or more, Shirley? Just tell me in as few or as many words as you like. Okay.

Okay. I have an older sister and her name is Beverley, Bev for short.

Excellent. Are you good friends?

Yes, we're very close although we're quite different. Bev's married and has two little boys. I adore my nephews. I like being an aunty, just as my boss likes being an uncle and I don't blame him!

Although relaxing before her eyes, Jackson had a job to do, especially with this staff member. Without pause, Shirley asked if she could have a look at the graph to see how it worked when she answered a question. It's so interesting, she said.

Next question now. Are you enjoying your job at Wallington Enterprises?
Yes, very much.
What do you particularly like about it?
Well, it's busy and demanding but never boring. Just the ticket for me.
Do you take drugs?
I like a smoke, that's all. I don't do drugs.
Do you dislike any of the staff here?
She giggled, hoping it would relieve her rapidly tightening heart. 'I like everyone, some more than others of course, but I feel very welcome here.'
Excellent. Is it true that you secretly fear or hate Pete and Mick Wallington?
She laughed openly. 'Gosh, my secret's out! No, Jackson. I don't fear or hate anyone, especially my bosses. They're very good to me. I think we work extremely well together and I hope they agree.'
I'm sure they do. One last question and we're done. If you knew then what you know now about America, and the job and all, would you have come?
'Definitely! Absolutely. It's a fabulous experience. I'm learning heaps, have made some friends and I look forward to every day.'

He thanked her very much and told her he wished he was based in OKC because he'd love to catch up with her socially. 'Could I call you next time I'm visiting home and take you to dinner?' His sincerity was real and unencumbered; he was an innocent at their bidding and was only aware of their need to know if she was lying. Whatever her test revealed, she knew his report would be favourable.

It was the first time one of 'the family' had approached her without being part of the game and it boosted her confidence. She'd acted her way through so many lies and would have a very large pimple on her tongue in the morning, but she wasn't sorry. She'd earned it.

At 5.30pm sharp they arrived at the OKC airport for the two inaugural charter flights of Golden Eagle Aviation. The planes had been booked by a dairy farmers' group and Bruce had insisted his two favourite hostesses were needed for one of the maiden flights.

Shirley was grateful for his support but quickly dumbfounded by Vickie's extraordinary lack of knowledge of Bruce and his new airline company. Their Martin 404, manufactured in 1941 with a decent World War 2 record before it was decommissioned, pulled out of the OKC hangar at 1.30am. It took Bruce and his co-pilot until 3.45am to get it off the ground. They were due to pick up their 40 passengers at Springfield Airport, Missouri, at 8.00am and from there fly to Chicago.

The propellers wouldn't rev and the fuel wouldn't flow. The air-conditioning wasn't working, it was 100°F in the cockpit and 90°F in the cabin. Shirley's first task was to survey the galley and cabin and it was a chastening, bloodcurdling inspection. The catering for breakfast was insufficient and there were no trays on which to serve it. The arm rests between seats were broken, the overhead lockers rattled the moment they began to taxi onto the runway and smoke started pouring out of the overhead vents and continued to do so for the next hour. The lavatory was a bucket affair, there was no running water, no towels, the curtains on the windows were filthy, crushed and torn, and the portable fire extinguisher was an original made in 1940.

Finally Shirley had to get off her feet and sit down; Vickie had been sitting for a while. Alone in the cabin, they waited and wondered if they should open the locked cabin door and flee for their lives. It was a close call when Bruce opened the cockpit door and shouted down the aisle: 'We've got everything under control now! Belt up Shirl and Vick, we're about to take off!'

The dairy farmers and their families, a well-dressed, tidy group, were clearly angry that the flight was running late. Shirley had welcomed everyone, the seat belt sign was on and they were waiting for clearance on the runway when she tried the public address system. Two minor electric shocks later, she moved to the front of the plane and yelled down the aisle:

'If your ears ache on take-off, open your mouths and yawn a lot. You'll look ghastly but you'll feel better. Once we're airborne, we'll try and put breakfast together without trays so it might be a bit messy but…I've got a few *Women's Weeklies* from Australia with me that you can pass around and we'll be in the Windy City in no time.'

They loved her accent and her attitude and gave her a round of applause. When they landed, those who could applauded again. She was sitting on the floor in the aisle holding an ammonia inhalant to the face of an elderly man who appeared to be having a heart attack. Her miniskirt, part of the Golden Eagle Aviation uniform, had ridden up to her waist as she fought to stay upright, her other hand held tightly by a woman in the opposite seat. Thankfully the old bloke was only having a panic attack.

The cockpit door remained open throughout the flight because of the lack of airflow and the passengers up front heard every word: 'How does this bastard work? Son of a bitch, the altitude gauge has gone! … Damn, I can't find the charts, where the hell are we?'

Shirley and Vickie managed to serve breakfast to every second person and asked them to share. There was a lot of spillage but they cleaned up and chatted away, 'snowing' the farmers as if experienced hostesses, with Shirley waxing philosophical about dairy farming in Australia.

They circled Chicago twice, trying to get permission to land. The cockpit conversation indicated they were missing an essential instrument. The air traffic controller was informed that the item was out of order and they were redirected to a commercial airport nearby.

It was now a painfully short 24-hour turnaround. The women were exhausted and decided to collapse in the airport hotel.

Thirty years later Shirley would come to love Chicago, but this weekend she was not 'betting her bottom dollar' she'd have 'the time of her life and do things they don't do on Broadway'. They actually slept for 12 hours. Shirley had a bubble bath but struggled to enjoy a pizza at the hotel restaurant before checking out with Vickie and walking back to the airport. Their check-in was midday and most of the passengers boarded at 1.00pm. The rest chose to fly with American Airlines.

The journey home was a nightmare. The weather had changed because the tornado season was approaching. The windy city was living up to its name and the 40 lunches plus all but four of the sick bags on their plane had been stolen. Apparently it was common in airports around America, something rather important they forgot to teach at the Golden Eagle Aviation Air Hostess course.

With no food, an unpressurised cabin, four sick bags and no towels, 20 of the 33 passengers were unsurprisingly sick. There was no choice but to empty the sick bags into the trash, clean them by hand with ice and hand them out again.

'At least we had class,' Vickie said later. 'Anyone sick twice got the same bag back!'

A little girl, maybe three years old vomited all over Shirley. By the time she got to the galley to clean herself up it was so rough that the ice chest and four gallon water flask fell on top of her, somehow opening the back door in the process. It was a grim challenge to get out of there before the flask and floating ice disappeared through the gaping hole and took her with them.

A pale-faced Vickie grabbed her as she was clawing her way out and promptly vomited outside the cockpit door. Shirley sent her to the back of the plane, instructing her to stay there until they landed.

The entire cabin smelt and looked like Kowloon Bay in Hong Kong in 1963, except here nobody was smiling. There was vomit everywhere. Shirley used some dirty seat-back covers soaked in ice to clean up the mess (and put on people's heads). The closer they got to Missouri, the worse it got…up and down, swerve to the left, up and down, swerve to the right. Finally secure in her seat when she heard the 'ding' of the call button, the only mechanism on the plane that worked, she grabbed an ammonia inhalant. Once again they landed with Shirley sitting in the aisle, mini skirt around her waist and a passenger depending on her for his life.

She learned later it was standard practice in America then to obtain airworthy certificates without inspection of the aircraft; all the owners had to do was send off the paperwork and pay the registration fee.

Vickie swore she'd never fly again, unless in business class on American or Qantas. Shirley needed time to think about it, acknowledging that Bruce had to be a bloody good pilot to fly that plane through a twister storm and get them down in one piece.

When she arrived at work next morning, yesterday's ordeal was quickly forgotten; Frank Sinatra was in town. His private jet from New York happened to arrive within an hour of the miraculous Golden Eagle landing in OKC, just before the storm was upgraded to a tornado.

At three o'clock in the afternoon, when the day had darkened sufficiently for all the lights to be turned on, Pete called Shirley to his office.

'The tornado's been downgraded so there's a window of opportunity to pick up Frank before it gets dark. He's been sleeping off a busy week and I'm expecting that call from Washington so I can't leave right now. Would you mind picking him up from the airport hotel and dropping him at the Hilton, Shirley? I'll pick him up later for dinner.'

'Well, as long as you think it's safe to drive?' she managed.

'No problem there. You'll enjoy meeting him. Just take the rest of the day off once you've dropped him at his hotel. Thanks a lot.'

For the first time she took the 12 flights of stairs to the basement, making her decision on the way down. She drove straight home and was surprised to find Vickie had been sent home early by her boss because he'd observed the worsening weather.

'Fuck!' she exclaimed, stunned to hear herself say the word reflexively.

'What's happened, lady?'

'I have to make a phone call. Don't go anywhere. It'll save me having to tell you.'

She called the office and asked for the boss.

'Pete, I'm so sorry but I could hardly see on the road, there's traffic jams in all directions and I kind of panicked, turned around and drove home. I've never been in a tornado before but I've seen them on the news and this looks pretty bad. I'm sorry but I think Frank should stay where he is until it's over.' She then volunteered to start early in the morning, asked him to put whatever had accumulated on her desk, and hung up.

'Bravo!' Vickie hugged her. 'Talk about luck being a Lady tonight! Let's have a glass of wine to celebrate.'

'Without you I'd be one step closer to my grave,' Shirley replied sombrely.

During the second half of her 10 months at Wallington Enterprises there were some unexpected highlights that kept Shirley sane, but all of Vickie's predictions came true.

She wrote to her father, telling him about the horses who were supposed to be in England, and that her phone was bugged. He responded by return mail that for the first time in his life he'd studied the racing pages of *The Age* and learned that two of the horses were at a stud farm on the Mornington

Age Three

Peninsula and one was already considered short odds for the Melbourne Cup that November.

I'm very worried about your safety, Shirley, he wrote.

In reply she summarised Vickie's advice, assuring him she was handling the situation carefully and would not take unnecessary risks. It was small comfort for a father on the other side of the world who knew his daughter only too well. The Victorian Education Department had just appointed him a District Inspector for Schools and he was obviously busy, but he'd board a plane tomorrow if she needed him. Famous last words.

Whilst the Golden Eagle Aviation planes were grounded to attend to some 'minor' repairs, Vickie invited Shirley to join her for a weekend in Nashville, Tennessee, at the upcoming Annual Gospel Singing Jubilee, insisting they travel American Airlines.

Vickie was still friends with her ex-fiancé, a guitarist named Lou Reed who starred in a world famous band. 'Lou always performs there "to keep in God's good books." Talk about double standards all the way to the top!' she laughed. 'But it'll be a dead cheap weekend, lady, because he'll get us into everything and we can stay with friends.'

The huge four-storey theatre was full to capacity: 10,000 people applauding rapturously between acts ranging from individual singers and musicians to large church choirs, country and rock bands to American TV evangelists preaching short and not so short sermons and leading the congregation in prayers. Three hours was enough for Shirley.

'Watch out for the quartets, they're the worst,' Vickie advised as they entered the back stage door. They were led into the male dressing room where ex-fiancé Lou offered 'true' Southern hospitality – an introduction to two of his friends, both clerics, who wanted to take them to a private party later.

'Thanks, but we have an appointment,' Vickie hastened to reply before Shirley could accept. 'Both married with kids,' she murmured aside.

On Saturday night they went their separate ways. Shirley was determined to go to the Grand Ole Opry. Several streets were lined with straggling queues of people so she walked alone on the other side of the streets and eventually fought her way through the crowds to reach the box office.

'I've come all the way from Australia and I just need one seat. Can you help me please?'

It worked every time.

She landed a front row seat on the 2nd floor balcony. That night stars including Dolly Parton, Porter Wagner and Johnny Cash were performing. She was joined by a very handsome young man who sat down beside her during interval, introducing himself as Tom Jones. They chatted amiably for 20 minutes until the warning bell rang and he said he'd wait for her after the show outside Tootsie's, an artists' bar downstairs, and buy her a drink. He loved Australians and his English agent was negotiating a concert in Sydney next year.

It was a classy sort of pick up and Shirley wanted to see Tootsie's. However, they never quite got inside the bar. Tom took her arm as she greeted him before leading her into the car park.

'It's far too busy in there tonight, we'll go somewhere quieter where we can have a decent conversation,' he said.

When they reached his car there was a folded page under the windscreen wiper. Tom opened and read it, apologised that he'd have to leave immediately and asked if she would be alright to get back to her friend at the gospel singing.

'I'll be fine, thanks, but would you mind if I read the note?'

He handed it to her and told her to keep it before jumping into his car and driving away. In large letters scribbled across a pizza restaurant advertisement, the note read: 'I saw you chatting up that woman and I never want to see you again. If you want your bag, you'll find it in my rubbish bin where you belong. Rosy.'

'You've missed nothing,' Vickie consoled her later. 'Frankie and Tom were born with talent, but they're so self-absorbed they'd be lousy lovers.'

On the 1st July 1970, Vickie insisted her Aussie friend witness a Ku Klux Klan parade down the main street of Oklahoma City, the identical route she would be taking a few days later on a float advertising Wallington restaurants. The KKK parade was an unnerving experience, with friends and family shedding tears as they edged through the crowds lining the street to embrace the Klan members they knew. Shirley's mind boggled; what on earth would the Independence Day Parade be like?

On the 4th July, dressed as a cowgirl, Shirley rode on the back of a four-meter iron bull fixed to the back of a large truck. Thousands of locals lined the streets waving flags, singing the *Star-spangled Banner*, more or less in tune with multiple piped versions booming from speakers on every other float. Again, many shed tears as they sang whilst embracing family and friends.

'Only in America!' Shirley laughed at the irony and waved back to the crowd, in company with Wallington's field manager, a bright and attractive man in his 30s who was proving to be a solid and empathetic friend. We'll call him Ray. He would have a big future with Wallington's, if he played his cards right.

A few days later, accountant Carl was dispatched to Washington DC for an urgent financial problem only he could solve, and Ray phoned in to advise that the manager of #12 steak house had gone absent without official leave and the restaurant was booked out for dinner.

At 4.15 in the afternoon Ray swung by to request Shirley's help with the rush hour, and two minutes later Carl waltzed back into the office bearing good tidings.

'To the White House and back in a day!' Shirley exclaimed.

'That's what we pay him for,' came a familiar voice behind Carl.

It was Mick, who'd arrived in the car left permanently parked at the airport, not realising Carl had landed at OKC from Washington ten minutes earlier.

'You look wonderful,' Mick complimented Shirley as he adjourned to the board room.

Five minutes later Pete screamed, 'Three Bourbons, Shirley!' and she delivered them on a tray with the 10-page business sale document she'd just completed tucked under an arm. He thanked her and asked her to leave immediately for #12 steak house.

'Order a cab, Shirley,' Mick instructed. 'I'll pick you up at 8.30 tonight and take you somewhere elegant for dinner.'

'You've made yourself indispensable to Pete in a very short space of time, Shirley, and I must apologise for my brother's manners. He's very grateful but has trouble conveying it. I know your history and you'll be off by the end of the year under these circumstances. Fortunately, I've got bigger plans for you.'

'I accepted that when you offered me the job, Mick.'

'I'm not talking about a management job in Australia! I know now that you'd be bored in no time with anything I could offer you there. I want to get you into the main game – personally and in my business in Nassau. You must know by now that I'm determined not to lose you. I have to go to Melbourne for The Cup in November but I can have a visa in place for you by the time I get back. I have Sympatico with you and believe I'm you're man, Shirley.'

'I'm beginning to grasp that, Mick. I just don't know what to do about it.'

'Let's go back to the office and discuss it.'

'My flatmate is visiting her sick mother in Little Rock for a couple of days. We could go to our apartment instead?' she suggested.

Mick got lucky, finally making love to the woman he was lining up to be his fourth wife, or so he thought. Shirley had been without sex for too long and was quickly responsive to the skills of this power broker cum lover. Hence when he left her apartment early next morning his intentions were affirmed and his hopes riding high.

The following day he spent with Pete and Carl in Pete's office. When everyone else had left the office, he took Shirley into the board room and they made love on the floor. The cleaning lady arrived, began vacuuming in reception and opened the board room door before they were done.

'Dear God!' she mouthed before turning off the vacuum cleaner and settling in to watch!

Horrified, Shirley later told Vickie the whole story, then added: 'I can't believe I allowed Mick to make love to me on the board room floor!'

'It's easy to believe what you did,' Vickie replied, 'but can you believe it of the cleaning lady!'

It was one of Vickie's best lines; Shirley still laughs whenever she thinks about any one of the long list of cleaning ladies she's employed down the years.

The day of reckoning was nigh.

Ray, the field manager, who was increasingly included in board room discussions, took Shirley aside to give her an oblique warning about how old traditions and operating practices die hard. He commented that it would be smart for her to be alert to brotherly loyalties.

It was difficult to know what exactly he was trying to tell her, but Vickie was all over it.

'Mick wants you and Pete's jealousy of his brother is long standing,' she surmised. 'He's the wild card and half his staff, well…the few you personally know have disappeared without trace and the police either haven't been informed or are doing an undercover search. You have to be very, very careful what you do next.'

Shirley responded directly. 'I'll be forever grateful for your support and advice, Vick, but I have to handle this myself. Mick's a contradiction in terms – a bad man with a good heart, and I'm counting on the latter. Please trust me now; I need time to think about what I have to do.'

Mick returned three weeks later and asked if she'd made a decision. Enigmatically she handed him a short poem she'd written titled *Sympatico*, the word he'd used to describe his feelings for her. He was an intelligent man and would surely get it.

> A random, fleeting blush, is not so very much –
>   For I have blushed before.
> A quickening of my pulse, can often times be false –
>   Not from my deepest core.
>   But if I laugh and joke
>   When I am lonely,
>   Be forewarned!
>
> An adoration in my eye, could mean my heart will easily lie –
>   Do not be too believing.
> A breathless kiss upon my lips, might just be a full eclipse –
>   So often it's deceiving.
>   But if I cry a lot
>   When I am happy,
>   Be forewarned!
> Sympatico may turn to love tomorrow.

He read it slowly, folded the piece of paper and looked at her with a mix of acceptance and shock. One large tear fell down his right cheek.

'I've underestimated you. I'm very sorry,' he said. 'I guess it's too late to say I love you.'

'Yes,' she replied quietly. She hadn't expected the tear, but stayed with the script she'd planned.

'I haven't buried my mother yet and my father hasn't either so I have to go home and support him. I can't come to the Bahamas with you. There's no way I could tell Dad I'm moving to Nassau with a still-married man more than twice my age – a man who feels 'Sympatico' for me. It would destroy him, and probably me. I'm sorry, Mick. I'll always be glad to know you, and grateful for everything you've given me.'

At 8am 13 lucky days later, a uniformed official from the Dallas Immigration Department presented himself at the reception desk of Wallington Enterprises.
'Shirley Joy McLaughlin?'
'Yes?'
'You have been working illegally in America for nearly 10 months and on behalf of the United States of America Immigration Department I am formally advising you that we are deporting you, as of Friday week. You will leave work now and meet me at your apartment where you'll give me your passport, which will be stamped accordingly.'
The official followed Shirley home and they entered her apartment in silence. He waited in the kitchen whilst she recovered her passport from the top shelf of her wardrobe, then duly stamped and signed the deportation certificate in her passport on page 13 - yes, page 13 - one page after the long expired, short term visitors' visa. She'd quietly obtained that visa on her last day in New Zealand when Mick had returned to the CBD without her passport. Did he genuinely plan to secure her a work permit, but change his mind when she rejected him? She'd never know.
Alan had offered to take long service leave so he could be with her, adding that a few international school visits would make the trip tax deductible. Once the immigration official left, she rang her father's office and left a message with his secretary. 'Please tell Dad I've just been deported,' she said calmly. 'I have to be out of here Friday week but I can get a one month extension…if he can come? He can call me at home tonight or tomorrow night, Sue.'
On Friday week there was no formal farewell for Shirley in the office; in fact there was no acknowledgement that she was leaving at all. Having sold her car two days earlier, she was dependent on Vickie to pick her up at the end of the day, however Mick turned up and saved Vickie the trouble.
'You owe me three weeks' pay,' Shirley smiled at him when the pleasantries were over.
'Yes, I do, and some holiday pay. Let's go to the bank and I'll drop you home.'

Her stomach churned as Mick parked the Cadillac outside the bank and gave her a cheque. He said nothing as she got out of the car, watching as she walked into the bank, collected the cash and returned to the car.

'We're square now?' he murmured, but she let that go for fear her voice would reveal her darkest thoughts.

'I'm grateful to you, Mick,' she recited from the script in her head. 'I'm sorry to have missed the chance we had…under different circumstances…' and her mind went blank and she could say no more.

At that precise moment he was about to jump out of the car to open her door when Vickie pulled into the drive. Vickie's boss's unfortunate past dealings with the Wallingtons, and the undoubtedly negative input she'd subsequently offered Shirley meant he had no desire to meet Miss Morris. Quickly he reached across to open her door.

'Keep what you've learned about us to yourself and I'll make sure it works for you,' he stated purposefully before kissing her on the lips, wishing her well and driving swiftly away.

Deportation, fate and *If it's Tuesday, it's Belgium!*

It would take 12 months for Shirley to understand the full significance of Mick's final words but at that moment she was acutely cognisant of her current situation. The following Monday morning she drove to Dallas to secure a month-long visitor's visa so she could remain in the States.

'My father, Alan McLaughlin, is a district inspector for schools and Special First Class Head Teacher of a major teacher-training primary school in Australia with over 1,000 students. He happens to have planned a visit to America and has educational seminars and lecturing commitments with several large schools around the country and would love to spend some time and money with me before we depart for a European tour.'

Shirley's smile and gushing admission that she'd broken the rules because she'd fallen in love with America were sufficient to convince the Texan public servant of her deep regret. He proceeded to confirm Alan's credentials and airline bookings via two international phone calls, stamp page 14 of her passport opposite the Deportation stamp, and wish her well.

The following weekend Shirley was to meet her father in Las Vegas – 'of all the places to meet my daughter!' he enthused to everyone before he left. Their schedule happened to clash with Shirley's last Golden Eagle Aviation commitment, a secondary school sports' team charter to Denver, Colorado. Although she wasn't proud of her decision, she offered the job to a colleague named Jennifer who was married with three children and was having an affair with Bruce. She allowed her obligation to Alan to appease her conscience.

Father and daughter were tired when they finally met. They spent three relaxing days in Vegas, barely leaving the Stardust Hotel where Shirley won a jackpot on a poker machine. With her winnings they were able to cover their entire expenses, including tickets to several shows and an hilarious evening with Jerry Lewis.

From there they flew to Denver at the invitation of a man Shirley had befriended during prolonged negotiations in the purchase of a Wallington business.

The sale had eventually happened but not before Pete had snuck in one Sunday after church and removed all the assets. It was the day before Settlement; Shirley happened to be in the office innocently typing the contract and witnessed it all. Purchaser Jim was left with an empty building and called to tell Shirley. It was two days after her deportation notice and they cautiously shared commiserations. Jim insisted that she and Alan visit him prior to their Washington and Niagara Falls plans en route to London.

They had been in his Porche driving up the spectacular, winding road to the peak of the Colorado Mountains when directly ahead, no more than a mile away, the Golden Eagle Martin 404 crashed into a mountain.

Shirley quickly discovered that both hostesses and the co-pilot were killed instantly. The passengers, all 36 students and four teachers were dead by the time the emergency services reached them. The only survivor was the owner and pilot of the plane, Bruce.

Shirley was in shock and Alan decided they should back-track to Oklahoma City to attend the funerals of her colleagues. Her memory of the days they spent in OKC remains a blur. She could recall Alan being a wonderful support throughout but the details of the funerals, where they stayed, how long they were there and who they met were lost to her. Only the headlines in the state and national newspapers and the fact that Bruce was being interrogated in a hospital bed remain with her.

Age Three

Many years later, Alan would recall the day of the funeral of the woman who had died in Shirley's place. He said he still had occasional nightmares about her three little girls sobbing with their father in the front pew of the church.

The extraordinary fate of it all was beyond comprehension but Shirley could no longer ignore her part in the events that had unfolded during her time in America. She had been complicit in several peoples' unfaithfulness, especially Mick's which had undoubtedly saved her life, but come at the expense of Jennifer's.

Margery's mixed metaphors would forever return to haunt her. *Life isn't fair, but whatever you choose to do, you'll have to live with the repercussions of your actions, darling, and two wrongs don't make a right.*

The first time Shirley used her passport after it included an American Deportation stamp caused her and Alan no inconvenience. Niagara Falls was spectacular, but if they walked across the bridge to Toronto, Shirley would not be allowed back. In fact, departing America was the easiest exit they would make before they arrived home in Australia two months later.

Their whistle-stop tour of seven countries in 30 days was demanding but the bus was comfortable, the driver excellent and the accommodation reliable. The company guide, a handsome Italian in his 30s, was erudite and obliging – especially to Shirley who was by far the youngest of the 38 tourists on board. The great generation made up the majority and Alan immediately struck an easy camaraderie with couples, widows and widowers. Shirley was allocated to share a room with the only woman in her 20s travelling alone, but ultimately teamed up with a woman in her 40s who was intelligent, trouble-free company.

At the first border checkpoint at Calais, Shirley was escorted from the bus to be interrogated in the small, official 'bathing box' (so dubbed because in those days that's what border offices looked like to Australians).

'But what did you actually do?' the guards pressed, insisting on great detail because they didn't understand the American code in her passport.

'I worked as a secretary without a visa,' she repeated, but it took two hours to convince them she'd simply been a lazy Aussie girl who'd forgotten to get a work permit.

It became apparent that if it was going to take two hours to get into every country, their timetable would be shot. The tour guide, who was well endowed with muscle, ideas and ego solved the problem, firstly introducing himself as

'Dino Crocetti', Dean Martin's name before studio producers came up with a Hollywood moniker. (Bizarrely, they'd just learned whilst in Vegas that Martin's co-star, Jerry Lewis, was apparently christened Joseph Levitch. Go figure.)

Brandishing the microphone on the bus with theatrical flair, Dino briefed his charges. 'At the next border, we're going to bury Shirley at the back of the bus under a pile of your coats. On approach, we'll turn up the heating, you will all take off your jackets and coats and our naughty little Aussie lady will remain silent and still until the officers have boarded the bus, checked your passports and let us go.'

And so it happened that Shirley was smuggled through Europe, leaving no evidence she'd ever been there.

Another tour guide by the name of Harry Keisler (the given surname of Heddy Lamarr, everyone was informed – truth is definitely stranger than fiction!) joined the tour in Paris. He'd been working for the company in Bangkok, was learning the European circuit and began an affair with Shirley's room-mate, Christina.

Naturally, Christina was unaware of the many evenings he'd spent in Bangkok's brothels and by the time they arrived in Lucerne she had crabs.

'I've got these things with lots of legs crawling all over me,' she cried and Shirley called the hotel doctor. He gave her some pills and told her to apply what looked like flea powder every four hours, adding that Shirley should keep her own towel and flannel out of the bathroom and ensure she didn't share any clothing, bedding, soap or snacks.

'Crabs are very contagious, dear,' he advised.

By this time Shirley was having a 'condom' affair with Dino. Light relief after the Wallington saga, with a final curtain known before the show began. It would be a one act play with a fated season of 30 days.

Alan bumped into her many times on his way down to breakfast as, high heel in hands, she climbed up the stairs still in evening dress, to shower. Fortunately he'd been so well trained by Margery that right from that first happenstance he managed a smile and a chipper 'Good morning'.

By the third week he was positively effusive. 'Did you have a good night, Shirley?'

Dino was a charming Italian with a glamorous façade, a generous wallet and an in-depth knowledge of the best nightclubs on the Continent, but he didn't have the maturity, quality or literary refinement of Andreas, the Chief Purser.

Never mind. It was good to be alive.

Somewhere in the midst of those 30 manic days and nights, three weeks' rooming with a crabs-infested woman of Afrikaans descent and half an hour spent gasping for air under a mountain of jackets and coats every few days, Shirley found time to begin plotting her new career. It was clear she'd decided to become a novelist and her first book would be a murder mystery.

We came across a titillating summary of the intended cast, closely based on her and Alan's travelling companions. The diverse, international list of bona fide characters were penned in shorthand in November 1970; it appears she was searching for a plot as she typed up her notes on her new portable Olivetti soon after they arrived home.

If it's Tuesday, it's Belgium.

Dorothy: Best of company, together on the bus. Sincere, lonely, regretful but with a dry sense of humour, sometimes sad, never bitter. Large frame, lovely face, warm eyes, giggler and independent. Business interests: 'Mr Gibson' Agency in Sydney with two clients (Mr Chang and Mr Yeung @ $50 an hour), toast mistress, clerk for Qantas.

Perhaps begin in London's China Town?

Christina: Room-mate with crabs, angular features, dark, masculine clothes but femme fatale eyes. Aged 28, commercial artist in debt for the last three years. 'Fuck all men I say. Fuck 'em!' South African joke…Little man walking along the street when someone threw a rotten tomato at his head. 'Are you joking or did you mean it?' he asked. 'I meant it, you fool,' came the reply. 'That's okay then, I don't like being made fun of.'

Bill & Marge: The Maple Leaves from Canada: Libra and Taurus. Talk to one another all the time, laugh and join in.

Tearful in Koblenz, travelling down the Rhine on their 25th wedding anniversary. Schnapps served straight-up at 9.30am and even got Alan into the habit! Genuine, mature couple with two adopted children.

The murder should happen on their anniversary, sort of Agatha Christie style on the boat.

Denis & Vera: At first pleasant, talkative, fun. By Cologne, had pulled out of group activities, found dislikes for everything and everyone. Suddenly a sour couple with sharp features and thin mouths. Denis moody, Vera bitchy; tough combination for close quarters.

Make good extras post the murder, or one could be the victim?

Denise: Two-faced large woman of leisure. Queenslander. Widowed after happy marriage. Frustrated, ready for anything but not inviting it, racing around making cups of tea and drinking cheap whisky and brandy. Student Castle in Heidelberg brought bad memories of wrongly imprisoned husband.

(Could a _woman_ be my murderer?)

Winston: Travelling American, missing his wife, reserved, sense of boyish fun but prefers to be left alone. 'I don't dance with anyone but my wife,' – or so he said. Later…drunk: 'I've been on business in Tai Pai, reminds me of my first experience at 17 with a pro in Amsterdam. "Well, are ya' going to get on with it, or aren't you?" she asked me, reading the paper. "Tell me when you've finished, will you?"'

Contradictory man… natural suspect?

John & Francis: Boring, bigoted hippy couple on their honeymoon, won Sydney lottery but spent the trip complaining and sponging. Booked twin rooms, it was cheaper! Francis' terrible skin covered in thick make-up. Salzburg and Bavarian Alps were glorious, and roadway built by prisoners whilst army built underneath tunnel from Austria to Germany was amazing, but they were disappointed with it all – and said 'The Jews earned what they got.'

Winnie & 'Click Click': Mr & Mrs Low from New Zealand, professor and ex-teacher. Gentle, nervous woman and unimposing man, racing up to front of bus to take photos, checking time and light meters constantly. In Milan, Padua, Venice…Winnie had never seen so many males on the loose. 'God damn it, they might be able to make love, but they're not the full lire!' Strange comments/behaviour for educated people.

Interesting possibilities?

The Bastard & Wife: Mr & Mrs…can't remember. Obese, beer drinking, stingy, false smile, wants to be liked, forces attention and then abuses it. Rude, ignorant Aussie with timid, abused wife reduced to tears most days. Naples to Pompei and God of Fertility: Porn sculpture, women forbidden (but Dino showed me and it was huge!) yet all they could say was 'All Italians are bastards. They're all bloody bastards!'

Mr & Mrs McCormack: Sir Rupert and Lady Janet, doddering, condescending old couple. 'Oh, let's not bother to take the tour, dear. Let the plebs go.' In Rome, to Tivoli Gardens: 'Poor priests, they must have some simple pleasures I 'spose?' Rupert more fun, but both suffering inferiority complexes, acting like they were superior in every way.

Barry: Smiling Belgian, retired, fat old bloke who liked his beer, unperturbed by anything much. Amiable enough, glad to mix with whoever would have him. In Monte Carlo lost US$2K travellers' cheques, no worries. Spoke fluent French, Italian, German and English, perhaps more?

Wild card, could be useful.

Natalie & Michael: Russian woman from Melbourne, shouting her intelligent, troubled son a holiday. When he lost heaps in Monte Carlo, he blamed his mother and decided to go home. Her 'ex' called two days later, their son Michael had landed but would live with him from now on. 'Great news. At last I can get a life!' she said, chatted up Alan over dinner in Paris and asked for his phone number in Melbourne. (Could hardly believe it when Dad gave her a wrong number – Mum would have been proud!)

Val: French/Italian. Arrogant, selfish, thoughtless, intelligent, capable of anything. At San Bernadino Pass we got caught in a snow storm, chains on bus wheels took hours, cars skidding down the hill, everyone ordered out to walk through narrow Pass. Val stayed, helped the crew, put up umbrellas in the bus as snow came through vents in the roof, secured everyone's property and expected no thanks. Don't judge a book by its cover!

A special character, essential part of the denouement? Bring her on the page early, set up a surprise. Much virtue in "if"…but a twist, perhaps. She could be capable of murder.

As it was Alan's first trip overseas, he wanted to add Athens and one must-see part of India to their itinerary. By changing their tickets accordingly, stopovers in Beirut and Hong Kong were also added to the list of destinations. They may have been travelling by air, but the detours proved to be more maritime in theme – it was anything but smooth sailing and they were lucky to get home together.

During a guided tour of The Acropolis in Athens, they were constantly surrounded by hundreds of men, a small group of whom dobbed Alan in for pocketing a lump of agate from the Parthenon. It nearly got him arrested. In

Beirut they were relentlessly trailed by the cab driver who'd taken them to the ancient ruins of Byblos when they first arrived. The man Ibrahim Yueseff obsessively followed them, insisting on taking them everywhere, introducing his family and pressing them to stay on at his home.

They'd booked an historic British Hotel for their time in New Delhi. They arrived early in the morning and found the staff were similarly invasive, opening doors, flogging their taxis, and hanging around with hands out for tips and Alan was unashamedly relieved to learn that their 'suite' was ready.

The large bed-sit arrangement was swarming with flies, bees and other unidentifiable creatures when they entered. The bathroom was grotty, the sheets on the beds likewise and the mattresses felt lumpy. Following a breakfast of lukewarm coffee and burnt toast with flies, Alan was extremely agitated and had had more than enough.

'The sooner we get out of here the better,' he grumbled.

An aggressive argument ensued between three men over who would get the job to drive them to Agra and the Taj Mahal, but luckily they chose a driver called Charlie and Alan's passion for the trip returned. According to Charlie, the Taj was a marvellous infusion of Central Asian, Ottoman and Safavid architectural styles, built by the Moguls post the first Muslim invasion in the 12th century. It was quite a build-up and they hoped he was right.

Charlie was an intelligent 'old soul' who in excellent English regaled his passengers with an infinite repertoire of local stories and jokes, both historical and philosophical. The journey to Agra was long and slow, the only route was a road shared by mountain goats, cows, donkeys, horses, camels, trishaws, scooters, bicycles, cars and trucks. The human contingent included lepers, begging children missing legs and arms, sexually ambiguous characters and two or three generations of families who lived on the sides of the road, their encampments scattered across the fields to the very foot of the mountains.

Charlie gauged his tourists' reactions shrewdly.

'India tolerates eccentricity and differentness like no other country,' he chatted away as if talking about the weather, catching their eyes in the rear-vision mirror from time to time.

'Eunuchs, impotents, hermaphrodites – we give them a special place here but no more or less than the animals and we common mortals. We're all different. We're all the same. Only on this earth for a short time.'

The Taj Mahal did not disappoint Alan and Shirley and his tender narrative of the love affair behind its inception, spiced with historical details of a British colony that was now emerging into a major civilisation in its own right gave them a new understanding of India and her peoples.

Before heading off to the airport, they visited the Agra market where Shirley found the most beautiful fabric she'd ever seen. Charlie obligingly changed her $US20 note in order for her to purchase three metres of glorious rainbow silk.

At the airport they went to the bank to change their left-over local currency and alarm bells rang. Alan had receipts from the hotel and the taxi drivers, but Shirley had none. It dawned on her then that, like most Indians he described so eloquently, Charlie had by-passed the money-changing laws.

Six uniformed men took them into a dingy little office. Alan was given a seat but she was made to stand whilst they accused her of being a criminal.

Half an hour into the hour-long interrogation they arrived at the quintessential point; it wasn't about changing money on the black market at all. It was about her passport! One of the officials attempted to get through to Dallas to verify her reason for deportation, but without success. It was the middle of the night in Texas.

Shirley nearly lost it, but just in time remembered the rules. Tears flowing, she gave them a heartrending rendition of her recent family tragedy and was mid-way through a rousing crescendo – 'I simply must get home because my sister is ill…and her children…' when the loud speaker interrupted.

'Last call for Hong Kong. Passengers Mr and Miss McLaughlin, please go to Gate 64 immediately.'

As if he'd been called, a mature man in a medal-studded uniform knocked on the door and entered.

'This way please,' he smiled, escorting them to the gate and waiting until they'd been cleared.

As soon as the seat belt sign went off, Alan pressed the bell and ordered two beers. It was not yet 10.00am.

'Was I set up?' Shirley finally broke their after-shock silence, 'like they were using me to learn to interrogate or something?'

Alan sipped slowly on his beer. 'There was a camera filming everything in that office, the last call timing was sheer luck and your performance was a tour de force. I'll drink to Mum and the Wallington brothers for that.'

Finally homeward bound, Shirley and Alan had mixed feelings about the last leg of the journey. They were missing home yet not wanting this hastily planned adventure to end. It had been a unique and unifying experience for both father and daughter. Margery had forever been her younger daughter's best friend, as Alan had been their older daughter's. Now they shared a close, personal friendship.

Hong Kong was a wonderful finale. The people were charming, the cable car ride up to the peak spectacular, Macau by hydrofoil in rough weather worth every minute, and a sentimental guided tour of Project Concern's floating clinics, shacks on the hills and the Walled City were a fitting end to a highly charged journey home.

On their last night they joined some Project Concern staff for dinner and their host ordered oysters for starters. Neither Alan nor Shirley had eaten them before. Alan tried one and spat it out; Shirley devoured her half dozen and Alan's remaining five.

'Fabulous, Dad!' she raved. 'At last I know what Will meant when he said the world's your oyster!'

On a makeshift desk in her bedroom at Alan's new Glen Waverley home, Shirley wrote her first novel. It took her six weeks, writing non-stop. At the start she told her father it was going to be a European-based detective story and hopefully not just a travelogue-cum-murder mystery, and he was thrilled.

'Go for it!' he encouraged her.

Living off her saved US dollars (most of the small inheritance from her mother had been spent on the world trip), she produced just over 50,000 words. Better a trifle short than a long, boring read, she reasoned to herself. The working title wasn't quite right so she renamed it *Thirty Days Hath September*.

Bugger! Not very original either. *'What's in a name? A rose, by any other…'*

For heaven's sake, it is what it is! Publishers change titles anyway, don't they? she declared and hit Print!

With 140 pages in hand, she sat down in Alan's favourite chair in the lounge and read the manuscript as if for the first time, pen at the ready. She told herself to be realistic. There were bound to be some clumsy bits, poor grammar, technical errors and typos.

Two days and dozens of corrections later the truth of the matter hit home. The characters were real enough, each of them different and seriously flawed, and the read had some pace to it. The plot even felt believable. But what she'd assumed would be the story's strength ended up being its irreversible weakness.

The only attractive, funny, flamboyant, talented character in the entire manuscript – sort of a mix of Dean Martin, Jerry Lewis and Heddy Lamarr, was the bloody murderer! *Fuck.*

'Better get a day job, lady,' she grumbled out loud. 'You're not going to make your living writing any time soon. QED.'

Except this time she was wrong.

Television productions, personalities and persecutors

In 1971 Channel ATVO was widely referred to as the fourth television station in Australia. ATVO, which later became ATV10, or Channel Ten nationally, was battling to compete with channels HSV7 and GTV9. Even the non-commercial ABC2 had better ratings.

The station was owned by Sir Reginald Ansett of Ansett Transport Industries, a man who knew a lot about transport and little about television, although probably more than the executives on 'Skid Row' who had been recruited from his diverse transport operations. The studios were located in the Melbourne suburb of Nunawading, a few minutes by car from Glen Waverley. The convenient location however, was not the reason Shirley chose to approach them.

It so happened that Reginald Ansett's first business had been financed by Norman Crean, the husband of Grandma Jones' younger sister. After fronting capital for Reg's first taxi outfit, Norman had backed Ansett's first plane and thereafter their investment relationship had continued throughout the rapid expansion of the mogul's multifarious empire. Shirley knew that if she managed to carve a career in television, the value of an advocate in high places could not be overestimated.

Unsurprisingly, the knowledge of Uncle Norm's contribution to Sir Reg gave her purpose and a new burst of confidence. Timing and luck were also on her side the day she called the station manager to sell herself and scored an interview for the next day.

It was a bourgeoning time in television in Australia. Most families had by then at least one large 'box' television set in their living rooms and national stations were broadcasting up to 12 hours a day to meet customer demand. Crawford Productions were beginning to take over the soap and serial market and Graham Kennedy's 'In Melbourne Tonight' live-to-air variety show at GTV9's 'Television City' had been capturing the nation's evenings five nights a week for more than a decade.

Live morning television was well established and the rapidly expanding purchase of successful overseas TV shows and films was changing the culture of family life. Picture theatres around the country, mainly showing American and English films were suffering because the entertainment at home was fabulous and free, and restaurants were closing down at a frightening rate.

ATVO's station manager, Peter English, would prove to be the most loyal friend Shirley would ever have during her time in the entertainment business. She arrived 15 minutes early for her interview. Five minutes after his secretary took her resume and references, she was called into Peter's office.

'Tell me what you're looking for,' he said straight up.

She hadn't scripted or rehearsed what she was going to say because she didn't know what he was looking for!

'As you can see from my resume, Mr English, I've never let school stand in the way of a good education,' slipped out and set the tone from which there was no turning back. 'I've done a lot of practical and creative things but haven't stayed long at any. Twelve months in America, and exploring the world with my father, have settled my travel lust. I've just completed my first novel but it's not going to make me a living. I'm looking for a position that stretches my creative skills and gives me a challenge I can't wrap up in a week or a month. Whether it's on camera or in the back room, I think you'd be mad if you don't employ me.'

English's face opened up like Alan's might have done, but he had another question and she sensed it was pivotal.

'What about a second novel? Don't you want to conquer the next one whilst you're hot, save being stuck with first novel syndrome?'

'It's a detached, lonely sort of job, Mr English, and I'm not yet 23. You've reminded me of my grandma's advice when I was growing up. She grew roses and plants for the local florists to supplement her pension and we visited her every Christmas in Mornington. Each year I'd beg to stay so I could tend and pick the flowers with her but she'd insist I go to the beach with dad and my sister. "You'll have plenty of time to garden when you're old," she'd say.'

'I get your drift, Shirley. It so happens I'm looking for a writer for our morning show,' he said. 'Our new producer, Marlene, is doing her best but the competition is fierce and the cast need new blood and fresh ideas. I'm going to create a position that will keep you challenged, and perhaps at the same time solve another problem I've got,' English reflected aloud.

'I'd like to offer you the position of Writer/Assistant Producer of *Fredd Bear's Breakfast A' Go Go*. How does that sound?'

Shirley had never been a morning person. When the alarm rang every weekday at 4.30am, she endured a warm shower to wake sufficiently to drive to the Studios by five.

She fell into the position *'in two shakes of a duck's tail'* as English commented later, her fast typing skills, ABC program experience and recently sharpened vocabulary rendering the practical aspects of the job a snap. Notwithstanding, it was her personality, drive and ability to write, produce and sell new ideas to the cast on a daily basis that brought about the sacking of the existing producer six weeks later, and her immediate promotion to the senior role.

The news surprised nobody except Shirley. Marlene was an experienced, gentle soul who'd given her new assistant every support and encouragement. English told Shirley the news in the privacy of his office after Marlene had left the building. When she asked him to explain why he'd let her go, he gave her an honest answer followed by some brutal, if cryptic advice.

'Marlene's been a competent, willing employee but she couldn't win the confidence of the cast,' he began diplomatically.

'It's tricky juggling professional and personal relationships in any business environment but in this game you're working with egocentrics…insecure, covetous, crazy individuals. It's tough. They've kind of fallen in love with you because you're making them look and sound better, and the ratings are going up accordingly. You're a lot younger than them but just as confident and capable and they know it. You're in charge now. Make sure you remain so. Stick to your guns, maintain your standards. You've got a big career ahead of you, providing you remember that your brief apprenticeship is now officially over.

'And don't forget that self-absorbed people fall in and out of love at the drop of a hat!' he added brightly, before asking if she was familiar with her new office. No. She wasn't; Marlene had worked behind a closed door.

It was a derelict stationery-cum-broom cupboard containing a desk that ran the length of one wall, the original shelves fixed to the other and holding a serious overflow of 'stuff'. On the desk was a phone, typewriter and portable TV, and a framed picture of Fredd Bear and the cast of the show on the wall. It was claustrophobic, but she'd keep the door open.

Brekky shows at the time were alluringly guileless and basically less predictable versions of todays. The formula was the same: a panorama of news, cartoons, pop star clips, competitions, cooking demos, guest artists of all genres and interviews with authors, politicians and anyone famous for any reason whatsoever. Most of the segments were underpinned by an overt agenda but the cast and crews at all four stations managed to deliver wholesome family shows. *Fredd Bear's Breakfast A' Go Go* was sold as a children's program that also catered to adults.

'Fredd Bear' was a talented pre boomer named Tedd Dunn. Concurrently he fulfilled the role of the station's senior wardrobe designer and worked from early morning to late afternoon most days. He was also in demand for public appearances at schools and shopping centres around Melbourne and volunteered to assist Shirley in her new position, which he happily did when he had the time. Tedd was gay and had a long term partner who contributed greatly to their busy social life.

Judy Banks hosted the show. A woman in her 30s, she was well known to Melbourne theatre goers following her many stints in lead roles of successful musical comedies. She'd also appeared in an ABC series during the 1960s. As hostess, she played the role of dear friend and close confidant to the title character, Fredd Bear, and was on camera for most of the two hours of the show each morning.

Judy and Fredd had already developed a special partnership by the time Shirley took over and they greedily embraced her scripts, delightedly doing what they did best in many themed comedy 'plays' that spanned the entire shows. Judy's partner was Bob Phillips. They'd met in early 1969 on the set at ATVO when Bob left GTV9 following Graham Kennedy's early (first) retirement from the highly successful national variety show *In Melbourne Tonight*. Previously a floor manager and producer at GTV, Bob was instrumental in creating *Fredd Bear's Breakfast A' Go Go* for ATVO in 1969, but had moved on to open up an entertainment agency.

Colin McEwan, journalist, radio announcer and ventriloquist (the voices behind *'Leonardo de Funbird'* and *'Cassius Cuckoo'*), was exceptionally talented and managed to surprise every day. He didn't need Shirley's scripting services because he wrote his own material, but she included him in many Judy and Fredd dramas, often with hilarious results. Colin kept his personal life to himself, although Shirley vaguely remembers he had a wife.

Michael McCarthy was the newsreader, a good-looking young man who'd attracted a strong female following. Blessed with the gift of the gab, he'd been in real estate for a while before stumbling into television. He was single, and loving it.

Despite the ungodly hour of the morning (make-up at 6.30) and an hour's drive from Melbourne's CBD, it was worth the effort for the guest performers and interviewees to turn up for appearances on the show. Shirley booked guests directly or through their agents and she was never short of talent. Regulars included Johnny Farnham, Normie Rowe, Judy Stone, Ian Buckland, Johnny Young, Ronnie Burns, Allison Durban, Colleen Hewett, Tony Pantano, Issy Dy, Ian Turpie, Johnny Chester, Chelsea Brown, Ian 'Molly' Meldrum, Ugly Dave Grey…and that's only a quick snapshot.

Many of the artists were in town on package deals. Locals turned up at short notice when cancellations occurred: *All publicity is good publicity!*

Few guest artists at ATVO were paid a fee to perform on the show. Johnny Farnham received $20 per appearance on the brekky show, thanks to his agent Glen Wheatley, but the majority of celebrity guests accepted the status quo which was to turn up and be seen. It was considered good experience and helped sell seats at their own shows. Live television productions enjoyed steady sponsorship but what little advertising time was allowed was strictly controlled. The country's population was smaller and the broadcasting hours shorter, and 'prime time' television was about an hour after 'tea'.

The fact that ATVO executives didn't pay professional talent for live TV performances was not publicly broadcast until the following year and Shirley was caught in the resulting backlash. A special second anniversary broadcast of *Fredd Bear* was already locked in by the time she'd taken over and every artist who'd performed over the previous two years had been invited to help celebrate.

The following day you could read all about it and the headlines and articles didn't hold back: 'STARS TRICKED INTO FREE SHOW. Rated as the number one 'Red Faces Story' of the year, nearly every top pop artist in Australia gave their services free-of-charge to Channel O's *Fredd Bear's Breakfast A' Go-Go!*'

The artists had been invited to a special chicken and champagne post-show soiree but the breakfast had been cancelled by management at the last minute. Instead they were taken to the Channel O canteen for a cup of coffee and toasted sandwiches, which they had to buy themselves!

Writing and producing 10 hours of live television a week was not for the faint hearted.

Managing a cast of talented yet insecure, egocentric, temperamental and sometimes downright impossible children masquerading-as-adults made every work day an interesting challenge. But for Shirley, 1971 was characterised by relatively harmonious relationships with her colleagues at the station, along with some generous support from a Skid Row secretary.

Without an assistant, Shirley remained responsible for typing the lion's share of the programs and scripts, but Jeanette offered her services (when her boss was playing golf). Her skills were exceptional and she went on to become one of the most successful television producers in Australia. 'Jeanette' is not her real name. Most names in Age Three have been changed to protect the innocent…and the guilty.

Another integral part of Shirley's job was to closely liaise with highly creative advertising executives and attend meetings with agency gurus and sponsors' representatives. In this, she was in her element, which she put down to her lengthy employment with H.J. Heinz. (Well, at that stage it had been her longest performance of nearly 18 months!) With her instinctive marketing and sales disposition and her belief that *the truth will out,* she had no fear of these worldly, fast-talking men. Indeed, she recognised herself as their equal, with the same strong self-esteem and healthy ego and an unwavering work ethic. At last she didn't have to act. She could just be herself.

Inevitably this sometimes presaged complications.

Tim Black, of Black & Blue Advertising Agency in Melbourne, was determined to pull off the first Australian live phone cross from radio to television and had been knocked back by Channels 9 and 7 respectively: 'Too hard. Radio runs to tight schedules, television is all over the place.'

Tim had already secured a family-friendly sponsor, Susan Day Cakes, and had also lined up a DJ at Radio 3KZ. He wasn't the type to give up. Over lunch, he and his partner talked Shirley into making it happen.

It didn't take much. She was excited, sure they could do it. All it would take was for her director to agree she could take the call 60 seconds before the cross from the DJ to Judy.

Shirley took the first call in the control room and it went precisely to plan. The director told Judy to stand by. Fifty seconds later the DJ was patched through for a two-minute conversation that aired simultaneously on radio and television. Tedd did a celebratory 'Fredd' dance around the host desk and a new, entertaining form of breakfast advertising (a la Graham Kennedy) was born.

The segment was a huge success. The cast and crew enjoyed Susan Day cakes for breakfast every Tuesday for the rest of the year, the Black & Blue Agency stepped up their sale of the show, prompting several new sponsors to come on board. And Tim Black began to pursue Shirley.

Tim was single and in his early 30s. Everyone who encountered him professed he was the most handsome man they'd ever met. With the looks and charisma of Paul Newman, he could stop a room before he got through the door. Shirley had long maintained a lack of interest in glamour boys and sex symbols, but how could she refuse? Given that her social life was nil and they were both too busy for a typical relationship, she was happy to get together with Tim every other week. So why not? It was only going to be a light affair anyway. She was sure of that.

Darren McKay was the advertising manager of a major toy manufacturer in Australia when he first approached ATVO to advertise on the show. In addition to his company's contract for weekly placement of commercials on *Fredd Bear,* Shirley set up a live commercial tied to a competition for children to win expensive toys they would otherwise never own. Steven and Dale were not long out of nappies when she set up Bev and Rob's phone number as the fall-back family to call to win the Toy of the Day, and they did quite well out of it. Darren became a close friend and remained so, on and off, for the next 45 years, usually tracking Shirley down via Alan or Bev.

Henderson Lamont was CEO of a major funeral parlour chain. He also owned florist shops and a manufacturing company renowned for fishing boats, coffins and babies prams. He was still working on securing his customer base – from the cradle to the grave, when he decided to make children's skateboards using left-over timber.

Television was the perfect sales medium for the product and Shirley recommended Tim at Black & Blue Advertising. A few weeks later the first commercial went to air. Henderson came by the studio to see the 30-second video and the hilarious five-minute live demo go to air. After Shirley took him into the control room for a first-hand look behind the scenes, the two established a professional friendship that day that would benefit, and stimulate them both for many years. He made no sexual overtures, accompanied Shirley to awards nights when she needed a supportive companion, gave her an unforgettable insight into how one makes dead bodies presentable and sharpened her wit every time they met.

On the home front, a mere five minutes away, Shirley's family were creatively busy and also adjusting to a new and changing world. Bev gave birth to her third son, Craig, a gorgeous little boy who quickly became known as the little pixie. Rob was again promoted, thus beginning his climb up the primary teaching ladder, echoing Alan's own progress before him.

By then Shirley had set up a base in South Yarra. Her flat was close to the city, which made it easier for her to squeeze in a social life. She reasoned to Bev that it was high time anyway that their father got a life of his own and didn't have to wake up to her alarm at 4.30 in the mornings, to which Bev promptly replied that he didn't mind and already had a life inspecting 40 schools a week whilst remaining Head of Ashwood Primary, not to mention his latest text book and his inauguration of The Glen Waverley Gem Club and future rock-hunting travel plans.

Alone once more, Alan missed Shirley's company but her absence triggered his realisation that work was interfering with his life. One night at dinner with his daughters, Rob and neighbours Betty and Jim Bradshaw, he reflected that the first 25 years of life takes (and feels like) 40 years, the next 25 takes 25, and the last 25 takes ten.

'Make the most of everything,' he said in his economical way. 'Life gets shorter.'

As 1971 was drawing to a close, rumours were circulating in the studios that *Fredd Bear* cast members were agitating for change. For two years they'd been getting up at 4.30 in the morning, the show was now on a high and paying its way. Why not give them an afternoon program? Their high profiles increased the likelihood of success in the tougher, more lucrative and civilised time slot.

English discussed the matter in confidence with Shirley. The Skid Row executives weren't interested but if she had any ideas for the cast that might work in the afternoon, he suggested she could pen a draft and he could float it by Sir Reginald. The magnate flew into the studios by helicopter on Mondays for a meeting with his executive officers and was bound to have been informed of trouble brewing in the brekky studio.

Just prior to a lunch party at a crew member's flat in South Yarra, Shirley completed a draft for a one-hour afternoon show. She arrived late and walked into the beginning of a séance. It was her first experience and would not be her last.

With the curtains closed and the lights dimmed, she could only just make out six men from the station's crew, including Jeanette, sitting around a table. Two of the men rested their index fingers on a down turned beer glass in the centre of the table, surrounded by square letters of the alphabet from a Scrabble Board game. Between A and M and N and Z the words YES and NO had been written in pen on the back of two playing cards.

'Is there anybody there?' Ted asked.

'If there's a spirit in the house, please move the glass to Yes.'

Nothing.

'Try again!' and 'once more!' also led to nothing. Somebody suggested a change of hands and when Phil removed his, Jeanette urged, 'Shirley, you have a go!'

'Is there a spirit in the house? Please answer if you're there,' she offered reluctantly, caught off guard with nowhere to go. The glass began to move slowly towards YES. Startled, Shirley reacted and took her finger off the glass. It stopped immediately.

'Okay, you're a contact at least, maybe even a medium!' Ted shrieked excitedly and everyone clapped.

Age Three

'Put your finger back on that glass, Shirley!'

The beer and wine flowed as the crew fired questions at the glass. It responded by spelling out correct answers, but whether there was a spirit in the house, or that it wasn't Ted or Shirley pushing it, remained doubtful.

'Three fingers at a time maximum,' Ted decreed.

When everyone had taken a turn, the mood and questions changed dramatically. The proof was there, yet it was still difficult to believe.

'Will the morning show continue next year?'

YES BUT DIFFERENT, spelled the glass.

'Will any of us get the sack?'

NOT YET.

'Is my marriage going to implode?' one of the floor managers asked.

IF YOU DON'T CHANGE YOUR WAYS IT WILL.

The questions were becoming personal and the answers getting longer. Everyone was asking questions now.

Ted eventually decided it was time to stop before everyone was drunk and the game got out of hand.

'Is there anything you'd like to say to us before we stop, spirit?' he asked.

Nothing, not even a slight movement.

'Anything important we should know about the past or the future before we say farewell?' he tried again and the glass began to move.

It spelled out SOMEONE AT THIS TABLE KILLED SOMEONE IN ADELAIDE.

Jeanette fainted and fell off her chair. It was a party stopper and whilst she recovered quickly and improvised that she was having a bad monthly, she gratefully accepted Shirley's offer to drive her home.

Over coffee in her flat she opened up. Whilst her sister was at work, her brother-in-law had sexually attacked her in the kitchen they shared. She'd stabbed him with a carving knife before fleeing for her life and he was dead on the kitchen floor when her sister got home. The judge went through the motions with the lawyers but it was an unwarranted trial and he recommended she change her name, leave the state and start her life anew. Jeanette took his advice, settled in Melbourne and carved out for herself a renowned career in television.

Not a word about the séance was uttered to anyone in or outside the station and Jeanette carried on as if nothing had happened. The crew behaved impeccably.

The year was thankfully drawing to an end. Everyone was tired and there'd been a few unpleasant verbal clashes amongst the cast, anxious for news of the afternoon gig. Shirley was looking forward to the Christmas break so she could reflect and recharge.

With 20 shows to go until the end of the year, she was invited to the board room for morning tea with Sir Reginald. Finally, she would meet him! Childhood memories flooded back of Uncle Norman's wake in 1956, the McLaughlins arriving to witness Aunty Flo toasting his life from where she stood in the middle of the dining room table, clutching a magnum of champagne.

'Here's to Norm, my beloved husband "The Baker", who left me a £100K buried in flour bags in the backyard!' she'd shrieked. 'There's a lot o' dough in bread!'

Shirley was welcomed by several executives and was escorted to her seat at the board table. She was introduced to the boss, who was already seated at the head of the table. Extending her hand, Reg rose to shake it and pleasantries were exchanged as coffee and scones were served.

Small talk dominated whilst everyone enjoyed the refreshments, then the CEO asked for attention. He thanked Shirley for her wonderful work this year before ceremoniously handing her an Ansett Airlines voucher for an all-expenses-paid two week Christmas holiday at his famous tourist resort on Hayman Island, off the coast of Northern Queensland. As the men applauded, he sat down purposefully and shared a little aside with one of them.

It was clear even to blind Freddy that Shirley's part in the morning tea had now concluded. There was not a word of her late Uncle Norm who'd put this man on the map and stuck by him through all the years of his life; not a word of the future of *Fredd Bear's Breakfast A' Go Go* or the top ratings one of the crew had told her they'd finally achieved; and not a word about her afternoon script that by now he must surely have seen.

'O, what men dare do! What men may do! What men daily do, not knowing what they do!'

Age Three

Numb but ever gracious, she thanked him for his kind words and generosity and added that she'd enjoyed her first year with ATVO and hoped there'd be many more. At this, several of the executives shifted slightly in their seats. She joked about having had bumpy rides on Ansett Airlines in the past but said she'd be right at home this time before quickly excusing herself to escape to her broom cupboard.

She was welling up when she heard her mother's voice. 'Pick up the cards you're dealt and play them like they're the best hand you'll ever get. Perhaps they are?'

Hayman Island was a long way from Melbourne. It took a day to get there and the last leg from the mainland to the island endured with sick children in a crowded boat on a squally sea. Notwithstanding, the resort staff were well trained and allocated everyone's rooms in record time. The threatening cyclonic winds had moved on overnight and the magnificent seaside, swimming pool and variety of recreational activities began to lift Shirley's mood.

It was just four days until Christmas and Shirley's accommodation was one of dozens of late 1960s-style motel units located independently at the back of the resort, a short walk to the main building and beach. In size and ambiance the unit could have been her broom cupboard at ATVO Nunawading, but that was irrelevant. She spent her waking hours swimming, sunbaking, listening to bands and entertainers, talking to tourists and at last relaxing.

On Christmas Eve she joined a party in the resort where she danced until midnight but needed help to open the back door to walk to her unit because of the wind. The threatened Cyclone Althea, north of Townsville, had made landfall on the island. Shirley reached the footpath when a large pot plant fell on her feet. She staggered into her unit, locked the door and took off her dress and shoes but remained in her underwear. There was no radio or television in the unit on which to check the weather so she decided to read until sleep came. But that was fitful at best. The howling winds increased and the banging and smashing of trees and flying debris soon became one long ear-splitting, terrifying nightmare.

She dreamt she was in OKC, alone on the drive home from Wallington Enterprises on the night of the Tornado-Frankie setup. In her deranged mind she reasoned that if this was another setup it was not going to be as easy to escape. Her watch told her it was 4.00am as her only window smashed and part of a unit's roof flew by. She dressed and packed her case. Whilst her walls and roof remained intact, she figured it would be best to stay where she was. Where could she go anyway?

The worst of it was over when security staff began knocking on doors. Shirley's knock came at 6.00am.

'Happy Christmas,' the bright spark grinned. 'Sorry,' he said, and gave her two choices. The cyclone was moving out to sea and the worst damage had been to the units, the residents of which were being evacuated immediately. Because she had a two-week complimentary booking, he reckoned that they would be able to find her alternative accommodation in the resort later in the day – if she wanted to stay.

For heaven's sake, not bloody likely!

The exit from the island was demonstrably worse than the sickening entrance, and the airport queues were endless. The charming and talented performing artist Matt Flinders and his wife happened to be in the queue, and after a great catch up a sense of normality returned.

Shirley arrived home on Christmas night and collapsed, remaining safely ensconced in her South Yarra apartment for several days.

Cyclone Althea took three lives, 90 per cent of houses on Magnetic Island were damaged or destroyed and the total cost ran to $50 million.

On Monday 3rd January 1972 Shirley went back to work, arriving at the studios at 9.00am.

Like her cast and crew, she was on paid holiday leave until the 17th but her evacuation from Hayman Island had focused her mind on survival and intuitively driven her to acknowledge the precariousness of her position.

It was a big international news day and the skeleton staff were busy. An IRA bomb blast in a Belfast department store had injured 55 women and children; Ken Rosewell was on his way to winning his fourth Australian men's singles titles in the tennis; the World XI cricket team led by captain Garfield Sobers was threatening to defeat Australia in the third test match; and rumour had it that President Nixon was about to sign a $5.5 billion grant to begin space shuttle research.

Peter English was on holidays and after she'd noticed Tedd Dunn's car was in its usual spot, she assumed he was back at his desk in the wardrobe department. Apart from the news, live shows didn't resume until late January or early February, which made her wonder what on earth was Tedd doing here on the third day of the New Year?

She entered the offices on Skid Row without a plan. True to form, executive secretary Jeanette, whose boss had checked in and out on his way to golf, was ready for a chat. Having typed countless scripts for Shirley last year, she was bursting with excitement. Shirley's brief for the afternoon show was being fine-tuned; Tedd was working on the script and his new role to ensure *Fredd Bear* captured the afternoon audience.

'No wonder the rest of the cast are coming back early for rehearsals. Next week, isn't it?' she continued exuberantly.

'What's going to replace the morning show is anyone's guess. Why are you looking at me like that?'

'Do you know who's producing the show, Jeanette?'

'It's you, isn't it?'

Shirley shook her head.

'Oh shit! I'm so sorry. Please don't tell anyone I told you this. I'd lose my job!'

Shirley smiled. 'I'm not here today so this conversation never happened. You have my word,' she smiled, gave her a hug and left the building, driving home thinking about the sage advice Peter English had given her, along with her mother's experiences in radio. Margery had pre-warned her that the entertainment business was a trade where a handshake rarely meant anything more than that, and English had confirmed it.

Notwithstanding, timing and being in the right place at the right time were everything; Cyclone Althea and Jeanette were just the catalysts. Sir Reg had been appeasing his conscience with an illusory thank you, a holiday that cost him zilch and a congratulatory handshake. He had done it to appease his 'gopher' executives. But Jeanette's unguarded comments and her fear of losing her job had unwittingly given Shirley enough ingredients to save her own, if indeed there was time.

'I went to the right place at the right time to discover the truth,' she said to the neighbour's cat on her patio, 'and I've got precisely four days to make the luck work for me.'

English, Judy Banks and Colin McEwan returned to work the following Monday. Mike McCarthy turned up to formally resign, having decided after all that real estate was for him, by which time Shirley had prepared a 20-minute 'audition' rundown for a new morning program that she would write, produce and host. She'd arranged to interview a couple of the station's live show comperes and had also scripted some short segments and live commercials. Several members of her crew, including the director, were quietly on side.

'You've obviously caught up with the news, Shirley,' English greeted her.

'In a manner of speaking, Peter. I've got no idea what I've done to deserve the knives in my back and assume you're sworn to secrecy too. Is it your task to let me go?'

'Yes, and no. It's entirely my decision to keep you on if I can justify it.'

'Great. The only details I know of what's transpired is that you have to deliver a replacement brekky show. I'm not going to be bullied out of television without a fight, Pete,' she declared before filling him in on her strategy.

'The crew are ready to pipe it live to every office on Skid Row this afternoon,' she said. May I proceed? If I'm not good enough, so be it.'

Shirley of the *The Early Birds* went to air on Monday 24th January. English secured Keith Livingstone as her newsreader and arranged for Roy Hampton, compere of The Morning Show to co-host with her for the first two weeks. Four shows later a state-wide power strike forced them off air until Monday week.

When the luck's with you, expect three hits before it runs out. Suddenly Shirley had the time she needed to fully develop a new morning show format.

If she was going to be working these crazy hours, she wanted there to be real purpose behind her product. She thought back to her time with Project Concern and her memories of the children she'd encountered who constantly smiled, despite living in poverty and poor health. Daily 'Early Bird Hospital Time' segments, comprising interviews with hospital staff and patients, mainly children, would make a difference. Hospital administrators would be delighted to cooperate and she could quickly build a strong viewer following.

Several weeks later she'd created a new, pre-recorded community service half-hour program titled *Happiness Is…* Following a good deal of research and meetings with principals of schools, hospitals and charities, Shirley would script each show in advance and spend one day a week on location with a backpack team of two. The brekky show was shortened to 90 minutes and ran from 7.00am to 8.30am Mondays to Fridays, the pre-recorded *Happiness is…* aired at 8.30am on Wednesdays.

In addition to the long days she worked to put six shows to air each week, she received a good deal of publicity and became a sought-after presenter at award ceremonies, fashion parades, show-biz functions and she loved her new high profile even if she was often too busy to accept many invitations.

The make-up department did her hair every day and she was dressed by the Myer Emporium, but she didn't have the time to choose her own clothes so it fell to the wardrobe department to order her outfits each week. Despite his change of manner, Tedd did a professional job. Judy and Colin's demeanours had also chilled and she suffered whispers behind her back wherever she was in the studios.

She had no idea what she had done. How could they be jealous of her? She was a novice and they were professionals!

Jeanette gave her hope that the blackballing would eventually subside.

'They're probably miffed because of the times you had to discipline them to stop blaming the crew and throwing tantrums when things went awry. You're in the same position now that they were and you don't do it. Maybe they're jealous because all the crew in this building love you,' she suggested. Yet Margery's words were the ones that struck home. *Don't take yourself too seriously – you're not going to get out of here alive.* Perhaps her cast were simply stressed out by the thought of settling into a new show?

During this period her personal life didn't suffer because she didn't have one. On Friday nights she would play cards into the early hours with Bev and Rob's neighbours, Betty and Jim Bradshaw, and she always made time to dine with the family. Little pixie Craig had by then started to walk but Steven and Dale were running around and still winning toys from her every other week. She usually gift wrapped them and delivered them on her way home. Spending what little time she had with her gorgeous little nephews was a joy, and a valuable leveller.

She chanced to bump into Allan Uebergang one day during the power strike as she walked into the CBD Myer store to meet her wardrobe contact. Few colleagues of Shirley's, and none of the media, had any idea she'd been married. She'd almost forgotten herself.

Allan had left the Navy and become a plain-clothes detective. He instructed Shirley to 'stay there' whilst he grabbed and handcuffed a man who was entering Myer at the same time, pushing him into the hands of a detective standing by the waiting car.

'Stay there,' he ordered the driver before walking back to Shirley.

'All in a day's work?' she asked with a smile.

They chatted amiably for 10 minutes. When they'd run out of individual updates and enquiries about each other's families, there was nothing left to say. 'It was nice to see you and all the best,' and then it was over.

No fault divorce legislation had just passed through the courts and she recognised that this was her opportunity to end that chapter of her life on a friendly note. A week later she'd filed for divorce via friend and lawyer, Agnes Wundell.

Her professional and opportune, if somewhat sporadic personal relationship with Tim Black continued. One night after they'd enjoyed a couple of business and New Year's Eve parties with mutual colleagues, out of the blue Tim suddenly asked her to have his baby.

She responded without discernible shock and was more surprised by her own reaction that the entreaty itself. For most women she knew, having Tim's baby would be the ultimate dream come true and the fact that the last thing on her mind was falling pregnant again did not register. Whilst Tim's was a more loving, valiant and arguably less life-changing offer than Mick Wallington's had been, it was also a bridge too far.

At 6.30 one Friday morning three weeks later, two dozen long-stemmed red roses turned up for her as she sat in her make-up chair at the Nunawading Studios. There was no card, but any mystery was well and truly solved seven days later when Tim called her from Sydney

He told her he had two children and that following her knock-back he'd decided to finally marry their mother, his partner. They'd wed last Saturday, the day after he sent the roses. He'd been in turmoil for months leading up to it and, suffice to say, had caught gonorrhoea from a prostitute.

'You need to go to your gynaecologist in case I've passed it onto you. I'm very sorry about everything. Please forgive me,' he implored.

Shirley has no recollection of how she responded in the moment, but their professional relationship continued unabated, on her part because he'd at least had the integrity to tell her (and no doubt his other lovers, especially his new wife). As far as she was concerned Tim had taken responsibility for his actions in a business not known for its accountability.

The inevitable questions drove her crazy for about a week. *Why didn't I know he had a partner and children? Why didn't somebody tell me? How could I have been so blind, dumb and stupid?*

But seven days is a long time in television. She was flat out and life rushed on.

It was 8.15am on a Tuesday in April. A live segment she'd created for the show called *Cartoon Carnival* had become an audience favourite. In it she would read a story she'd written herself, usually concluding with one of her favourite poems.

This particular morning, following a commercial break, one of the crew walked into frame to surprise her with several beautifully bound books of encyclopaedic proportions. In a voice somewhat higher than usual, Shirley read the titles on the spines and immediately twigged: it was meant to be a joke. The four volumes covered case studies in Matrimonial Law, providing legal and governance examples and solutions for divorce lawyers. She concluded the segment with her usual élan but her stomach was churning and she wondered if she was going to be sick.

How had the crew known she was leaving straight after the show for a CBD divorce court? As the credits began to roll, the floor manager divulged that he'd overheard her talking to Jeanette about it; he and the crew had seen her court date as the beginning of a new life of freedom and accordingly proceeded to wish her a quick and happy divorce. As they thanked her for being a good sport, she managed a laugh and returned their sentiments. But when she left for the hearing, instead of jumping into the front seat of the cab for a chat with the driver as she normally would, Shirley sat silently in the back seat lost in thought.

Am I becoming paranoid? she wondered, before trying to determine exactly when she'd lost her sense of humour.

Agnes Wundell had assured her it was a simple case. Shirley had been separated from Alan for two years, they had no children, there were no outstanding financial issues and neither party had any objections to the divorce. With all these factors considered, there was every reason to believe it would be a matter of 'Just a simple *Decree Nisi Absolute* thank you, Your Honour'.

Whilst divorce laws in Oz had changed for the first time since their British inception, the great generation judge hadn't adapted yet. It soon became clear he never would. To him men were men, fighters and providers at the centre of the universe, in charge of the world. Women were home-makers, mothers and companions through thick and thin. Some even worked these days, until they became 'the wife'. The suffragettes in England might have revolutionised the western world 70 years ago, but the judge hadn't changed at all.

The lawyers had cordially completed their duties on behalf of their respective clients and the *No Fault Divorce Decree Nisi* was ready to be stamped when the Judge decided to interrogate 'the wife'.

Agnes was initially more traumatised than Shirley. She hadn't briefed her friend for a spell in the dock because the law no longer required it. The judge was out of line! Shirley was immediately escorted by a clerk to the witness box and sworn in on *The Bible*.

The judge began with a five-minute invective on the irresponsibility and total lack of premeditation demonstrated by privileged young women today. They jumped in and out of marriage without a thought for the young men who had pledged to love, honour and keep them in the manner to which they'd become accustomed. He required answers from this particular 'wife' before he could, in all conscience, grant this divorce.

Her interrogator stated in as many words that she had abandoned her dedicated Royal Australian Navy sailor during his horrendous experience on the HMAS *Stuart*. She'd obviously received a 'better offer', and moved on yet again when another presented…that of chasing fame and fortune in television!

'What I want to know, Miss McLaughlin, is why you left your marriage so quickly, and why you weren't prepared to wait for your husband to return so you could work on your marriage?'

Shirley was profoundly humiliated. Allan and his mother watched on, pale faced, and she could feel their pain. Despite his contribution to the selective information submitted on his side of the case when it was no longer required under the law, she knew it wasn't Allan's fault she'd been put in this position, any more than it was Agnes' or hers. Allan's lawyer was a great generation man and no doubt a friend of the judge's.

Age Three

It didn't occur to her to move into automatic 'acting' mode, trapped as she was in the power and inequity of the law. Nor did she mention the losses she'd experienced, instead attempting to explain their differences and incompatible goals, forever mindful of not offending.

Ultimately, the judge's chauvinist, Machiavellian conduct would be a turning point in her life. It was a disgusting, debilitating, destructive end of the death of a marriage of two sincere, inexperienced, already traumatised young people who'd made a mistake and were moving on with their lives.

The Judge begrudgingly declared a *Decree Nisi* and Agnes took Shirley to a long, alcoholic lunch at which they speculated how the world would operate when men finally accepted women as equals.

Shirley's weekly, pre-recorded *Happiness is…* program quickly developed a loyal following and lived up to the lyrics of its theme song: *Happiness is… different things to different people.* It was a perfect medium for a much wider field than children's health and education. People connected to community services came out of the woodwork to contribute.

Her first international guest was London actor Maurice Kaufman (husband of the very beautiful actress Honor Blackman) who spoke on the topic of epilepsy, followed by an interview with the federal health minister, the Rt. Hon. John Rossitter, who turned out to be a surprisingly good subject.

She did a special feature on Project Concern; filmed one of her best programs in Fairleigh Women's Prison in Melbourne (and in the process nearly lost an eye); and during the week of the third anniversary of Margery's death recited a version of her mother's 1937 radio feature, *The Seven Ages of Woman,* reimagining each act as a poem.

According to files in her study, she declined an interview with Hollywood star, Omar Sharif, who was visiting Melbourne for the second time in as many years. What contribution he had offered to make to a *Happiness is…* program, or why Shirley responded negatively wasn't stated, but that didn't stop the media rumour mill.

'ON THE GRAPE VINE,' a column written by a good mate who was also the editor of one of Melbourne's favourite TV magazines ran a five-line piece on how she'd originally met Sharif at the Princess Theatre, and that they'd since formed a close friendship. According to the rag, he was sending her post cards every week. The story gathered momentum and she was astounded how many people in the business believed every word.

Bearing the brunt of more hostility from members of her former cast and a few other conspiring insiders, she began to wonder if this 'close Hollywood friend' was the origin of whatever lie had started the whole sorry business.

As the animosity increased and the afternoon show's ratings dived, Shirley's profile and audience grew. Whilst the *Fredd Bear* cast acknowledged her in the company of English, directors or executives, they didn't speak to her when their respective commercial or publicity bookings coincided or when sitting next to each other in make-up. The atmosphere was clearly uncomfortable for support staff and crew, but they were a solid lot who needed their jobs and somehow they managed to remain courteous to everyone.

The month of May was fast approaching. Shirley would turn 24 on the 13th and she realised with relief that this year there would be no birthday candles to blow out on a Susan Day cake. Her diary was already full until late May and weeks ago she'd arranged to board at home again with Alan for a while. Subsequently she gave her landlord notice of her intention to vacate the South Yarra flat upon the expiry of its lease in April.

Everything was in place for a change of life. She just hadn't had the time to think it through, or the energy to consider what on earth she was going to do next.

After the move back to Alan's, she decided to take a day off.

She made sure she left nothing to chance at the studio, having late last year stayed home from work with the flu and in doing so copped a punishment worse than the crime. The programs had already been written and the cast were capable of carrying on without her for a day, but 'she'd let them down'. Perhaps that's where it had all begun when she had so irresponsibly caught the flu?

This time she advised English and her director that she was taking a day's leave, wrote herself out of the running sheet, instructed the girls in the library to select additional cartoons she'd scheduled and scripted some 'intro' lines for newsreader Keith. She'd also lined up Jeanette and Penny to take her calls.

Alan went to work with a furrowed brow and Shirley went back to bed with a second cup of coffee and a foolscap pad, although a notebook would have done. By the time she got up at 10.30 she'd made a decision.

Age Three

Two weeks later English found a note on his desk and had a knot in his stomach when Shirley arrived for the 9.30 meeting she'd requested.

Immediately she handed him a letter of resignation, effective from the last Friday in May.

'I'm sorry, Peter, but I've decided television is not for me,' she said. 'Perhaps it would be best if we keep this from the staff until then?'

Peter read the three-paragraph letter twice, put it aside and asked why she'd come to this decision.

She explained that ever since Sir Reg had kindly dismissed her to Hayman Island whilst the program reshuffling occurred, she'd been caught in cyclonic weather. She'd requested the day's leave so she could chart a long-term forecast for her life, adding that she'd since secured a national PR position with one of her show's sponsors, Sarah Coventry Pty Ltd (the largest direct sellers of costume jewellery in the world at the time).

'It's a transitory plan, Peter. It'll be easier for everyone that I've accepted a position elsewhere, outside show biz altogether.'

'I'm very disappointed…very sad, and I feel guilty,' he responded heavily. 'You're the most talented, dynamic woman I've ever had on my staff and I've been praying you'd get on top of the bullies…I should have done more. It's all down to jealousy – it's part of the business. I told you that.'

'Yes, and the words of thanks in my letter are unequivocal.'

'Presumably a long-term forecast where your stay in television doesn't look good. How did you arrive at this?'

'I created a map entitled "The world's your oyster",' she replied, 'intending to list all the sunny days at ATVO and all the reasons I should stay. I was brought up to turn negatives into positives, Peter. Life's full of good and bad weather, but for the first time in my life I stopped to examine the negatives.'

She didn't detail the bullet points she'd drafted that led to her decision. Instead she simply said that she didn't like herself much anymore. 'The business' had changed her, and not for the better. While she was grateful for the extraordinary experience and skills she'd acquired and the lessons she'd learned, it was time to repossess herself and the values she held dear.

'No regrets, Peter. It's all part of the rich tapestry of life,' she concluded.

Many years later she would discover the charted 'map', yellowed with age and written in her left hand *with a thumb nail dipped in tar*, in one of her publicity scrapbooks.

The world's your oyster   *May, 1972*

You're paid 40% less than Bob Phillips was 18 months ago when he resigned as a producer of five shows a week. You're writing, producing and compering six shows a week, and working 15-hour days, seven days a week! It might be the way it is, but it's a cop out for a capable woman who could stop working for The Man and work for herself, and get paid what she's worth!

Tedd, Judy and Colin are classic professional artists and personalities → egomaniacal and eccentric. Tedd's gay and Judy's ambidextrous; they've worked hard for a long time and probably copped heaps of shit. Miss Straight Lady breezes in full of dynamic energy and talent minus tantrums, succeeds behind the scenes then breaks the rules and succeeds on camera literally overnight – thanks and no thanks to them. What were you expecting? Love and support for helping them achieve top ratings in their last year on the Brekky Show?

You always dreamed of following in your mother's footsteps and you've done it, but did she really leave 3BA because she blacked out on-air? The Phar Lap story and her colleagues using it to cut their friendships rings cyclonic bells. She was an alien Miss Straight Lady too → and it was a <u>totally</u> exclusive men's club then. She drummed into you *Never reduce your standards to suit the people you're with.* Can you maintain them and forge a rewarding career in a business where the CEO and Skid Row and therefore half the bloody staff shake hands and stab you in the back at the same time?

Bev says you've changed. Have you? If so, why? You didn't get into this business for fame or fortune so how and why have you changed? And stop deferring to your mother! She's gone. You're on your own now.

You've always liked your own company, and been content in your own little world. You couldn't have invented Wendy Barr if your dreams were based on being the centre of attention. Face it.

Age Three

You're a one-on-one individual, not the extrovert you and most people think you are. Everyone says the camera loves you but it's not because of your pretty face and sparkling eyes, stupid! It's about your viewers who think you're talking directly to them.

So how and why have you changed? Nowhere to run lady. Too much on your plate, exhausted, lack a' nooky → insecure in a hostile environment but always acting happy. Dead-set good reasons for insecure people to feel threatened. And still reeling from The Judge? Maybe you've become a pain in the ass to family and friends for mindlessly boring them with your so-called glamorous life and commitments?

You've got time for a good cry today. Might help you get real again. It would certainly relieve your sister.

Can you imagine living and working in this industry for the rest of your useful life? If the answer's no, what the hell's left to learn in Nunawading worth knowing? You've packed five years into 18 months by anybody's standards and will be lucky if you're missed for five minutes. Goodbye and break a leg.

You've got a handle on it now so what's the verdict? Want to finish up a bitter and twisted old bag in a nursing home after working for 'the man' for 50 years on the wages of a cleaning lady with your only personal possession a camphor chest full of memorabilia? On the positive side, you won't be able to see any more to read the fucking reviews of how talented and brilliant you were let alone remember how many Hollywood lovers you were supposed to have had before you die in nappies following years of dependence and indignity…*Sans teeth, sans eyes, sans taste, sans everything.*

During a farewell party arranged by English, Colin McEwan took Shirley aside moments before the speeches began to apologise for his distance in recent times.

'You were the best thing that happened to us last year and I wondered from the start why we all got caught up in the gossip,' he admitted before lamenting, 'It was just that one jealous porky that caught on like a bush fire.'

'Thanks, Col, but what was the lie? Nobody's ever told me.'

He didn't seem surprised. 'When you met Tedd's Hollywood agent, at the Logies I think, you asked her privately to represent you. He was livid, felt his friendship with you had been abused. Did you ever meet her?'

'Yes I did, but at a dinner party at Tedd's,' she whispered as English called for attention. 'She asked me to contact her if I was in California because she'd love to catch up again.'

Peter made a moving speech, then on behalf of the 200 staff who had turned up to wish her goodbye, gave her a gift-wrapped box containing a Royal Doulton dinner set. A large accompanying card, designed and painted by 'the boys' in the art department, featured a caricature portrait of Shirley, her near-naked body adorned with strategically placed jewellery and padlocks. Around her likeness they'd written: 'SHIRL'S A PRO-MOTION EXPERT IN COSTUME JEWLERY DARLING!'

The illustration, which depicted her as an easy-go girl who was leaving them for fake jewellery, was intended to be as much a compliment as it was a cheeky ribbing.

'Lady Shirl', she of the work ethic, the laugh worth bottling and the pocket full of dreams, then took to the stage where she waxed lyrical as only she knew how:

> *Our revels now are ended. These our actors,*
> *As I foretold you, were all spirits and*
> *Are melted into air, into thin air…*
> *And, like this insubstantial pageant faded,*
> *Leave not a rack behind.*
> *We are such stuff as dreams are made on…*

'We're barracking for you, Shirl!' a couple of her crew called from the audience and everyone applauded.

When she read the missives inside and on the back of the card she wondered if she'd ever dare dream again. There were more than 100 comments and to read them brought a stream of tears. She found it strangely unnerving that so many people had identified both her good and not-so-good traits:

'I wonder what would happen if you ever said Yes?'
'Watch out for the little men, Shirl.'
'Glad you did it, wish I could!'

'*To the biggest and most beautiful hustler (next to me) wishing you every happiness and sweet memories of an incredible experience!*'

'*Whatever happens, you'll come up laughing…*'

And from director Rob Weeks, who'd spent the best part of a day coaching Shirley for one 30-second dog food commercial: *I'll never forget Meat Blox Chub!*'

Director Bob Loxton wrote: '*We'll all miss you, the industry will miss your talent.*'

And from her film crew: '*Happiness was knowing you, Shirl.*'

Her old cast contributed with genuine thanks, love and best wishes, as if their friendships had never soured.

Had it just been a bad dream? What if…?

Much virtue in "if"… 'Don't even think about,' she snapped herself out of it. 'It's over.'

The last words on the bottom left of the back of the card, next to Judy's loving thanks, were consistent with the leitmotif and she cried again, this time from laughing.

> AUSTARAMA TELEVISION PTY LTD
> Cnr Springvale & Hawthorn Rds Nunawading 3131
> TO ORDER QUOTE: *Sex & Hard Core*
> *All the very ~~best~~ breast to our Shirl from the Porn Boys*
> **COPYRIGHT**

Husband No. 2

Her first assignment for her new employer was a three-day jaunt to Brisbane for a business-expanding conference. She travelled with the current 'Miss Australia', an intelligent, mature young woman whose services had been secured by the CEO of Sarah Coventry whilst sponsoring the national contest.

During the three-hour flight the two women discovered a connection on a much deeper level than fake diamonds whilst talking about little else.

'What do you think of this jewellery?' her new colleague enquired cautiously. 'Do you like it?'

'I think it's trying to be something it isn't, but it has a huge market. I wouldn't wear it by choice,' Shirley replied, proceeding to tell a story she'd forgotten until this moment.

Last year the company had given her several boxes of jewellery to select for their commercials and she'd taken them to her flat in South Yarra to sort. A few days after the first scheduled live commercial she was burgled and, along with a few personal items, the boxes were stolen. It wasn't worth claiming insurance, and the company was understanding and replaced the product. It was unsettling to come home to a targeted robbery but the agent installed new locks on the doors and she dismissed it from her mind.

'I find it hard to believe now that I was so cool about it!' she exclaimed.

'Didn't the cops tell you the robbers had to be juveniles who lived nearby, fans who probably saw you flogging it on telly, knew your movements and went for it? Professional burglars don't take risk stealing fake jewellery! It's the only reason I can think of right now for buying mutton done up as lamb in the first place.'

The conference was a huge success but both left the company a few weeks later. It wasn't that they felt cheap exactly, but agreed it would be wise to leave before they did.

Baby boomers were getting a reputation in Australia. Nearly everything about them, from their opinions of themselves, and their parents to their choices of friends, was increasingly seen to be flawed.

At 24, Shirley figured this didn't apply to her anymore: *Been there, done that,* she thought. *New start coming.*

She had one year left to make good on the promise she'd made to herself to be self-employed with a roof over her head and a mortgage in her name. She'd also added ownership of a dishwasher and her own cleaning lady to the conditions. Given, as Alan had said, that the first 25 years of life takes and feels like 40, she didn't have a moment to lose. She'd experienced the truth of Kipling's poem: *If you can meet with triumph and disaster, and treat those two imposters just the same…* and was grateful for her success. In fact, she had begun to realise that the sabotage of her television career had been fated from the start and she was doubly lucky it had happened quickly and not taken up anymore of her valuable time.

Always the ingénue, she imagined similarities between her situation and that of a returned soldier and started to read anything she could get her hands on about the Vietnam vets. They had made it home from an unwinnable war and into a hostile environment where there was no acknowledgement of their experiences, not even so much as a 'thank you' for their efforts.

Her research was humbling; almost 60,000 Australians served in Vietnam, 19,000 were conscripted, 3,000 were wounded and 521 died. Were she to persist with her metaphor, it would be more accurate to say that she'd volunteered for service, suffered shrapnel wounds only, won a war that would be forgotten in five minutes and, bizarrely, been thanked profusely.

Alan rarely initiated deep and meaningful conversations with his younger daughter. He'd learned long ago that she'd ask for advice when she was ready, and this time it didn't take long.

'I'm a bit lost Dad,' she began. 'I don't miss the constant battles but I miss the crew and staff who've been my friends and colleagues seven days a week for 18 months. I need a new vocation but I can't even think where to start.'

She told him how she had found herself unexpectedly missing the ocean at Mornington, and Grandma's flowers, and country towns with little lanes and rivers running through them, and trees and hills and neighbours talking over fences.

'More than anything, I miss Mum, even though I talk to her nearly every day. I haven't buried her yet. Have you, Dad? I don't know if I ever will.'

Words failed him momentarily.

'I never thought I'd say this to you, Shirley, but I think you should stop worrying about the future and spend the next 12 months putting your life back together. Your mother did that when she left radio. She worked nine to five and utilised her people skills without having to deal with stress. Then she met me,' he smiled.

'Why not stay on here so you can save some money to start your own business when you've got a salary coming in. Something will crop up. It always does.'

If Shirley had known then that following her mother's providential lead was destined to be disastrous for her, she might have accepted a recent invitation to jump a plane to Alice Springs in search of gold.

Whilst researching for a real job, it suddenly hit her that there was one irksome loose end she hadn't attended to that might become troublesome.

Her contaminated passport would be valid for another four years. Carl, Wallington's accountant in OKC, was an old hand at registering false names and obtaining passports for illegal immigrants and could also make deportations on fake passports magically disappear. Surely that would apply to real ones too? Mick had promised to look after her if she kept her mouth shut, but that hadn't come with a guarantee.

'Forgive me,' she whispered to her parents' wedding photo above the fireplace. 'I'm going to have to tell lies, and keep on lying for the rest of my life, but it's the only way.'

Waiting patiently in a queue at the Immigration office in Melbourne she rehearsed her script, aware that face-to-face deception would be the hardest. She clutched a new passport application form on which she'd ticked a number of boxes including 'Never been deported' and 'Never been married'.

She began her story in an animated, feminine rush. 'I can't believe it! I'm so sorry but I've lost my passport. I didn't report it because I didn't know it was missing until now. Mum had just died and I'd left my widowed father to move into a flat…and I was working 15 hour days but that was two years ago and now I've just moved back in with Dad and it's simply nowhere to be found.'

The young man behind the counter was enjoying the performance and said he thought he recognised her. She gave him the paperwork, suggesting with a sexy grin that perhaps he did.

'Shirley of *The Early Birds*! Of course,' he exclaimed. *'Happiness is*…what a great program. Why has it stopped? You must have something pretty good on offer instead,' he speculated as he checked her documents. 'This is good, no probs. It'll be ready in four days, you can pick it up or we'll post it?'

'Thanks so much, I'll pick it up,' she said. 'Maybe we'll have time for a longer chat then?'

Four excruciatingly long days later she collected her new, clean passport. It was impossible to know whether they'd checked her credentials and travel history, not that there was any way they could have discovered her illegal entry into seven countries in Europe anyway. Phone calls did then what computers do far more thoroughly now, plus she was a known entity and her application had probably been stamped 'approved' by the man who served her.

Age Three

She then boarded a tram to St Kilda Road where the American Consulate was located. As she reflected on the riskiness of her next move, Shakespeare's Brutus came to mind, the final lines of his *'tide in the affairs of men'* repeating in her mind.

'On such a full sea are we now afloat,
And we must take the current when it serves,
Or lose our ventures.'

She filled out the application for a visitor's visa, requesting three weeks to 'visit a friend'. Her hand shook as she ticked another half-dozen lies in little boxes, glad of a 10-minute wait in a comfortable chair before she was called to the counter.

'I'm so excited,' she raved as the handsome young New Yorker (who didn't recognise her) flicked through the new passport and application.

'I've got a wonderful American girlfriend I met when I was in New Zealand two or three years ago and she's invited me to Nashville for the Gospel Singing Jubilee. I can hardly wait!' she gushed excitedly, then ventured, 'Should I hang around for the visa?'

He told her he had an appointment for lunch but would get to it this afternoon, kindly suggesting she return to the city for lunch herself and come back no later than four.

She did just that, via a spontaneous detour to the ABC studios where she invited a friend of hers, the station manager's secretary, to join her. Over lunch she was brought up to date with staff movements. Keith Podker, by then one of the fabulous Seekers, had finally left; the newsreader who'd regularly kissed her between the airlock doors had been lured to GTV9 where he was making his mark at Television City; her former boss of alcohol, long lunches and wandering hands fame had been retrenched. Apparently nothing much else had changed.

At 3.30pm Shirley returned to the consulate. She took a deep breath and waltzed in, all broad smiles and confidence. The reception area was empty; New York beckoned her to his desk.

'I decided to give you a five-year multiple entry visa, Shirley. Yer goin' to the best country in the world more than once in the next half decade, aren't yer? All I had to do was wait for a call back from New Zealand, confirm you were there. Easy. By the way, one of the staff recognised you. Her kids are fans. She reckons you must have a job offer on US TV?'

'Well, that's a nice compliment!' Shirley laughed.

'Thank you very much' would have been quite sufficient, but instead 'I'll be forever grateful,' slipped out of her mouth. He didn't flinch but it was a wake-up call for the rest of her travelling life.

By the 1970s, the Melbourne office of Drake Personnel was an integral part of Drake International's rapidly expanding global empire. The competition was strong, but Drake's temporary and permanent recruitment agencies around Australia were leading the field.

Shirley secured an interview with the CEO of the international operations, based in Monte Carlo, who was currently on business in Melbourne. His name was Ron Irwin and he discussed a position coming up in Monte Carlo as his private secretary. His current secretary, Ainsley Gotto, had been with him since 1971 when her previous boss, Australia's 19th Prime Minister, John Gorton resigned.

Her contract with Drake was about to expire and Irwin explained succinctly and directly.

'Miss Gotto is highly regarded in Canberra and a position back in politics has already been offered. What I'd like you to do is spend three months here in Melbourne learning our business of sustainable HR practice and talent management, with a view to coming to Monte Carlo to work directly with me. Are you interested?'

While surprised and flattered, Shirley responded carefully.

'I'm honoured by your offer, Mr Irwin, but I'm not ready to contemplate an overseas posting right now. I need a normal life and would be glad to take on a consulting role here and learn the business. Could we leave the question of Monte Carlo until next time you're home?'

'I have great respect for level-headed women and that's perfectly agreeable to me,' he responded and proceeded to call for his branch manager to come to his office.

'Shirley, I'd like you to meet Nick Bond. Nick, this is Shirley McLaughlin. I've just appointed her to your consulting staff.'

The next nine months, as always for Shirley, were action-packed. Yet it felt to her like she was on a treadmill, caught in a *pea and thimble trick* that could not be readily stopped.

Age Three

Nick was a pre boomer, a 32 year-old Englishman who was tall, slim and attractive in a respectable sort of way. He was brought up in India, the only child of an officer in the British Army, posted there after the Second World War. With a firm handshake and refined speaking voice, he came across as an intelligent, cooperative man who would make friends easily, which he did. Unfortunately, though, they didn't stick around any longer than his wives.

He was single and declared he always had been, and since moving to Australia three years earlier had been living with an old school mate and his partner. Before long he began courting Shirley, engaging her in conversation every day, telling her about his parents who lived in Dorset in the UK and his relationship with a former girlfriend.

One evening, as she drove home from work in her new, beautifully polished white MGA, it ground to a halt. Nick happened to be following in his second-hand Jaguar, pulled over to help and followed her to Glen Waverley to be sure she made it home safely.

Their friendship developed from there. Three months later, when Ron Irwin offered him a side-ways move to manage the Drake office in Adelaide, he asked her to come with him. When Shirley had introduced him to her father, he'd said, 'My name is Bond – Nick Bond,' and Alan had immediately felt apprehensive. He'd met him several times since then and acknowledged his intelligence, and arrogance. He wasn't the 'James' he thought he was, but beyond that Alan couldn't quite pin down why he didn't ring true.

He kept his thoughts to himself and wished Shirley well.

They secured a flat on Anzac Highway, a short drive or tram to the city and Glenelg Beach, and Shirley secured a position that was made for her: personal assistant to Gil Brierley, director of the newly founded South Australian Film Corporation. Appointed by the Premier, Don Dunstan, she became the first staff member of the corporation.

Gil had been recruited from Sydney to set up the business and ultimately put Australia on the world map as film makers, which he and his selected producers and directors irrefutably did.

Nick's Drake personnel staff were a welcoming lot and the best recruiter in the team, Helen Keightley, extended a friendship to them both. Helen was a Barossa Valley girl who'd recently been crowned Queen of the Barossa. Her boyfriend, Peter Wearing-Smith, was a petrol head like Nick and the four began to meet socially via the Adelaide Jaguar Car Club.

Peter proposed to Helen before Nick proposed to Shirley, but Nick had been singing 'I love you, I love you!' under the shower every morning for weeks so it was pretty much a done thing.

Following an attempt by Helen's sage mother to counsel them jointly about their naive judgements of character when it came to men, her famous 'last words' were never forgotten. 'Neither marriage will last,' she'd concluded decisively.

Mrs Keightley's warning must have had some impact on Shirley because she decided not to invite Alan or Bev and Rob to the wedding on account of it being a quick, low key affair. Suffice to say, the family were very disappointed, and worried.

On Friday 23rd February 1973, the Deputy Registrar of Births, Deaths and Marriages in Macquarie Street, Adelaide, duly solemnised the marriage of Nicolas Kirkpatrick Bond and Shirley Joy McLaughlin in accordance with the provisions of that Act, and in the presence of the undersigned witnesses, Peter Wearing-Smith and Helen Keightley.

At the end of the day the newlyweds threw a party at their flat. The Drake Personnel's and the Premier's staff and their partners attended, along with members of the Jaguar Car Club and danced until the early hours of the morning. However, a guest accidentally scraped the back of Nick's Jaguar on the way out and that ruined any chance of a romantic end to an otherwise perfect day.

How 'the man of the hour' had kept a lid on his alarming temper until the bride said *I Will* was inexplicable and unsettling, but a mere bagatelle to the shocks yet to come.

Three days later Nick told Shirley he hated Australia and had done so since the day he arrived three years ago.

'I've decided we're going home to England to begin a new life,' he informed her in his superior tone. Shirley's shock was patent but he ignored it.

'My ambitions haven't been totally destroyed yet but I'll contribute much more to our lives in a country where I'm rewarded for my efforts,' he continued, and in the next breath told her that from now on he was going to call her 'Jo'.

'Shirley is an old fashioned, belittling name in the UK.'

Thus Mr and Mrs Nick and Jo Bond gave notice to their respective employers and arrived in Melbourne four weeks later.

Age Three

Of course Alan agreed that they could camp with him for the weeks needed for 'Jo to pack up forever', and Nick to make their travel bookings, sell his Jag and 'clean up a few loose ends', whatever that meant.

Once the Jaguar was sold, Alan offered them the loan of his Toyota Hi Lux outside school hours. Nick took full advantage without a word of thanks, or even a top-up of fuel in the tank. He also lied to Alan on several occasions – face-to-face, and confident in his deception. Finally Alan shared his concerns with Bev. Together they decided that he had to have a conversation with Shirley before it was too late.

Getting her on her own was difficult but 10 days before the couple was due to depart an opportunity presented.

In his quiet way Alan told her what was worrying him. He'd said he'd empathised when she rushed into a new love affair after having been so highly productive and needed by so many people then suddenly finding herself alone again. He'd understood when she'd followed in her mother's footsteps all the way from leaving a promising show-biz career to meeting and marrying a man in personnel. But that man had lied and deceived her and now she was moving to England without consultation, collateral or any discernible consideration.

'You can still say "no"!' he appealed to her.

Although she knew her father spoke the truth, Shirley argued that there were extenuating circumstances for Nick's behaviour: he was under pressure to make this major move to London work for them both, and was worried about money after he'd spent quite a bit on reservations for a three-day honeymoon in Singapore en route. Plus he'd had a falling out with his former flatmate, which had not been his fault.

'So he's a bit off-balance Dad,' she explained.

But even as she spoke, she imagined both her parents issuing a warning.

'If you've only heard one side of a story, you know considerably less than half!'

Father and daughter said their private farewells, with Alan reassuring her that he would always be there for her.

'If you need me, pick up the phone,' were his final words.

After three days of non-stop tours and lengthy walks in Singapore, Shirley begged Nick to allow her a morning of rest at their hotel. He acquiesced but then divulged that he'd acquired a parcel of opals from a jeweller in Adelaide and had plans to establish contacts with opal dealers through their agents in Singapore and the Bahamas.

After Nick departed, Shirley started to sweat profusely, alarmed by this latest development. She decided to have a bath to try to relax. But as she lay in the warm, soapy water she developed crushing chest pain and shortness of breath and was barely able to get out of the tub to call reception.

By the time Nick returned to the room hours later, the hotel doctor was in attendance. He informed him that Shirley had suffered a severe panic attack before turning to her and sternly repeating what he had already said to her in private. 'You must deal with your problems and fears or the next time you get chest pains you may not be so lucky.'

A few days later they arrived safely in London, before driving in a hired car down to the small country town of Poole, Dorset, where Nick's parents lived in a quaint river-front cottage.

Welcoming 'Jo' with open arms, Nick's mother expressed how happy she was that her son had found a wonderful Australian girl. She asked Nick if Jo had given him the lovely emerald signet ring he was wearing on his little finger. Nick replied without thinking that he'd bought it at a second-hand shop in Melbourne.

No liar's memory is perfect. He'd told Shirley when they first met that it was his grandmother's engagement ring.

Shirley had already transferred all AU$49K of her savings to a bank in Poole before his parents' innocent questions and comments began to make her wonder if she'd married a pathological liar. While Nick continued to keep up some appearances, insisting they use his cash to buy a second-hand car and rent a flat in Dorchester, her fear that his opal trafficking would see him stumbling upon Mick Wallington proved unwarranted.

Having been in Dorchester for three months, none of his plans had progressed; he'd sold one of the parcels of opals he'd procured 'on commission' in Adelaide, and Shirley was now paying the rent. Not that her money was hers anymore.

It was a Tuesday when she was advised by a bank clerk that her husband had transferred her funds into his account and that subsequently she'd need his signature to make withdrawals. England's men still ruled the world, the bank manager was happy to have done his duty and Nick was solvent again as any man had the right to be. Of course she could consult a lawyer, but *only the lawyers win*…and she had no money to pay for advice anyway.

Age Three

The following day she called Alan to say she was in trouble. If she decided to come home, she asked him, would he be prepared to loan her some money so she could set herself up in business?

Without question or judgement, he agreed. 'Do whatever you must do and I will support you.'

On the Thursday she kept an appointment at the local medical practice in Dorchester to secure a new script for the contraceptive pill. The doctor was chatty and offered her a job at £20 a week with an immediate start. Crest fallen at the realisation that now this was all she was worth, she immediately declined.

It all came to a head on Friday night. They'd had a regular dinner date on Fridays with the in-laws in Poole since they moved to Dorchester. Mother-in-law, Alice, greeted Shirley warmly but commented that she seemed to be a little off-colour.

'The tummy's a bit upset,' Shirley replied calmly, 'but it's nothing serious. There's no reason why you three shouldn't enjoy a beer at the pub, though. I'm happy to watch the oven and look after the dog whilst you go to Happy Hour.'

The moment they were out of sight she took the four-step ladder from the kitchen and climbed into the loft above the guest bedroom. Nick's boxes of 'stuff' were carefully labelled and she quickly located a document she'd become certain existed – an original Certificate of Marriage to a woman in Pennsylvania! There were many letters from the woman, and a letter from her solicitor, but no follow-ups and no *Decree Nisi*.

I married a bigamist, she announced to the dog as she climbed out of the roof 10 minutes later. He wagged his tail and barked appreciatively.

'What a fool I've been, Toby, what a bloody fool!'

When her feet hit the floor he jumped up to be patted. She picked him up and hugged him.

'You're just a dog, Toby, but you're a lot smarter than me. I'll always be grateful to you for being my witness on the day I decided to break all the rules.

'All I have to do now is accept failure, let my mother lie in peace and grow up and learn from my mistakes!'

With a one-way ticket home and £25 in cash 'courtesy' of her soon-to-be-ex, she set off on the long journey home to Melbourne.

Three trains later she staggered into Kings Cross Station under the weight of two suitcases, one carry bag and her portable Singer sewing machine, with a toothache so severe that she hadn't been able to eat solid food for five days. With little cash to get her all the way home, she was anxious about the odds of finding a dentist who'd bill the UK's National Health system for whatever it was going to take to stop the pain.

And then the penny dropped; she had a British passport now!

'That's two valuable assets Nick Bond gave me!' she exclaimed to her reflection in the train window, tears streaming down her face. 'Dual citizenship and learning how to make a decent Indian curry can't be underestimated.'

It's more than most men have left you with, lady, Shirley reflected wryly to herself.

She found a phone box to call her friends in London who were standing-by to put her up overnight, checked her luggage into a traveller's locker and headed off to catch the Tube into the city. 'Life Savers' are usually bad for your teeth, but she really needed one now.

In search of a dentist on the streets of London

The irony of Shakespeare's words in *Much Ado About Nothing* was not lost on her;

For there was never yet philosopher
That could endure the toothache patiently.

Had she known the technical terms for her malady – 'a pulpless upper right central incisor', it wouldn't have made any difference. The nerve in a front tooth had died. She knew that because it wasn't the first time it had happened to her. But no-one believed her.

She walked the streets of London, knocking on every dentist's door she came across. She did her best to convince the receptionists, sometimes crying whilst thanking them for their time, then walked on. She kept knocking until it was afternoon and Big Ben struck four.

Finally she came across a sign for a dental practice on the fourth floor of an old Georgian building. The lift was out of order and when she arrived at the reception desk her running nose had started to keep pace with the tears. The receptionist handed her a box of tissues, at which point Shirley burst out with a raucous hoot of laughter that was still reverberating around the room when her delirium subsided enough for her to mumble 'thank you'.

The receptionist recognised the accent the moment she spoke and listened attentively to Shirley's self-diagnosis. She was about to summon her boss, a dentist from Adelaide she said, working part-time in London whilst doing his Master of Science in Restorative Dentistry, when he walked up to the desk.

He introduced himself as Dr Jack Cavander and told her he'd overheard most of her story. After instructing his receptionist to re-schedule the day's remaining check-ups, he led Shirley to his dental chair.

'So you think the nerve has died,' he asked as he applied a stick of dry ice to the tooth in question.

The shock of the sensation made her jump out of the chair, in the process bumping her head on the overhead light.

'Sorry!' he too responded with feeling, settling her back into the chair and lowering it until she was almost horizontal.

'The good news is that your diagnosis is correct,' he said after a close inspection of her mouth. 'The nerve is irreversibly inflamed and dying.'

'At last somebody believes me!' she laughed and cried as Jack began the root canal procedure that would put her out of her misery, starting and finishing the endodontic treatment in one session over the next couple of hours.

Later she figured it must have been whilst she was under anaesthetic that he'd decided to take her to dinner. She had just taken a delicious sip of coffee when he returned to the surgery to advise he'd booked a table for two at The Dorchester that evening. He added that whilst he wouldn't recommend steak yet, apparently they did an excellent Indian curry that would be perfect for her first meal in a week.

The encounter with Jack was a bizarre coincidence she knew she'd never forget, and accepted gratefully. She called to advise her friends she'd be there after dinner, but it wouldn't be late.

They had a great evening together, comparing notes on a number of shared interests including Premier Don Dunstan and his South Australian Film Corporation initiative. Jack told her that he planned to head home to Australia the moment he'd finished his Masters and ultimately would settle in Melbourne. He said he wanted to pursue the friendship with her and gave Shirley his parents' address and phone number in Adelaide. She promised to call them, and write to him when she was settled at home; she'd never be able to thank him enough for making it possible for her to fly home the next day.

The only problem they faced during their eight-hour dalliance was finding her friends' house in Ilford. The address was right but Jack drove around the district for nearly an hour before he found it, by which time he was anxious for a kiss or two and his patient was nearly out of patience.

The next morning, after Shirley had slept fitfully on their couch, Denise Everitt, her old friend from Camberwell High and her husband Rodney Davidson helped her retrieve her luggage from King's Cross before dropping her at Heathrow airport, with little time to spare.

She checked in immediately but just as her luggage, along with that of a dozen other passengers in the queue disappeared through the curtain, a change of gate was announced. By the time the frantic group reached the new gate, the flight had closed.

No thanks to Nick, Shirley's flight had been booked by a travel agent in Dorchester which meant she'd have to go back into London to have her ticket reissued. With no money for a taxi she travelled by tube to the agent's head office and managed to get onto a flight via Dubai late that day.

Free of pain and with time on her hands, she called Alan 'reverse charges' to update him on her arrival time. She then went to Harrods to buy a 'thank you' gift for Mr and Mrs Bond to acknowledge their kindness to her. Though the gesture almost exhausted her remaining funds, she felt much better when she finally boarded her Qantas flight.

She arrived in Melbourne on Wednesday 25th July 1973, minus her luggage, with £3.50p in her wallet and in the same clothes she'd been wearing for the past four days since she'd begun her journey home. Alan was waiting at the international gate at Tullamarine Airport and greeted her in tears that just kept coming.

But it wasn't his younger daughter's dishevelment that caused Alan's sobs when he met her at the gate. It soon became apparent that his deep distress related to his older daughter – or, more specifically, her little pixie Craig. The Gosbell family were flying back from a holiday in Queensland and would touch down on the Tullamarine tarmac in 20 minutes, where an ambulance was waiting to rush the desperately ill boy to the Royal Children's Hospital.

Age Three

A tragic homecoming

Rob had decided to apply for a month's long-service leave and take the family on a relaxing holiday to Queensland, in company with close friends, Brian and Jan Webster; Brian was also a teacher with leave due. The two families left a very cold winter in Melbourne in their respective cars and unwound quickly during the long drive north.

Bev and Rob's three sons were similar in ages to Brian and Jan's three daughters and the six of them played happily together from sun-up to tea time in the hotel's playground and pool.

It was another beautiful day in paradise one afternoon three weeks later when Steven came running into the Gosbell suite from the sand pit calling 'Mummy, Mummy!'

'What's happened, darling?' Bev opened her arms to greet him.

'Craig's bleeding!'

'Oh, Steven! You boys have to be gentle with him! He's much smaller than you.'

'We didn't do anything, Mummy. He's just bleeding.'

Bev and Rob rushed Craig to the nearest doctor, 40 miles away, who promptly gave his diagnosis (based on treating one such case during his internship 20 years earlier), and proceeded to make the arrangements necessary to get them home as quickly as possible.

'The Royal Children's in Melbourne is the only hospital that can help him,' he said.

As Bev carried her youngest son from the plane to the ambulance, blood poured from his nose and mouth. He was two-and-a-half-years-old and gave his older brothers a heart-rending smile and a lingering wave with his tiny free hand as the medic took over.

The ambulance departed with Bev, Rob, Craig and Alan, but it would be the last time Steven, five, and Dale, three-and-a-half, would see their little pixie.

Craig died three days later from a very rare, sudden onset leukaemia.

It was a terrible shock for everyone, but it was Bev and Rob who set the paradigm. During the longest week of their lives, their extraordinary courage and determination to help Steven and Dale cope with their loss was an example to everyone.

Whilst Jan and Brian respectively drove the two cars home with their devastated daughters in time for the funeral, family, neighbours and friends stepped up their love and attention to show how much they cared. But as Bev and Shirley had learned long ago, people handle shock and distress in different ways, and not always fittingly.

Shirley spent most of the week at the Gosbell's and felt Bev's pain directly when a friend dropped by with a bouquet of flowers and concluded a short conversation at the front door with the thoughtless remark: 'At least you've still got two lovely boys.'

In the Gosbell lounge room a couple of days prior to the funeral, the Methodist minister was visiting to pay his condolences. Bev welcomed him warmly and opened a subject that was heart wrenching in itself.

'I can't stop thinking about whether we did the right thing agreeing for Craig to have a blood transfusion, Bill. We had to make a decision quickly, and he died shortly after it. Should we have left his life in God's hands?'

The Reverend had no answer! He rattled on about how difficult it must have been for them, and how it was hard to know whether the doctors were right to recommend it…on and on he went, leaving Bev more disturbed than before.

God would approve, Bev. You did everything possible to save your son surely wouldn't have challenged his faith, or his understanding.

The church was full and the service was beautiful. Everyone cried, but Bev and Rob smiled valiantly as they welcomed family and friends for the refreshments that followed.

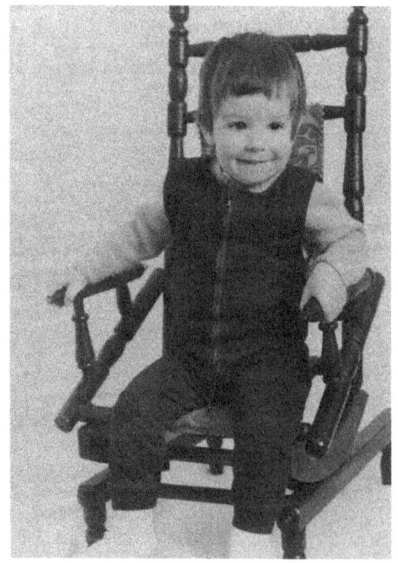

Craig Ashley Gosbell …

23/02/1971 – 28/07/1973

Rest in peace, our beautiful little pixie.
We will always miss you.

3rd Intermission

Oklahoma City

Golden Eagle Aviation

Vickie

If it's Tuesday, it's Belgium

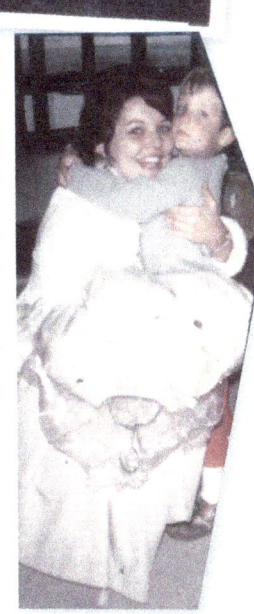
Welcome home from Steven

AGE FOUR (1974 – 1986)

And then the justice
In fair slim belly, resilient unlined skin,
With eyes more wise, and hair cut short.

Justice may have been coming for Shirley, but it was not yet in the stars for the Gosbell family.

Shirley thanked her lucky stars that she'd left London when she did and was especially grateful for the Heathrow stuff-up that caused her to miss the booked plane. Alan was devastated but it would have been worse if he'd had to make two trips to the airport in as many days to support his beloved daughters.

Of course Alan, and Bev and Rob's neighbours, Betty and Jim, were also concerned about Shirley's health following her recent traumas, but hers paled to insignificance in the face of her sister's incomparable loss and she determined to get a life as quickly as possible to ensure no sympathy was wasted on her.

During the last few weeks in England she'd completely forgotten she'd left AU$3,000 in a fixed deposit account in Australia, and a few days before the funeral her luggage had arrived. They were shocking days but having some money in the bank and her personal affects and own clothes again went some way towards rekindling her self-esteem and independence.

The changing times

Somebody once said *Human reason needs only to will more strongly than fate and she is fate.* Shirley knew that even with a loan from Alan, she was not going to be able to start her own business by relying on fate, luck or destiny, whatever she called it.

Or was it?

The thought that she was nearing the end of her first 25 years, which continued to feel and look like 40, was unrelenting. She combed the newspapers, from the bad news on the front pages to the good on the back for a self-determining opportunity or even just an idea that might lead to one.

Since her 16th birthday she'd been updating her resume every year but this time didn't bother. A professional change of life meant it shouldn't be necessary, and there was nothing good to add that anybody needed to know.

The first-born baby boomers were now adults, technically speaking, and had come to be associated with a long list of contradictory attributes. They were variously described as self-centred and full of their own importance, independent, morally equivocal yet obsessed with utopian ideals (however fleeting), predictable – and street smart. Having been mentored by mothers and fathers who wanted their offspring to have more fun as kids than they'd had in their own childhoods had produced rather more tempestuous, renegade progenies than they could have imagined.

As a classic baby boomer, Shirley acknowledged that her generation had endless opportunities and was much better off than their parents had been. Boomers were healthier and safer and so would almost certainly outlive them, but she was also aware that a long life does not necessarily make a happier one and so she'd better get cracking.

Her mother may have exited the stage four years ago but she continued to have the last word: *Concentrate on your strengths so your weaknesses don't show!*

It was still winter and ratings time in television. The medium itself was attracting massive audiences during prime time, in fact most of the time. Aided and abetted by constant promotional activities, diverse media point-of-sale initiatives and 'celebrity' pictures and features, it was as if half of Australia's 13 million people had given up recreational activities in order to stay home and watch the telly.

Age Four

Despite the local film industry beginning to take off at home and abroad, many of the country's cinemas were struggling to meet their overheads.

On the international front, Shirley's friend Vickie Morris in Oklahoma City had been right in predicting that Nixon wouldn't last his term. When *The Washington Post's* Bernstein and Woodward broke the Watergate story, nations were glued to their screens for daily updates. Terrorists had opened fire at the Athens airport, killing three people and injuring 55 others bringing TV journos from around the world in the hope of acquiring a scoop. Even 'Sesame Street' had reached Moscow, where Soviets denounced it as 'imperialistic'.

The power of the Fourth Estate, both serious and sensationalist, was expanding at a rapid pace, the latter blurring the truth and making the detection of bullies and abusers more difficult. Small and large businesses jumped onto the bandwagon to sponsor live shows and serials featuring all-Australian talent. Pioneers such as Hector Crawford (of *Prisoner* and *Neighbours* notoriety) and Reg Grundy (*Sale of the Century* and *Wheel of Fortune*) sold their products into countries around the world.

Naturally all this new content demanded more staff to meet ever-expanding quotas and opportunities abounded.

In Adelaide HSV7 was looking for a producer/host for a woman's program. It was, potentially, an idyllic role for Shirley if only she could contemplate re-entering the dog-eat-dog business. During her time in the UK, Graham Kennedy had come out of his first retirement and was back at GTV9, bringing with him Bob Phillips as producer. A third potential opportunity was a Victorian country TV station in the midst of expansion who would likely regard Shirley's skills as spot on for their requirements.

What should she do? Take one step at a time…that'd be a major change in itself!

Although she was offered the position at HSV7 in Adelaide following a successful audition, she didn't want to be away from her family. In addition, she'd finally 'got it' that despite being a gifted producer and well-trained performer, and loving the industry itself, she simply didn't fit the celebrity mould and never would. The fact that the salary offered by HSV was half that of male newsreaders reminded her of the gross inequality of it all and was undoubtedly the final clincher.

It was only a couple of weeks after Craig's funeral and there wasn't much time to contact old friends before she left Adelaide. Gil Breirley at the SA Film

Corp had just left for the airport and Helen Keightley at Drake Personnel (who might be Mrs Peter Wearing-Smith by now) was on leave.

But her greatest regret was that she'd lost the address and phone number of dentist Jack's parents on that fateful journey home. She couldn't recall his name beyond 'Jack' and was deeply upset because she'd given her word. Surely she'd remember his surname when life settled down?

So much for *going back*, especially to Adelaide! She knew then it was time to go forward.

She'd not had time to move in any direction at all when Bob Phillips called to ask if she'd like to run the agency he'd left to produce Graham Kennedy's show.

Over lunch Bob expressed his regrets about her exit from ATVO. He acknowledged his partner Judy's unwitting involvement in the lies and bullying that he realised must have influenced Shirley's jumping ship. She was the ideal person to manage his agency, he was very busy producing *In Melbourne Tonight* and she'd have free reign to run it her way.

The offer was financially ambiguous but definitely promising. She'd been gone such a short time and knew all the talent personally, along with most of the key clientele who booked them. Despite it having been vacant for months, Bob had continued to pay the rent on an office in the Allan Eaton Recording Studios in Carlton, close to Melbourne's CBD. It meant she could literally walk in there on Monday and begin to build up the business again.

Bob was a good salesman. More importantly, he was also a decent sort of bloke and offered to guide her whilst she settled in, suggesting she could offer bookings on the Kennedy show as an incentive to talent she wanted to represent. He was prepared to pay her commission for every booking she made in or outside the industry.

Too easy, she thought later, weighing up the pros and cons. All she had to do was pay Bob's percentage monthly, plus the office rental and telephone bills. Travel and general expenses were also her responsibility, but of course they'd be tax deductible.

Shirley bought a car and then told Alan about Bob's offer. He was greatly relieved to learn that she'd decided to stay in Melbourne, and especially glad that she was taking on a business she knew well. It was a forward plan that sounded like security at last.

She put him on standby to loan her whatever she would need to buy Bob out, hopefully in time to allow her to celebrate her 26th birthday in style.

24/7 Flesh-to-Flesh enterprises

It took almost 12 months, a good accountant and some reasonable give and take on the part of both parties for the agency to become truly hers. By then Shirley was not only running the business, including paying all the bills, but was also starting to see it grow.

A settlement was quickly agreed upon when she offered to give back the name 'Television Entertainers of Australia' in the event of Bob wanting to return to the agency business when Graham Kennedy decided to retire again. The cash price minus the brand was something in the vicinity of AU$10K and they maintained a professional, friendly relationship thereafter.

The S&J Entertainment Company incorporating *Shirley McLaughlin Enterprises* was registered, new letterhead designed and another phone line installed. Allan Eaton gave her free use of an empty dark room next door to her office, which she designated to her secretary.

Expanding her stable of artists and clients would finally give her a commanding, independent career. She'd always been complete in her own company, needing only a commitment to a project to maintain her happy disposition and interest in other peoples' lives and livelihoods. Despite the vulnerability that was forever just beneath the surface, with the driving force of a seasoned creator and the freedom to diversify and take risks, she knew she could do it.

With the able assistance of Heather, mother in law of Glen Wheatley, Shirley quickly doubled the talent and clients lists.

Selling flesh to flesh is a fitting epigram for the primary duties of a show biz agent. Their only product is people. Talented, egocentric, capricious and sometimes perfidious people, at that.

The commodities that talent agencies deal in can't be handled, trialled, guaranteed or gift wrapped, owned, loaned, eaten, worn, used or exchanged if they don't work. There are no refunds on purchases, short of disaster or non-appearance.

Agents generally take 10 per cent of the talent's fees and personal management representation ranges from 15 – 25 per cent.

With sufficient talent on a theatrical or entertainment agent's list, the opportunities to secure a range of permanent purchasers increases, whilst those with production experience are able to pre-package shows for a limitless range of clients and consumers that multiply the rewards exponentially. Notwithstanding, the very nature of the game is fraught with jeopardy, unpredictability, disagreements, jealousies, failures and successes and all people striving to achieve success *in public* are prone to step out of character now and then.

An entertainer's agent works erratic hours, rarely has a day off and good days often run into the early hours of the next day. Shirley's easiest business was negotiated in the wee small hours of the morning, directly following a successful performance. When an artist concluded with tumultuous applause, the publican or nightclub owner would shout her a drink and confirm the next recommended 'product' booking. Notwithstanding, her biggest deals and most rewarding relationships came from clients of a different hue.

Shirley's access to current and up-and-coming artists of the day was established during her television career and whilst doubling Bob's inherited list, she needed an innovative business plan. Quickly establishing herself as a major player in the game would only happen if she could rely on client loyalty across both distinctly different groups. That meant securing regular work for them all.

She needed to sell more talent *simultaneously* so she could maximise her own time. With bold handling of carefully selected talent, and a wider range of clients, she could book multiple acts and 'shows' that would lead to exclusive, contracted work. By producing shows herself she could boost her income and provide more work for everyone. Her established artists would do well and the new talent would gain experience as support acts.

''Win-win,' she whispered, her blue eyes shining with excitement.

There are so many stories in the S&J Entertainment Agency and SMcL Management scrapbooks, diaries and albums that we needed an idea, or a POV as Shirley would say to direct our selection. We wanted to cover the good, the bad and the ugly succinctly.

The S&J Entertainment Company and SMcL Enterprises management lists in the mid and late 1970s were challenging, but we finally selected a

AGE FOUR

baker's dozen stories (lucky 13!) that we loved hearing and being a part of during our growing up years.

The S&J Entertainment Company
Incorporating Shirley McLaughlin Enterprises
Tel: (03) 347-4535

SHIRLEY McLAUGHLIN ENTERPRISES

Kerri Biddell
Geraldine Doyle
Eric Pearce
Hugh Stuckey (Writer)
Zi Zi
Sue Coles
Col Elliott
Gerry Ford
John Lisle and The John Lisle Set
Suzanne McGuffie
Enza Pantano

THE S & J ENTERTAINMENT COMPANY

COMICS
Marg, Mel & Johnny Arthur
Marg & Johnny Arthur
Ron Blaskett
Tommy Deane
Brian Doyle
Ugly Dave Gray
Syd Haylen
Irene Hewitt
Paul Hogan
Miss Daphne Fitzherbert
Lester & Smart
Paul J. Peters

ENTERTAINERS : MALE
Greg Anderson
Greg Bonham
Gordon Boyd
Johnny Chester
Richard Claptan
Frankie Davidson
Edwin Duff
Smacka Fitzgibbon
George Hegan
Kamahl
Lionel Long
Bill McCormack
Johnny O'Keefe
Doug Owen
Tony Pantano
James Pegler
Marty Rhone
Randel Ross
Normie Rowe
Sandy Scott
Simon Smith
Al Styne
Gerry Thomas
Ian Turpie
John Williamson

PERSONALITIES
Ian Buckland
Hunphrey Bear
Maria Beyen
Denise Drysdale
Garry Meadows
Ian Meldrum
Judy Nunn
Myrtle Woods

ENTERTAINERS : FEMALE
Dorothy Baker
Mary Jane Boyd
Chelsea Brown
Dawn Dixon
Lynne Dutton
Dianne Faulkner
Renee Gayer
Jenny Green
Linda George
Bev Harrell
Shirley Jacobs
Marcia Jones and The Cookies
Dinah Lee
Markeeta Little Wolf
Liv Maesson
Marlyn Martin
Renie Anne Martini
Seona McDowell
Helen Noonan
Julie Robinson
Patricia Stephenson
Judy Stone

FEMALE IMPERSONATORS
Eric Raven : (Jullien Tome)
Tracey Lee

GROUPS
Allan Eaton Big Band
The Blue Echoes
Cobbers
Dove
Frank Traynor & The Jazz Preachers
Jigsaw
The Four Kinsmen
The Hawking Brothers
Max Causon Big Band
Mega Set
Mulga Bill's Bicycle Band
The Mixtures
The Pied Pipers
PT 74
The Rondalls
Springwater
Tony Hedges Trio
Yarra Yarra New Orleans Jazz Band

STRIPPERS
Judy
Doodie

MUSICAL DIRECTORS
Pianists, Guitarists, Drummers, etc.

DUOS
Bill & Boyd
Double Tempo

VENTRILOQUISTS
Bob Fillman
Chris Kirby

221 Pelham Street, Carlton Australia 3053

THE WORLD'S YOUR OYSTER!

Personal Management:

Shirley McLaughlin Enterprises

13 MACARTHUR PLACE, CARLTON. 3053.
PHONE: (03) 347 4535

or

SHOWBIZ ANSWERING
PHONE: (03) 347 9888

ENZA PANTANO
Versatile, exciting cabaret and T.V. performer.

* Don Lane Show
  Ernie Sigley Show
  Mike Walsh
  Paul Sharrott Show

* Rooms include:—
  Mandarin, Sydney
  Paprika, Adelaide
  Top Hat, Galaxy
  and Carols by Candlelight, Melbourne
  Romano's, Perth
  Blinkers, Brisbane

COL ELLIOTT
Australia's answer to Benny Hill!

* Penthouse, Melbourne.
  BTV 6

* Toured with:
  Johnny Chester and
  The Jigsaw

* Paprika, Adelaide
  Galaxy, Melbourne

* Lions Sportsman's Breakfasts, Football Clubs, etc.

PAUL O'GORMAN
Performer with great "presence" on stage.

* Don Lane Show
  Ernie Sigley Show

* Runner Up Australian
  Popular Song Festival

* Original Compositions
  Recorded by —
    Kamahl and
    John Farnham

* Major Clubs, Restaurants,
  Functions.

THE JONES GIRLS
Close harmonies, subtle humour, slick glamourous floorshow.

* Originally with Daly
  Wilson Big Band.

* Dina & Donna in 'The
  Magic Show', Melbourne.

* All major Clubs and
  Functions —
  Show is a mixture of
  Modern thru' Nostalgia.

SUSIE COLES
Warm, lilting voice and charm.

* Don Lane Show
  Ernie Sigley Show
  Penthouse

* "So Little, So Much",
  EP. Released January '77

* Support to:
  Roy Orbison,
  Festival Hall, Melbourne.

* Paprika, Adelaide.
  Civic Centre, Brisbane.
  etc.

JOHN LISLE
Compere/Vocalist with natural ability to "involve".

* Penthouse, Melbourne.

* Originally with highly
  successful "Raiders".

* Toured —
  Singapore, Thailand,
  Malaysia.

* All major Clubs and
  Hotels in Southern States

Also representing **Matt Flinders** *and* **The Chancellors.**

A run of firsts...

For the first time in her life Shirley was totally in charge and sold her 'flesh-to-flesh' without compromise, particularly when it came to money. Her opening line to new clients never varied.

Age Four

'My artists' fees are not negotiable and I charge 15 per cent commission for packaged shows. You'll get 110 per cent return on our work because we're in this game not only to entertain your customers but also grow our individual businesses in the process.'

Australia's first casino opened in Hobart, Tasmania in 1973. Although the team at Wrest Point Casino had from the start booked individual talent and packaged shows, Shirley found it a hard gig to crack the exclusively male competition in the agency game. But crack it she did, in the process becoming the first female agent in the country to break through at Wrest Point.

It all came about via a sheep farmer. She'd managed to book a packaged show into the Working Men's Club on King Island, which is situated in the middle of Bass Strait, and a light plane trip from Melbourne. Danny, the manager, was a fourth generation local farmer whose wife and children had watched Shirley on the telly.

While the first of her packaged shows for Danny's club opened doors for Shirley into almost every large venue in Tassie, it also provided a memorable example of why the Working Men's Club on King Island quickly earned a reputation that Australia's male agents didn't covet. It proved to be a one-off gig for John Lisle and The John Lisle Set, ventriloquist Ron Blaskett with his famous Gerry Gee, and Irish comedienne/vocalist/guitarist Geraldine Doyle, despite the fact that the show was a resounding success, the numerous encores extending the two-hour show to three.

The following morning Danny and his family took Shirley and her cast to the airport for the trip back to Melbourne.

The wind was blowing at cyclonic speed and yesterday's yachts and fishing boats had gone to ground. A single pilot would fly their 12-seater airplane to the mainland and his seat alone was in place. They soon discovered they were to share with a truckload of live crayfish that also needed quick passage to Melbourne. By the time the wheat sacks of crayfish, an export integral to King Island's economy, were stacked in the cabin, a mere seven of the original seats were able to be reinstalled. Just enough to seat them all.

Ron Blaskett sat in the co-pilot seat, John and his band of three managed to squeeze into seats behind them and Geraldine fell into the only back seat they'd managed to reset, directly behind Shirley and crammed between thousands of very busy crayfish, squealing as their copious legs danced through the ropes securing the sacks.

'Gerry Gee is about to narrate a eulogy of my life!' Blaskett yelled to Shirley from the front seat as the plane took off.

'I'm going to be sick all over you, McLaughlin!' Geraldine contributed from the back seat as the plane began a sharp ascent to 6,000 feet, the pilot's attempt at avoiding the storm.

'Better get Gerry to begin the eulogy, Ron,' Shirley called to Blaskett up front, and 'For God's sake start singing, Gerro!' she laughed hysterically to Doyle at the rear.

John Lisle and his band picked up their instruments from between their legs and began to play. Everyone, even Shirley, sang all the way home, drowning out the crayfish chorus. They landed safely at Essendon Airport in Melbourne with a story to tell to their children, and grandchildren.

Gerro's husband Patrick Fitzpatrick, known as Paddy to friends and 'Horizontal' to Gerro's audiences, greeted them on the tarmac.

'Thanks to you, I'll never eat crayfish again!' Geraldine quipped to Shirley in farewell.

Paddy, possessed of his wicked Irish humour, added his own classic rebuke. 'Missy Shirley, I'm gonna whip you! I'm gonna whip you like you never bin whipped before!'

When kindred spirits share the same sense of humour, their friendships are usually enduring. Over the next 40 odd years, Gerro and Shirley would continue to chat like sisters during their intermittent meetings and phone conversations. And Paddy still concludes most of their interactions with, 'Missy Shirley, I'm gonna whip you!'

The Working Men's Club was the scene for many a riotous interlude involving Shirley's clients. She booked a gig for another of her life-long friends, comedian Col Elliott, only for him to come home with his face badly sunburnt. The spotlight hadn't been working on the night so he'd instead been lit with an infrared lamp, the kind physiotherapists use for 30 seconds at a time to penetrate and warm sore muscles and increase blood flow. Despite being blasted with heat the equivalent to that of a blow torch for 45 minutes, Col later relayed the story laughing like a member of his audience.

However, neither Shirley nor the agent of Judy Stone, the pint-sized performer with the titanic voice, were laughing when she got home to Sydney after her turn on King Island. They never learned what happened at the Working Men's Club that night because Judy refused to discuss it. The only related words she did utter were to her agent: she would never work for Shirley McLaughlin again.

The diverse business men who'd backed Shirley at ATVO became clients of a different kind, several of them remaining friends for decades to come.

Ex-lover Tim Black, who had both divorced and re-married in the years since the unexpected red roses and *that* phone call, asked her to recommend an artist for a national advertising campaign he was running for appliance giant, Sanyo.

Tim needed an exotic, non-commercial singer who would do justice to Sinatra's hit, 'That's Life', in a theatrical, product-enhancing way for multiple 30 and 60 second national TV commercials. Shirley was one of several agents who were briefed and there were many big names put forward for the contract.

In contrast, Shirley pitched a little-known singer who worked the jazz clubs and pubs of Sydney. Kerrie Biddell, with her intelligent face, sylphlike body and a three-octave range appeared on the Graham Kennedy show a few times but otherwise she'd had no commercial experience.

It was for mostly personal (perhaps contrite) reasons that Tim wanted Shirley to have the job but he also took the risk on her because she had been the only agent who'd met his brief precisely.

She managed Kerrie thereafter for some years, flying her to Melbourne for Sanyo shoots, cabaret and TV bookings. Their agent-artist relationship was dynamic and sometimes difficult, but both saw good money from the advertisements, which also established Sanyo and Kerrie as household names.

Henderson Lamont of funeral parlour, florist shops and skate board fame was inspired by Sanyo's success and decided to run a series of TV commercials to lift the profile of his parlours. After he told Shirley he needed a well-known, dignified man to front the ads, she recommended Eric Pearce GTV Channel 9's long-standing, nationally revered newsreader. A mature, and beautifully spoken man, Sir Eric (as he would one day become) was perfectly cast in the role, although he would question that many times before the contract concluded.

Henderson invited Shirley and Eric to lunch at his head office so they could meet his executives and get 'a feeling' for the business at the centre of the advertising campaign. He took them on their first, and last guided tour of a funeral parlour, accompanied by an in-depth running commentary covering every element of the death business most people could live without needing to know.

By the time they entered the dining room, Eric was looking decidedly pale. But he settled as lunch progressed and it became apparent that people in the funeral game have good senses of humour. He seemed to finally be enjoying himself, despite barely touching his food.

Before dessert was served Eric looked purposefully at his watch, graciously thanked everyone and apologised that he would have to rush off at that point or otherwise be late for work. On the short walk to Shirley's car he made his position clear. 'I'd laugh if I could risk it, but I'm fighting off the urge to be sick until I get home. Please excuse me from any further invitations to the house of death, Shirley, and after I've thrown up I'm going to instruct my wife there's to be no bloody viewing of me when I'm gone, with or without makeup!'

Another financially rewarding opportunity of a different hue came via Ron Cotton, head of the Australian petroleum company Mobil. This thriving business sponsored a variety of large and small functions throughout the year, attracting a 'who's who' of Australian business leaders from across the corporate, union, government and charitable sectors.

Ron needed Shirley's services to round up a mix of comperes, bands and entertainers for all such major events.

Bob Hawke was often present at the Mobil functions and on these occasions it was difficult for her to concentrate on anything but him. At the time he held both of the Australian Labor Party's top jobs, i.e. federal president of the ALP and president of the Australian Council of Trade Unions. He was also well and truly still 'off the wagon' and consumed enormous quantities of alcohol. The way he behaved towards Shirley at these events was usually offensive and though clearly unacceptable, his colleagues and friends would laugh off his 'capers', as they called them, and look the other way. Bob may have been an influential and proud Aussie larrikin when he was sober, but he was a woman's nightmare when drunk.

As no Johnny-come-lately to lecherous men, Shirley's initial defence against the assaults was to just quickly move away from him. She had come to accept that such form was the culture of the day, given her experiences abroad and the litany of inappropriate advances she'd put up with from the local stars she'd worked with, including Paul Hogan, Ernie Sigley and Don Lane, (one of whom had accosted her in a corridor in a television studio in Melbourne with the words 'I can make you come in 30 seconds'.)

Sexual harassment was neither acknowledged nor discussed in public in the 1970s and whilst the unprovoked incidents still shook her, she walked away those days rather than confront them. Nevertheless, it was becoming difficult to mix with her Mobil clients because of Bob's escalating lewdness. Something had to give.

The moment when Shirley took control came during the wrap-up of a highly successful Mobil show. As once again she felt Bob's roving hand in a place it shouldn't have been, something inside her snapped. She raised her arm in full view of half a dozen VIP guests and with a strength she didn't know she had slapped his clammy mitt with a resounding 'thwack!' She then turned on her heel and left the venue without looking back.

Bob would probably forget it by morning but the witnesses would remember it for life, as several told her when they saw her at the next function.

Her artists who'd performed at the gig that night may have had to wait for a cheque in the mail, but Shirley had finally made good on her mother's maxim from that drive on the way to Grandma's when she was a child: 'Stop the bully at the start or he'll just keep bullying!'

And with that she vowed to never let any man reduce her again.

In her experience, offenders like Bob were almost always pre boomers and it struck her later that the 'me' generation might be the catalyst for the previous generation's behaviour.

The baby boomers were redefining youth with free love, drugs, rock 'n roll and constant sea-changes, blowing family stereotypes apart because it was their right to do anything they liked. They were born to have it all! The great generation stoically accepted their lot but the pre boomers had suddenly got a taste of freedom and wanted a slice of it whilst they were young enough to get a share.

She thought about Alan too, her beloved father who'd become her best friend since Margery died. They'd never discussed her constant battles with men. 'Those bastards live on another planet from you and it wouldn't have served our relationship well,' she explained to him in the framed wedding photo on the mantelpiece. Despite more than 20 years in country Victoria where Alan had lived with the horrendous, factual knowledge of paedophiles and rapists in churches and schools of all denominations, she'd convinced herself he'd never have believed her.

'Firsts' in the flesh-to-flesh business continued to be a constant for Shirley, and there was one pre boomer client and friend in the mix who was always a gentleman. Despite an unstable marriage, Darren McKay of Toltoys fame was a genuine friend and sought her professional services and company whenever he could.

Unfortunately for him, and perhaps Shirley, when his marriage finally broke down she was being courted by her landlord, Allan Eaton. A girl has to eat.

News flash

Gareth Gosbell was born on the 25th of September, 1974. Bev and Rob didn't plan the pregnancy. They were still adjusting to the loss of Craig, but as Alan always said, life happens when you're looking the other way.

Gaz was a perfect baby. He had a calm about him that suggested he'd landed on terra firma; as a result he hardly ever cried. His parents assured their older sons that he wasn't a replacement for Craig. He was his own little man who'd arrived like magic from Mummy's tummy and was happy to be here with them.

Steven and Dale were too young to know how life happened then, but they knew Gareth's arrival was an awesome thing. Their new baby brother was a gift that even Santa couldn't deliver with a hundred reindeers pulling his sleigh.

A friend, for life

Friendships develop quickly in showbiz and often unravel at the same pace. Shirley had been around long enough to be more selective and less easily duped when it came to those she chose to pursue relationships with. Ergo, men and women would end up either her best friend, or worst enemy, with only unthreatened business associates in the space between.

Age Four

She of course valued their company, mutual respect, loyalty and commercial rewards engendered by all her friendships, but the one that stood taller and stronger than all of them was a woman named Beris Underhill.

Beris was a theatrical agent who rented offices about 100 metres from the Allan Eaton Recording Studio. Her agency was called Frog Promotions and her list of theatrical talent boasted many famous actors, both at home and abroad. If you picked an Australian television star from the '60s, '70s, '80s or '90s, Beris would have been their agent or manager for at least one of those decades. She was flat out five, sometimes six days a week, even with the support of her full-time assistant Felippa Rock, the wife of successful actor Michael Pate.

Industry outsiders may assume that selling and managing actors contracted to be on film or TV sets for weeks, months and/or years would be less time-intensive than the lot of entertainment agents, whose performers work one-off bookings at all hours of the day and night. In reality, the workload is often greater for actor agents.

Beris was constantly submitting and booking potential actors for auditions, following up on rejections, negotiations and contracts, and managing theatrical careers across stage, screen and television. She had a monopoly on TV serials including *Prisoner* and *Matlock Police* that ran for years and were watched and loved by millions of Australians. Managing these actors' temperaments, year in and especially year 'out' (when their contracts are terminated), is not a job for the faint hearted.

A vivacious woman of strength and substance, Beris was a single mother to Jason, whose father Jeff Underhill was an artist and inaugural member of the Push movement. Jeff Underhill had died when the boy was still in nappies.

Shirley and Beris met at the pool table in Allan Eaton's studios, a popular rendezvous for all manner of clients; musicians, tenants, friends, neighbours, national and international stars and would-be-if-they-could-be hopefuls who knew somebody who knew Allan. The beer and wine flowed freely and there were often more deals done around that pool table after 5pm than over the phone in the heat of the day.

Shirley had at last found a ball sport where being left-handed was no handicap. She had already played a round of pool and lost, without disgrace, to world champion Eddie Charlton when a short blond woman challenged her to a game. The first time she and Beris played together, just the two of them, it became clear that neither had a chance of winning three games in a row. For both women, this amounted to 'boring' so they adjourned to the local pub for dinner.

Five games of pool launched a friendship devoid of rivalry or duplicity and based on shared, competitive traits. Their associated businesses and like ethics were a given, and that they'd both lost their mothers helped them form a natural bond. On reflection, it was probably as much their vertically challenged five foot two (with eyes of blue), outrageous, quirky senses of humour that made the friendship stick, for life.

From that night on, when Shirley had an entertainer who was also an actor, she took Beris to lunch to get the inside gen of Who, Where and How much to charge for her client. When Beris had an actor who was also an entertainer, she took Shirley to lunch for intelligence.

It didn't take long to emerge in conversation that Beris was a close friend of Tim Black's ex-wife, and that she'd studiously calculated that Shirley had become his lover several years after the birth of their second child. Apparently he'd only married his long-term partner to give the children his name, but beyond that Beris was discreet when talking about her friend. She did however divulge that the marriage wasn't going well and wondered aloud if Paul Newman's double would be knocking on Shirley's door any time soon.

'I think you're a bit of a femme fatale,' she added frankly.

'Thanks for that, but no way,' Shirley retorted, 'even if I hadn't just agreed to move in with Allan Eaton.'

A friend in business, but not for life

Allan was a pre boomer and well into his 30s. Their friendship developed over time, mainly through their landlord/tenant relationship and growing business association.

Shirley was booking acts to perform with the Allan Eaton Big Band, often referred to as Australia's Glen Miller Big Band. They'd earned a huge following over many years playing Friday and Saturday nights in a large dance hall in Albert Park, an inner suburb of Melbourne. At the same time she was scouting and signing potential recording artists to her management list to maximise every opportunity Allan's exceptional musical abilities and diverse business offered.

She wasn't blind to the feelings Allan was developing for her, but their friendship remained platonic. He'd had a live-in lover for years and Shirley was fed up with amorous men who came with complications.

One afternoon Allan rushed into her office at the studios, imploring her to drop everything and come with him to the hospital.

His partner Natalie, who worked on reception at the studios, had yesterday gone in for minor surgery. Only that morning Shirley had visited the ward to wish her all the best and had found her in good spirits.

'Something's gone wrong!' Allan gasped, struggling for breath, before they rushed to his purple Mustang.

He drove at 100 miles an hour until a police car forced him to stop. When he explained his haste the officer gave them an escort at similar speed to the Cabrini Private Hospital in Malvern.

As they arrived a nun in traditional black waited on the steps. She went to Allan immediately and put her arms around him, tearfully declaring that Natalie had 'gone to God'. Moving between the stunned pair, she took one of each's hands and led them into a private office where the surgeon endeavoured to explain the tragically inexplicable.

Several days later, Shirley flew with Allan to Brisbane to attend Natalie's funeral and the devastating wake that followed at her family's home.

Natalie's parents were not well off but her mother was determined to get answers as to why and how this had happened. Some weeks later, renowned Melbourne lawyer Frank Galbally offered to represent them pro bono in a civil suit against the hospital.

When the case went to court many months later, despite some documented staff mistakes including the head nurse leaving the operating theatre to call a heart specialist following Natalie's 'blue' reaction to the anaesthetic, the judge ruled that Natalie had died as a result of a rare allergy. He found it wouldn't have been possible to identify prior to surgery, and that everything possible had been done to resuscitate her.

Shirley's decision to move in with Allan a few months later was based on her admiration and respect for him. And also because it suited her.

She'd been living with her father Alan all this time, commuting daily to the other side of the city for work. She'd just paid back the money she'd borrowed from him (including interest at the going bank rate of 10 per cent) and had recently taken out a mortgage for a one-bedroom flat in the suburb of Caulfield. Following some minor repairs she'd installed a tenant, in doing so taking the first step towards setting herself up for an independent future.

A born bachelor, Allan didn't make any promises or declare his love and Shirley had no false or wildly imaginative ideas about him. He was alone again, and life wasn't much fun alone. They'd shared his loss and could now share their friendship and mutual business interests within an intimate relationship.

It went well for a couple of years. They were a good team, entertained regularly, worked long hours at the studio and ate out on the way home two or three nights a week. They took holidays together, sometimes with friends or clients.

By late 1975 Allan was restless and his eyes were beginning to rove. Shirley didn't pick up on it at first, she was too busy, but one Sunday when they threw a lunch for Allan's best friend and his family it became clear.

They welcomed their guests, a family of three, and settled pool-side for champagne, beer and an hors-d'oeuvre platter for starters. It was a beautiful day and the young son swam merrily as the adults talked shop, music and the advertising business. Lunch was planned for 2pm but was served 15 minutes later. There was no reason to hurry.

Allan had decanted one of his finest reds and it had gone down fast. He was a generous host yet he seemed agitated as he adjourned to the bar for another. Shirley followed to top up the water jug and he grabbed it from her, pushing her out of his way.

'You aren't coming down with the bloody flu, are you?' his mate asked.

'Yea, could be,' Allan shrugged, put down the water jug and poured himself another wine.

Shirley lightened the conversation to ask about the family, particularly directed to the son who was extremely well mannered and had to be bored by now. The convivial atmosphere continued and it was about 4pm when she served dessert.

Allan had started to berate her about the delay. From there the drama quickly escalated. Suddenly enraged, he crushed with one hand the crystal goblet of claret he'd been nursing much more often lately. Fragments of glass, red wine and blood shot in all directions.

Age Four

Extraordinarily, everyone except the hosts laughed it off. Animated chatter resumed as Shirley attended to the son's shirt, which had caught the brunt of the wine and blood.

Equally incredible, it was well after dark before they finally left. Allan turned on her the moment they pulled out of the driveway.

The phone was ringing when they re-entered the house and Shirley gratefully raced down the passage to the kitchen to answer it. But Allan followed her.

'Hello?' she said breathlessly into the receiver before turning around. He was standing behind her with his right hand raised, fist clenched.

'It's your mother!' she gulped, thrusting the phone at his closed fist hovering just a couple of inches from her face.

The reference to his mother seemed to strike him like lighting, overwhelming his physical power.

Shirley seized the moment, walked down the passage to their bedroom, grabbed her handbag and car keys and closed the front door behind her.

She drove to her father's house to seek a familiar refuge. Alan woke from a bad dream to the heavy knocking on the front door.

Shirley sat by the side of his bed for a long time. He listened attentively as she talked through what had happened. Her monologue ended when she guessed out loud that Allan had found somebody else and had fallen to his line of least resistance. He wasn't a violent or abusive man, she reasoned. He'd just never been good at asking women to leave.

She slept fitfully and told her father over breakfast the next morning that she'd be grateful for accommodation again until she found somewhere new to live and work.

It was still early so she stopped by the house in Caulfield on the way to work, told Allan she'd move out of the house by Friday, and give him two weeks' notice at the studio as soon as possible. He was somewhat chastened, and greatly relieved.

He stayed home on the Friday to make sure she didn't take anything with her that was his. 'For heaven's sake, Allan!' she eventually exclaimed. 'Quit judging me by your own deceitful standards. Go to work so I can get me and my stuff out of here!'

Flushed with embarrassment, he grabbed his briefcase and fled.

There was now an unspoken leitmotif, an instinctive motivation if you like, that drove Shirley's life. With acknowledgment to Uncle Norm, she'd taken on the responsibility of making her own bread and the experience was transforming her in a way that dough could never do.

Throughout her nearly five years of personal management, the list remained solid. It included a number of high-income artists, writers and personalities, several of whom she'd nurtured from the start. But she continued to sell her own management skills to up-and-coming entertainers, which would lead to her 'discovering' a talented teenager with a unique image and enough potential to one day rock the world.

Markeeta Little Wolf had won the 1974 national Grand Final of *Young Talent Time,* the top-rating weekly ATVO series. She had also taken out the Nine Network's *Showcase '74*. On top of that, her support performances for Matt Monroe and Rolf Harris won her a nomination for 'Best Teenage Personality' of that year's TV Week Logie Awards.

It was a magical year for Markeeta and her mother Dona, a professional seamstress who created the colourful American-Indian costumes that played an integral role in her daughter's success.

Yet, whilst essentially tuneful and full of heart and soul, Markeeta's voice didn't quite rise above the impact and presentation of the singer herself. The judges on Australia's TV talent shows apparently hadn't noticed this – they certainly hadn't referred to it – despite the fact that several of them were professional singers. Shirley had observed it straight off, even though she couldn't sing in tune for love nor money. Perhaps she was wrong? Perhaps it didn't matter? The girl was on her way and already had a following.

One afternoon Shirley had been on what was known as an 'agent pub crawl', checking on her acts working the circuit, when she happened to drive past a hotel with a fairly uncouth reputation. A sandwich board advertisement out front caught her eye and she pulled over for a closer look: Markeeta Little Wolf was scheduled to perform at the venue that very evening.

Only just that morning Shirley had read in her week-old *Melbourne Age* that Australia's population had surpassed 12 million people, of which more than half were between the ages of 15 and 64.

'Jesus!' she cursed aloud as she parked her car slightly outside the lines. 'What on earth is Markeeta doing working in a pub with drunks and hippy baby boomers?'

Shirley knew it was the wrong market for the girl and that performing in such places could destroy her career before she'd even got one.

Following Markeeta's floor show she approached Dona with outstretched hand, introduced herself and made an immediate offer of management.

Dona was a bright woman. She responded like a classic, protective *'don't put your daughter on the stage Mrs Worthington'* mother. But she was also a listener and it soon became evident that she liked what she heard. Matter-of-factly Shirley explained that agents charge 10 per cent to book acts into paying gigs. Without professional management, that's all Markeeta would ever get.

'Managers work tooth and nail to grow talent, raise the artist's image and open up a national and sometimes international career that justifies a much higher asking price.'

Dona and Markeeta duly arrived at Shirley's office the next day where the deal was struck; 15 per cent until Markeeta 'made it', with a bottom-line figure determining what 'made it' meant in dollar terms, and 20 per cent thereafter.

To keep up her end of the bargain, Shirley knew all she had to do was get Markeeta back on television and sell her into appropriate venues.

But what she really personally wanted to do was *'Lift her up where she belonged'*. And with her established relationships around the country, she had no doubt she could put this gorgeous girl on the map.

Most cherished of all Shirley's television affiliations was BTV6 in the town of Ballarat, the birthplace and home of Margery Daw's 3BA program in the 1930's. Her strong working relationship with the station had led to her standing in as writer and producer of *Ballarat Tonight* when BTV6 CEO and manager, Gary Rice, was away on business. Gary was a pre boomer and a true gentleman.

The local *Tonight* show had a massive following in country Victoria and was a prime opportunity for emerging artists. Dona Little Wolf wasn't thrilled about the regular Ballarat bookings Shirley was lining up for Markeeta. She'd done her time in the early years when her American husband was making his name and didn't need to go there again.

Chief Little Wolf nee Ventura Tenario had married Australian-born Dona Corner in 1952. She'd borne him a daughter, Markeeta, and supported him every step of the way in his pursuit of becoming a world champion wrestler and showman. At the top of his game, a series of strokes paralysed half his body, leaving him physically twisted, wheel-chair bound and entombed in a special hospital for the aged.

Dona didn't talk about the Chief, and most people including Shirley thought he was dead. Her precious daughter was her protégé now and nothing, absolutely nothing, was going to stand in her way.

'Ballarat is just a country gig, Shirley!' she protested. 'The small fee surely doesn't justify the effort?'

Shirley replied, 'I'll be doing the driving and the money's irrelevant. It's about growing confidence and the gaining of experience, Dona – think of it as Off Broadway on the way to the top.'

Unsurprisingly, BTV6 became one of the mother and daughter's favourite sojourns.

Markeeta's first album, *Sunbird*, was produced and recorded by Allan Eaton and sold to Festival Records by Shirley. The title was an abbreviation of a song written especially for Markeeta by Bruce Rowland, Melbourne music scene all-rounder and member of Allan's band. *I Am A Sunbird* sequenced well with *Native North American Child* and several other numbers written by Jim Weatherly of US record label Image Records from which Shirley had procured the rights.

By the following year Markeeta's star had risen so much that Shirley landed her a one-off contract to perform at the 44th Annual Hollywood Parade of Stars. While the gig didn't come with a pay cheque, the potential for international exposure was huge and Dona, Markeeta and Shirley flew to California for several action-packed days.

Robert Wagner and wife Natalie Wood lead the glitzy, theatrical procession of floats down Hollywood Boulevard. It was televised across the country with 25 million Americans tuning in to watch, and afterwards Markeeta was presented with the 'Talent Queen of the Year, Hollywood International' award at a glamorous industry lunch. The three Aussies recognised most of the celebrities in attendance and Markeeta even got some autographs!

Shirley spent the next day walking Hollywood Boulevard cold calling on record companies, a bag of *Sunbird* albums under her arm. She'd not had any takers and was about to head back to the hotel when she chanced to meet an executive record producer at the reception desk of a major company.

Age Four

He invited her to his office on the spot, where he perused the succinct marketing package and commented on Markeeta's unique image. Shirley sat quietly on the other side of his desk, barely daring to breathe as he played several *Sunbird* tracks.

Finally, he said, 'She's got some talent, but not enough. Her voice doesn't match the image, and maturity won't change those vocal chords. It is what it is.'

At her visible disappointment, he apologised, adding, 'I've always wanted to go to Australia, too, but it's so far away … tough luck I'm afraid.'

Next on Shirley's list was a meeting with Liberace's agent, Seymour Heller.

She'd telephoned Heller before leaving Melbourne to arrange it. He'd booked another *Young Talent Time* alumnus, Jamie Redfern, as a support act for Liberace's last tour of Australia and it was known in the industry that Lee (as Liberace was called at home) had agreed to an encore Australian tour.

Upon arrival at Heller's suite of offices, Shirley was gobsmacked. While the exterior was an avant-garde version of a royal English castle, the rooms inside were dominated by huge, multifaceted, blindingly sparkling chandeliers. Liberace memorabilia covered the walls and on the quick tour Seymour gave her, she spied not one but two gold grand pianos holding their own in what she assumed were staff offices.

Inundated with strange aromas from the large, exotic floral arrangements in every room, Shirley launched into an embarrassing sneezing attack. Seymour, an amiable man, handed her a box of tissues.

'Happens all the time,' he admitted, laughing.

Just as they were getting down to business, a call came in from London. Apparently there was a problem that needed his immediate attention. He asked the caller to give him five before apologising to Shirley for having to cut the meeting short.

She knew that Jamie Redfern's 'Mr Worthington' father had given Seymour and Lee hell during the last tour, but when he suggested a breakfast meeting at her hotel the following morning, she thought she must have succeeded in reassuring him about Dona. In any event, the meeting was to conclude discussions between agents prior to proceeding to meet the Little Wolfs.

When she returned to the hotel, she updated Dona and Markeeta, explaining that Seymour was joining her for breakfast in the morning to conclude their interrupted agents' meeting. In order to meet the normal standards of privacy in these discussions, she asked them to depart earlier and suggested they breakfast at the cafe they'd discovered the day before.

Unexpectedly, Liberace had decided to join Seymour and they had just been seated when Shirley joined them. Both men stood immediately, shook her hand, Seymour apologised for her sneezing attack and Lee explained that he wanted to meet her so they could make a quick decision about Markeeta's suitability.

The Jamie Redfern disaster was first on the agenda. Shirley reiterated that although Dona contributed a great deal to her daughter's career, she listened to frank advice. In fact, they hadn't had one disagreement in the two years she'd been managing Markeeta.

At that precise moment Shirley's heart stopped. Mother and daughter were entering the dining room, walking towards them feigning surprise, as if it was a huge shock for them to see their manager seated at a breakfast table with Liberace!

Dona immediately arrested a passing waitress to bring more chairs, Seymour and Lee once again stood up, shook hands and slowly seated them. Their disappointment was palpable.

Shirley was mortified. *If only Dona had been able to let go of control and leave her to…*

It was a long flight home. She talked silently to herself most of the way. *Hollywood had been listening, but at the critical moment the stage mother had mindlessly blown her daughter's chance of an international career. They were so close…*

Shirley had just arrived in her office direct from the airport when Seymour phoned.

'I'm extremely sorry,' he said, 'but you were leaving the next day. Time was short and a test was essential. Lee couldn't handle another tour like the last,' he explained, again.

'We wanted to negotiate a deal with you first. Lee had asked me to invite you all to lunch or dinner before we made a firm offer,' he added.

'We loved Markeeta, and Dona seemed pleasant enough, but the damage was done.'

It was a sobering end to a trip underpinned by huge expectations – both for Shirley and, in different ways, the Little Wolfs. The relationship between artist and manager didn't instantly change, life went on and bookings for Markeeta continued at a pace, but Dona's ready laughter and constant communication was fading fast.

Shirley's attentions were diverted too. She'd spent so much time on Markeeta's bourgeoning career that she'd neglected to follow up on several important assignments. She'd appointed John Lisle, musician and compere to take over her personal contract to produce the illustrious, outrageous Vi Greenhalf's morning show at GTV9, and fortunately that was going well. She'd created another brief for Mike Brady to write a 'footy' theme song for his guest appearance at the Melbourne Cricket Ground for the AFL grand final and had produced 'Up There Gazally' that sounded to her like it was going to be a hit.

But not everything was running smoothly. She decided to close her door, get Heather to take all calls, and write herself a detailed list in order of urgency. For the next three weeks she put out bush fires, repaired relationships and got back in control.

The Little Wolf business and personal association remained professional but when word came to Shirley that Dona had been overheard blaming her daughter's manager for a 'cancelled' tour with Liberace, it was clear that she had decided to change managers. Markeeta's continuous exuberant thanks for everything were much appreciated, but it was over.

In the aftermath Shirley was sad, but overwhelmingly grateful for all she had learned from the experience. She used her new typewriter to draft a letter to her mother, and filed it in a two-ring folder labelled 'Death'.

```
Dear Mum,

We all miss you every day, especially Dad.
He's a passionate mineral and gemstone
collector these days and sets a fine example
of how to make a new start when you've lost
the love of your life.

It's been seven long years since you left me
without notice a week before my 22nd birthday
and I'm writing this now because I've just
managed to bury you in my head.

Of course you'll question the accusation,
given you collapsed three days before you
died in the same bathroom in which I'd lost
```

a baby only a few months earlier. But the doctors repeatedly told us you wouldn't walk again, wouldn't survive the year, wouldn't live through the night – and you always did. And then you up and drowned in the bath! Okay, you had a heart attack – that *wasn't* planned – but up until then you were always in control.

I'm grateful for everything you did for me, Mum, including giving me a Christian upbringing, despite the fact that I'd buried God before you died. *You* gave birth to me, not him! I suppose it's ironic, but you were my god. The Gods of all religions were invented by men who are still killing men, women and children in their Gods' names. But thanks to you, I still love men.

And finally I love me too.

Sorry that I was a slow learner with a low boredom threshold. You taught and mentored me with such passion and resolve that I couldn't bury you until I saw you and me in a mirror – as Dona and Markeeta!

It's crazy but I'm praying to the heavens that Markeeta will quickly come to the realisation I've just grasped. She needs to start driving her own life in order to become herself, and has to let her mother go before she can be at peace and they can become beloved friends. I hope it happens for her before Dona dies.

You'll always be with me, Mum, keeping me honest! I will always love you.

PS: If the late Mrs Worthington happens to be wherever you are, give her a miss. She was never in your class.

The S&J Entertainment Company and Shirley McLaughlin Enterprises moved from Pelham Street, Carlton on a Friday afternoon and opened for business in MacArthur Place, Carlton on Monday morning. Telstra re-connected the old line and installed a new one and the removalists were still hauling desks and furniture up the stairs of the small terrace home when the phone began to ring. Good sign.

Following the departure of her longstanding secretary Heather, who'd recently become a hands-on grandmother, Shirley engaged a bright, articulate 18 year old named Gail to be her receptionist. As well as doing some of her typing, her new employee would staff an answering machine service she was planning to launch. Gail lived with her unemployed boyfriend who had an unexplained, constant supply of money and took her to the local pub several times a week. As a result, she regularly turned up to work hung over, but always arrived on time and attacked every day with enthusiasm and a rare competence for one so young.

Shirley's social life was virtually non-existent and she considered phoning Darren McKay. She'd turned down his last dinner invitation what felt like a lifetime ago. After the breakdown of his long-suffering marriage he'd turned up on her doorstep in Caulfield with two of his four children in tow. He'd managed to track down where she lived, but not with whom she was living.

She'd also declined approaches from several other clients and the only new friendship she'd formed was with a neighbour who lived at the other end of Macarthur Place. Heather was a single mum, her ex had weekend custody of their child and she was hot to trot to join Shirley on the nightclub circuit. When her businesses eventually sold, she would take Heather up on her offer to rent her guest quarters.

Shirley had made the decision to sell up in 12 months and was determined to get a good price. Whilst the business was financially solid, it was entirely dependent upon her long-established, intimate associations with the entertainers and clients on her list. The agency's name could stay, but given that she was the management business, its brand would have to change, taking with it a fair slice of goodwill. Potential buyers, probably already in the agency business, were unlikely to be interested in taking over the lease of a small terrace house cum office unless there was added value to justify expanding.

The idea she'd arrived at was so patently obvious she was amazed nobody had thought of it before. A new business' first advertisement generally puts it on the map, she thought to herself, so she kept to a simple format, launched the service and thereafter obeyed the golden rule: 'Don't begin to advertise unless it's your intention to stick to it.'

> *At last!* *A national answering service, exclusively for the entertainment industry.*
> **SHOWBIZ ANSWERING 03/347 9888.**
> *We'll take your calls, keep your diary and pass on bookings and messages to you, or your agent. $2.50 per week includes full answering service and continuous advertising to 2000 prospective clients and bookers as well.*
> **Get listed!** *Phone 03/347 9888 NOW.*

For no particular reason beyond there being a special on airfares at the time, Shirley took a week off at Christmas to go to Bali.

It was a classic Shirley-style journey of alien experiences as enlightening as they were at times harrowing. Given that she'd watched a witch doctor perform an exorcism on a small boy in the tiny Malaysian village of Kota Baharu and worked for the very poor on the sampans in Hong Kong, as well as the very rich in the deep south of America, it was pretty much compulsory that she partake in a Balinese cremation ceremony. She joined a procession from a village at the foot of the Kintamani Mountain to witness the burning of a dead man's body. As the man burned – and, presumably, his soul released – and the acquaintance she'd met at the bus stop continued to throw up, she determined to continue the passionate pursuit of a life worth living for as long as age and health allowed.

Her fifth year in the agency business was rushing by and Shirley's new independence and quiet confidence was subtle but noticeable to those who knew her well. She was interstate when a large envelope from lawyers in London arrived for her at Alan's. He immediately figured that Nick Bond must have met somebody and that his parents had insisted he get a divorce this time before having another shot at *until death do us part*.

Sure enough, as Shirley discovered on her return, five years after their marriage Nick had filed for divorce. The papers were to be signed and returned by 'the wife' within 30 days. If the documents were unclaimed and/or returned to sender, the divorce would go through uncontested in due course and no further communications would be entered into.

She met Agnes Wundell for dinner to discuss the divorce papers and the recent sale of her apartment in Caulfield. She had rented out her first property investment for four years by that stage and had made a substantial profit. Shirley also briefed her lawyer friend on what to include in the contract of sale for her businesses, adding that they would be accompanied by a detailed 'How to' operating manual covering every aspect of both enterprises.

As she watched Agnes drive off afterwards, the signed documents safely on the back seat of her car ready to be officiated and returned to London, she exhaled slowly.

It had been a liberating evening and she was looking forward to being able to let her hair down a bit when the business sold.

She didn't have to wait long. A few weeks after her 'for sale' advertisement appeared in several appropriate publications, and following five enquiries with no follow-ups, a musician in his late 20s and leader of a band Shirley had never heard of responded, inspected the house, operating systems and unexpected Manual that came with the businesses and expressed interest. A week later a price was agreed, a deposit lodged and the date of handover settled six weeks hence.

'How easy was that?' Shirley reflected to Agnes and Heather who'd joined her for dinner when the contract became unconditional.

'When you've got your act together and put in the work, you make your own luck,' Agnes replied and raised her glass.

The farewell party was held on the night of Shirley's 30th birthday, a week prior to her exit from an industry she'd called home for nearly a decade. Predictably, it was an outrageous success.

Upstairs and down, the house overflowed with people both famous and infamous. The dazed new owner, his band members and a few of their wild friends not usually seen at agency parties joined the fracas and the caterers did a sterling job in confined, if not cockamamie, conditions.

Shirley had invited several personal friends and business clients, as well as a couple of constables from the local police station. She'd struck up a friendship with them during the year by plying them with free tickets to shows to ensure they 'handled' complaints from her neighbours about the constant stream of visitors parking across their driveways. She waited for them to accept then informed them their invitation came with a few cryptic catches: they had to come dressed in their uniforms and be willing to fire a gun on Shirley's signal.

Midnight came and the cops took their places on the balcony, their two guns at the ready. At Shirley's instruction about 20 of her clients lined up across the centre strip of Macarthur Place.

As the guns went off, performers of all shapes, sizes and states of inebriation lurched onto the road, eggs balanced precariously on spoons clamped between their teeth. Col Elliott and Susie Coles were in the lead when it suddenly hit Shirley that she'd forgotten in the rush of the day to boil the eggs!

Before her eyes the race became a cacophony of flying eggs and screams of laughter that woke every neighbour in the street. The shortest competitor in the race by a long shot was Beris. Yet despite being overwhelmed the entire length of the race by eggs and much larger bodies tripping and tumbling over her, she struggled across an imaginary finishing line, got to her feet and called up to the balcony that she'd earned the booby prize.

It was impossible to know if anybody had actually won so Shirley awarded her the winner's prize for sportsmanship and survival skills.

Beris laughed and cried and everyone applauded.

At about two in the morning, as Agnes was in a position of power on top of the fridge discussing with the constables the abused legal rights of people arrested and thrown into cop shops overnight, the two constables offered to prove her wrong.

She accepted blindly, metaphorically speaking, and they lifted her off the fridge, handcuffed her, thanked Shirley for a marvellous night before driving off with Agnes in the back of the car, lights and sirens (briefly) wailing.

They delivered her back to 13 MacArthur Place next morning. She was obviously tired but gave the cops a hug and thanked them for their hospitality and professional insights. Over two cups of coffee she told the story of sitting in a cell drinking beer with the cops until 4 am, collapsing into the stretcher-bed and being woken five hours later to a hamburger they'd bought on their way in. She was given a fresh towel for a shower and driven back to Shirley's in a daze whilst the men raved about the best party they'd ever attended.

'I'll never forget it, Shirley!' Agnes exclaimed before, as was her way, promptly redirecting the conversation to an unrelated topic.

'Is the new owner going to make it?'

'Don't know. He's surprisingly shy, might have been nervous? Showbiz parties can't be new to him, but I suspect he was overwhelmed by what he's taking on.'

Agnes rambled for a while about how much she'd enjoyed the party, speculating that with the drug-free environment and all the networking that had gone on during the night, the new owner must surely have realised how much opportunity was available to him.

Her eyes widened momentarily. 'Maybe that's it? No drugs! He chatted amiably enough but didn't quite rise to the occasion…didn't connect.'

Shirley gave one of her hooting laughs, which brought Agnes back down to earth.

'Forget my thoughtless musings,' she changed tack. 'It's not your problem anymore. Let him go, Shirley. *Let It Go.*'

Bull's-eye! Agnes was a judicious lawyer but an exceptionally discerning friend.

Déjà vu…close to home in the underworld

When Johnny Pasolini, one of Shirley's long-standing clients and owner of a large hotel in Carlton learned she'd sold her business, he asked her to drop in for a drink. He had an idea he'd prefer not to discuss on the phone.

By their second beer he'd offered her the job of re-opening and managing his nightclub. It would fit her plans perfectly, providing he accepted her terms: a fixed-term contract from July to December 1978, after which she would be moving on.

Johnny agreed. She gratefully accepted his additional offer of a company car. She'd be boarding with Heather less than a mile away, but the second-hand bomb she'd bought on return from England five years ago was about to detonate.

With the proceeds from the sale of her Caulfield flat, she purchased a beautiful old terrace house in Carlton. It was in need of renovation but as she worked at the nightclub from mid-afternoon until around four in the mornings she'd have a few hours most days to supervise the work. As luck would have it, she had to hire tradesmen to make some changes to Johnny's venue and switched them to her private payroll after opening night.

The hotel itself – we'll call it 'The Evergreen', was a very busy establishment with several bars and kitchens, accommodation and an excellent bottle shop accessible from inside and outside the building. 'Upstairs at The Evergreen' had previously been managed by a well-known Australian entertainer and was losing money at a frightening speed. When the debt hit $150k Johnny had been forced to sack him, close the club's doors and examine his options.

Naming a nightclub that was notoriously patronised by Carlton's underworld figures 'Upstairs' at The Evergreen was incongruous, certainly. However, the name had been coined in reference to the wide, deep, old-world timber stairway that led from the street up to the venue. Queues of party-minded patrons would meet on the stairs and flirt as they made their way up.

The venue was large and well-equipped for its purposes. It boasted a central 100-seater dining room, a stage, a dance floor and a long bar with enough room for 60 standing customers at any one time; and there was an extensive kitchen at the rear.

In the weeks leading up to the opening Shirley worked on bread and butter tasks. She recruited staff, checking on the suitability of their personalities and skills by dropping into pubs where they already worked. She planned and implemented a marketing strategy to publicise the 'Upstairs' resurrection, and oversaw a variety of essential repairs and additions.

With the leeway she'd been given to lift the décor, she opted to install half a dozen classy, large potted plants to enhance the venue's ambiance and create unity across its several cross-functional spaces. At the start of it all she'd called Showbiz Answering to check availabilities of bands, comperes and singers for opening night and revelled in the full circle she'd come.

In the meantime, Johnny had recruited from Italy a highly recommended chef, the first-born son of a friend of a family friend. He was due to arrive in Australia a week prior to opening night. In addition, an excellent young downstairs chef had been promoted to the next floor as his assistant.

Age Four

Throughout the preparations Johnny took Shirley at her word, putting her in the bar downstairs whenever he was short staffed. She needed to learn to make cocktails and pull beer, not only to become competent herself and to be able to teach the staff, but because the tills would be her responsibility. After a while it became the standard for Johnny to call her into work early to help with the lunch crowd and the busy bottle shop. She'd often arrive upstairs with several hours behind her and a 12-hour shift ahead.

It didn't end there, either.

'Shift three' as she called it, involved cooking bacon and eggs in the kitchen as the sun came up to feed Johnny and any of his lingering friends. She has vivid memories from one stormy Sunday morning when one of the aforementioned told her she'd cooked a great breakfast for his brother the previous week. When she enquired why he hadn't returned for a fry-up since, she was informed he'd been shot dead yesterday.

Johnny's demands may have been excessive, but the gratis downstairs' beer pulling, bottle shopping service and breakfast duties weren't just grist to the mill. They were for Shirley an education in themselves. And after her many years of self-employment it was all fun – well, mainly fun! She still took plenty of care, but didn't have the burden of responsibility.

Six days before opening night there was only one outstanding issue that troubled Shirley greatly.

Her hospitality staff were trained and locked in, she'd booked the band and guest artist and the excited assistant chef was busy stocking the kitchen. Johnny had decided to be her 'assistant host' and run the bar during the first week, and had completed selection and negotiations with the bar staff. It was all good. Well, almost.

Shirley, 'the manager', sighed heavily as she considered the last hurdle between her and a seamless opening night, and it was a significant one. *What the hell was she going to wear?*

At that time, evening dresses were the work attire of choice for the few and far between female managers of sophisticated nightclubs. Shirley owned two.

Finally she resolved to take a day off to prepare a suitable wardrobe for the duration of her contract.

When Allan's fiancé Natalie had died she'd left behind a wardrobe full of exquisite clothes. Her mother hadn't wanted them and months after Shirley moved in with Allan he'd asked her to keep anything she wanted and give the rest to charity. Natalie was her height and size so everything would fit, but she hadn't been sure she could wear a dead woman's clothes and live with herself.

'You two were good friends. She'd be happy if you wore them,' Allan had encouraged her at the time, not quite dismissing her reservations.

Shirley duly donated everything to the Salvos, bar Natalie's evening gowns. Somehow she couldn't give them away. She'd carefully packed them in a tea chest and they now sat in Heather's shed, silently willing her to free them from their inappropriately shabby confinement.

She opened the box tentatively, but the first gown was so magnificent that she jumped up, held it close to her body and swirled around like a ballet dancer. Tears streamed down her face as she quickly gathered them all up before she could change her mind, bringing them out into the sun in all their glittering glory.

'Thank you, thank you, Natalie,' she cried as she skipped to the laundry.

Late in the day, just as she was unpegging the hangers from the line, Heather drove into the carport from work.

'Christ!' she cried, admiring the row of beautiful gowns blowing gently in the breeze. 'Wear the gold one for opening night. You'll steal the show!'

The advertising was working, the phones were ringing hot and the restaurant was booked out for most of the first week.

Old faithfuls of Upstairs knew they could turn up anyway and stand around the bar all night so Shirley called security to check sufficient staff were rostered on.

'She'll be apples, dear. We're not amateurs,' the male receptionist dismissed her condescendingly, said 'bye' and hung up.

Gun laws were still as slack as America's and she was well aware that Carlton's reputation as the Italian food centre of Melbourne was eclipsed by its notoriety as the mafia protectorate of Australia. She'd already glimpsed knives and guns on men's belts, and tucked down their trousers while assisting them to remove and hang their jackets. When she'd told Johnny as much, he'd echoed the advice Vickie had given her in Oklahoma.

'Accept it, pay no attention and carry on as usual,' was his reply.

This time, however, there were two inalienable reasons why she would never do that again and they both came down to accountability.

Firstly, during work hours she was responsible for the welfare of her staff; she'd accepted that five years ago when she became an employer.

Secondly, she had a personal responsibility to ensure that men treat her equally on the job; that included business security, integrity, confidentiality and respect.

Running her own business had given her the freedom to be herself, where there was no need to slip into character and act her way through difficult times. But it was becoming clear that this short contract was going to test her every step of the way.

Perhaps, it occurred to her, it would be smart to don a persona again…and stick to the script in order to maintain my ethics and survive?

The opening night was a huge success, although not without incident.

With Johnny occupied elsewhere at the time, Shirley naïvely sat the members of two recognisable – and infamous – families within a few tables of each other, only to quickly discover they were the Hatfields and McCoys of the Carlton underground. The Italian head chef hadn't materialised, apparently delayed in Singapore thanks to a bomb scare, and the food was below par but only the celebrity chef/food critic she'd invited seemed to notice.

Peter Russell-Clarke was an Australian legend known for his television cooking shows, racy, luminous articles and restaurant reviews. His laconic wit and fluent repartee ensured he was frequently a guest on countless local and national talk and variety shows. He and Shirley had met through Allan Eaton, and they had occasionally joined him for dinner at his Carlton home. The food was always outstanding, and his company unfailingly outrageous.

From the start he'd called her 'The beautiful Shirley McLaughlin with the wonderful laugh' and began sending her single, long-stemmed red roses when she moved to Carlton, to no avail (he already had a city girlfriend and a wife installed in his weekend home in the hills).

Although she'd been surprised and pleased when Peter had accepted her invitation to the Upstairs opening night, she fretted for the entirety of the following week about how he would describe the mediocre food.

His full page review began with his intention to write a wickedly biased narrative on account of his undying, unrequited love for the beautiful SMcL etcetera, along with his plan to get down on bended knee before the night was over. 'But the chef from Italy hadn't arrived in time and the food was frankly awful,' he wrote before describing it in detail. Thankfully he finally divulged that the chef had now arrived and a late licence was imminent so 'soon you'll be able to dine, booze and thump about Upstairs until three o'clock in the morning.'

'And how did I fare with Shirley?' he concluded. 'No good. She was still laughing when I left.'

The following day, Diego, the missing chef, staggered into the downstairs bar with two enormous suitcases and an assortment of over-sized hand luggage. The men at the bar promptly stepped back, not only to give him room.

He may have been visibly jet-lagged and infused with the reek of cigarettes and the stale funk of long-haul air travel, but these factors in no way detracted from his swarthy good looks.

It wasn't his animal magnetism alone that prompted everyone to quickly forgive and forget Diego's late arrival. His work ethic and chef skills exceeded their expectations and his unassuming personality and come-to-bed eyes triggered giggles and blushes from the hotel's female customers and staff. This may have been the reason for a sudden increase in needless questions about the menu emanating from the dining room during service, but the attention didn't move this Latin baby boomer: he'd already set his sights on Shirley.

It took a couple of weeks for the hotel's long-term and infamous customers to revert to form.

One night an argument between two brothers at a table quickly developed into fisticuffs. When Shirley finally peeked out over the bar, behind which she and the staff were crouched, she saw one brother spread-eagled in the middle of the dance floor. The other had picked up one of her ambience-inducing pot plants and was swinging it around his brawny body. He then hurled it across the dining room.

Fortunately, all the huge botanical projectile took out was an empty chair in the corner, but its journey there made a sight for sore eyes. Soil from the pot exploded into a thousand flying particles, whilst broken branches swiped glasses off tables, indiscriminately slapping the shocked faces of some customers and devastating the hairdos of others. Tears sprung from the eyes of patrons seated under the plant's flight path, but not because of the bone-crunching violence they'd just witnessed. Showered with debris and dirt, some customers were momentarily blinded, but most were left blinking frantically at each other in an attempt to rid their eyes of grit.

After the brothers had been escorted out by security, it became apparent that 95 per cent of their diners felt that the free grog Johnny offered, along with a performance by a guest artist, were sufficient recompense.

As she watched them settle back to enjoy the rest of the evening, Shirley thought back to her time in OKC. How many times had she seen staff at restaurants owned by the Wallingtons carry on regardless after a colleague had 'disappeared' mid-shift, never to be seen again. It surprised Shirley that Aussies were just as prepared to turn a blind eye when it suited them.

Victoria's Deputy Police Commissioner, Bill, stopped by The Evergreen later the following night. As was his habit, he came straight upstairs.

Quietly spoken and intelligent, Bill had a well-developed sense of humour and had taken to dropping by to chat to Shirley over a drink or two. Though always framed as a social interaction, their one-on-ones were primarily a laboursaving initiative – a cost-effective way for the cops to keep track of the underbelly of Carlton. More than once there'd been an interrogatory air to Bill's side of the conversation: Who's in town? Who isn't? Which families are currently friends, or enemies?

Shirley ordered their standard fare, a weak gin and tonic with lots of ice for her and a neat single malt Scotch for Bill. He would down three that night. He was on an important mission.

Earlier in the day two of the local constabulary had dropped by the hotel to issue Johnny an official warning. They'd received several complaints about the events of the previous night and had no choice but to follow up. Bill didn't mince words.

'They don't want to lose this meeting place any more than we want them to and they know that,' he told Shirley. 'The Evergreen is their second home. I'm not sure if they've got anything on Johnny – he's certainly clean as far as we're concerned – but along with the way he caters to them, I've no doubt it suits them well.'

'To what degree of danger am I, my staff and patrons exposed to when two members from one family can completely lose it in a place they call home?' she pressed.

He replied matter-of-factly that Johnny had broken the rules appointing a woman to manage Upstairs and it was important she join him for a drink whenever he turned up. These guys kept their women folk at home and would never accept her management authority.

'Of course they don't want trouble with their male, or female hosts,' he smiled. 'But this can change in an instant. Stay sharp!' he muttered as an afterthought.

One Saturday, Shirley had just started to seat customers for lunch downstairs when who should walk in the door but Dr Jack Cavander!

The fact that he was accompanied by a woman didn't stop him from showing his joy at seeing his dentally challenged London flame again.

Shirley briefly explained her tragic homecoming, and that she'd somehow lost his and his parents' contacts in the trauma of it all. She hadn't had a chance to apologise or thank him when Johnny called her to the bar. She quickly sat the couple down and told Jack that lunch was on her.

An hour or so later she was called to the bottle shop and Jack grabbed the opportunity to follow her with a business card in his hand.

'Call me,' he implored, placing his card on the side of the till.

The shop was busy and it was at least 10 minutes before she was able to pause to pick up the card. But it wasn't there, wasn't on the floor, wasn't in the till, wasn't in the bin. The other staff on the shift hadn't seen it, but one suggested she ask Johnny.

'I think you were in the fridge when he dropped in briefly...'

'...*having observed the initial meeting and the young man following me into the shop,*' she concluded silently.

She'd been aware for some time that Johnny fancied her. Even if she told him she had no romantic interest in Cavander, there was no way of getting that card back without accusing him of rather creepy and certainly childish sabotage. That would lead nowhere and likely set her up for a nasty exit. Her contract would conclude in three weeks.

Jack had told her he was working 'locally'. It took Shirley a week to ring every dental surgery in close proximity before she expanded the search to the suburbs.

Perhaps he'd said 'Oakleigh' not 'locally,' she considered, her hopes rising.

When she'd exhausted that line of enquiry without success Shirley despaired. Though Jack now knew why she hadn't contacted him or his parents when she'd first returned home, this time there was no way he'd interpret her silence as anything other than rejection. There'd never be another chance like this.

Age Four

It was a cruel blow – one she knew she'd never quite get over.

The second last Saturday night of her contract would surpass every example of criminal-induced mayhem she'd witnessed during her tenure at the Evergreen. Just after 10pm the sound of gunfire from the stairway reverberated through the venue. Panicked patrons both Upstairs and down shrieked and ran for cover, a number suffering asthma and panic attacks in the process.

Within minutes the cops from the local station arrived. An ambulance followed almost immediately, flanked by six or so police cars and paddy wagons. By that time the bodies of two men lay splayed and lifeless halfway up the stairs, their blood spattered everywhere. The two victims were taken to hospital and the perpetrators who'd inflicted the wounds were handcuffed and taken away with an escort of uniformed men.

One of the medics stayed behind to attend to several customers' minor distresses and a couple of police officers remained to support the Evergreen security personnel as much as the customers. The show Upstairs went ahead as planned and downstairs rocked with almost the same intensity.

There was no doubt about Johnny. He sure had a way about him.

'Meeting you has been invaluable, Bill,' she said to her friendly deputy commissioner, not knowing then how prophetic that comment would prove to be in the not too distant future.

When Shirley's contract concluded, Christmas had come and Upstairs at The Evergreen was thriving, its loyal following remaining intact despite the loss of an imperious few regulars who were no longer of this world.

She gave Johnny back the company car. It was the right thing to do. She'd been well paid, trusted and always treated with respect. He owed her nothing. She put the rest of it all 'up' rather than 'down' to experience.

If anyone it was she who owed Johnny. His offer of a job had been the catalyst for Shirley experiencing the most astonishing, bizarrely beneficial six months of her life to that point.

Quoting a commissioner of a different kind, the old general factotum at Melbourne's ABC radio studios who'd seen it all, literally and metaphorically speaking: 'If I ever get over this, I'll never have another!'

Burying icons, placing executives, dismissing lovers

Her first week back in the real world saw Shirley negotiating a second mortgage with the bank (the renovations running to form at 30 per cent more than quoted), throwing a dinner party, offloading heaps of 'stuff' at a garage sale and joining the local library. She spent hours poring over the news that she'd missed during the last 12 months.

That she'd opted to take the next month off so she could 'smell the roses' was ironic, as always. Death, in its many forms, was a compelling page turner.

Australian actor Peter Finch had died at the age of 60. Born in England, he'd come to Australia aged 10 and achieved a string of stage and screen successes. Margery and Alan had taken Bev and Shirley to see *A Town Like Alice* and Shirley had never forgotten it. Not long after his death, then unknown Australian writer Colleen McCullough's *The Thorn Birds* was sold at auction in the States for an unprecedented $1.7 million and McCullough said Australians would hate it because she'd written it for Americans.

Why on earth would a woman on the brink of international success declare herself dead in her own country? Shirley wondered aloud, turning the page and shaking her head in disbelief.

She resumed reading and discovered that in June 1977, three of Australia's protestant denominations - Methodist, Congregationalist and Presbyterian – had joined to form the Uniting Church. She read that the historic joining of the protestant family was achieved after more than 70 years of planning, the mean life expectancy of Australians at the time.

Suddenly she wished she was at a dinner party with friends rather than in a library where silence reigns. She wanted to shout a rhetorical question, very loudly. How could any God wait for hundreds of generations of human beings to die before any of his supposed family decided to act like one, or perhaps two as in Protestants and Catholics in the Christian religion?

Indulging herself a bit further with the dinner party idea, she realised that if she was the host of the event, she'd have to moderate the arguments or face losing friends. For instance, would Almighty God who created men in His image be humbled that His devotees in colonial Sydney had finally negotiated their differences?

Her outrage was interrupted by a headline proclaiming the death of Elvis Presley. How on earth had she missed that? She'd been too busy to know, let alone mourn his loss. The undisputed King of Rock 'n Roll had amassed $1,000 million entertaining the world and had accidentally killed himself, aged 42! She remembered how she'd fallen in love with him, aged about 10, and how she'd asked her mother why he was called 'Elvis the Pelvis'. For the umpteenth time she felt regret that she'd missed him by one day in Vegas when working for the Wallington Bros.

Muhammad Ali, previously Cassius Clay was still winning titles around the world. He'd refused to go to the Vietnam War, his steadfast commitment stirring America's rumbling discontent.

'War is wrong,' he said. 'I will not fight and kill. Bring on the firing squad! I'm ready to die!'

In early May 1978, the Queen of England announced that her sister Princess Margaret's marriage to the Earl of Snowdon was over, hastening to add it would not affect her official position and she would continue her public engagements.

A few days later Ma'am sent a poignant public message of condolence to Dame Pattie Menzies and the people of Australia. Pattie's husband, Sir Robert Menzies, Australia's longest-serving prime minister and founder of the Liberal Party had died in Melbourne, aged 83. He had been the leader who enabled the great and pre boomer generations to bring up their baby boomers in a secure, multi-cultural environment and rapidly expanding economy.

Australia's own King of Rock, Johnny O'Keefe had lived one year longer than his American hero. 'The Wild One' had died at age 43 following a massive heart attack. He'd formed Australia's group, Johnnie and the Deejays, and compered the first national rock television show in Australia on the ABC's *Six O'clock Rock*.

Shirley had been a fan since she'd worked at the ABC, aged 16. In her 20s she'd booked him regularly and their last meeting had taken place a few weeks before she sold her business.

It seemed to her a cruel death and brought her full circle from the loss of so many of her own family to the sheer luck that she was alive and well and living at a time and place in history where she could do anything she wanted, *as long as you want it badly enough, darling.*

Aldo Moro, who served five times as Italian prime minister, was shot dead by his Red Brigade captors. A bomb exploded killing two men at the Hilton Hotel in Sydney where Prime Minister Malcolm Fraser and leaders of 10 other countries were attending a Commonwealth Heads of Government Meeting. Pope John Paul was crowned in Vatican City and 33 days later died of a heart attack. The first female prime minister of Israel, Golda Meir, described as a 'stalwart lioness' and one of the great women of the Jewish world, died at the age of 80. An American man charged in a court in Oregon for raping his own wife admitted he'd beaten her, but the sex had been voluntary. Following a three-hour deliberation, the jury found him not guilty.

'Must be God at work again,' Shirley snorted, eliciting frowns from others who'd joined her in the reading room.

So this news is what happens when one views the world through dark coloured glasses at night! she continued, silently. *What about the birth of the first test-tube baby in a hospital in Manchester, lady? Or the Australian Government giving title to 95,000 square kilometres of land to two Northern Territory Aboriginal tribes?*

The mourning was over. So too was showbiz for her, but she needed to make a living. All she had to do now was find something she really wanted to do.

Chandler and McLeod Management Consultants (C&M) were a national, Melbourne-based company specialising in human resources. They offered the full suite of services from executive and office staff recruitment, psychological testing and head hunting to management consulting. Until the early '80s they had been unrivalled industry leaders in Australia for many years. When the Recession hit their clients' shrinking staff requirements forced them to dramatically reduce their own workforce in order to stay afloat.

C&M's recruitment modus operandi put every applicant to the test, resulting in safer decisions by employers and employees alike. Alf Chandler and Doug McLeod were the first students to graduate with Psychology degrees at Melbourne University prior to the end of the WW2, Alf had recently retired and handed the business over to his son, Kevin, whilst Doug continued to co-manage the company until his retirement.

Following a successful first interview with the manager of Staff Services, Shirley met with Kevin Chandler at head office in Kew.

'Shirley of The Early Birds!' he greeted her warmly as if they were old friends. Kevin's children were of similar age to her nephews and had loved her shows. He went on to explain that feedback from her first interview had made

him think she might be the ideal candidate to launch a new C&M executive placement service.

Until the 1960s employers had tended to hire their own staff but as companies grew and the founding of consulting firms such as C&M arrived on the scene, retaining the services of an independent recruiter became popular.

Kevin's plan for a new division was still in its infancy but basically what he was offering was a business development gig in executive recruitment with an innovative company who underpinned their approach with psych testing. The main gist was that she had to build relationships with client companies and secure the talent to fill their vacancies.

'Sort of mini-head-hunting, isn't it?' she asked instantly, seeing the correlation between this opportunity and her former career.

'At least I come with an extensive client base!'

First things first, Kevin said. 'It is our practice to give you a psychology test in order to get an in-depth knowledge of your IQ, aptitudes and temperament.' Four or five hours later, after she'd answered hundreds of questions in what felt like an exam room environment, they reconvened in his office where he gave her a summary of the results.

> Ms McLaughlin is in the upper quartile for managers and professional people, with strong control of her temperament, i.e. consistency of behaviour. She is able to take a highly objective and analytical approach toward other people, in consequence, is rarely personally affected by criticism or unfair remarks.
>
> A primary characteristic is that she carries the respect of others and is highly effective in picking up ingenious ideas and novel strategies and making them work; her ideas may sometimes be radical and practical constraints may be overlooked.
>
> A typical extrovert, she is socially confident, full of fun, likely to be the centre of attention whilst simultaneously being especially considerate and caring of others. However, whilst she doggedly finishes everything she starts, she bores easily and her need for people is not particularly high. She often prefers her own company.
>
> She is creative, adaptable and resourceful. She is no poker face, but is not prone to outbursts either. Her depressive is low and her manic only average, she doesn't always play to win but is by no means ready to compromise either.
>
> Ms McLaughlin's ambition is directed towards herself rather than others and she tends to make decisions very quickly. She's not particularly critical and her optimistic outlook lets her make these decisions a little too hastily.

She listened as he read her profile out loud, wondering how one test could possibly have revealed so much about her.

Finally, Kevin summarised the findings. 'You're a sensitive, negotiative leader with insight into what makes people tick. You should fit in well.'

'I've being selling flesh-to-flesh for most of my working life but you've just given me serious insight into how much I've yet to learn. I'm excited!' she gushed the moment he stopped talking.

'Good…err excellent…forgive my semantics but I'd say we refer *people-to-people*, Shirley. We don't sell flesh-to-flesh.'

Oops, she thought, chalking that up as Lesson No. 1. The salary offered was ridiculous, about 200 per cent less than she'd been making for years and it only took two weeks on deck for her to learn she was being paid about 60 per cent less than the youngest male consultant, who also had his own secretary.

Never mind, she told herself resolutely, determined to focus instead on the many benefits of the job: it was a new challenge in a professional environment, there was ongoing training, C&M was an innovative company and for the first time in a very long time she'd be working relatively normal hours.

She'd make her mark first and demand a fair deal then.

During weekly drinks in the boardroom on Friday nights a couple of months later, she asked a friendly colleague a burning question.

'I've heard some of the guys musing about why Kevin employed me when it's apparently clear that I don't have the "two Ds". What on earth are the two Ds, Gary?'

'You don't have a Dick. And you don't have a Degree,' he replied. 'Happy now?'

It had just meant to be a part-time gig to supplement her meagre C&M income. She would work there three nights a week from 6.00 to 10.30, and take an occasional Saturday shift when she could.

On her second night behind the bar in the North Melbourne pub, Shirley reconnected with an acquaintance from her past who would be the next man to turn her world topsy-turvy.

She'd met Patrick at Allan Eaton Studios. He was a leviathan Melbourne bookmaker and a very handy pianist/singer and had dropped in to confirm he could play Friday nights for the next month. Shirley poured him a beer on the house at the boss' directive and he asked her to dinner the following night.

Patrick, yet another pre boomer was at least 10 years her senior. She didn't remember much about him from the Allan Eaton days except that they'd shared an interest in horses…of the speculative kind. He'd offered her a job pencilling for him in towns close to her heart like Ballarat, Yarrawonga and Warracknabeal, and had also said he'd teach her how to bet and when to take a trifecta with a win almost guaranteed. (She must have been living with Allan at the time to pass up an offer like that!)

The position was still open due to the difficulties of finding a scrupulous, nippy bookkeeper for casual, out-of-town hours. It would sure beat pulling beer in a pub where the great majority of customers seemed to be pre boomer married men on-the-make. No point in counting your chickens before they hatch, though. Just accept the invitation. You have to eat and it might lead to a trifecta.

Patrick became her part-time, live-in lover and Shirley learned to pencil, bet and win on-the-nose, plus quinella and trifecta in no time at all.

Patrick was a gentleman of the old school with a quick wit and a sociable, generous nature that led to romantic and quirky dinners with colleagues and friends 'in the business' who never quite turned out to be who they portended to be. For Shirley there was no stress, lots of fun and a free education in gambling. As one example, on the first Tuesday in November for the next 13 years she managed to place a bet 'on-the-nose' of the winner of the Melbourne Cup. It had to be an amateur gambler's world first and worthy of a Guinness record or some such accolade, but she consoled herself each year that it was a fair return on what it cost her to aid and abet Patrick for a mere 13 months.

By the time Patrick had declared his love for Shirley and his willingness to commit to their relationship, he was 'staying over' most nights of the week. During said declaration, he had also confided that he was still technically married and had an 11 year-old son.

They both left around eight in the mornings, but Shirley always arrived home first. One night as she opened the front door she instinctively sensed there was something awry, but she couldn't pinpoint it. The following night she noticed the quilt on the double bed was rumpled. She hadn't left it like that, and Patrick had left before her.

By the end of the week she was convinced there was somebody living in her house during the daytimes. The kitchen was disturbed; fresh food had been eaten and dishes stacked in wrong places in the dishwasher. So who was sleeping in her bed, eating her food and bringing in the mail and placing it on the kitchen bar every other day?

She'd begun to wonder if she was losing her mind when the plumber phoned to apologise for disturbing her boyfriend in the bedroom! He'd let himself in via the hidden key to renew a couple of taps and sure enough, when she got home the bed linen was pulled back, her pillow indented and when she reached for a brandy the bottle was empty.

Patrick was in Sydney, flew home immediately and spent a week doing his paperwork and business calls behind closed blinds in the lounge room until he caught the bastard, which he duly did. Well, in a manner of speaking. He'd managed to punch him in the face as he was quietly letting himself in via the French doors, but the squatter had broken loose and run for his life. In earnest pursuit Patrick had chased him down the back lane and onto the main road before losing him.

Shirley knew by then that bookies tell lies; big ones, little ones and what some folk call 'porkies'. Telling anything but the truth was a game in itself, so naturally she couldn't be sure the intruder story happened exactly as it was told to her, but the locksmith changed the locks and the uninvited house-sitter was never seen again.

During 1979 Patrick accepted a gig from a Melbourne radio station to fly to Auckland, New Zealand to call and commentate at the races during the annual Inter-Dominion carnival. When Shirley received a magnificent bouquet of two dozen red roses a week after he'd gone she felt an all too familiar sinking of her heart.

A rose, by any other name… but 24 long-stemmed red ones! *No way*, she thought as the realisation set in. It was likely guilt that had prompted the effusive gesture, not the love it had been intended to convey.

Not sure what else she could do, she phoned his hotel. The receptionist advised that he'd checked out but would be back on Saturday.

'Oh yes, of course!' Shirley surprised herself with her immediate and devious rejoinder. 'I'm so cross with myself. I've lost the name of the other hotel. Do you happen to have it?'

'Sorry I can't help you,' the receptionist replied. 'He did tell me he was taking a few days off in Fiji but didn't mention where he was staying.'

It's moments like this when it's not what you know, but who.

Bill, her friend from The Evergreen, was still the state's second top cop. When he returned her call two days later, he gave her a quick precis about confidentiality and not revealing sources before confirming what she'd already come to suspect. The wife of her 'friend' had applied for a passport two months ago and was currently holidaying at a 'particular' hotel in Fiji.

Shirley picked Patrick up from the airport a week later and told him she'd booked a room at the airport hotel. She reasoned that he'd had two hectic weeks, and that she had too, and they had lots to catch up on.

Despite her acting ability, she'd never been good at hiding her emotions so he very quickly deduced that there was something wrong.

He opened his suitcase in the bedroom and gave her a couple of trite gifts clearly purchased at the last minute, all the while chatting away about New Zealand and the people he'd met and how much he'd missed her. As his awkwardness increased, she felt sorry for him and discursively cut to the chase. Had he received her thanks for the roses when he got back from Fiji to his hotel in Auckland?

His face turned grey and he fumbled in his briefcase for his cigarettes.

'I sent them…because…' he faltered, her knowledge of his deceit hitting home. 'I…my wife knew it was over but she deserved a holiday so I decided to…'

'…join her for a few days for old times' sake,' Shirley quietly concluded.

'No!' he snapped. 'To ask her for a divorce! I should have told you in the first place. Please understand…and forgive me?' he begged. 'Let's go home. I love you!'

Shirley took a deep breath and handed him the keys to his Mercedes.

'I've packed your clothes in the boot. Get some sleep and take a cab in the morning to pick up your car. It's parked outside the house.'

'I'm sorry too,' she mouthed as she closed the door behind her in a labyrinth of tears.

It had been a long time since she'd had so much fun with a man as she'd had with Patrick. He had treated her like a princess, was a great lover and friend, and had taught her a good deal about gambling and music. She felt empty and lost and was unable to bear the thought of staying in the house in Carlton. It was time to sell up and move on.

At C&M she was flourishing, just as Kevin Chandler had predicted; she was in the right job to maximise her strengths. A born finisher, she set plans and followed through, re-wrote everything from advertisements to job descriptions and resume's to increase the chances of success for everyone and never let an opportunity pass to open another door and make another match.

Her house in Carlton sold quickly, she paid out the two mortgages and purchased outright a freestanding house in the suburb of Hawthorn. During the school holidays she employed Steven and Dale for their first work experience, during which time they cleaned gutters, painted walls, tidied up the garage and gardens, and learned to drink beer and puff a cigarette. Bev sighed a lot but reminded herself and the boys that their Aunty Mame was a one-off, and that laughter was the best medicine.

Shirley hunkered down to focus on her career, but after suffering more than a decade of symptoms undoubtedly caused by the inexperienced intern at the Frankston Hospital, she reluctantly accepted that a hysterectomy was her only solution.

She remained in hospital for seven days because of complications, but there were compensations too. Girlfriends brought her snacks, beer (kept in the blood fridge by empathetic nurses) and cigarettes. Kevin and her colleagues from work visited regularly and she stayed with Bev for a few days after being discharged.

Five weeks later she was back at the coalface. It may have been a bit too soon, but Kevin had given her six weeks leave on full pay and she was very grateful.

Patrick renewed his pursuit a few months later.

The marriage was definitely finished and he was doing a deal to take over a tourist resort in far north Queensland. He begged her to reconsider, join him and begin a new life together. She kept him at bay, but had not given him an outright 'No'. He figured she was waiting to see if 'the deal' was a bookie's wager, or the real thing.

The inscrutable prerequisite was that he couldn't make the deal without Shirley to share the job of running the resort. He would have to commute from Queensland to Victoria every week until he was financially stable enough to apply for a Bookmaker's Licence in Queensland.

Age Four

Shirley was beginning to waver and wrote herself a timely reminder of her experience of bookmakers.

> *Don't forget what you learned at The Flower Drum restaurant in China Town. Frequented by late diners who finished work when most people had long finished dinner, you were privy to bookies telling fellow bookies everything but the truth.*
>
> *They always discussed the evenings meeting's winners and losers as they related to the bottom line, but you knew the truth – and not just from pencilling.*
>
> *Some evenings you'd hide $50 or $60k in the fridge and/or washing machine or dryer for safe keeping until morning. Other nights there wasn't enough cash in the kitty to pay the 2 per cent turnover tax. It was a **great**, or **better than evens**, or **lousy bloody** night, regardless of whether the favourites or long-shots were first over the line.*
>
> *They had to know that they lied to one another, so why do they do it? Is there such a thing as an honest bookie?*

With Hawthorn quite close to work and Shirley with more leisure time than she'd ever had before, she decided to work on improving her game of tennis.

She was looking for a fourth player to set up a weekly commitment when Diane Tiffin presented.

Di was born six weeks later than Shirley, an English woman who'd been working for a UK Ambassador in Brazil when an opportunity arose in Canberra to work for one of Australia's Federal politicians. When he was voted out and Di had fallen in love with Australia, Kevin snapped her up as his private secretary and Di was delighted to be invited to become a member of a regular, or more precisely inimitable doubles quartet!

Robyn Irvine, also born in the late 1940s and, like Shirley, already with a couple of marriages behind her, was a consultant in C&M's Staff Services division and they quickly discovered they had much more in common than birth dates and poor choices of men.

Beris Underhill (the pre boomer of the team) and Di Tiffin discovered they shared more than their current, much younger lovers and the fact that they'd never married and had no plans to do so.

Di, Robyn and Beris's loyalty, stamina and passion for life matched Shirley's and it was the beginning of life-long, joint and individual friendships. They laughed and cried together and each went out of their ways to share the good and bad times on an equal, uncritical basis, within Australia and wherever any one of them was circumnavigating the globe.

Beris continued her highly successful Frog Promotions agency, becoming the long-term lover of the charming, entrepreneurial Frank, son of Lord Baden-Powell who had started the worldwide Boy Scout movement in the early 1900s. She eventually sold up and retired alone, with son Jason and his wife Jacquie close by.

Robyn married again, this time to an American. She left C&M five years after they'd met, during which time Shirley twice stepped into her shoes. Baby daughter Bobbie was nine months old when Rob decided she'd had enough, returned home and eventually redirected her future by becoming a Chaplain and manager of a major charitable organisation.

Di went on to become manager of the exclusive women's Alexandria Club in Melbourne, followed by tour guiding in Australia and Europe which she continues to this day.

'Trusty friendships come first,' Alan used to say. 'You're looking for love, Shirley, but you won't find it without friendship first. Make the most of everything!'

The evening Patrick arrived on her doorstep at Hawthorn, 'the moon was a ghostly galleon, tossed upon cloudy seas.'

With all the chutzpah of a burgeoning bookmaking business boss he made her a proposition that, ultimately, she wouldn't refuse.

She resigned from C&M, installed tenants in her house and four weeks later she and Patrick moved to North Queensland.

Cardwell By-the-Sea, midway between Townsville and Cairns, was a multi-faceted tourist business with a caravan park and cabins, petrol station, laundromat and café. The reunited couple lived in one of the cabins and soon discovered that it was a seriously big task for two sets of hands to keep the business alive.

Shirley drove Patrick to Townsville or Cairns every week to catch a flight to Melbourne, and picked him up a few days later.

With flat feet, scorching days and only one part-time assistant, it wasn't exactly what Shirley was expecting. But she was busy and that helped.

Age Four

Most of all she enjoyed feeding the truckies to help them on their way. Cooking hamburgers at eight in the morning or eight at night was unpredictably rewarding. The men were grateful, down to earth, honest and funny.

The laundromat was a nightmare. Customers lacked basic standards of cleanliness and manners. The petrol station where service was always given was a constant battle to ensure the customers paid, and the guests in the cabins reduced the cleaning ladies to tears several days a week.

Three months later Patrick's father died unexpectedly whilst he was in Melbourne so he called Shirley to drive the Mercedes home. Unbeknownst to her at the time, he'd already decided to bail out of the contract in Queensland.

It took her three days to drive from Cardwell to Melbourne, inclusive of a terrifying 30 minutes caught between two sadistic truck drivers, ahead and behind her. The truckies had made her life fun in Cardwell and now seemed bent on killing her. Eventually they drove her off the highway and into a ditch as they approached a country town. Visibly shaken, she checked into the first motel she came to and the receptionist alerted the police.

She met Patrick at a North Melbourne hotel in which he had a financial interest, and had booked a room for a couple of weeks – just for her! He was going alone to his father's funeral in Ballarat, of all country towns he could have lived and died in, and she was predestined to stay in North Melbourne without a car until he returned.

Her last hour in North Melbourne was spent in a phone booth outside the pub, largely motivated by her first call to Beris.

'He hasn't embraced me in his loss, B,' she said. 'His wife and son will be there, along with many friends I know.'

Beris's reply was philosophical. 'He'll always go a'roving and you'll never be sure where he is. He might bury his dad but don't bet on him burying his wife anytime soon. Scratch him and get on with your life.'

Shirley unexpectedly smiled and recited the first verse of a favourite Kenny Rogers' song to B. *'You've got to know when to hold 'em, know when to fold 'em. Know when to walk away, know when to run…'*

Her second call was to her property manager to check on the tenants. They were leaving but the Hawthorn Football Club, one of the top AFL teams had applied to rent her house on behalf of an up and coming star relocating from Perth.

Her third call was to her father Alan. She needed a bed again.

The fourth was to Kevin Chandler. She'd sold her car before she left town so after she hung up she took a bus to Kew to meet him.

The day Shirley left C&M, Kevin had given her a reference he'd written two days after taking her and Patrick to a thank-you dinner.

> 25 January 1980
>
> TO WHOM IT MAY CONCERN
>
> It is with great pleasure that I take this opportunity to comment on the performance of Shirley McLaughlin. Shirley was employed by Chandler & Macleod Consultants Pty Ltd to establish a new recruiting activity in the middle level executive area. Testimony to her skills in the development of this area was the fact that in the six months prior to her leaving, the Division returned 40% net profit on revenue.
>
> I do not believe that without Shirley's enthusiasm and dynamic attitude towards the job, this would have been possible.
>
> Shirley has high levels of skill in any persuasive activity. Her job function with us lead her into contact with many senior executives, all of whom spoke highly of her and communicated their thoughts directly to me.
>
> We viewed Shirley's leaving with disappointment and would re-employ her in the future. As testimony to my belief in her ability, we would create a job for her were another not available.
>
> (Signed) Kevin Chandler

'Yes, I'm a gambler with my life, Kevin, and make decisions too quickly!' she laughed when they'd settled in his office. 'All I know is that I have to move a long way from Melbourne to cut loose from Patrick. How far can you send me?'

The Western Australian capital Perth would be the setting for the next two years in Shirley's playbook of life.

Age Four

She negotiated a self-employed contract with C&M this time, purchased a new car, drove to Adelaide and took the train to Perth.

During the two-hour stopover in Kalgoorlie she walked into a pub in the main street and met the man who owned it, and who was about to board the same train to Perth. He had two horses running on Saturday. We'll call him Christopher.

They played Black Jack and had dinner together in the dining car before adjourning to their cabins. Christopher proved to be an intelligent, single, pre boomer gentleman with a ready smile and a gentle personality. When they parted at the Perth railway station, he invited her to join him at the races the following day.

Naturally Robyn was waiting for her. She'd transferred a few months earlier to manage the Staff Services division and was overjoyed that Shirley had left Patrick and come to Perth.

'You'll be Upstairs again!' she hugged her, 'and we'll be playing tennis when we're not playing up, lady! There's an energy here that I haven't experienced before,' she rushed on. 'I put it down to Perth's transient population… countless newcomers from all corners of the globe walking St Georges Terrace in the hope of finding their nirvana. Maybe we'll find ours!'

The mining boom hadn't quite happened. The locals referred to it as 'the boom you have when you're not having one' but there was plenty of work all over the state and Shirley's placement service grew accordingly. Clients in the Eastern states recruited from the West too, which added a social dimension when they flew over to interview her selected short lists.

Her new boss, Gary, the consultant who'd nonchalantly disclosed the 'two Ds' she didn't have, was now State Manager for executive recruitment. He set her up in her office, introduced her to the staff and several clients and left her to run her own show.

Unsurprisingly, pre boomer men from all walks of life kept coming, some adding more than they detracted.

Christopher became a genuine friend and semi-regular lover. He had some delicate health problems that no doubt contributed to his dependence on alcohol, but he was a placid, caring soul with a generous disposition. Nothing was too much trouble when Shirley was available to visit Kalgoorlie, including private plane pickups and returns.

She and Robyn were his guests for one wild weekend, primarily to attend the annual Kalgoorlie Cup race meeting, a very dressy affair matching Flemington's Melbourne Cup. There was a lot of new money in 'Kal' by 1980 and with the influx of tourists, plus many mines re-opened and large companies drilling 24/7 like the old days, the Tote alone took $76,000 on the Cup that day, in a town with a resident population of 20,000.

A major client at Alcoa's Head Office also befriended Shirley and nearly killed them both one night driving home from a party. He couldn't remember what happened later but he'd side-swiped a truck coming the other way and miraculously both drivers kept driving.

Yet another pre boomer from C&M, Sydney's General Manager of executive recruitment and psych testing (we'll call him Barry Ewan) visited Perth semi-regularly and was gently edging towards a more intimate relationship. He'd used the word 'Sympatico' when describing their association, bringing flashbacks of Mick Wallington to mind.

At least she wasn't alone in being befuddled at why pre boomer blokes continued to take up entirely too much space in her life. They tended to swarm like flies around Robyn too.

'Perhaps it's just our sex appeal and unlikelihood of falling pregnant?' her friend suggested dryly.

Shirley obviously decided to put her thoughts on paper.

> <u>What are the common characteristics of pre boomer men?</u>
> They're mainly married, successful in their careers, most have children and are not exactly living lives of quiet desperation.
> They've got large egos and probably don't get accolades at home anymore.
> They're bored with their marriages.
> Their children are closer emotionally to their mothers due to the lack of time their fathers spend with them.
> Sometimes they actually fall in love and decide to make the break, but their dependence on lies usually destroys them.
>
> <u>What do they see in us baby boomer women?</u>
> We're single and come without baggage.
> We are successful, attractive women who have a driving force to achieve.

Age Four

This makes us exciting yet paradoxically safe. There's no risk of us getting pregnant, little chance of mixing in their social circles, and it'll never be likely that we'll bump into 'the wife' whilst picking up kids or shopping at the supermarket.
We're fun, we're a challenge, we provide regular sex and we are low maintenance. Just dinners, the occasional short holiday, and dozens of bloody roses.

<u>Why do we persist with them?</u>
We're dying to fall in love with a man who adores us.
We can choose vocations rather than childbearing these days but we yearn for both.
Our best friends are single and still looking for 'The One'...
We've always overwhelmed men of our own age and those of us who married baby boomers did so because we chased them. And they still leave us alone, unless they're married.
Pre boomers are all grown up and searching for their youth again, and
We've lowered our standards to suit the company we keep because that's about all there is. They can afford us, entertain us, lie to us and cheat on us, and we kid ourselves that it's better than nothing.

For the first six months in Perth Shirley lived in a rented apartment on the ocean front. By the time the lease was up she'd purchased a small 'fixer-upper' house in the riverside suburb of Applecross. Her renovations took six months to complete, due entirely to her business and social commitments. Her cynicism of men was all but forgotten; she had a life now and it showed.

During her last week of holidays she called Fred, a friendly and conscientious plumber she'd contracted to work on the upgrade, if he could recommend an electrician. She needed some new lights installed.

Fred lined up a sparky who arrived promptly that afternoon. He'd been in her home an hour when he called her into the bedroom for advice about the wall lights above the bed. As she entered the room he threw her onto the bed, whacked her across the face and into a state of shock. In her daze, a glance up at the luminous hands of the wall clock convinced Shirley it was three in the morning. He'd also closed the curtains, which had darkened the room, and she remembered thinking for a moment…or perhaps an hour … that the neighbours would be asleep and wouldn't hear her scream. And that she couldn't scream anyway because her bleeding mouth wouldn't work. She didn't stand a chance.

When she regained consciousness she could still feel his hands and body on her, but after a moment or two she deduced he was gone. She recalled kicking him but otherwise had no recollection of how she'd survived the attack until another hour had passed. She only knew she was alone, half naked and freezing, despite the hot day. The power was off – and she had not been raped.

She threw everything she'd been wearing onto the floor of the shower and scrubbed every inch of her body under the running hot water for a long time. When she was dry, she put on a dressing gown, poured herself a Scotch and phoned Fred.

Twenty minutes passed before he was at the door. Tears in his eyes, his unbridled display of emotion unwittingly gave her permission to cry for the first time.

'You were lucky to smash his knee,' Fred said. 'He's had it repaired twice. You'll never be attacked by this man again, and neither will any other woman. I promise you. You have my word.'

It transpired that the man was a convicted rapist who'd been released 12 months earlier from several years in prison in another state.

Margery's words came to her then; how life was a numbers game and that sooner or later there'll be a bad egg.

The experience didn't put her off renovating. She had more houses ahead of her than she could possibly have imagined at the time that would need tradies.

She did, however, tell every woman she knew who lived alone to never be lured into a bedroom by an electrician to 'check the lights'. Get the plumber to do it.

It was nearing the end of 1980 when Shirley took over the Staff Services division in Perth, with Robyn heading back across this wide brown land to head up the function in C&M's Sydney office. Whilst her executive colleagues warned her that the temporary and permanent staff placement job was a backward step, she was confident it would enable her to work to her strengths.

Her decision was also a great disappointment on a professional and personal level for her Sydney boss, executive GM Barry Ewan, but she was able to do

Age Four

just that when she discovered that the office lease was about to expire and could not be renewed.

New offices had to be found, the move had to happen virtually overnight and, per Kevin's instructions, she had to restructure her entire workforce in the process.

She took it in her stride. The move came and went, existing and new staff settled in with Shirley at the helm. The business grew.

When towards the end of the year Robyn resigned to marry an American and relocate to the US, Shirley was again offered the role vacated by her friend. If she took the chance, she'd be back in the big smoke but under very different circumstances, both professional and personal, from her last Sydney sojourn with Allan Uebergang.

Without question, there were plenty of positive aspects about her life in Perth, two special members of staff in particular. She'd recruited and trained Lois Wood as a temporary staff consultant and become private friends with her and husband Alan. And there was Jenny Casson, a 17 year-old who came to her first interview straight out of school whom she'd appointed on the spot as her secretary. What began as boss and apprentice relationships had quickly evolved into enduring friendships.

But the fact remained that it had always felt to her like another planet, light years away from all she knew and loved. In the end it was the desire to be closer to her family that compelled her to leave. She missed her father terribly, and yearned for us all. She had even started to lament her inability to forge the same special relationship with the now eight-year-old Gareth that she had with her older nephews.

Th' hast spoken right, 'tis true.
The wheel is come full circle, I am here.

The Sydney office may have been in the city's heart but there was little discernible passion in the staff services team that resided within. It was immediately obvious to Shirley that managing the Sydney practice was not going to be easy.

Robyn's last few months had been unsettling for the staff and not much in the way of presence or support had been forthcoming from head office. A looming recession and the subsequent drop in recruitment activity meant C&M's large executive recruitment, psych testing and senior management groups on the other side of town were battling, desperately preoccupied with developing new products to meet the changing financial climate.

Unsurprisingly, of the six consultants and three reception, secretarial and psych testing staff she'd inherited, several were known to be seeking work elsewhere. With a diminishing marketplace and 20 per cent drop in core staff services business, Shirley had to let a couple of people go and retrain the remainder to 'pound the pavement' and market their services face to face. This personal service prompted growth in the temporary staffing market, with companies opting for short-term contractors over permanent employees. Juggling all this on top of doing her best to maintain an up-beat environment took Shirley at least 10 hours a day. But everyone was under pressure and it was beginning to show.

Most days of the week Shirley was also charged with conducting one-hour exit interviews with senior executives for major clients. These interaction 'outplacement' consultations, usually with men in their prime who'd held positions of trust and responsibility for years, in some cases half a lifetime, were stressful, exhausting and often heart breaking for both parties.

Adding insult to her injury, the fees for this work went onto the activity sheets of head office, not her own department.

During one fiery exchange, she put it to Barry that the arrangement 'unfairly bolsters the pay packets of men who generate less profit than I do, and yet they are paid 40 per cent more! Does this explain why I'm doing the head office dirty work, Barry?'

He responded that her head office colleagues were paid more because they shouldered the responsibility of interviewing and appointing executives who would inevitably become new clients. In addition, the executive search consultant was fundamentally a conduit to top management status, a problem solver and decision maker, hence more demanding than obtaining suitable people to fill positions.

The inexplicable introduction of the 'search' consultant, a different kettle of fish altogether, surprised Shirley but she let it go. Barry was obviously stressed out too.

'The fact remains that your executive recruiters' workload has dropped dramatically,' Shirley said quietly. 'It seems to me that it's beneath two-D consultants to notify and counsel other men who are being made redundant through no fault of their own.'

Age Four

Barry conceded the point and reminded her that 'a girl has to eat' before extending an invitation to lunch.

As luck would have it, Shirley's personal financial situation at the time was surprisingly good.

The Hawthorn Football Club tenancy of her Melbourne home was ongoing and an agent in Perth had secured a short-term tenancy with an option to purchase her house in Perth. The tenant was a newly appointed bank accountant who would be eligible for a staff loan in a few months. This went according to plan and she transferred the total cash price of the sale into a fixed deposit that paid 16 per cent interest for some years to come.

Around mid-1982, when Australia was well and truly in the grips of recession, Barry opened a C&M-affiliated corporate consulting company specialising in the prestigious, international executive-search market.

Already closely connected to C&M's Seattle offices, he spent many months formalising affiliations in Europe and South-East Asia. But despite the dynamism he must have displayed to get these deals over the line, there was little of the usual upbeat spontaneity about him when he was back on home soil.

Developing a new company is of course demanding, even at the best of times, but Shirley sensed his obvious dysphoria wasn't work related; executive search is essentially germane to organisational change and rapidly changing market places. Barry spoke so little of his problems, those at home and in business. She would likely never have known the man's true disposition had she not seen it completely unmasked one night when she stumbled upon him in a legendary club in Sydney's infamous red light district.

She'd arranged to meet her former client, Kerrie Biddell, who was singing in the particular club that night. She'd been elsewhere for dinner with friends and was heading towards the bar when she saw him, sitting alone, crying gently into his beer.

Fleetingly she mistook him for her favourite uncle, Jack, who'd secretly lived with depression for years and had finally killed himself after six months of psychiatric counselling. Shirley couldn't imagine what might have happened to her successful, intelligent, former boss to be crying, alone, hunched over a public bar in a Kings Cross club late on a weeknight.

In the moment, she froze. Should she approach him, or leave him be? If he'd lost a loved one, or been diagnosed with cancer, would her presence be welcome? If his current despairing state was a manifestation of his genetic makeup and she invaded his private hell, would it add to his misery? Unlike Uncle Jack, he was an educated man who counselled others for a living. No way would he want her to know he needed help.

Kevin's words of counsel following the findings of her psych test came back to her.

When in doubt, don't.

'The recession Australia had to have' had happened and 1983 was well underway when Kevin and his senior executives began to close offices across Australia. Shirley still had a job, albeit with a reduced staff who, whilst grateful for their jobs and managing to pay their way, were a far cry from the happy team who'd welcomed her to Sydney with a 'Gorillagram' for her 35th birthday 12 months ago.

Kevin had decided to close down the national business as it stood and re-engage a select few of his consultants to take on increased responsibility. The offer he put to Shirley to become a partner in the new Sydney operation shocked her and it took her 24 hours to respond.

Her astonishment was quickly followed by scepticism and ultimately relief. She wrote to Kevin, thanking him for five priceless years in the people business and explaining why she'd be declining his offer.

The last year in Sydney had been a long and challenging one. She'd often felt adrift, with little support from 'over The Bridge'. Or, more hurtfully, him. She had no reason to believe that even with the financial input she'd be required to make to become a partner, that she would receive the same returns as her male colleagues. She'd never been paid equally as his employee, despite being openly measured against other consultants' performances and profit contributions to the company.

Kevin offered to fund her relocation back to Melbourne, and after she paid out the lease on her car, she started planning her drive home to 15 Kiah Street, Glen Waverley.

She'd been moving since she was born and yearned to be in her own home in Hawthorn, but it wasn't yet vacant. How many houses had she lived in already? Had to be 20, maybe 30. How many careers had she had? At least half a dozen. Was she born to keep moving on?

There's money in oysters

The old tennis team reconvened at the Albert Park courts, minus a pregnant and US-confined Robyn. With so much to catch up on, the three of them adjourned to a local wine bar for drinks and oysters, reminding Shirley of her European trip with Alan in 1972.

Di Tiffin remained single. Kevin had been forced to let her go but had sold her into a new career as manager of the exclusive women's Alexandria Club in Collins Street, Melbourne. Beris continued to run her successful theatrical agency, Frog Promotions, and remained ensconced in the long-distance relationship with Frank, her wealthy, unhappily married man. Shirley was working freelance under her now greatly diversified 'Shirley McLaughlin Enterprises' business, and still under Alan's roof as she waited for the end of the lease in Hawthorn.

After arriving back in Melbourne, she'd taken work with a national personnel agency where she spent a few months training consulting staff and writing advertising material and speeches for the multi-talented boss. Following several diverse, but appalling incidents, she walked out of Head Office one morning, never to return.

The worst incidents were too close to home for Shirley, but it wasn't a case of a pre boomer subjecting women to Russian hands and Roman fingers in a social setting. She chanced to witness the two young women she'd short-listed for a secretarial position respectively exiting the boss's office in tears and dishevelled messes following lengthy interviews.

The first had reappeared straightening her skirt, avoiding eye contact and escaping into a lift before Shirley could get to her. The second reappeared an hour later blowing her nose and wiping her eyes whilst stumbling towards the lift. Shirley reached her as she tripped and fell. They went down in the lift together but she refused to speak, and shook her head vehemently when Shirley asked if she could drive her home. She pulled her parking ticket out of her bag and walked quickly away, having not said a word.

Shirley was also speechless by then. There was nothing to say. The victims had been silenced and there were no witnesses to whatever happened inside that office.

Two days later the boss turned up at Alan's. He was deeply sorry for whatever had caused her to leave the office without notice, trusted she was over it and offered her a permanent contract in the state of her choice. Following a short, civil conversation Shirley politely declined and showed him out the door.

With the short time left to repossess her house, she did some freelance work for a major accounting company, Bird Cameron Consulting, where she trained a fabulous woman named Julie Steele who'd been flown to Melbourne to learn executive recruitment in order to manage their Sydney office. Following an intense week of one-on-one training at the boardroom table, and partying most nights, they became bosom buddies and went on to share some mainly stunning experiences, at home and abroad.

It was an unexpectedly cheerful end to her chequered career in the management consulting business. 'Time to go home and recreate a new life,' she laughed out loud. 'Time to make the world my oyster!'

It was a catastrophe! Well, that's how it seemed at first. In retrospect, it would just be another unforeseen problem she'd need to resolve before starting anew.

The house she'd entrusted to a real estate agent and in turn the Hawthorn Football Club (HFC) for three years had now been vacated. When she arrived to assess what needed doing before she moved back in, the shock at its condition overwhelmed her.

The HFC had poached the young footballer from the Perth team, offering him a three-year contract in a top AFL side. The lad, however, had failed to make the grade.

He and his new wife had barely settled in Melbourne when they found themselves alone, and cruelly isolated in a house literally five minutes from the action at the Hawthorn club house. Instead of beginning an exciting life together, making friends and being part of a successful team, the club put the lad in the seconds and found him an office job nearby that only exacerbated the injustice of it all.

In the first year they had a baby. They also adopted a couple of Alsatians, which soon spawned and produced a pup. Two cats had wandered in over Christmas and taken up permanent residence and two fish and two birds were recruited at some point and also lived inside. The following year a horse was added to the menagerie and installed in the backyard. Then the couple had another baby.

According to the neighbours, the mare sometimes got a workout in the park that backed onto the property, but it wasn't the horse Shirley was feeling sorry for as she surveyed the chaos of her once pristine back garden.

Major repairs were needed throughout the house, yard and garage, but the most distressing damage was the opaque silhouettes of footballs on the roof of the master bedroom. Given the agents had clearly done no more than collect the rent and pay the rates, she insisted they obtain the quotes for repairs, which she would then follow up directly with the Club.

Following submission of quotes that ran to a couple of thousand dollars, she arranged a meeting with the President, Ron Cook.

He was waiting for her in reception, ushered her into his office and offered her a flute of chilled Moet. He'd also ordered two dozen oysters from the kitchen, which duly arrived on a large platter surrounded by strawberries.

In light of Shirley's trashed house and garden, and the couple's undoubtedly disintegrating marriage, the paradox of the president's gesture would have been laughable if it hadn't been so arrogant.

'I'm extremely sorry for the state of your home and offer our sincere apologies,' Ron began. 'The couple were young and rather busy with babies and animals from what I've been told,' he sighed, handing over a cheque. 'I've been wondering why you wanted to meet me after so much inconvenience.'

Shirley replied she felt compelled to talk to him about the Club's recruitment policies.

'You shipped a young, just-married "star" with high expectations all the way from WA to Melbourne and when he didn't perform to your expectations, you abandoned him in the blink of an eye. When I saw the football marks on the ceiling of my bedroom it was clear the marriage was under considerable strain. I must admit I couldn't help wondering if your treatment of the young man influenced his treatment of his animals.

'Apparently they broke up the moment they got home to Perth.'

The president had the look of a chastened school boy as he topped up their glasses. 'How can we avoid this happening again?' he asked her.

'Offering contracts to players without flying them in for a trial run first is irresponsible at best,' she summarised bluntly. 'You're making promises you can't always keep. Any young man leaving home a hero and becoming an unknown overnight would be devastated. Finding him an ordinary job and putting him in the seconds was callous compensation. Imagine how it would have impacted his new wife and their relationship!

'He had the ball at his feet, Ron. He was a willing horse, but you put the cart before the horse. They're back home now and he's in the doghouse and she's left holding the babies. Got it?

'Football may be your product, sir, but you're in the people business and it is not a game!'

Six weeks later Ron called to advise they'd changed the VFL's recruitment rules. Potential imports from other states would have to complete a month's trial prior to being offered a contract.

'It was great to meet you,' he concluded. 'Drop by the club anytime…are you available Thursday? For dinner?'

Yes, she needed to eat, but had no appetite for yet another pre boomer on the make. She graciously declined.

'There has to be oysters,' she told her new assistant, Gini Versluys.

'Whatever selection of starters I settle on for dinner parties, oysters have to be included. There's got to be strawberries too, but we won't charge for them.'

Shirley had hit upon the idea of **gourmet away** when the fringe benefits tax had been introduced. Instantly she'd recognised the opportunity that existed in bringing food and service into the board rooms of Melbourne executives who were no longer able to claim lunch and entertainment as tax deductions.

The catchy name and branding for her mobile catering service were created by freelance artist Alan Wood in Perth, husband of her former consultant C&M Perth colleague Lois. She sold her car, purchased a little kombi van and had it customised to accommodate food trollies, portable equipment and buckets of food, the lessons she'd learned down the years about buying wheels serving her well every day for the two years she owned gourmet away. The chocolate-dipped strawberry logo adorned the marketing materials and was printed on classy t-shirts, which her part-time and casual staff wore on the job. For formal events, male staff who didn't own a dinner suit with the requisite red or black bow tie would be fronted the money to hire one.

Keen to give gourmet away a flying start, she would conclude lunches and dinners with the service of complimentary, chocolate-dipped strawberries, which usually sealed the next booking.

Age Four

Goodwill spreads quickly. Convenient, delicious, competitively priced and well-presented food served by two stylish women with personality plus covered everything required by the usually male occupants in the board rooms of the day. These jobs led to other gigs and in next to no time gourmet away was catering for all manner of activities, from 18th and 21st birthdays to product launches, corporate parties, weddings and wakes.

Shirley was so busy running the show that she lost 16 pounds in weight in the business's first year, and another half dozen in the second. The constant shopping, maintaining close liaison with regular clients, keeping all her casual staff on side whilst supervising, preparing, cooking, travelling, feeding and supplying everything from menus to glasses to grog for hundreds of people most weeks, and more in the lead up to Christmas was enough to put anyone off their food.

Thankfully she had Gini to keep her sane. Gini had replaced Allan Eaton's fiancé on the front desk when Natalie died, lived close by and had been raised in a home of gourmet cooks; *Gini's of Toorak* was her father's renowned Melbourne restaurant.

'A girl has to eat,' Gini would remind her, and they would both giggle.

Despite major repairs, new paint throughout and a renovated kitchen, the house still smelt like a dog's (and cat's and horse's and bird's) breakfast.

She certainly didn't need a menagerie, but a dog would be good company and she and Gini came home via the pound from a gig one afternoon with a one-year-old, black and white castrated cross between a King Charles spaniel and a border collie.

'Finally, I have a child!' she wrote in her annual Christmas newsletter. 'He's got big brown eyes, super intelligence, is a wicked wrecker of all things and a mummy's boy – I suspect for life! I've called him Sunshine because that's what he is.'

Following early morning bouts of barking sessions for his first 10 nights in Shirley's garage, Sunshine had no choice but to adapt. He soon settled into his new owner's rules and became a joyful, sometimes riotous feature of Shirley and Gini's working lives.

During the first year, Jenny Casson from Perth turned up, and stayed. She'd lost her mother early too, and decided it was time to leave home.

Shirley was overjoyed to see her and offered her board in the guest bedroom. Jenny secured a nine to five secretarial position and naturally became a gourmet away part-time waiter. Sunshine was delighted to welcome another member of the family, but slept outside and missed the semi-regular, dead of night guest who made her presence felt to the newcomer a week after she'd moved in.

'There's someone in the house!' Jenny shook Shirley awake, having crept out of her own room and jumped into her keeper's bed at two o'clock in the morning.

'Listen!' she whispered as the footfalls in the hallway came closer.

Shirley turned on the bedside lamp and wrapped her arms around her friend.

'It's okay, everything's okay, Jen,' she smiled. 'I'm so sorry I forgot to tell you! It's the lady who used to own the house and died here. She walks up and down the hallway first. Calm down, Jen, and listen to her soft, slow footsteps. She's an old lady ghost…listen…she's doddering back into the lounge…now she's opening the crystal cabinet. She does that every time. The cabinet was my Mum's and I think she must have had one just like it. Maybe your Mum did too? She'll go away in a minute. Would you like me to make you a coffee?'

'Something stronger would be good, Shirl, but not in a crystal glass if you don't mind.'

Late one afternoon in 1984, a few months after Jenny's 21st birthday on the 12th May and Shirley's 37th on the 13th, there was a knock at the door. When looking back later she would acknowledge just how extraordinarily lucky she'd been that day. Not only had Sunshine (inexplicably) been asleep in the garage, but the sole bathtub in the house was for once empty of its usual ice-packed panorama of salads and buckets of pre-cooked party foods.

The man at the door had a serious task to execute.

'Gourmet Away is your registered name,' he informed her before he'd even stepped over the threshold, 'but you're operating outside the rules. It's illegal to cook professionally from a home without a licence to do so, Miss McLaughlin.

'Operating within the prescribed health and safety rules of food preparation and delivery must be done in a professionally approved venue. Surely you knew that?'

Fuck.

She couldn't believe it, but even with all her business acumen she'd actually forgotten this prerequisite.

Faced with a potential disaster, Shirley's sense memory kicked in and almost unconsciously she summoned her inner damsel in distress.

Age Four

'I started the business cooking in companies' kitchens,' she began cheerfully, taking him into the lounge and offering him a coffee, which he declined.

'One booking led to another,' she took up where she'd left off. 'Soon I had company executives referring me to family and friends. I'd just renovated my house and haven't stopped working since. As you can see, I'm passionate about cleanliness. I used to be in the entertainment business and of course I did get some thanks for my efforts, but I've never had as many letters of gratitude as I have since I started gourmet away. Would you like me to get them? I still don't understand why people I've simply fed are so profuse in their thanks when those I literally and metaphorically speaking fed were few and far between.'

The man blinked at her, visibly overwhelmed. She grabbed the moment.

'May I ask how you discovered I was operating illegally?' she asked over her shoulder as she retreated to the kitchen to put together some light refreshments.

Her adjudicator was a little man in the vertical sense, but tall of character. Whilst she was busy in the kitchen, he remained behind and drifted off into the other worlds depicted in the beautifully framed, old black and white photos on her wall.

They'd sipped, chewed and chatted for 20 minutes before he answered her question.

'One of your competitors dobbed you in,' he divulged. 'That's how it usually happens, but this one had a couple of mates who confirmed the allegation. It's a compliment of the cruellest kind, of course.'

At her offer to refill his champagne flute, he shook his head, apparently remembering why he was in her house in the first place.

'Miss McLaughlin…excuse me. Shirley. I have no alternative but to set a deadline by which your business must have vacated these premises.'

With genuine regret in his voice, he laid his terms on the table, next to his empty plate.

'You have six months to sell your business, or reinstate it in a professional venue,' he said as he signed off on the file before standing and buttoning his coat. He then thanked her for the fresh oysters and delightful champagne, hastening to add that neither had influenced his decision.

'It's been a pleasure to meet you. I do hope this extended time frame will make things a bit easier for you,' he concluded kindly.

Fighting tears of relief Shirley bid him farewell and waited for his BMW to disappear before heading to the garage to fetch Sunshine.

'I've just met a little man with a big soul and a soft spot for pretty women. The fate of it all, eh?' Shirley exclaimed to the dog once they'd adjourned to the fireside in the lounge.

Sunshine wagged his tail. Excited conversation was always good.

'Unfortunately we have to move, or sell,' she added dolefully, patting her beloved dog's now lowered head.

Somehow Sunshine seemed to sense that there was change in the air, whilst Shirley thought about George Orwell's *1984*. Big brother was watching alright but she considered what a lucky break it had been that the Ministry of Love had sent Winston to do their bidding. Who else from the department of law and order would have given her time to flee?

Christmas was coming and the gourmet awa^y schedule was nearly full. Last year's festive season had been busy enough and she realised she'd be lucky to get through this one without additional help. Gini wasn't interested in taking over the business so Shirley's decision to sell up was a fait accompli. She couldn't afford to lose any more weight, and she needed to get a life.

A business agent and friend found her a buyer in early 1985 and the deal was settled in March; gourmet awa^y was well established in Melbourne and its clients, plant and equipment and SMcL Manual were included.

The new owner, who had a small catering business on the other side of town that she was ready to expand, arrived at Shirley's with the removalist truck. Whilst the driver loaded up her new assets, Shirley and Gini helped her fill the kombie van with empty trollies, buckets, eskies and boxes of linen, menus and stationery, kitchen and service paraphernalia. Gourmet awa^y's new proprietor was so excited she almost took a rose bush with her as she reversed out of the drive, and then she was gone.

Shirley gave Gini a bonus with her final pay packet, and then she too was gone.

The house felt empty and eerily still, but Jenny would be home from work soon and tomorrow was another day!

She'd asked Jenny if she'd like to go overseas with a seasoned traveller, perhaps take a 12-month sabbatical and work in London?

Jenny jumped at the chance, but her face fell at a sudden realisation. 'But what will happen to Sunshine?'

Shirley decided to offer him to the neighbours. Everyone in the cul-de-sac loved the friendly dog and several had wanted him, especially the widow at the end of the street whose dog played happily with Sunshine in the park. But the young couple over the road were friends of Shirley's and had always wanted a dog. They were ecstatic and didn't hesitate to agree.

Having renewed her British passport in her maiden name (thank the gods again for Nick Bond) and secured two highly recommended tenants for her house on a 12-month lease, the big day finally arrived.

As arranged, her neighbours appeared as the taxi was pulling into the drive, ready to take Sunshine into his new home.

The dog had been very clingy during the last few weeks of comings and goings, packing and cleaning, and was visibly upset when the driver put their suitcases in the boot. Shirley was handing over the house keys to the neighbours in the lounge when Sunshine jumped up onto his mistress's back, front paws clinging to her shoulders, and began to howl frenziedly.

It took Jenny and the neighbours to wrench him away and hold him still.

Heartbroken, Shirley said they needed to leave straight away.

'Get into the car, Jen,' she instructed before tightly hugging the warm, furry body of her faithful companion to her chest and returning him into the arms of his new owners.

The piercing howls began again as Sunshine watched Shirley climb into the cab.

By now they were all crying and as the taxi pulled out of the driveway Shirley muttered her lately ubiquitous quote. 'If I ever get over this, I'll never have another.'

'Of course you will, Shirl!' Jenny rallied through her tears.

'A dog needs security and stability, Jen. Am I ever going to be able to offer that?'

Jason Bourne, eat your heart out!

The planned 12-month overseas adventure for Shirley became 15 months. Jenny stayed two years.

The itinerary read like most Aussie baby boomers' overseas travel schedules, although Shirley's low boredom threshold and susceptibility to bizarre twists of fate always led to atypical, unexpected experiences. Alan and the Gosbells waited with anticipation for the regular letters, not that there was anything conventional about them. Steve was heading to uni next year and Dale was only two years behind so they were allowed to read them uncensored, but Gareth would have to wait awhile.

The nephews quickly decided that Bourne's scriptwriters must have read about or witnessed some of Shirley's escapades, stolen them and made them Bourne's own. It wouldn't be the first time.

Getting there…

EGYPT: We spent the first week as guests of the Consul at the Australian Embassy in Cairo. Pete was an old friend of Di Tiffin's during her British diplomatic career so we dropped in to say hello. Over a few Fosters beers Pete insisted we check out of our hotel and move in with him.

It was the month of Ramadan and a good time to visit, not too many tourists, but the temperature was 40 degrees daily so we savoured the elegant accommodation and Consular social life. Speaking of foreign affairs, Pete was a generous host who hopes I'll welcome him in London later this year.

During an excursion to the city bazaar we saw cats being skinned, thousands of men stopping to pray every few hours and women submersed in black buying sexy underwear, amongst other less salubrious items.

The Pyramids by night dwarfed five of the other six wonders of the world, perhaps on a par with the Taj Mahal by day…but how can one compare? At least I wasn't caught with black market money this time. We travelled by overnight train to Luxor for a few days to visit The Valley of The Kings and Queens and met two young Egyptian men who taught us how to pray, and play (in a private casino, nephews!)

GREECE: We arrived on the day of Papandreou's second or third election. Our hotel overlooked Constitution Square so we experienced the all-night razzmatazz from the balcony…the faithful communist stalwarts of Papandreou's party, tourists and thousands of unemployed youth took to the streets with whistles and horns, interspersed by police sirens and fireworks. By the time we got to the Acropolis later the following day, clambering over strewn flags, food, drink and execrable refuse from the night before, I fell asleep sitting on the pinnacle looking out over Athens!

Many of the male locals are chillingly aggressive but a cruise to three islands – Paros, Hydras and Aegina, where time stands still and the bougainvillea and roses cover almost every house was wonderful. Unfortunately our departure was not. We left amidst virtually no security three hours after the Shia terrorists hijacked the TWA airline from Athens en route to Beirut, proceeding to hold the 39 American hostages for 16 days. I doubt we'll return to Greece.

ITALY was an eye-opener this time around, but the cost of everything, the rip offs and trauma whilst searching for reasonable accommodation didn't stop us having a great time.

Two Italian guys befriended us in Naples, travelled with us to Sorrento and Positano, a town on the edge of the world that you can only enter by foot, walking down hundreds of steps and along alleyways single file until you reach the sea. At three in the morning the beach was white, the yachts' sails dotting the harbour were lit by a full moon and the water was warm and clear. When I could stand it no longer, I stripped to my undies, dived into the ocean and swam with the lads to the rock music from the disco high up on the cliff's edge. You should try it sometime. You'd never forget it.

In Rome another two Italians befriended us (read accosted) and took us to several night spots, a misnomer because they're open 24/7. By the time we got to Venice we were grateful for some peace. Keeping Italian men at arms' length is exhausting.

VIENNA captured us next. I stood on the stage of the Amphitheatre Hitler re-built in the late 1930s and recited a Shakespearean sonnet (*Shall I compare thee to a summer's day…*), the acoustics so perfect I could hear my words reaching the most distant stone seat 100 metres away where Jenny sat, applauding wildly.

GERMANY gave us our most exciting time in Central Europe. Heidelberg wouldn't let us go, nor four fabulous guys from the

Commando Unit of NATO's forces stationed there so we decided to stop worrying about our diminishing travellers' cheques and relax and enjoy it. We drank a great deal of beer with the men, and too much Schnapps and wine on a trip down The Rhine on a luxury boat with virtually no tourists, apart from a brass band of 150 Americans! So much for Allan Eaton's *Big* Band.

The people you meet when you travel the world! It's all about the people. What would be the point and how would we remember the sights without them? We were running out of ready cash and decided to skip France and Switzerland and do them later. By boats and trains we arrived two days later in London and waited six hours for a hotel room.

Settling in…

LONDON: It took four days to find two bedsits at 193 Gloucester Place NW1 and we're here for three months. It's a great address (famous last words) close to the tube station and heart of the city, has a laundromat and a wonderful little pub over the road…but oh dear, it's colourful! After all those years working with the two Ds at C&M, I'm now living in a building in London with the three Ps - prostitutes, poofters and pimps.

One of the Ps set fire to the building last week. We were evacuated when the smoke was curling its way up the stairs of our four-storey house but apparently it's not uncommon and just bad luck to be evacuated! The P who lit the fire was taken to jail and charged with arson and drug pushing but was released through lack of evidence. We also have a black flasher who became a basher soon after we moved in. A day later his wife became a trasher and threw everything including the TV into the courtyard (more like a pit) that backs onto my window, all this in the middle of a rainy night, the screams and banging and crashing competing with police sirens approaching. The cops had left when gun shots ricocheted around the pit, they stormed back into the house but left five minutes later: no one was dead. Last but not least, there's a female '2nd floor Quickie' who works just above my ceiling; she moved in the day after a male P and his 10-minutes-a-pop boyfriends vacated. Pretty good turnover for everyone involved.

We're expecting a suicide or at least one or two murders any day now. If you're wondering why we don't get the hell out of here, there are two reasons. We'd lose our bond money and we don't want to miss whatever's coming next.

When the going gets tough…

Following three gruesome weeks temping for Alfred Marks Bureau Limited, I wrote to the CEO advising why Jenny and I were severing our association. Not for the first time I'm guilty of not reporting an appalling incident to the police, but it wouldn't have achieved anything, any more than it would have done in Oz.

I was booked on a three-day secretarial assignment for an Arabian prince from Dubai who was co-chairing an international conference at another venue. The agency had given me the prince's name and hotel, despite learning later that he'd told them to give me the room number.

Alarm bells should have been ringing in an experienced consultant's ears! Two hours later, following several calls back and forth to the agency, the prince duly arrived and took me to a room.

He was an athletic, handsome pre boomer with excellent English and professional manners, gave me a key to the door, dictated yesterday's meeting notes and left me in the bedroom with desk, phone and typewriter, instructing me to leave the typing on the desk when I'd finished and meet him there tomorrow at midday. Day two went according to plan and he was happy with my work. Midday was also set for day three, he arrived on time, picked up my typing and pocketed my key from the desk, selected a wine from the fridge and poured two glasses.

'Thank you for your excellent work,' he said with raised glass.

I thanked him, took a sip and picked up my notebook.

'No dictation today,' he said. 'You typed my last conference minutes yesterday. I'm going to make love to you today.'

It was a terrifying moment, I stood up instantly and walked towards the door. He jumped in front of me, pushed and held me against the bathroom wall and unzipped his trousers under his flowing Arabian gown. I broke free and reached for the door, but he'd locked it behind him when he arrived. I was stuck, but somehow had the presence of mind to grasp that so was he.

'Many people know I'm here – just as they know you are. It's in your interests, sir, to take your hands off me at once and let me leave. You'll never get out of England alive if you take this criminal behaviour any further. Unlock the door please.'

It's difficult to write what happened next. He pushed me back into the room and onto the bed, masturbated in front of me, unlocked the door when he'd finished and told me I could go.

I probably saved myself from a much worse fate but it was the most sordid, mortifying experience of my life at the hands of a man of privilege and title who'd decided to take revenge for defeat of his original plan. All I could manage was to report to the agency that the prince was a sexual harasser, minus the details. I simply couldn't tell them, and certainly couldn't contemplate telling a lawyer and then a judge!

All the horrific stories Dad used to tell Mum of abused children when I was supposed to be asleep rushed back and I suddenly grasped why most of them couldn't tell anyone. The horror and shame runs too deep.

Given the agency was complicit in the incident, with the obvious lack of scrutiny they subjected their client to, I knew they'd let it go. So why did I bother at all? Because I'd never sleep soundly again if I didn't, and they'd already referred me to the job I'm in now.

…the tough get going!

I've landed on my feet as a writer/personal assistant to the MD of an expanding sports sponsorship business, Sports Bureau International Ltd (SBI). It's a brisk 10 minute walk from Gloucester Place.

SBI connects commerce with big sporting events ranging from all ball games to car and motor boat racing and Commonwealth and Olympic Games teams. One of SBI's major sponsors is Guinness so the over-consumption of beer continues. It seems no matter where a girl travels in Europe there's always free beer, however we also have the Gordon's Gin account for British Skiing, Heinz (my old employer) for international school sports, Long John Whisky for athletics and I even managed to negotiate Paul Hogan for a Fosters' Melbourne Cup Day/BBC hook-up, but he couldn't make it. Besides a free liquid diet I have a choice of T-shirts for every day of the week, advertising World Snooker through to Superman and 'Going Places with Gordon's'. Coming up I've got the task of escorting 150 VIP's on the Orient Express to Edinburgh for the Commonwealth Games. Fun, eh?

I hope you guys, especially Rob and Dad will be impressed that Denis Compton (a rather alcoholic version of his former self) bought me a port at Lords Cricket Club yesterday, and Nigel Dempsey really has got something more to talk about than hot gossip.

My direct boss is a bright, funny, appreciative bloke called Roy Mantle who broke the association with Alfred Marks at my request, employed me on contract and is paying me cash via a marketing slush fund. It's a mad house, frantically busy, the work is different and challenging and, as noted, there's lot of perks. I'm enjoying it immensely and even Roy's ex-wife driving me crazy with phone calls every other day has not marred the freedom of all care, no responsibility – a rare and beautiful thing!

The showbiz scene....

I think London still offers more entertainment, pomp and 'live' extravaganzas than any other city in the world. I'll round up theatre experiences at the end of the year but for now, we managed to con our way into two great seats at Wimbledon and watched the day's semi-final matches – Navratalova and McNamee in the mixed doubles and Lloyd and Durie, Shriver and Navratalova in the singles. Mid-afternoon we sat like school kids on the lawn sipping a beer as Cash, Jaryd and Connors et al walked by from the practice courts to the main stadium. Jenny got autographs and could have had a date with Cash, if only she hadn't been side-tracked by Connors.

So what about the male scene?

Plenty of them, one in particular whom we met at our local via a friend of Jenny's from Perth. His name is Alex Quinn, he's from Belgium, owns a travel agency in West Kensington, speaks five languages, is an excellent chef, and assures me he's divorced with two children. He's taken me to a couple of functions, invited me to dinner at his place last week and dropped me home around midnight (not before asking me to move in with him), but I didn't get a wink of sleep! The P in the bedsit above mine was entertaining a man who must have 'snapped' because he hurled every piece of her furniture at the walls.

Within minutes the noise woke the entire building and my ceiling was about to collapse when he came yelling down the stairs, dragging the girl behind him, stopped at my landing and proceeded to put a boot to my door. By the fourth fierce hit the lock had become unhinged, I recovered from shock and screamed 'Stop that at once!' The guy reacted, grabbed the girl who was now sobbing on her knees, and literally hauled her down the remaining stairs, wrenching the poorly attached front door off its hinges as he dropped her on the pavement and disappeared. The cops arrived too late but called an ambulance.

Jenny bunked in my bed until it was time to shower and go to work, except that yet again the water was off and the toilet in our bathroom was blocked so we left early and cleaned ourselves up at our respective jobs.

Jenny's boss, the fabulous American movie star and film director, Gene Hackman, who operates out of his UK offices most of the year, is very protective of her, as Roy also proved to be when he heard our latest 'P' news. I think Roy's already a little in love with Jenny, but concerned for both of us and suggested I give notice immediately and accept Alex's invitation to move in.

What he has in mind for Jenny I don't know but I wrote a second letter to the Landlord, Mr Devonshire of Devonshire Properties, concluding with our notice to quit at the end of the week and my intention to report him to the police if he refused to return our bonds. A tradie fixed my door and the front door immediately and we received our bond cheques in the next mail. I moved in with Alex (see West Kensington address, above) and Jenny is renting in a CBD flat with a girlfriend from work.

The prostitute survived with a broken arm and multiple bruises and apologised to me on the stairs the night before we left. She cried as she spoke of her two daughters who happened to attend the same school as the landlord's children and asked me why some kids get all the luck.

AGE FOUR

FRANCE, BELGIUM, SPAIN…

Alex's travel agency jaunts are usually hosted by him and I join him when I'm available. Living with this man is one adventure after another, despite a few dark moments. I've made it clear that I'll be returning home in June 1986, but he's in love and thinks he can change my mind.

In France we walked the green, war-torn fields along the coast between Bologna and Calais, stopping to explore the remaining air raid shelters and view the white cliffs of Dover from across the sea. In Ostend we attended the weekend-long Mardi Gras (rivalled only by Rio's). All the visitors were masked, I was dressed as a black and white cat and had a big win at the casino at four o'clock Sunday morning. In Barcelona we attended a bullfight, but that means eight (8!) bullfights in one afternoon and we walked through the slaughter house at the back of the Stadium on our way to the car. I thought I was going to be sick and will never go to a bullfight again.

SOVIET UNION, IRELAND and WALES, SCANDINAVIA, MOROCCO…

My long weekend solo journey to the Soviet Union was startling, from beginning to end. When I landed in Moscow I felt subjugated immediately. Uniforms everywhere, at -10° the population not in police or army uniforms were so rugged up it was hard to observe any national traits.

Moscow is spacious and quite beautiful and the Russians are helpful but they don't smile, perhaps a result of the high divorce rate? Or maybe it's the food? I counted 16 variations of ashen cabbage in four days. As tourists, we had to stay within a 22km range of our landing point but following a walk through Gorky Park with another woman travelling alone, we decided to escape for a few hours by train into the country. We had no idea we were being followed until we couldn't find our way home. There wasn't much choice. Few Russians speak English so we approached the two plain-clothes' men and they escorted us back – to the front door!

We were just in time to attend The Barber of Seville, sung in Russian and performed to a packed house by The Bolshoi Opera Company in the 5,000 seat, magnificent Lenin's Palace. Just before interval a man (ex-lover) sitting behind us tapped me on the shoulder. 'I'd know that laugh anywhere!' he exclaimed and shouted me and my companion champagne and nibbles (thankfully no cabbage) for supper.

Dublin was stunning, but also startling. I spent three days in and around the city, visited Geraldine Doyle's sister and family and the breathtaking Trinity College and Long Room where the original Book of Kells lies open to read.

I dropped into Slattery's grand old pub in the heart of the city and Slattery (Senior) himself was honouring me with his company and a pint of Guinness when one of the staff screamed 'bomb scare!' The Irish Rebel folk group left the stage immediately whilst some of the guests ignored the warning and kept on drinking, but Slattery took my hand, marched me into the kitchen and instructed a chef to whisk me out the back and take me to my hotel. He invited me to return the following day for lunch and I said I'd try. I think he knew he'd be eating alone.

Being half Irish, half Welsh no doubt makes me biased but the countryside in Ireland and Wales (and England and Scotland, of course!) is magnificent and the people warm and hospitable. Everybody should visit the UK at least once in their lives. Jenny and I spent a weekend at Ruthvin Castle in Wales and attended a medieval banquet in the dungeons below. It was like landing on another planet. The entertainment was out of this world too.

Jenny's and my White Christmas '85 Scandinavia holiday began as no other, a roller-coaster sail to Copenhagen that took 26 hours on the Longship and heightened our appreciation of nature's extraordinary beauty, and terror. Sitting on the upper deck, crossing the Channel as the waves crashed above the windows of the bar and froze instantly they hit the glass, and the ship crackling and groaning its way forward through the icy sea was terrifying and exhilarating.

Age Four

The return journey was a snap because we were so relaxed following a week of good living in a fabulous hotel. Alex had upgraded us and there was champagne, a cheese platter and bowl of fruit waiting for our arrival. The generosity of the locals was also exceptional, making it a memorable, inexpensive trip. Well, cheap actually. We didn't have to pay for anything much.

My solo journey to Morocco didn't begin or end well, not to mention what happened in the midst of the seven-day packaged tour. The wing flaps of the 707 Charter jammed 20 minutes after we'd taken off and we shuddered and dropped, rose and fell and shook on the emergency return to London before another plane could be sourced.

Getting out of Tangier a week later was worse because of the US bombing of Libya. Two days after the tour began the bombers began flying over for most of the daylight hours and our Syrian tour guide spent hours on the phone talking to affected family and friends. Alex tracked our course and called my hotel rooms every day to insist I get a plane home immediately. I couldn't pacify him, despite explaining I was safer in the group than I would be alone. Every town we visited was battling a surge of violence and murders within communities because of the war and the tour group applauded the pilot who got us safely out of Tangier and home to English soil.

I must admit I'm beginning to feel the odds shortening on my extraordinary luck and will be glad when my Qantas plane lands on Oz terra firma.

ENTERTAINMENT (and leaving it behind)

I promised a comprehensive list, but here's the memorable shows, guys. Caught the last night of Deborah Kerr in 'The Corn is Green' at the Old Vic, and a fabulous performance by Liza Minnelli at The Palladium. Then there was the opening night of 'Chess,' 'The Judy Garland Story' and 'Les Miserables'. 'Is There Life After High School?' at the Donmar Warehouse was also wonderful, an off-West End theatre where west end actors perform when not in leading roles.

In tune with the culture of the day, ammunition seems to be all the rage. The Viennese New Year's Day concert at Royal Albert Hall left my ears ringing for days because of the cannons fired from the upper boxes during the last rousing London Philharmonic Orchestra march.

At 'Fantasia', out in the heart of the Sahara Dessert in Morocco, Alex and I sat under a starlit Arab sky eating Berber style couscous whilst being entertained by snake charmers, belly dancers, singers and musicians when, finally came the charge of 60 Berber tribesmen on their mountain horses, firing their rifles a few metres from us whilst pulling their mounts up dead from charge-to-stop in five seconds.

Alex bought the best seats in the house, three rows from the front to see 'Are You Lonesome Tonight?' Set during Elvis' last days and played by the superb Martin Shaw, he sang all the old songs and could have been a double for Elvis when he fired the gun in a moment of rage and the bullet landed in my lap! Of course I screamed in shock, as several others did around me until we all realised that I literally had the blank in my hand! Alex whispered 'put it in your handbag' as 'Elvis' gave me a little wink from the stage. (I'm going to buy an old printer's tray at Covent Garden to house all the miniature souvenirs I'm accumulating.)

Alex also took me to three formal balls in the best of British tradition at The Waldorf, Grosvenor House and The Dorchester. One had an Australian theme and there was a large, painted map of Oz on the central dance floor, MINUS Tasmania! As a guest on the CEO's table, I couldn't help saying that if I had a gun, I'd raise it to him. Ten minutes later a lackey appeared with a cut-out map of Tassie!

Leaving Alex is not going to be easy…

I haven't told you about the downside of our relationship but I guess it's time and will help you understand my decision.

For all his caring, generosity and genuine love for me, he's a man of multiple personalities. The worst for me is his jealousy, but I've recently learned that his ex-wife and children suffered abuse and a restraining order issued years ago ensured he would never have access to his children again. Several incidents involving business or personal friends of mine have created problems, despite my total openness in arranging to meet them over lunch or dinner.

On the first occasion I went to an SBI girls' night out and he sidled into the restaurant, was escorted to a table and watched me like a hawk until he'd finished his dinner and stormed out in full view of us.

The most frightening incident occurred when the Consul from Cairo turned up. I told Alex who he was, how he'd looked after Jenny and me in Egypt and that I'd accepted his dinner invitation. I arrived home around midnight, put my key in the lock but the door was latched on the inside with no choice but to bang and yell until he was forced to open it. He was drunk, could barely walk back to bed and slept loudly but soundly until morning when he apologised profusely, brought home red roses (yes, two dozen!), took me to Le Touquet for the weekend and proposed over lunch.

On the way home we got stuck in a lift for 90 minutes at Calais Port, a claustrophobic woman screamed throughout the ordeal and an elderly man had a heart attack. Alex was completely out of control by the time three men from the local fire brigade hauled us out through the roof. My left hand was burnt during the exit and I looked like I'd slashed my wrist but my 14 NEW TEETH, thanks to an Aussie dentist and the National Health Scheme, stayed put so I'm grateful and will be smiling all the way home!

I've given notice to Roy and committed to help Alex move his travel agency to a new location prior to flying home mid-June (when my tenants vacate). Roy's friendship is solid and he plans to visit Australia next year, wherever I happen to be. Alex hasn't accepted yet that when I say NO, I mean it. He's upgraded me to First Class for the journey home and I have the uncomfortable feeling he'll turn up uninvited before the year is out.

P.S. I still reckon the world is my oyster.

Life happens when you're looking the other way

Shirley had always been fond of the quote 'What's it all about, Alfie?' the movie she would never forget, despite both she and Bev being mere youngsters when they saw it with their parents.

Margery had taken a turn on the street outside the theatre whilst they were waiting as Alan collected the car. Predictably she'd fought the convulsion, no doubt instead answering the girls' questions about Alfie searching for his life and then taking the opportunity to offer some oblique advice.

'When you have a passion or a dream, make sure you give it a shot or you'll always regret it,' she'd said. Shirley had written this down in her private notebook the moment they got home and it had been a maxim in her life ever since.

Shirley would meet the one real Alfie she'd ever know just after she'd arrived in London.

He was an 18-year-old Saudi prince who had been on holidays from uni in Riyadh, and staying with relatives not five minutes from her and Jenny's digs in Gloucester Road. Alfie was 'tall, dark and handsome', as well as intelligent, well-mannered and gregarious.

Shirley met him at the local pub. He had been looking for an experienced woman with whom to have a holiday fling. She hadn't been looking for anyone…but a short affair with a youngster of his class was hard to refuse. She'd never been to bed with an 18 year old and realised that given her 38 years of age, the opportunity was not likely to present again.

There had been, however, a caveat to their arrangement. Alfie took recreational drugs and insisted she join him. Shirley was against drugs, always had been, and despite having received plenty of illicit offers in her time, she'd never crossed the line.

(On the other hand, for a girl brought up on a regimen of *'Be good sweet maid, and let who will be clever'* interspersed with the likes of *'You'll never know if you don't have a go'*, it's possible she was just waiting for the right one.)

'Give it a go. You're a writer,' Alfie persuaded pragmatically, 'and experience is the best research.'

The clincher came when he assured her that one 'mild' pill would give her a high during sex like she'd never had before.

It was to be a one-off and she insisted on keeping a written record of her feelings and thoughts during the experiment, with his help if necessary. He kept his word and she learned a good deal about her strengths and weaknesses.

Age Four

As time and space slowed, she lay on the floor of her bedsit and scribbled notes in an exercise book. The page was oddly fuzzy yet clear, and in her typical hand writing she wrote that the world was spinning, that she felt unreal as if she was in another life and her watch was stuck on a quarter to one. The taste of the apple Alfie had given her to eat was juicier than any she'd ever tasted, yet later she was sure she'd been drinking champagne instead.

Propped up by her right arm, her left hand moving the pen across the paper, she tried to tune into the classical music Alfie was playing; he was laughing and she asked him to stop. Suddenly, as if by magic she could identify the music of individual instruments, separate the violins from the guitars, trumpets from trombones…everything! It was an orchestra like she'd never heard before.

'At last I know what people with an ear for music can hear…thank you, thank you!' she exclaimed.

'I'm pushing myself hard, just as I've pushed myself all my life. But it's not as good…it's not my choice,' she realised and abruptly stopped writing.

With that the high went swiftly to a low.

'I'm not in control…' she gasped, the tears began to flow and she picked up her pen again and sang as she wrote.

> …And I look at you and you're laughing.
> And you're asking me how do I feel?
> And I'm asking you, how long does it take
> And what do we do
> When the world starts coming down?
>
> And I'm wanting to have it all at once,
> And I'm wanting to make love now.
> And I'm wanting to eat and wanting to sleep,
> And wanting to know
> What do we do
> When the world starts coming down?

Her experience of the come down guaranteed she would never take drugs again, even though she'd been glad she'd tried it. Alfie had dismissed her reaction by saying she was overly conservative, and stuck in old society's rules.

She'd acknowledged this, yet under the influence had written: 'I've arrived at a freedom of heart and soul and the lesson was greater than the sum of its parts.

'I've been acting all my life but I don't want to escape anymore. I don't feel free. Tripping might be fun but you can have that without drugs and you don't have to die a little every time you stop laughing!' were her last words as the world came tumbling down.

The great generation *Alfie*, played in 1966 by scrummy British actor Michael Caine, and the gorgeous 18 year old Gen-X Alfie had somehow erased the trauma inflicted by the sexually deviant pre boomer prince and, in doing so, had raised Shirley up for her melancholic return home.

She'd always wanted to write books, but unless you were one of the dozen or fewer writers around the world who managed to produce an international best seller, there wasn't much money in it.

She knew she didn't have that kind of talent. Additionally, she was too young to give up her business and social life for the insular, isolated life of a full-time author, sitting at a desk in a bedroom writing 12 hours a day without any guarantee she'd ever be published.

Yet, *If you have a passion or a dream…*

'All I need is a plan!' she murmured, gazing at the photo of Alfie he'd given her before he flew home, but not focusing on the image at all.

She'd managed to pay her way without drawing funds from home and owned her house and a growing share portfolio, but it would not be enough to support a few years trying her luck writing books. Self-employed through Shirley McLaughlin Enterprises, freelance consulting and selling her business writing and PR skills to a national market, she'd be in control, having fun and working towards her goal.

'Three or four years,' she wrote on the back of the real estate agent's final tenancy statement. 'By no later than 1990 I'll have a decent share portfolio, will probably sell up, scale down and go somewhere cheaper and quieter to write.

'And if I haven't sold a manuscript three years later, I'll give it away and buy back into the city.'

The tenants left everything in good order and she'd been back in her house long enough to draft a PR brochure for the new business, put out a few feelers and secure a stock broker in Sydney when the first short-term offer came.

Age Four

A Human Resources consultant from her previous life called from Sydney to ask if she was available for three to six months to help get his new business off the ground. He'd opened his executive consulting business whilst she was overseas. Whilst it was doing well, his sales manager had left without notice.

'The business is out there but without decent sales direction my new staff jobs are at risk. I need entrepreneurial input fast,' he exhaled heavily.

Shirley was interested but unsure on-the-spot if she was ready to relocate for a few months. His offer to pay her accommodation and commuting airfares enhanced negotiations considerably.

She slept on it and phoned the employer next morning. It would be a contract position commencing one week hence.

Early on the afternoon of her second Thursday back in Sydney she was exiting a building in Pitt Street following a morning of successful 'cold call' meetings when she literally bumped into her old 'Sympatico' boss from C&M, Barry Ewan.

In a city of several million people, Shirley figured the odds of them running into each other had to be longer than winning Tatts Lotto.

Had it been fate…or just an extraordinary coincidence?

Both stunned and openly excited to meet again, they soon discovered that their worlds had changed, but nothing between them had.

Shirley's affairs with intelligent, successful, double-standard pre boomers had reduced her trust in men of that type to cynical jokes (like the one Patrick had stupidly told her against himself about why you'll never see a bookie going to the races on a bus – it was simply too crude and not funny enough to retell). But what really slayed her was the realisation that she'd likely been complicit in their infidelities. She was done with men who lined up their next wife whilst 'shouting' the current incumbent to a flash vacation in order to appease their guilt.

Was Barry capable of this? she wondered, suddenly visualising a T.S. Elliot quote from her diary: 'Am I damned to spend the rest of my life exploring in order to arrive where I started and know the place for the first time?'

Like a couple of life-long friends they hugged spontaneously and for an indeterminate time chatted there on the footpath.

Eventually he asked her to join him for dinner, but not before admitting why he'd finally stopped pursuing her.

'You were always surrounded by men. Half my staff were in love with you and then I discovered you'd slept with two of them! I was disappointed…and I s'pose I couldn't take the risk of rejection.'

'Oh dear,' she sighed, and recalled one of the guys in question.

They'd gone for an early swim in Fremantle Harbour on the morning of the office move. When she was bitten by a stingray, her arm swelled to three times its normal size, he'd rushed her home to smother her in powdered meat tenderiser and it had worked a treat, in more ways than one. In the frankness of the moment she divulged there'd been a venereal disease to balance out that brief encounter, but didn't comment on the other man he'd referred to. She couldn't remember at the time who he was!

Before the evening was over Barry laid his cards on the table, urging her to move to Sydney.

'We've always lived in different states and never had time to develop a relationship. I've missed you…I can't explain how much…' he implored.

'I've often thought we were unfinished business,' she replied.

4th Intermission

Geraldine Connor & Patrick Fitzpatrick

Susie Coles

Hugh Stuckey

Allan Eaton

The egg & spoon race at midnight

Col Elliott

Chandler & Macleod Consultants Pty Ltd
Industrial Psychologists
Consultants to Management
5 Wellington Street Kew Victoria 3101

Robyn

Allan & Lois, Perth

Jenny

Season's Greetings

Gini

Roy from London with Robyn

Cardwell by the sea   Bookie style

Beris   and with John Cameron

Beautiful Sunshine

Alex Quinn

Jenny

AGE FIVE (1987 – 2000)

Full of wise saws and modern instances
And so she plays her part.

On Good Friday 1987 Shirley woke up in the lounge of her new home in Sydney under a leaking tarpaulin where she slept during three weeks of intermittent, torrential rain. With Barry beside her during Easter, they laughed as they emptied the strategically placed plastic buckets around the bed in the mornings.

The cottage at 8 Waite Avenue, Balmain, was a renovator's dream that turned into Shirley's, and every Tom, Dick and Harry's nightmare before it was done.

It was the third in a row of three terraced houses that were built in the mid-1880s as stables for the first Governor of New South Wales. Across the road the original manor house, known as *The Grange,* stood proudly on its double block, having been kitted out with a pool and cabana. The occupant was the governor's great, great grandchild. They would occasionally wave to Shirley from the safety of their Rolls as they pulled into their driveway. Otherwise they remained aloof, which was in contrast to the rest of her new neighbours who welcomed her with open arms.

The other two terraces were home to a young couple and a single gent respectively. Another bachelor lived in the freestanding house on the other side of Shirley. The single gent, divorced Aussie John of John Cameron Aviation, the largest helicopter and light plane service centre in Australia, and bachelor Max, an engineer and entrepreneur from Finland brought her up to speed on the harrowing history of her new home.

She'd purchased it from a man whose suicide attempt had been interrupted by a neighbour as she'd left her house. He'd been in his car, which had been parked outside her front door. As the police dragged him into a paddy van he'd screamed, 'I've got a right to die if I want to! My girl's left me, I've run out of money to finish the house and I'm going to bloody kill myself, whether you like it or not!'

Before him, a wealthy hermit had lived there for 20 years in indescribable squalor. There'd been no bathroom and no kitchen, and 'Old Paul' had been dead several days before being discovered by his favourite niece.

The niece was the ex-wife of the guy who ran off with the Russian 'Red Bikini Girl'. She'd jumped off a Russian ship in Sydney Harbour and was eventually granted asylum – you may remember the headlines? Red Bikini and Old Paul then had a torrid affair before she dumped him as well, and went on to become a successful model. After Paul left his niece his entire fortune, she moved to the North Shore, leaving her ex to squat in an ironically similar state to that of her late uncle.

Perhaps the history of her new home should have served as a warning of things to come, but Shirley was an old hand at renovating. How hard could it be?

In the real world now

Geraldine Doyle and hubby Paddy Fitzpatrick were the first old friends to welcome Shirley back to Sydney, and had recommended the builder. We'll call him Tom. He'd recently completed major renovations for them and had agreed to undertake the transformation of 8 Waite Avenue.

Two months after commencement, and not long before Easter when the framework and a new side brick wall between Number 8 and the young couple's upstairs deck next door was completed in readiness for the addition of two bedrooms, a walk-in robe and balcony, the downstairs floor began to cave in! White ants. Throughout.

Margery's words that 'only the lawyers win' were ringing in Shirley's ears when she remembered she'd kept a copy of her letter to the real estate agent requesting a building inspection pre-purchase. We'll call him Dick. She made an appointment and presented him with a copy of the letter and the quote to rip up the carpets and re-concrete the floors. Balmain is an old, 'tight' suburb, more like a country town, and the last thing Dick needed was a negligence case that might open up 'a can of white ants,' so to speak. He wrote a cheque immediately, shook her hand and apologised profusely.

A week shy of Easter, and just after the concrete had set and the old roof had been removed, she was served with a 'Stop Work' order by an officious little man on her new doorstep. The next door couple – we'll call the man of the house Harry – had discovered the new dividing wall upstairs was positioned four inches over their boundary and Harry had decided to sue. A date was set in the Balmain City Council court 10 days after Easter.

Barry accompanied her to court. The judge spoke at length and the couple's solicitor demanded a litany of fees including compensation for stress and loss of income!

When Shirley finally got a chance to speak, she expressed disappointment that her young neighbours, and Harry in particular, hadn't approached her directly; so many people had unnecessarily become involved. 'I'm trying to develop a new business whilst living under a leaking tarpaulin during the heaviest rain recorded in Sydney for several decades,' she said, 'but all that matters here, Your Honour, is that my builder made a mistake and the wall has to come down and be put up again in the right place as soon as possible.'

The judge had already made his decision and dismissed the case in a few words.

Barry took her to dinner and over dessert he told her that he'd be away for a couple of weeks at the annual headhunting conference in Seattle.

The timing was fortuitous. Tom the builder was booked to start the renovations again on Monday and she'd need every minute of the next few weeks to get started on three new contracts she'd won.

The next morning their farewell was brief.

'We should plan our future when I get back,' he said before driving away.

As she watched the car disappear from view, she thought of a quote from *All's Well That Ends Well.*

'Oft expectation fails, and most oft where it most promises.'

Her new take on SMcL Enterprises had started slowly and the house extension had cost double the original quote. (So much for the 'expect 30 per cent more than planned' tenet!)

The money was going out faster than it was coming in, with Shirley admitting it in her 1987 Christmas newsletter.

'I'm fairly desperate for 'luxury' items like toilet paper, milk and petrol… reassuring myself that I'm saving fuel by staying home today in case the phone rings. I posted the second wave of flyers and it's been non-stop ever since. Now I'm having trouble working out what to accept and what to decline.'

Whilst picking up a project brief at her old C&M stomping ground, she ran into a former colleague who regaled her with the latest company gossip. Inevitably, the conversation soon turned to Barry. Shirley's poker face remained intact up to the point when her friend commented that he'd heard their old boss was 'off at that annual shrink symposium' in the States again.

'You know, the one where the exquisitely dressed wives go on tours each day so their husbands are free to compete with each other as to how superior their understanding of the human condition is,' he scoffed sarcastically with a roll of his eyes.

By then, Shirley wasn't listening.

How had she been so gullible? she wondered. *Why hadn't he called since he left? Was Barry leading two lives?*

When he turned up at her house in Balmain 16 days later, he was clutching a bunch of two dozen long-stemmed red roses.

If he'd actually spoken when he handed them to her, Shirley hadn't heard him, the irony ringing in her head drowning out all else.

'Did you miss me?' he asked after they'd sat down at the kitchen bench to catch up over a glass of champagne.

'Yes, very much,' she replied, 'but I need to ask straight up – have you lied to me? By way of omission?'

She hadn't known she was going to say it until the words rushed out of her mouth. But there it was, on the bar with the roses and neither could be retracted.

He turned pale and his eyes welled up.

'What do you mean?'

'Why do you look guilty and terribly sad all of a sudden?' she asked him, putting a comforting hand on his arm.

'I took my wife to the conference…it's one of those summits where wives are expected to come along,' he muttered into his glass, avoiding her eyes.

'I didn't tell you,' he continued, gathering momentum, 'because I knew you'd be upset…I've been planning to tell her that the marriage is over and wanted to give her a decent holiday first.'

Fuck, fuck, fuck! The only thing I've learned from history is that I haven't learned a bloody thing.

She'd been swearing a lot lately, putting off facing the truth.

They'd known one another for 12 years and had spent most nights together for the past four months.

But where did his wife believe he was all those nights?

They'd been the best of friends from the start, but never quite the best of lovers. He was tentative, usually leaving her to initiate intimacy. He was somehow naive in his love making…as if he didn't have the experience to take the lead.

Perhaps guilt diminished his libido because he was still sleeping with his wife?

He was almost child-like, always conscious of others' expectations and what they wanted of him, seeming never able to do what he wanted to do. How many times had she heard him espouse the dangers of 'forgetting yourself' to the staff psychologists at his C&M training sessions? As Margery had often said, 'You have to learn to be selfish before you can become unselfish.'

Shirley reflected that Barry had probably long ago got hooked on the masochistic pleasure that mindless compliance can bring. But she couldn't have this conversation with him. He was the master of the game and, try as he might, he'd never be able to make a genuine commitment to her. His omissions and deceit would continue until he was too old to stray. He and his wife would grow old together, unhappily acquiescent with the status quo.

It was over and it fell to her to call it like it was.

The knife plunged into each other's hearts. Neither was innocent; both had brought about this inevitable end.

The fabulous forties

Despite an arduous start to 1987, Shirley's long-term dream to write books was now a driving force.

'…I can but hope!' Shirley wrote to Alan a couple of weeks before she turned 40. 'On Tuesday, 13th May 1947 Margery McLaughlin gave birth to me and I'm sorry it's taken so long, Dad, but I'm going to fulfil yours, hers and my hopes this decade.'

There was gloom and doom all around and the year would certainly prove difficult for many members of the great, pre boomer and baby boomer generations, but Shirley had become her own woman and was determined the last few years of the 80s were going to be the most liberating of her life.

Even the sad and bad news didn't ruffle her. Danny Kaye of 'Walter Mitty' fame died, aged 74. Fred Astaire, 'king of the hoofers', had also shuffled off this mortal coil, aged 88.

In Australia, five Sydney men were found guilty of the abduction, robbery, sexual assault and murder of 26 year-old Anita Cobby; former liberal party leader and federal speaker Sir Billy Mackie Snedden, was found dead in a bed in a Sydney motel, having suffered a heart attack; and Michael and Lindy Chamberlain were pardoned by the Northern Territory government over the disappearance of their baby daughter Azaria at Ayes Rock in 1980.

The event that rocked the world in 1987 was also somewhat lost on Shirley. The day the stock market crashed, Black Monday, 17th October, had even caught Alan Greenspan off-guard – but her savings were safe! £50 billion, or 10 per cent had been wiped off the value of public companies in London and the Dow Jones had followed, wiping 22.5 per cent off share values. No country was spared, with accurate predictions of credit squeeze, recession or depression to come.

Whilst many of her generation were doing it tough, Shirley was enjoying Sydney as never before. The mix of creative projects and a busy social life with old and new friends were keeping her stimulated and fulfilled. Well, in the case of the latter, not quite…but she was onto it.

On the project front she was deeply involved in a PR assignment for an ocean sailing club looking to capitalise on Australia's 1988 Bicentennial next year; a major writing assignment for a section of the public health system in Sydney; and essentially self-serving commutes to Melbourne to train staff for a national recruiting firm

On the social scene, the locals took up most of her spare time. Neighbours Max and Aviator John, plus Qantas steward John and his wife who lived over the side fence, Julie Steele from Bird Cameron, Gaby Dongès and Chris Fletcher whom she'd met via a friend of Barry's, plus all the usual suspects from her showbiz days kept her busy.

She threw a party for her 40th, and Beris flew up from Melbourne to join the crowd.

'I think this one beats the egg and spoon race at your agency farewell party,' Beris mused quietly whilst they were cleaning up when everyone had gone. 'I wish I'd made more of my forties…they went by in a flash and now I'm on the downhill run.'

'Rubbish! You've made the most of everything and will probably outlive us all, B.'

'I wish…' she replied.

'Are you okay?' she asked and Beris shrugged, leaving Shirley very uneasy about her best friend's health.

Shirley was accepted to study a bachelor of arts, majoring in English at the University of New England (UNE) in Armadale, commencing in 1989.

She attended an orientation weekend, loved what she saw and heard, and committed to knuckling down to the required 15 hours of weekly study in the first year.

Alan was over the moon that she'd finally embraced the importance of a solid education. He had been saying so when Shirley interrupted him.

'I'm not doing this to get a degree, Dad,' she clarified. Registering his confusion, she elaborated. 'I'm doing it to brush up my English and writing skills so that I can focus on writing what I want to write.

'All my life I've been writing what men have paid me to write. That won't mean a damn thing to any publisher considering a manuscript from a first-time author. Uni is going to be about learning how to motivate my readers to keep turning the pages!'

Alan smiled through wet eyes, relieved and proud.

'That's our girl, Lovely,' he murmured, gazing into the distance.

Despite the fact that she wasn't starting until next year, Shirley had purchased the 20 books on the BA list, inclusive of plays, poetry and novels and was momentarily overwhelmed by the substance and commitment she was taking on. Albee, Auden and Austen, Bronte, Chaucer, Chekov, Coleridge and Conrad, Dennis, Fielding, Gaskell, Gardner, Lawrence and Malouf, not forgetting Paterson, Plath, Walker, White, Wordsworth – and Shakespeare.

She'd decided to spend the long weekend in January reading when neighbours John next door, and John over the side fence independently insisted she join them on Australia Day for the bicentenary celebrations of the arrival of the First Fleet 200 years ago.

'There'll be plenty of time to read when you're old!' aviator John exclaimed, reminding her of Grandma Jones' advice a lifetime ago about gardening.

'I hope you're not going to become a bloody boring university student on me,' Qantas John groaned.

For the day's activities Shirley joined aviator John and his friends on his boat on the Harbour. That afternoon it was one of 8,000 small craft already afloat in preparation for the evening's extravaganza. Around them, the harbour's every vantage point was crammed with the 1.5 million spectators who'd come to partake in the celebrations.

Whilst they cruised slowly, precariously around the Harbour, she struck a friendship with Alessia Bighi, fashion designer and heir to Marfy Patterns which was based in Ferrara, Italy.

Alessia's Australian lover was the skipper of a yacht owned by a US billionaire who was a friend of John's. She'd joined his yacht in France and he'd dropped her off in Sydney en route to America. One week's holiday prior to flying home was sufficient for them to become life-long friends, visiting each other at their respective homes, or in London where they always reminisced about meeting at the Bicentenary.

For the evening's celebrations, Shirley joined Qantas John.

Prince Charles, Prince of Wales, paid tribute to Australia on the forecourt of the Opera House but most Sydneysiders missed his address, content to watch the maritime spectacle of sailing ships and the now 10,000 small craft engulfing the Harbour. A Royal Australian Air Force fly-past and a gigantic fireworks display lit up the Harbour Bridge and turned the sky into a blaze of colour. Shirley and John saw it all, having walked down to the waterside with an esky of food and grog to wait for the show.

It was a proud, extraordinary day and night and Prince Charles concluded: 'As history goes, 200 years is barely a heartbeat, yet look around you and see what has happened in that time – a whole new free people, a people of a whole new free country, Australia.'

The financial crash may have sucked the life out of a number of Australian industries but sales and marketing firms had increased in demand. As permanent staff were laid off to reduce overheads, the 'gig economy' boomed and there was plenty of money to be made for multi-skilled freelancers and temps of Shirley's calibre and background.

As her free time trickled into non-existence, it became apparent that she needed a dedicated space in which to work and organise her uni, freelance and writing commitments.

Tom the builder, who'd become a regular fixture at her house since embarking on an affair with a friend of hers, proposed a kitchen modification that would do the trick. Extending the wall opposite the kitchen bench out onto the side walk-way, he erected a wide glass roof and floor to ceiling windows. He then built in a desk that ran the length of the room but still allowed space to walk through to the bathroom and laundry.

Ironically it was her new desk, or rather how she'd felt after a concentrated week behind it, that prompted her to change her business plans completely. From the time she'd shut up shop for the day, the phone hadn't stopped ringing. The deluge of freelance work offers had made her understand exactly how Banjo Paterson felt when he wrote to Clancy (of the Overflow), that *'the drover's life has pleasures that the townsfolk never know.'*

She continued her metaphor in a letter to Alan, conveying her growing dismay.

'I'm probably mixing my metaphors again, and becoming eccentric and tired of *sitting in my dingy little office, where a stingy ray of sunlight struggles feebly…*

'I may be driving my product to market like Clancy did, but I'm not really working for myself. I'm at everyone's beck and call, setting them up then moving on. I'm a born finisher, Dad, but I'm tiring of even starting!'

Forty electrifying days…

Most of the work she took on in 1988 was doable and relatively stress-free, perhaps because she was becoming disengaged.

Whilst remaining aggravated by the sexism, discrimination and injustice she saw all around her, there seemed to be nothing she could do about it.

Women continued to be underpaid, people who were 'different' were still treated appallingly, sexual harassment and bullying were as rampant as ever and the word 'feminism' remained a term of disparagement and stigma, muddied by association with lesbianism and separatism. Nothing she could do about that either.

Paradoxically, and inevitably, her BA reading commitments were beginning to stir her conscience and driving force to do something. Rosalind in *As You Like It* had struck home in more ways than one: *'Do you not know I am a woman? When I think, I must speak.'*

A short-term contract to help a former colleague launch a new recruitment arm for his HR business, including recruiting and training staff, may initially have struck her as another Banjo-esque assignment but it wasn't dingy at all, and into the bargain she met Kristina Rixon, known as Boppy (short for 'teeny bopper'), a country girl 20 years her junior with whom she would forge a lasting friendship.

Thanks to Rosalind, the next job she secured was destined to be different from any other she'd known. To Shirley, speaking meant doing.

For the second time in her life she'd answered an advertisement in the daily press. The manager who appointed her explained the duties involved but acknowledged it was hard to know where they might lead until the program got underway.

She'd become one of 80 government-appointed 'watchdogs' deployed into mental wards across the state to scrutinise records and facilities in an effort to prevent 'another Chelmsford'.

The media had been instrumental in sensationalising the exposure of a dozen deaths in Sydney's Chelmsford Mental Home due to neglect and excessive Electroconvulsive Therapy (ECT shock treatment). The public outcry had prompted the government to launch an inquiry, and the immediate result of that was the part-time appointment of 'Official Visitors' to the secluded (closed) psychiatric wards of mainly public hospitals.

In groups of three, the watchdogs would attend their allocated institutions to thoroughly examine the ECT record books, looking for evidence of excessive treatments administered, plus interview and communicate with staff, patients and family members. As a nonpartisan official visitor (no qualifications or associations within the medical or legal professions), Shirley would accompany an appointed medical practitioner and a lawyer. They would then submit a written report (within 24 hours) of their findings, including any person/s who approached the Official Visitors with complaints or concerns. Suspect or actual findings would be reported back to the NSW Minister of Health.

Prior to commencement, Shirley had attended a seminar, the first held in eight years, and was briefed by various department heads, including the officials who would evaluate their reports, the lawyers representing patients at committal hearings in the magistrates court, and the guardian board who supervised patient after-care.

So many cogs in the wheel, so much indecision, so little funding.

Initially it had seemed miraculous to Shirley that their watchdog jobs had been approved. But any doubts she had as to the necessity of the initiative disappeared when a psychiatrist informed her about the state of mental health in Australia.

He began with the fact that a mental disorder strikes one-in-four people.

'One per cent of the world's population is incurably schizophrenic, but 10 per cent is affected by schizophrenia to some degree. We all know one or two, perhaps without knowing it.'

Shirley reverted to shorthand to keep up with him.

Then there was suicide.

'More Australians take their own lives than die on our roads; during the last decade the numbers hovered around 2,050 a year. Men commit suicide four times more often than women; it's the leading cause of death for males under 44.'

'Several of my family, and two friends took their own lives,' she couldn't help interrupting, 'and several tried but failed.'

'Yes, it's all too common,' he continued pragmatically.

'One of every 29 deaths investigated by the state is a suicide. An estimated 55,000 people attempt suicide each year, but Suicide Prevention Australia estimates that the number of people who contemplate it is likely 20 times higher. The vast majority of people who commit suicide are parents.

'Are you a parent?' he suddenly addressed her personally.

'No,' Shirley replied quietly.

'That's good,' he said brightly, 'although you don't seem to have any depressive in you so you may not have passed on the family genes if you'd had children anyway.'

Her first day on the job was like no other in her career. She arrived at the Prince of Wales Hospital in Randwick to meet solicitor John Connelly and medico Harry Haber in reception. Flanked by an armed security guard and a male psychiatric nurse, they embarked on a silent journey into the bowels of the hospital. The further they went, the more doors they encountered that needed to be unlocked by the security guard. After filing into an elevator only just large enough to hold them all, they descended to the floor that housed the psychiatric ward. Another locked door later and suddenly they were in a new world.

The secure wing was a maze of concrete walls punctuated by broken faces and aimlessly ambling ghosts. The more coherent among them leant against the walls smoking, but the majority of the patients just sat gazing into space. Shirley would occasionally receive a smile in return for hers. Engaging them in conversation was rare, but when it happened it was always portentous.

The official visitors were crammed into the nurses' station for a briefing about the current occupants of the ward. This included not only their psych history and length of internment, but also their family support or lack of, and any physical health issues that weren't blindingly apparent.

On being dismissed, Shirley and her co-visitors would head off to perform their first inspection facility – the ECT treatment room, followed by the padded cells and the recreational area for visitors to meet with family.

It didn't take long to realise why the minister's inquiry into these modern-day bedlams had been given the thumbs up.

Whilst the head nurse had said there'd been few ECT treatments administered during the past month, the record book stated otherwise. When Shirley read that one patient had been submitted to 17 rounds of convulsive therapy during the past week, she felt a creeping unease.

'Why had she lied?' she wondered aloud. Her colleagues shook their heads.

They'd discovered several anomalies by the time they'd completed their first rounds and agreed between each other what feedback they'd share with the minister. The doctor had picked up some irregularities in a number of padded cells, his legal counterpart would report the ECT situation and Shirley would relay the content of a disturbing discussion she'd had with a patient, as well as noting the absence of ECT information sheets for patients' families.

Besides breaking up the occasional scuffle between patients or visitors or both, the security guards were trapped in the most depressing of environments, their shifts amounting to countless hours of utter boredom. Feeling sorry for them, Shirley would sometimes pass on an inside story of a patient they'd rescued who was now doing well, endeavouring to reassure them that if they weren't on the job, the official visitors wouldn't be either.

For the next two and a half years Shirley worked one and sometimes two eight-hour shifts a month inside the mental wards of The Prince of Wales hospital – precisely 40 days service in the pursuit of *making a difference*. When the results of the inquiry into Chelmsford's horrors were finally published, she had reason to wonder what contribution she'd made.

The fatalities had continued to occur 'at a death average of about one or two a year, with a total of 27 individuals dying as a direct result of the deep sleep therapy, and 24 others committing suicide following the treatment, or due to it'.

She counted her blessings for a unique experience, but was relieved that that philanthropic journey was over.

Shop and cops

It was the perfect solution!

A year or two running a nine to 5.30 shop, Mondays to Saturdays, with time to study and pass exams in order to meet a 1990 deadline to sell up and go bush to write full-time? If Margery had been around to be asked, she might have quoted Disraeli…*Life is too short to be small.*

Whilst Shirley had no experience in retail, she'd always been a shrewd shopper and reckoned she knew enough about selling to make a quid! A recession was almost certainly coming but she could handle that and be back in control of her life. It was a people business after all. How could she lose?

She purchased the goodwill and chattels of a tiny gift shop in Darling Street, Balmain, from a shopkeeper called Kerry Washington, who ran a large gift shop at the city end of Darling Street and quickly become a supportive friend.

She renamed it 'Shirley's Place' and on the signage added the tagline 'It's not the thought that counts, it's the gift behind it!'

She employed a part-time assistant, Jaquetta, recruited Boppy to work Saturdays, and rostered two experienced temps who would help with the pre-Christmas madness and cover her during short-term periods of absence.

Jaquetta was a local lass who was good on the job, and good looking too. She was dating a star in the TV soap opera, *Sons and Daughters*.

Many famous film and television identities lived along the Balmain waterfront. Those who visited her shop, among them journalist George Negas, Olympian Dawn Fraser and the hot-shoe-shufflers David Atkins and Rhonda Birchmore, were mostly pleasant and polite. She would gladly display flyers for their performances when requested.

Others were not so agreeable. John Singleton was a regular and unfortunately so were his demanding sons. They wanted everything. Dad would fork over hundreds whilst the two of them jumped around wildly, and more than once she'd needed to discipline them to prevent the destruction of yet another item on her shelves.

Before she knew it 1989 was on the horizon. In the lead up to Christmas she quadrupled her bottom line and it was little wonder why.

Each day over those three weeks she was on the floor for 10 hours straight. Jaquetta worked five days a week and Boppy's Saturday shifts also had to be extended to cope with the rush. Shirley had been prudent in ordering sufficient stock for the peak trading period but the shelves were nearly bare when Shirley's Place finally closed on Christmas Eve. Her profit for the month was a tidy $20K, which when she looked at her poor, dreadful feet, she knew she'd well and truly earned.

Straight after Christmas she took the phone off the hook and enjoyed two 'Shirley McLaughlin days', meaning she gave herself sick leave to stay home and recuperate. There were no repercussions or knives in the back this time. She was the boss!

She'd booked a flight to Taiwan on 29th December and spent three days casing Taipei's wholesalers' trade centre (the largest in the world), purchasing unique gifts and hundreds of greeting cards at rock bottom prices whilst establishing accounts for future mail orders. There was no resistance in Balmain to Made in Taiwan if the gift and the price was right.

En route home she spent a few days in Honolulu with relatively new friend, Julie Steele, sharing Julie and Tom's luxury apartment on the beach at Diamond Head where Tony Curtis time-shared an apartment across the passage. Having trained Julie for Bird Cameron in Melbourne, she knew what to expect. Julie was a party girl.

Their plan to run out of sugar and knock on Tony's door was the only disappointment. He was there alright, but the party-pooper refused to answer. Naturally they later agreed over a glass of champs that he was the looser.

Already over-committed for 1989, Shirley's first month of the year was chockers.

Roy, ex-boss from London was visiting and she would need time off to show him around. He was seriously thinking of opening a Sports Sponsorship Bureau in Australia. Ken Moon, her tutor-to-be at University New England, whom she'd met during the orientation weekend in Armadale, owned a home nearby in Balmain and he and wife Elaine (who was head of the English department at UNE) spent their holidays there. They'd invited her to dinner and Ken had arranged a lunch to give her some insights about the degree she'd taken on.

On top of this, a sergeant from the local police station had befriended her and locked her into a meeting during the second week of January. She'd suffered several shop lifting incidents in the early months as a rookie learning the ropes, and had met several constables from the local cop shop, but the reason for the sergeant's solo session was unknown.

Shirley had yet again landed on her feet, but the shop was her first experience of dealing with the general public day after day and she conceded that she still had a lot to learn. Whilst Balmain had more than its share of the famous and fortunate, there was also a number of men and women bashing and abusing children and/or each other, and miscreants' shop lifting and/or suddenly lunging over the front desk to steal her till. There were also lost youngsters, Alsatians without muzzles, and patients from the local mental home who'd somehow escaped their padded cells.

Just as they'd done a decade ago in Carlton, the local cops knew an operator when they saw one.

Sergeant Geoff Cavanagh had decided that Shirley had the skills and street smarts to form a Business Watch for Darling Street, and of course it struck her immediately as another 'watchdog' experience. How could she refuse?

Geoff and the newly appointed chief inspector, a man named PJ McLaughlin, stressed the importance of a united business community and the Balmain Council in particular needed a wake-up call on many issues affecting shopkeepers. Shirley sent out flyers and held meetings every couple of months, Cavanagh always attended and the shopkeepers benefitted greatly. A Business Watch sticker on the front door was a warning that owners in the street talked to one another. It didn't change everything, but it made a difference for shopkeepers.

Three small initiatives inside the shop could reduce shoplifting to a trickle and the rules were so basic it was difficult to comprehend why somebody hadn't initiated it decades ago.

1. Eye-ball everyone who walks in the door, say good morning and keep them in view.

2. If you're at the back of the shop, move forward immediately and acknowledge them. If you're busy with a customer, excuse yourself momentarily to greet them.

3. Remember good customers will feel welcome. Potential shoplifters will feel uncomfortable because you've looked them in the eye. You know they're there, will call the police with a good description and pass it onto the shopkeepers along the strip.

In the meantime Cavanagh signed Shirley onto a committee to help stop drugs and crime in the district, and put her on a police call-list to counsel youths they thought could be saved.

However, her dealings with the local constabulary didn't stop there.

Aviator John had a weakness for women, and seemed to prefer those of Chinese or Vietnamese heritage. He'd been having a bad run in the relationship stakes for a couple of years and a few domestic incidents at his house (two down from Shirley's) had instigated calls to the police, on one occasion by John himself.

A long-term, on again, off again girlfriend had been at his home threatening to commit suicide, having already used a kitchen knife to refresh his wardrobe. She'd slashed several of his suits into tiny pieces, cut the sleeves off his shirts, sliced up six pairs of shoes and sprinkled the resulting concoction across his small front garden. During a previous breakup she'd chalked 'Kill John' on the front door and burnt the seat covers of his car with a cigarette.

When eventually he'd discovered that her family were involved with a Chinese triad, he was seriously spooked. The police dealt with it somehow and she wasn't seen again.

Shirley got to know John's next girlfriend quite well. She was a charming Vietnamese woman who regularly invited her to join them for dinners and boat trips. She had dared to hope that her hapless neighbour had chosen well this time, but all women are, of course, capable of retributive behaviour when their man cheats.

On a windy Sunday afternoon Shirley was at home hanging out the washing when the first bundle of women's clothing flew over the back fence from the old 'night lane' that ran the length of the three terraces.

A second clothing projectile followed shortly and then an assortment of smaller bags, a hairdryer, portable radio and several shoes followed suit. Next came Aviator's girlfriend, who had just straddled the top of the rickety fence when it collapsed.

If there was a silver lining it was that she'd thrown her clothes over first; her sensational horizontal landing, face down onto the ground, was at least partially cushioned. Her radio came on spontaneously with Elvis's *Rock Around The Clock* and Shirley figured even Shakespeare couldn't have topped this farcical scene.

'When you want to finish a relationship, John,' Shirley sighed some time later as they surveyed the damage to the fence, 'acquiring a new girlfriend is not the way to do it.'

'Yes, yes,' he mumbled with a sad nod. 'Never been able to do that.'

'You're such a decent bloke, John,' she replied, 'but could justly be accused of being a masochist.'

He responded thoughtfully that the cops had told him that last time.

Old friends and new

The New Year at 8 Waite Avenue Balmain brought pleasures and surprises.

Robyn had re-entered Shirley's life, bringing Bobbie, her five year-old daughter with her, and Roy arrived from London soon after. The rush of friends and social interaction helped Shirley regain her fervour and contributed greatly to a grand start to the New Year.

Roy conquered the tourist sights of Sydney whilst Shirley worked, but together they took a long, scenic drive to the south coast, sailed on the Harbour at sunset, and John took Roy on a joy flight in his fully restored de Havilland Tiger Moth.

A farewell party at home was de rigour and once the neighbours had accepted, it seemed appropriate to invite other friends. Suddenly the party became a 30 guest barbeque in her tiny backyard.

Beris didn't seem quite her usual self, but she flew up from Melbourne and had to stay elsewhere because Roy was in the guest room. Gerro and Paddy and Susie and Carl were the showbiz contingent, Robyn, Kerry and Gaby and Chris led the local friends, and neighbours Qantas John and wife Lynne, Max, and Aviator John completed the scene.

'I'm *happy as Larry* – no current threats!' John laughed, repeating his thanks to her for advising him so well. She had no memory of giving him advice, only an honest assessment he'd heard before.

Perhaps it was the spectacular sunsets whilst sailing on the Sydney Harbour that channelled Cupid? Or maybe the swashbuckling flight in the Tiger Moth? Or, most likely, the aphrodisiac properties of Shirley's favourite crustaceans. But after the soiree Shirley dismissed her fantasies and faced the facts.

Please, please, she asked an imaginary god, *let my matchmaking be good!*

It was over the prawn and salmon starters that Roy fell in love with Robyn. Before dessert had hit their plates, he'd asked her to join him in London. Their host hadn't been privy to either development when, at the end of the night, she declared the gathering a 'celebration of friends from near and far'.

When she added, 'No matter where we are in the universe, let's always treasure our good fortune in life to have met at all,' she had no idea that her words would remain poignant to Roy and Robyn for many years.

Shirley had posted her first essay to Ken Moon at UNE prior to driving to Armadale to attend the first of two compulsory live-in lecture sessions per year. She'd spent the three days in the lecture hall being stimulated and astounded; one of the evenings at Ken and Elaine's table at home enjoying erudite conversation sprinkled with university gossip; a night at her desk in her *dingy little office;* and the final night on the town with a fellow correspondence student.

Ken Moon was a man like Alan McLaughlin – the same quiet intelligence, same qualifications, same sense of humour and very similar upbringings. Ken, who had lived a disciplined, conservative life, often expressed his admiration for Shirley's vivaciousness and her ownership of herself, flaws and all.

Like Shirley, Elaine was a country girl. Also like her, she'd climbed to the top of a male dominated professional biosphere. Elaine's PhD in psychology had earned her distinctions and she'd rejoiced in finding a female soul mate who wasn't possessed of academic approbation.

During their first dinner together the women had taken over the conversation discussing the musings of Rebecca West, turn of the century feminism, and how far they surprisingly hadn't come since then. They'd canvassed man's history of fighting and killing men, women and children, and bullying, harassing and demeaning women since time immemorial. They agreed that what most disgusted them in this modern age was the pitiful failure of too many women to stand-up and say, 'This has to stop!'

Contrary to his usual quiet manner, Ken loudly agreed. He feared for his children and grandchildren's future.

'We've done our best with our one daughter and three sons, having always set equal standards. But one family can't change a culture and the dogma isn't equal.

'Men don't carry and birth the babies but without our sperm and muscular domination there's no life…we're superior, in control of the world. Its fate is in our hands and we were born to fight. C'est la vie,' he sighed. 'Women will probably never be equal, despite the fact that they surpass us in every way other than brawn.'

Unbeknownst to Shirley, Ken got into the habit of leaving her essays till last to read. He wrote to her once that for all the thousands of students he'd trained in his lifetime, she took the cake for originality: it was always a surprise to read 'her take' on the human condition.

An association that began between a student and her tutor became a veritable, evolving platonic friendship. For life. Interspersed with meetings and phone calls, they regularly wrote idiosyncratic, impassioned long letters to one another for nearly 30 years.

Show time

Shirley's Place was paying its way but the recession was biting and there was no relief in sight.

Since selling her smaller gift shop business to Shirley, Kerry had become her mentor and whilst they talked shop on the phone during working hours, they'd struck a friendship and met socially when they could. Kerry had been working as a bookkeeper for Sydney's Royal Easter Show for several years and had somehow convinced her new friend to become a carnival coupon seller!

Inexplicably, the money was exceptionally good. And…well, it would be a new experience, wouldn't it?

It was a five-day contract. Jaquetta was available for the week, and Boppy could help on Saturday.

Shirley was very uncertain about her hasty decision when Robyn called to tell her that she'd accepted the job too! Having also been tipped off from a friend about the money, she couldn't refuse because she was doing it tough and had a young daughter to support.

'I feel much better now!' Shirley shrieked and Robyn agreed that she did too.

Shirley should have known by now that dealing with the general public at a showground carnival where families were let loose and animals were constrained was not going to be a picnic.

Once on the job, she acknowledged her recklessness. Physically, it would be a decent workout for an Olympian. Mentally, it would drive a psychiatrist mad.

Suddenly an evocative response from Vickie in OKC reverberated in her ears.

'But would you believe it of a carnival coupon seller!'

There were only two things during those five days that Shirley cared to remember. Her fellow workers, an erudite lot, used to tell jokes to one another to keep their sanity, but she'd never been able to get the punch lines of jokes right so she didn't tell any. Instead, she'd offered to read their palms. The shared laughter and individual palm reading impacted on them all, so Shirley's memories of the unattractive behaviour of the carnival goers that they constantly encountered was quickly forgotten.

Of course, she was not alone in that, but most of the team went back year after year.

Shirley missed their company and couldn't recall any of their jokes, but when she found herself still in Sydney and available at Easter the following year, she decided to go back too.

She figured her palm reading had been done to death so she searched for one of Vickie's best anecdotes, and learned it off-by-heart.

Delivered in recitation style to the clique of carnival coupon sellers who could keep the team laughing…all the way to their banks without her, she got broad smiles, giggles and applause.

> You see a gorgeous girl at a party. You go up to her and say, 'I'm fantastic in bed.'
> That's Direct Marketing.
>
> You're at a party with a bunch of friends and see a gorgeous girl. One of your friends goes up to her and pointing at you says, 'He's fantastic in bed.'
> That's Advertising.
>
> You see a gorgeous girl at a party. You go up to her and get her telephone number. The next day you call and say, 'Hi, I'm fantastic in bed.'
> That's Telemarketing.
>
> You're at a party and see a gorgeous girl. You get up and straighten your tie; you walk up to her and pour her a drink. You open the door for her, pick up her bag after she drops it, offer her a ride, and then say, 'By the way, I'm fantastic in bed.'
> That's Public Relations.
>
> You're at a party and see a gorgeous girl. She walks up to you and says, 'I hear you're fantastic in bed.'
> That's Brand Recognition.

If at first you don't succeed…

The sale of Shirley's Place was never going to be easy, let alone during a recession.

Hurdle number one: yet again she'd put her name to the business. In her excitement at the prospect of taking on a new venture she'd overlooked the lessons she'd taken from earlier iterations of Shirley McLaughlin Enterprises. Buyers who are novices in that field may well go broke 12 months after they purchase. Smart ones will steer clear; gourmet awa^y had sold quickly, the new owners may have lost a few clients but they were still in business.

Hurdle number two: over-cautious lenders. After she'd hired and fired a couple of overpriced and/or arrogant agents, she orchestrated her own advertising and received four hot potential enquiries. The two who went on to accept the asking price were subsequently knocked back on their respective loan applications. Savings and business interest was ridiculously high in 1989 and whilst banks naturally wanted to loan, most of their customers were already over committed.

Shirley was forced to acknowledge that she was unable to manoeuvre or manipulate the world around her. The tide was going in a different direction. She decided to retreat, taking the business off the market and digging in for a long, cold, profitless winter.

The drunks increased as the economy decreased, emitting alcohol from their pores and dropping cigarette ash everywhere. Some started crying, others begged for money because their pension wasn't due until tomorrow, and the same old blokes continued to vomit on the doorstep – if she was lucky. 'You've got to get out of here!' she instructed herself one day when she'd cleaned up the doorstep and 10 minutes later had to empty half the lapidary cabinet and wash all the spheres, pyramids and shelves to remove the splattered sick.

Fortunately spring was approaching and she spent a quiet morning plotting a course.

Her last advertising tilt had drawn serious buyers but they couldn't get a loan. It was valuable information, but what was it telling her?

Shit! she muttered to Fred Astaire and Ginger Rogers on the wall in front of her counter, a large print of the idols she'd bought at an art studio in Sydney and finally framed when her last Taiwan shipment arrived. (David Atkins was picking it up after lunch.)

How did they get there? she asked herself. Fred was too short and clueless at the start, and Ginger was stunning and exceptional. How did *they*…?

Overcome the objections! she winced as if she was a fool to have taken 10 minutes to get it.

She stuck to the previous placement of ads, wrote for the market, and cut to the chase.

> **Christmas is coming…**
> **and the 4 weeks leading up to it**
> **will guarantee a happy one!**
> **Buy now, receive 2 weeks' free training,**
> **and pay out your finance on Christmas Eve!**
> **Comprehensive manual included.**

Age Five

The first of six phone calls she received in response turned out to be the only one that mattered. The woman who would eventually take the reins of Shirley's Place had recently been retrenched from the public service. She had the cash to cover the asking price, knew of the shop already and had been dreaming of running her own for 20 years.

By the end of their second meeting, she'd started referring to the business using her own name and by November was champing at the bit to finally be her own boss.

It was a magical moment when the vendor and purchaser signed the contract of sale.

The timing, and sheer chance of it all, that two very different women who had obsessed on one goal for most of their adult lives, were about to realise their dreams.

When things are going your way, everything seems to fall into place.

The New South Wales city of Albury, on the border with Wodonga in Victoria, was crystalising in her mind. The Murray River ran through it, the Great Dividing Range framed it, the farming community and vineyards nearby were thriving, and it was only 3½ hours' drive from Melbourne.

Shirley jumped into the car, drove to Albury, found a house with a view of the river and mountains on Riverside Drive at a price she could well afford, paid a deposit, negotiated a four month settlement, returned to Sydney and put 8 Waite Avenue on the market.

Kristina (Boppy) and her boyfriend Andrew White, born and raised in Albury and later to marry and return there, volunteered to be the agent's dummy bidders at the Balmain auction. When the price had dramatically surpassed the reserve, the auctioneer gave Andrew the 'stop' sign and a keen Englishman unwittingly bid twice more!

Shirley gasped, put up her hand and arched her thumb backwards. The auctioneer nodded and brought down the hammer on the buyer's previous call.

Whilst waiting for the respective house settlements and preparing for her move, Shirley worked freelance for John Downs at RMK Voice Productions, writing biographies and publicity 'grabs' of nationally in-demand talent and assisting with their management. On her final day, John threw a showbiz party to thank her, and he and his wife promised to hit the road to Albury to attend the party she'd wildly suggested she'd throw to celebrate the launch of her first book.

Fuck, she said to herself. *I hope I haven't tempted fate.*

Full circle

Rudyard Kipling's *If* occupied Shirley's mind as she drove to Albury ahead of the removalist van, especially the line: '*If you can meet with Triumph and Disaster, and treat those two impostors just the same…*'

Of course it all began when she was a little girl, writing stories on the kitchen floor whilst Margery prepared the meals, dreaming of the day she'd become a famous author. Scribbling poems and stories was an inherent response to her mother's intense and unique recitation coaching, but merely the first of countless imaginings, most of which she realised – until the boredom set in. Passionately focussed on growing up and getting experience in the wider world, she hadn't entertained going to university to learn a profession. There were too many options and too little time.

Following a credit for one year's formal study of English as an adult student and two-and-a-half years serving the unpredictable general public, she'd finally accepted that some people just have to do things the long way around, and that 'No' from a woman would always be more powerful than 'Yes…' providing it's delivered with feminine panache!

Thus was the eclectic road Shirley had travelled, from a creative childhood with a dying mother she'd been unable to bury for nearly a decade, to a resourceful woman with the audacity and self-worth to tread her own path.

Bev, too, would get the chance to realise her childhood dreams that year…

She had been selected as one of 150 choristers in Australia who would join the United Nations' World Festival Choir for a performance of Verdi's Requiem at a 2000 year old amphitheatre in Verona, Italy. With Luciano Pavarotti performing the tenor solo *Ingemisco* and Princess Diana's attendance already confirmed, it was a once-in-a-lifetime opportunity – particularly for a woman with inherent musical talent, who'd devoted most of her adult life to being a wife and mother.

Age Five

For the first time Bev would leave her men at home to fend for themselves. Though her sons were by then 22, 20 and 15½ years respectively, and Rob was perhaps not as domestically challenged as most of his fellow pre boomer blokes, she prepped them for every eventuality during her absence. The day she left, the Gosbell residence was a sea of Post-It notes bearing operation instructions for every household appliance, along with tips on the frequency and extent of cleaning and grocery shopping. There'd also been a comprehensive demonstration of how to use, and empty the vacuum cleaner, which had left the four awe-struck spectators wondering who'd be a woman if there was choice in the matter.

It was the final weekend of July when Alan and Steve rolled into Albury in Alan's rock-hunting Toyota ute. A visit with Shirley would be fun and she'd be glad of some help with one or two minor repairs, like a collapsed back veranda for starters. They settled in over some beers, a roast dinner and 'a few rattling good yarns,' as Alan called them.

After a solid morning of work on Shirley's new digs, the three of them pulled up stumps for lunch in the late winter sun.

As they finished eating, Alan murmured that tomorrow would be the 16th anniversary of Craig's death. In that moment, any intentions of returning to work were forgotten. Instead, Alan, Steven and Shirley settled in to reflect on the short life of their dear little pixie, eventually finding themselves reliving the final moments of his life. Steven had just started school and Dale was three and a half, Shirley was 26 and Alan must have been 62. It was disturbing, yet oddly riveting when they each related a spontaneous memory of those shattering three days.

Steven, now a young man of 22, recalled the horror of flying home from Queensland.

'It was my first time on a plane and a part of me was excited, but I ended up hating the whole trip because Craig was so sick, and all I wanted to do was land so we could get into the ambulance,' he admitted, adding how hurt he'd been at Bev's insistence that only Alan would go with them.

'He was a beautiful little boy. He smiled through his tears right to the end,' Alan said, turning to Steven with shining eyes and, in a rare show of raw emotion, gripped his grandson's shoulder.

'And it was your mother,' he continued in a voice cracked with bittersweet pride, 'my first-born girl…it was her love and courage that gave the rest of us strength.'

Half a world away, Bev (the object of Alan's reverence) had arrived in a country rich with outlets for her myriad passions and creative abilities.

After the long journey to Verona, the World Festival Choir's Australian contingent had spent a few days traipsing through the museums and art galleries of Florence before getting down to the raison d'être for the trip with a rehearsal. Final rehearsals for the entire ensemble, including singers from all around the world, were scheduled to take place in Verona two days later.

Following a day of sightseeing in fair Verona, Bev had just indulged in a long shower and was about to enjoy her first decent night's sleep since she left home when the hotel phone rang.

It was Rob, with the dreadful news that young Gareth had died in his sleep.

Dale had gone into his room to wake him because they were due at karate practice in 30 minutes. Rob was at church. Neighbour and trained nurse Marlene took immediate control. The coroner later confirmed that the cause of death was a virus of the heart.

There is no pain quite as devastating as the loss of one's child. If that parent is a mother, the grief she feels at seeing her child die before her is unbearable. But when fate cruelly delivers the deaths of two of a woman's children, both without warning and well before their time, there are no words to describe the blow.

'I don't know what I'm going to do without him,' were the first words Bev had uttered to Shirley and Alan after arriving back in Melbourne.

Many people had been instrumental in facilitating her quick return to Australia. But Bev's odyssey homeward had been as isolated as it was surreal. The only known quantity was that her Gareth was dead.

There was a bus trip to Milan, then a flight to Frankfurt. From there she flew to Singapore and then on to Melbourne. She had no idea how long she spent waiting around for the various connections. And even if the interludes had been quick, they would have been just as excruciating, imbued as they were with the faraway finality of the loss of another beloved son.

Hundreds of people attended Gareth's funeral, including all of the students from his form and most of his teachers. As Bev had told her older boys right from the time he came into the world, Gareth was his own man. He'd taken a different path to his academically inclined brothers and had lined himself up with a plumbing apprenticeship. But far from being any kind of black sheep, he was everyone's friend.

Age Five

As the service drew to an end, Rob stood to ask the mourners to join him in singing *For He's a Jolly Good Fellow*.

Variations on *'How on earth are we going to do this?'* ran through most heads in that church. But as each person involuntarily expelled an audible breath, they found a collective strength. And sing they did.

Everyone was crying by the time they finished the slow, sad rendition of the celebratory song, but the air of gratitude and love was palpable. It was almost as if Gareth was in the building, listening and quietly groaning, but admiring their courage and thanking them for coming in his gentle-hearted way.

None of the family ever got over losing him, but his spirit lives on.

Gareth Craig Gosbell ...

25/09/1974 – 29/07/1990

We have lost his presence but will never lose the memory
of his capacity for loving, caring and giving.

Becoming an author

It would be 12 months before Shirley got back to her usual happy self after the heartache of Gareth's passing and her sister's loss. Her grief wasn't helped by her involvement in a serious car accident just before she'd left Sydney. And she had also found herself battling to adjust to her radical change of life as a writer.

She'd moved on from the people business that to date had been her forte, centre and purpose. She'd re-charted her course, striking out on her own and embracing the unknown in order to give herself a real chance of succeeding at something she'd coveted since she was a child.

Albury was proving to be a town of cliques and moth-eaten social stereotypes. Single men were few and far between and mature single women were considered threatening. On top of it all she was actually frightened but couldn't fathom why.

Every morning she got up, had breakfast, did domestic chores, made phone calls, sent faxes, talked over the fence to the neighbours…anything, absolutely anything other than walk across the threshold of her study to start writing.

When she'd exhausted her litany of avoidance practices, her tears would begin. Most mornings it took her an hour just to sit down at her desk. Strangely, once she'd begun she could write all day and well into the night; sometimes she'd glance up from the keyboard and be stunned to see that the sun was coming up over the mountains.

That she kept the TV on quietly, constantly, was a valuable clue to her wretched, unprecedented fear and loneliness and helped her get over it when she realised how desperately she missed people. The soapies, movies and morning and afternoon live shows worked best, sort of like her staff were 'over there', working away in the general office. The fact that the TV was sitting on her L-shaped desk was irrelevant. She wasn't listening or watching it, just doing her own work with company in the background.

Eating alone also depressed her so she got into the habit of taking her lunch and dinner to the desk, with the volume turned up to watch the news.

The isolation of the career path she'd chosen was the inescapable element that challenged her commitment every day during the first year, despite her early success.

She had found a publisher for her first non-fiction manuscript and had just received the proofs. It was a strange feeling, as if somehow it had been written by someone else.

Wrightbooks in Melbourne were going to press later in the year, but there was some work to be done before then.

She was struggling with the title for starters: *Employees are not as Dumb as They Look!*

Geoff Wright, the publisher, and his daughter Lesley, the editor, had come up with a suggestion that embarrassed her: *Appointing People.*

It was so perfectly obvious that why hadn't she thought of it herself?

As a novice author, having her work edited was the next eye-opener. For about the 10th time Shirley started at page one, but for the very first time with dozens of sticky notes of suggestions and scribbles throughout the manuscript to guide her. There were so many recommendations for improvement – from additions to deletions and everything in between – that she reflected to her 'colleague', the TV, that she couldn't think why they wanted to publish her book in the first place!

When *Appointing People* had been transformed into a book, and she had received her six free copies in the mail and quickly flicked through one, she called Lesley to thank her for improving her maiden work by at least 10 per cent. Lesley seemed surprised with her gesture, and the compliment, and Shirley naturally wondered why. Surely any new, or established author for that matter, would be thrilled and grateful?

It was a lightbulb moment in her early days in the author business.

On her first book tour Shirley knew some of the media interviewers from her previous life and they certainly contributed to an early flurry of sales, but the recession was not going away anytime soon and Geoff, Lesley and Shirley had to conclude that the subject matter was ill-timed. Geoff had planned to sell *Appointing People* to his old publishing company in London but England wasn't in any better shape than Australia. Employers around the world were sacking people, not appointing them!

Never mind, the author said to her brand new computer, having just re-jigged her second tome for the hundredth time. *Minding Your Own Business* was geared to the market. The title was spot on this time and nearly ready for Lesley's magic.

'In memory of dear Gareth, and all the dreams that might have been…' she re-read on the acknowledgements page before bundling up the manuscript and heading out to the post office.

Life was good. Puzzling, but going okay. The books kept coming, as did the book tours, and the visitors from near and far – with and without invitations.

The view outside her window continued to inspire. A misty dusk faded over the distant mountains and gums most days, often deep blues and greens between rich yellows and autumn reds even in summer. After last year's floods they'd taken on a ghostly look and now the river was so low that her friend, the paddle steamer, had stopped operating.

Shirley missed her; she'd used to toot when she passed three times a day.

Albury was an elitist town which had bestowed upon Shirley all the cachet deserved of a 'published author'. She was regularly invited to contribute to panel discussions at the local university and to speak at book clubs and community functions. She knew that these weren't exactly overtures to life-long friendships or the sense of belonging she so craved, but her loneliness would compel her to oblige.

One such invitation was extended by Sandra, the beguilingly effervescent grande dame of the most popular book club in town. She'd been keen to develop a friendship with 'the new author' and threw a dinner party in Shirley's honour to introduce her to her friends.

That evening the conversation flowed and the food and wine were excellent, but there was a moment whilst the eight guests were concluding the main course when the subject turned to the working class in the outer suburb of Laverton, a blot on the landscape in every way. Shirley was quietly repulsed by the arrogance of the conversation, grateful nobody asked for her opinion, and offered to clear the table.

She'd purchased a couple of investment flats in the suburb and felt decidedly unsettled by their disparaging remarks. On the one hand she was offended, on the other worried. She'd had no knowledge of the rampant drug scene in Laverton, or the large numbers of residents who were living on the dole. The tenants she'd installed were paying their rent on time and her first six monthly inspections had been fine. She was living on the income from the two properties and the last thing she needed was another Hawthorn calamity.

Shirley had been in the kitchen a few minutes when Sandra's husband appeared, threw his arms around her, kissed her on the lips, ran his hands down her sides and grabbed her crotch, the full force of his body crippling her against the kitchen bar. She shrieked in shock and her scream shocked him. It was a sickening moment and there was nowhere to go. The guests must have heard her scream and she thought *quickly, quickly…how do I handle this when somebody comes?*

But nobody did. Was he everyone's favourite host – or was it more the case that they knew him too well and expected that she'd be able to handle it?

Age Five

Without missing a beat, he turned away to start stacking the dishwasher. She was still shaking as she stared at his back, wondering for the briefest moment if the assault had been just a figment of her imagination. Then she thought about herself, and why stay another minute for the dubious support of a woman who could be an abused wife and happens to be the first booklover in this unfriendly town to invite me to dinner?

She fled the kitchen and acted her way through the rest of the evening, departing with the other guests and a very heavy heart. She sent Sandra a thank you card the following day and did her best to put it behind her.

A few weeks later they bumped into one another in the supermarket. There was no doubt she'd been removed from the pre boomer's guest list and was greatly relieved on that score. But when Sandra apologised for her husband's rudeness and explained that he didn't read female authors and thought they were all cheap chicks who'd chanced to get a break writing shit for no-hopers, Shirley had heard enough.

Upon reflection, whilst her new profession had afforded her status and authority among these dreadful people, the fact that she hadn't spoken up and left the house immediately was probably evidence enough to them that she also viewed herself as merely a woman – just a female shit chick writer at that. Why hadn't she exposed the bastard and left them all to their just desserts? What was the matter with her?

This wasn't her first 15 minutes of fame, but it had certainly thrown her off balance. She felt ashamed and disappointed in herself, and was pondering over how she'd allowed her long-yearned success to change her when she remembered the first rule about *never reducing your standards…*

She couldn't remember when she'd last talked to Margery, but it was plainly well overdue.

Making a Living, her third non-fiction was picked up by Allen & Unwin and hit the shelves at the right time in early 1992 and was reprinted later that year. The national book tour demanded a month of Shirley's time and she was quietly beginning to feel like it was a job for a younger woman

She badly needed a holiday and was becoming bored with writing 'How To' books. She'd thrown out the three unpublishable works of fiction she'd completed in her 20s, but there was one story she'd desperately wanted to write for years. It needed some research before she could begin so she took a plane to Alice Springs, and then a bus to Ayres Rock.

It took a year to write and another year for the English agent Geoff Wright had recommended to her to line up a publishing deal with HarperCollins UK.

A Good Reputation was published in 1995, its 40,000 print run comprising hard and paperback formats. The following year, the publisher's Australian outpost repackaged it as *Billy Batchelor* and committed to an initial print run of 10,000 paperbacks.

As the author's lot goes, the literary agent Shelley Power had made some editing suggestions prior to accepting the manuscript, Shirley took them up quickly and returned the relevant sections by fax, receiving a contract in the mail a couple of weeks later. Then she jumped onto a plane to Paris and a fast train to Bergerac in the Dordogne to meet her new agent. How can you represent someone if you've never met them?

Shelley was a short, thin-lipped, greying blonde with a measured smile and an assertive personality. She would have been in her 50s, and was a generous host. She spoke eloquent English, but didn't mince words. She also spoke fluent French. Her flirtatious husband barely featured during conversations at the dining room table; she was definitely in charge.

Shirley stayed as a guest in Shelley and hubby's country cottage for a few days and they got on well; they had a mutual goal. Shelley had been determined to sell the manuscript from the start.

By the time she had sold the translation rights to Areopagus Publishers in the Netherlands, and their version *DROMEN DIE nooit vervagen* had sold out on the first print run, mainly to book clubs, she was recovering from breast cancer, her marriage had disintegrated and Shirley had secured an appointment with the managing director of Harper Collins in Sydney.

'I wrote this story about my mother who was a well-known Australian in her time, and an irresistible heroine. Europe loves it, but why am I dead in my own country before I've begun? What do I have to do to get *A Good Reputation* published here?'

In the course of half an hour they discovered they'd both tried their damnedest to influence the London staff to change the artist's cover of the book, a close up of two women who looked nothing like the white heroine and her Aboriginal best friend, to no avail. The MD subsequently bought the rights from the UK parent company and despite it being a best seller, Shirley received not one penny from HarperCollins, Australia. The price the colonial child had to pay the English parent to buy the rights, plus the costs involved to rename, package, sell and deliver it to the marketplace ate up all the profits.

Ironically, or perhaps unsurprisingly, Shirley found it a salutary experience. Yes, you can judge a book by its cover! Yes, she'd finally made it and the story would be remembered long after the price had been forgotten. And best of all, Margery would be so proud of her.

Billy Batchelor was nominated for the Kibble Award in 1997, but the politically correct of the day put paid to a win. Margery would have been deeply disturbed to read that the director of Australia's Council of Aboriginal Arts, who hadn't even read it, described the book as *'insulting and disrespectful…this latest example of Australia's willingness to embrace second-rate white interpretations of indigenous experience.'*

In the meantime, Shirley's appetite to write about real people had picked up a pace when the idea came to her.

The Driving Force, 200 Years of Australian Success Stories was published by Angus & Robertson, an imprint of HarperCollins in 1995, and reprinted in the second half of 1995.

Shirley McLaughlin is an enterprising woman and has a driving force of her own…She wondered what drove people to high achievement and further wondered why Australia provided what seemed to be a disproportionate number of such people. Why should it be?

She selected a list of champions and asked them: 'Who or what is "the driving force" that made your success possible?'

She asked 208 people, a mix of artists, writers, entertainers, politicians, business moguls, sporting heroes, education gurus, religious leaders and many ordinary Australians who overcame obstacles by sheer determination…

More than half did not respond. Others demurred. Some dithered (are they driven by somebody else?). There were 36 final acceptances and our undaunted author resurrected another 20 famous Australians who by some recorded declaration or written comment, had divulged the factors which led them to success. Her list includes Dame Judith Anderson, Maina Gielgud, Sir William Dobell, Phillip Adams, Slim Dusty, Sir Arvi Parbo and Peter Allen…

Others nominated a thirst for knowledge, a search for truth, a vision, the love of challenge, a will to win, and a sense of humour…

Phillip Adams wrote in his inimitable style: 'Oh, people will give you all sorts of formula for success…it all boils down to that four-letter word. Luck.'

And the last word belongs to 'Weary' Dunlop who said 'I believe we should have heroes and follow them – beware of mediocrity!'

Shirley's last non-fiction, *Money for Life,* was published in 1997, having begun its life in 1995 as a 10-lesson course for Stott's Correspondence College, an adult education off-spring of her alma mater Stott's Business College where she'd completed her Diploma of Commercial in 1963.

She'd begun tutoring, updating courses and writing new ones for Stott's since the early 90s and continued working for them into the 21st century. The students came from all over the world but most had lived in Australia, reluctantly returning home when their visas expired. Many continued in the hope of achieving a certificate that would help them secure permanent citizenship.

Money for Life was a classic Wrightbooks' non-fiction and one of the last Geoff published before he retired. Shirley had also caught a kind of retirement 'itch'. As her seventh book inside eight years hit the shelves, she was just about over it.

She'd taken her chances, had enough money and needed to *get a life!*

You could write a book about it!

Transcript of a speech to members of a book club, country NSW, circa 1995.
(40 mins or less, 20 mins questions)

(Shirley McLaughlin) Good evening ladies and gentlemen, and thank you for introducing me, Bill, and of course for so kindly standing-in for the president who's unable to be here because his farm is under water.

I hate to disappoint you all, but I'm not Ms Swain and I won't be launching a memoir of my life in television tonight…and though I was in the business during the 70s, our paths never crossed.

Unfortunately your highly anticipated guest speaker is stranded in Singapore because of a Malaysian pilots' strike. I'm her last-minute stand-in. Bill rightly complimented Ms Swain for still taking chances in her 70s and, coincidentally or perhaps just due to bad luck, I was caught in a similar predicament during Confrontation in Indonesia 30 years ago. But my name is Shirley McLaughlin, I'm a baby boomer in my late 40s and I'm not launching anything tonight.

(Male voice in background, undecipherable)

(Shirley McLaughlin) Please don't be embarrassed, Bill! I had short notice too and decided to adapt an address that I delivered in Western Australia recently that could certainly be titled 'Taking chances!' This, and the appalling weather in the last 24 hours must go some way to explaining a not entirely hapless introduction…

My original title, *I could write a book about it,* is specifically directed to book club members who dream of writing a book one day. I hope I can do justice to this capacity audience and know Ms Swain will be complimented to learn you came out in force on such an unforgiving night. My recent days have been fraught with drama too so she, Bill and I have quite a bit in common – especially the knowledge that things don't always go to plan.

I've just completed a book tour covering 2,000 miles by road in my reliable car and roughly 20,000 miles in dependable aeroplanes. For the statistically minded I slept in nine beds in three or four-star hotels and talked to 57 print, radio and TV reporters – some good, some not so good. I didn't count the hours I spent waiting in airports but I delivered 14 speeches in four states and completed eight of 16 planned book signings.

Sunday night I arrived home to a fax from my publisher advising that the rushed second print-run of my latest book was stuck on a container ship in Singapore's harbour throughout the entire tour. Laying irony upon irony, whilst Ms Swain should be home promoting her memoir, I've just marketed a re-print of my sixth, now out-of-stock book that isn't available.

What can you do? Blame the aviation and shipping executives in Singapore? Blame the publisher for poor planning or follow-through?

Life's a risky business and if we don't take chances, nothing happens at all. Might as well be dead. The good news is that Ms Swain and I don't have to do any flogging or signings tonight!

For many of us, from our earliest memories someone we love reads us a story. Blessed to be born at a time and place in history when literacy is mandatory, we start devouring books early, subconsciously learning that literature enriches our lives and heightens our ability to interpret the world around us. Timelessly crafted books answer our questions about the meaning of life on a conscious and subliminal level, fine-tuning us to the complexity and simplicity of human nature and our own strengths and weaknesses in the process.

To dream of creating something memorable in the scheme of all our schemes is an aspiration worth having. Whether fact or fiction, for adults or children…or perhaps a memoir to make sense of your life and leave a record for your grandchildren…

May I have a show of hands please from everyone who is currently writing, or planning to write a book one day?

Don't be shy! You're one of 75 book lovers here tonight and can share the dream.

(Male voice in background). That's about 50, Shirley!

(Shirley McLaughlin) Thank you, Bill…so about 50, and a few more hands went up, then quickly down – still deliberating? That's okay, hopefully you've got plenty of time!

A sample group of this size is anecdotal, of course, and as book club members you're naturally predisposed, yet two thirds of budding writers in a group of 75 people is only marginally higher than universal figures. Ask the question at your next dinner party and test these stats. If you're keeping honest company, you'll quickly discover most people you know believe they've got a book in them. It's a paradox because most will never write one, but firmly believe they can *and* will. It's an instinctive dream, more akin to faith than to actually doing, but most dreams are worth having and sometimes come true.

The best I can do in the time allotted is to give you a condensed insight into how I finally became an author, followed by some statistics about the publishing business.

I've had many occupations but they all started with: *When I grow up I'm going to be*…not 'do', you understand, but 'be'. *Be!* Regardless of the perplexing range of careers I dreamed of pursuing, my Mum always said: 'Concentrate on your strengths so your weaknesses don't show,' and she was still passing on this advice two weeks before she died in 1969.

'Under the circumstances you're doing okay,' my Dad reassured me a few days ago when I arrived home from the wasted book tour.

'What's three weeks and a truckload of lost sales out of your life? Make the most of everything!' he beamed.

Knowing smiles and positive attitudes from indomitable parents appreciate down the years. When life deals a tough hand and the smiles and reassurances continue unabated, the word courage resonates and reminds us that it's up to us to realise our dreams.

The life of an author is one long paradox: successes and failures, extraordinary highs and devastating lows, moments of celebrity followed by years of anonymity. These quintessential contradictions are preordained in the writing business.

A huge chasm exists between the imaginary life of the writer and her every-day responsibilities and domestic routines. Of the high points, there's the escape of it all, sitting at a desk writing facts or dreaming up fantastic stories using composites of known people – family, friends, neighbours, enemies, lovers…you're rarely lonely and nobody is safe!

On the down side, assimilating the real world with the unreal can be tricky. Taking a phone call, answering the door or checking the oven in the middle of a murder, suicide or rape can be devastating. Suddenly you're forced back to reality: the spouse, children, parents…life demanding your attention NOW.

When the demands of the real world have passed, you still have to go back to the story you're creating and begin again, forever reliving, retelling, correcting, never quite reaching perfection. Whilst I was writing *Billy Batchelor* I was nearly raped, and almost lost the best friend of my protagonist (who happens to be based on my mother), when the power went off and I lost 20 pages. The re-write was never quite as good as the original… *hey, who turned out the lights?!*

(Crowd noise; yelling, banging and crashing)
(Male voice in background, yelling) Remain seated everyone! It'll be back on in a minute!

(Shirley McLaughlin) Thank you very much for your patience, ladies and gentlemen. For a moment, I thought something worse than rape was about to happen. Working late into the night, alone, with aching back and squinting eyes can do that to a lady author when the power fails…

It takes time to produce a professional manuscript. All we need at completion is someone to like it, decide to publish it and fling it out on an unsuspecting public.

Unfortunately, the chances of early success are thousands to one. Writers live with failure both before and after they've been published, daring to believe this new manuscript is good, yet nobody wants it.

And rejection slips are rarely enlightening. 'Thanks, but no thanks' is the norm. A dozen rejection slips and another year or three later, it can be overwhelming to receive a personal note from an editor with a few negative comments and a final line: 'With some major rewriting, this flawed manuscript might possibly work…'

I'd completed my third (unpublished) novel in the late 70s after selling my entertainment agency. I carefully researched local and international publishing houses before sending my manuscript to half a dozen of them, and then dared to hope.

Many months and a few rejection slips later I chanced to read a story about Charles Dickens, who legend has it, submitted over 100 manuscripts before one was published and whose work still sells in the millions every year. Dickens' first published novel, *The Pickwick Papers,* was published in monthly instalments while he was still in his 20s, yet he continued to receive critical rejection letters for his ongoing work. This struck me like lightning – he was a man after all! What if a change of gender would help me?

After World War 2 publishers began to employ women to read, recommend, reject and edit manuscripts. We were better at it, and provided cheaper labour, but the men still made the final decisions. If I were a man, would I be read and at least given an insight into why I had been rejected? Only one way to find out. I ran off another six copies *by Sean McLaughlin* and sent them to my second choice of publishers.

Four months later I'd received three detailed reader's reports, each covering what was and wasn't working in my manuscript. It was a shock to the system, and everything I'd been brought up to believe about justice, equality and creed.

The insights and critical comments in those long reports were pungent… but ultimately liberating. One assessment from an international publishing house reported that I was making all the usual mistakes men make when writing about women!

'You seem to think all your reader wants to know about the heroine is that "she fell in love! Just like that, eh?"' the editor wrote, proceeding to tell Sean how it should be done.

So this is the help and encouragement men have been receiving all these years! I ranted to myself – and anyone who'd listen before returning to the manuscript with renewed purpose. I put in the hard yards to rewrite and learn, but didn't send that novel out again. It felt 'over-worked' and I didn't feel I could handle another rejection.

Instead, I consoled myself that every writer is said to have unpublished manuscripts stashed away in their bottom drawers. *Let it go and move on, woman,* I told myself sternly. *You're not just a pretty face anymore…you're a writer in the making!*

It was 1990 before I sold up in Sydney and moved to Albury to have a crack at writing books for a living. A good friend suggested I begin with non-fiction. 'Write what you know,' John said. 'It's the best way to get your foot in the door.'

My Dad agreed with John's sage advice, reliving memories of Mum's history as Margery Daw on Radio 3BA in country Australia in the 1930s. She had been truly alone in a man's world then and Dad, quickly shifting into school-teacher mode, agreed that nothing much had changed since Dickens' time.

'On the other hand, even Shakespeare today would probably write that women too have seven ages, and the right to an equal footing in the game,' Dad said, then got to the point.

'You're a work in progress, Shirley. Get on with it.'

(Crowd laughs)

Age Five

After having several non-fiction books published, I moved into fiction, got myself an English literary agent conveniently located in France…

(*More laughter from the crowd*)

(Shirley McLaughlin) …and HarperCollins UK published *A Good Reputation*. Hopefully the Australian version will be on the shelves soon.

Thomas Edison said genius is one percent inspiration, 99 per cent perspiration. Learning to survive in the cut-throat world of publishing certainly requires a lot of sweat. It's also good to have a thick skin and a well-developed sense of humour. It's probably ever been thus, although the business is in a constant state of flux and most authors are blessed with long memories and aren't known for being particularly forgiving creatures either.

For mine, these traits have been indispensable in all of my professions. If you already possess them when you come to the book game, you'll have a head start.

This is all subjective of course, but might stimulate some interesting discussions at your next book club meeting.

Becoming a published author is a unique adventure; I have to admit that a lifetime of experience in many diverse occupations was of no use to me whatsoever. Here's the process as I have encountered it.

You receive a phone call or letter offering to publish your work. The next few days are spent in a kind of euphoria, quickly diluted by the hangover. The contract arrives next and whilst it should be checked by an agent or solicitor, it's customary to sign it and return it immediately by express post (just in case the publisher comes to his senses and withdraws the offer!) A typescript of your work arrives a week or two (or often months) later with a congratulatory letter. When at first you see the number of deletions, corrections and recommendations for improvement the editor has suggested, you can't help wondering why they want to publish you at all.

You return the pages to your editor and everyone you know congratulates you as if success is a foregone conclusion. It's a lofty, powerful moment when you realise you're one of the reasons all those publishing people are employed, and why family and friends are so proud you've finally 'made it'. There are demented butterflies in your tummy that screech unceasingly: *What if it's a flop?* But you silence them, making plans to apply for leave from your day job and get busy sorting your wardrobe in preparation for the invitations and interviews that will hopefully inundate you shortly.

As the author's 15 minutes of fame moves towards its climax, your freebie books arrive in a box. There's only six of them and everyone you know is expecting a free copy. You rip open the box and flick through one book to see how many errors the editor missed. It's a strange anti-climax, coupled with a sense of exhaustion that very soon you're going to have to start all over again. Human nature is a dependable beast. The finished product is in your hands and all you can think about is a blank page, perhaps an idea but not much else. *Can I do this again?* There are no guarantees and times are changing so fast that if I don't get a move on I'll be out of fashion anyway.

Finally, the release date is in sight and you can't help but hear the 'ka-ching' of cash resisters after every increasingly exciting interaction with your editor. Then, suddenly, you're just the author! The publisher needs 90 per cent of the RRP to pay everyone else and maybe (but usually not) make something resembling a profit. The 10 per cent that's left over is what your contribution is deemed to be worth. And that won't land in your bank account until June the following year. At an average recommended retail price of let's say $25, this leaves you with $2.50 per book. If you have an agent, they pocket 10 per cent (or more) of your 10 per cent.

The following sales statistics from the 20th century are edifying, and levelling. The term 'best-seller' was not coined until 1912. The market place was still provincial and the likes of Dan Brown, Wilbur Smith, Barbara Taylor Bradford, Jeffrey Archer, Stephen King, Danielle Steele…and J.K. Rowling hadn't been born yet. At least there's a few women up there, one of whom looks like beating the lot!

- Every day of the year across the globe 300 books are published in English, i.e. 109,500 – that's 25 every daylight hour.
- In 1995 a massive 25 new books were published in Australia every working day. That's one every hour. One of those 6,481 local titles published was mine. Kind of puts things into perspective, don't you think?
- In 90s Australia, a bankable print run is 5,000 copies. Whilst 5,000 sales may return a profit for the publisher (and approximately $12,500 royalties for the author), 10,000 copies is this country's best seller milestone.
- Only five per cent of the professional writing population *worldwide* ever achieve 10,000 sales or more of any book.
- I've had a few best sellers but it doesn't take a mathematician to estimate my earnings at less than $30,000 per book. Royalties from public lending rights, education rights and the Copyright Agency continue annually for as many years as the book survives in shops, libraries and educational institutions, but it's not enough to live on.
- With few exceptions, first print runs of Australian fiction and non-fiction average 2,000 to 3,000 copies. The market (chains and bookstores) usually take between 800 to 1,500 on release and the

average rate of returns for Aussie non-fiction publishers from retailers run around 30 per cent.
- The great majority of books (of all genres) are not re-ordered, if and when the initial print run has sold.
- In more densely populated markets first print runs are obviously higher, but returns often are too. In the USA return rates are 40 per cent from chain stores and around 15 per cent from independent booksellers.
(The first print run of my novel in the UK earlier this year was 40,000, I was paid a decent advance but have no idea what, if any, royalties will follow.)
- An international study found that one tenth of one per cent (0.1) of titles published in a year will sell 100,000 units or more. That's between 102 and 125 per year.
- Fewer than 12 authors in any year, worldwide, sell 1,000,000 or more copies of any book and are rarely Booker Prize winners; however, this could be interpreted as being encouraging for those of us who recognise we'll never produce a literary masterpiece.

Finally there's the book tour,
    'Good fodder' is a term reporters, TV hosts and DJs use to describe people who answer questions with more than yes and no answers. They have programs and pages to fill with credible material and authors are not renowned for their stunning personalities or stimulating repartee. Only 10 per cent of published authors get the gig. Should you happen to be good fodder, overnight you'll go from a reflective, essentially private person to a full-on media talking head. There'll be days when you feel that if you have to repeat the same thing one more time you'll scream, but you don't. You simply carry on.
    By the time you get home everyone and everything demands your attention. You need a break but you also need regular income. (Besides, that 'fabulous holiday you had whilst you were on your book tour' should surely be enough!)
    I do freelance writing/editing and tutoring for Stott's Off-Campus College and also have investment units that make it possible for me to remain solvent, which allow me to take a holiday a few months after every book tour. It's essential for sanity and rejuvenation of the creative juices.

(Loud crashing noise on the roof/chairs scraping on wooden floor)
(Woman yelling) Was that a tree?
(Gasps from crowd/muffled shouts) Jesus, it's hailing out there!
(Man screaming)

(Shirley McLaughlin) The publishing industry is facing its greatest challenge since the printing press was invented. With the multinationals now dominating Australian publishing, lists have already been cut by 20 per cent. The great majority of books on the shelves today have the life of cultured yoghurt – about three months if you're lucky. Will the 21st century bring an end to the book as we know it, or will a way be found for old and new to co-exist? I can't visualise this beautiful town library of yours bursting at the seams with DVDs, e-books and USB sticks, can you?

A book is a friend, a personal, hands-on companion. As we turn each page, the smell and touch and feeling of ownership is surely impossible to replace. Time spent reading books is never wasted.

Plus, how will we get to sleep without them?

If you really want to write a book, stop talking about it, start planning for it, do some research on your subject matter, make copious notes and set a time to begin!

Getting started is the hardest part. I avoid taking that fearful step across the threshold into my study for weeks, but when I finally start I begin at the beginning!

What's the working title for this great idea? What's my opening line?

It takes passion to do anything worthwhile but writing is an egocentric craft and the passion ebbs and flows, and sometimes dies in the process. Until you try, you'll never know whether you're a person who can endure quarantined hours, days, months and sometimes years without any confirmation that what you're doing is actually any good.

When a writer gets stuck, unable to continue producing anything substantial, it's called 'writer's block'. But this can be a copout. What 'block' usually means is that the life you're living isn't in tune with your current needs, responsibilities, plans…that something, somewhere is awry. It could be serious relationship or health issues, however the usual reason is that you're over-committed to other things. Other things that aren't harmonious with locking yourself away in a room so you can turn ideas into actual words on paper and stories worth telling.

It's also entirely possible that you're not a writer and never will be. You might just be dreaming and that's healthy. But a word to the wise: avoid regaling authors you meet with long diatribes about 'the fabulous idea for the book I'm going to write…if only I had the time!'

Sorry, but you're wasting mine; we all get the same amount and it's what we do with it that counts.

Ladies and gentlemen, we've come full circle. Who's got a book in them? And are you going to write it?

Age Five

Whatever your dreams and future plans, taking chances is an essential part of achieving them. It usually means surrendering, and surrender is only possible if you're prepared to let go – and have a go. Bon chance!

If I've inspired any budding writers to begin the great novel of the 20th century tonight, I urge you to go straight home, weather permitting, and begin immediately. This century is nearly over and the best literature ever written took years to produce, mainly at a time when people were nowhere near as busy as we are today.

If you're stuck for an opening line, go for something real that you've experienced. Write what you know! Make your beginning timeless, brief and topical and change it later when you're up and running. What about: 'It was a dark and stormy night?'

Any questions?

(Lots of hands went up, mostly the usual questions. Near the end of the time allotted, Shirley got a persistent woman, about 60, at the rear of the library.)

'While you were speaking, Bill found your c.v. and circulated it to the back rows and I could hardly believe my eyes! You've lived and worked all over the world, had fabulous careers, been married and divorced twice – an extraordinary life! How could you give it all up and move to a hick town like Albury to write? How can you stand being locked away in a study and only coming up for air to flog your books and entertain your fans?'

'Oh dear,' Shirley sighed after a pause that felt like eternity.

'I'm afraid the answer would take time, and even if we had it, I haven't worked it out myself yet. Please forgive me…'

As she was floundering, a man called out from the back.

'You could write a book about it! Your life and how you've survived alone. It'd sell heaps more than 10,000 copies. I'd buy it!'

When the laughter eased she thanked him and responded philosophically.

'I'll never write a memoir, don't have children, have a wonderful sister and two fabulous nephews but most of my family are dead and I'll be gone in a minute and it won't matter a hoot. What would be the point?'

'Because a writer writes to be read?' a quietly spoken young woman, maybe 20, returned from the front row.

(Good old Bill told her later that the woman's name was Sally McIllwraith and she was working on her first novel. 'Must keep an eye out for her,' Shirley smiled. 'I hope she won't have to change her name from Sally to Sean to get somebody to read it.')

The shifting times

By 1997 Shirley had established a new home base in Avoca Beach, a beautiful town on the Central Coast, about an hour north of Sydney.

Her decision to leave Ultimo had been spontaneous and the local police had agreed that it was wise. A woman had been bashed to death with a meat cleaver in her apartment and Shirley was the only neighbour who could give them a detailed description of their chief suspect. He'd seen her as clearly as she'd seen him exiting the complex, he was on probation and the constabulary were pretty sure he was still in Sydney. They just had to find him!

Once Shirley made the break she'd realised how much she'd needed to get out of there.

The previous 18 months hadn't been without incident either. She'd sold up in Albury after returning from a three month break down memory lane in the States, only to discover that the suburb of Laverton had lived up to its reputation. The tenants in one of her furnished flats had gone, having emptied the entire unit and taken the back door with them. By the time she got home, a horse had moved in! She couldn't help wondering what the odds would be of yet another neddy making himself at home in one of her properties.

Her house had sold at auction, the sale fell over, a new buyer turned up a couple of months later and needed a quick settlement. Both of the apartments were sold by an agent and what she lost on the one hand, she made up on the other.

Shirley had made a hasty decision to move to Corrimal, near Wollongong in NSW, when she reconnected with pre boomer John Downs from RMK Voice Productions, dating back to her Balmain days. She agreed when he asked her to move back to Sydney to have a shot at building a relationship, with the caveat that they live separately until the finalisation of his recent divorce.

Whilst Shirley loved his intelligence and blokey sense of humour, she wouldn't ever have said she was in love with him. But she had been lonely. And as John had been coming from the same page, having just severed ties with his wife of 27 years, she'd taken her chances, albeit with eyes wide open.

For him, it was a complex situation. Shirley, on the other hand, could see it clearly for what it was: he'd made a grab at happiness by hooking up with his long-time friend, only to be dogged by guilt and the regret of having blown his chances with the woman he'd been with his entire life.

Inevitably he'd returned to the marriage for a while, but had eventually 'fallen in love' with someone new and moved to Queensland.

Shirley had been glad for him, but sad to be back on page one. In the plentiful unguarded moments enjoyed in her new idyll in Avoca Beach, the same old question surfaced: why did she continue to fall for much older men?

She recalled Margery's advice to 'Never underestimate early experiences. They can influence us for the rest of our lives.'

Not for the first time she wondered to what extent the much older Andreas, her first lover, had influenced her. But regardless, what did she expect to reap from older men now? She didn't need their money, didn't want their baggage and was tired of their macho egos.

So, she'd settled into Central Coast life, in a house that sat high on a hill overlooking the town and mountains beyond. She concentrated on keeping productive, writing and tutoring for Stott's, taking on other freelance work and watching her investments grow.

In telephone conversations with Bev, the carer for everyone, Shirley was kept in the loop about their father's declining health. But it wasn't until Alan asked for her help directly that she fully grasped the weight of the mission her sister had taken on.

Aged 84, he'd decided to compile a book of articles he'd written for the national *Gem and Treasure* magazines over the past 20 years.

Shirley worked on the layout and initial editing with him and parcels of manuscripts went back and forth between Melbourne and Avoca.

His one and only eye started troubling him first, followed quickly by fear of failure and 'What if it doesn't sell?' He'd become afraid to let anyone begin a serious edit of the manuscript and the whole thing overwhelmed and obsessed his life. Shirley didn't share this with the Gosbells initially, suffering personal guilt. Alan had made it clear that if only she was there, on the spot, he'd get her to edit it and be relaxed about it.

He had never shown any signs of depression before, or had he? Unconsciously Shirley flashed back to Warracknabeal, and the tears began to flow: her parents were in the lounge room and 'the girls' were in bed, fast asleep. She could hear her father crying, and hear him begging Margery to forgive him, because he couldn't forgive himself for bringing her to this God forsaken place.

Shirley took a week off and drove to Melbourne, a fair slice of the way arguing with herself about why her mother had never succumbed to depression. Was her extraordinary ability to fight on, regardless of wretchedness, tragedies and 24/7 physical pain, the result of her genes, or her upbringing, or perhaps her life experiences?

She also thought about how the great generation was living longer lives than any before them, and how the medical innovations in the late 20th century were still largely trial and error. What troubled her most was the increasing need for care during the diminishing physical and mental health of loved ones. It was sometimes life-changing for entire families who suffered for years in the process. Love was Bev's motivation, but how long would she need to be their father's prime carer?

Ten minutes after Shirley arrived at Alan's, by which time she'd grudgingly accepted that the psych at the Prince of Wales was probably right about heredity, they sat down at the kitchen table which was covered in mountains of meticulously categorised articles.

'I don't have the heart to go ahead with it, Shirley,' he stated happily. 'I'm over it! It's wonderful to see you.'

It was a metamorphosis. The moment he'd declared his decision to abandon the commitment, and all that entailed including his mates' high expectations, he seemed to just snap out of his depression and they enjoyed a terrific week together.

Six days later, when Shirley was pulling out of the driveway of his retirement village apartment, he leaned on her open window and asked if he could send her the final corrections to check before he sent them to the publisher. Shirley managed to reply that she'd be delighted, but drove back to Sydney with a heavy heart and the first undeniable evidence to her that he would not recover his joie de vivre again.

Sequels of an author's lot

It had taken two years from go to woe for the UK publication of *A Good Reputation*, and another two years for the Australian release of *Billy Batchelor*.

Just for the record, and leaping forward into the 21st century, film director Baz Luhrmann was sent a copy of *Billy Batchelor* when it was first published, but he did not reply. A decade or so later he garnered an Oscar nomination for his film *Australia*.

Age Five

Apart from two character changes and one or two outback scenes, in every other way the film was a direct steal from the story of *Billy Batchelor*. Even the *Batchelor* family homestead (featured on the cover of the book) was the exact family homestead in Luhrmann's film that Shirley had researched near Alice Springs. Had the stars of the movie known (old acquaintances of Shirley's, Hugh Jackman and Nicole Kidman), they might have influenced Baz to stick to the novel because the film didn't prosper, despite its global promotion.

Revised versions of original works rarely do.

Similarly, years after *Minding Your Own Business* was published, and when computers had taken over our lives, a couple of smart lads came up with the simple, extremely clever MYOB accounting package for small business.

A lawyer friend suggested Shirley should sue. With a laugh, she declined.

'I've been pinching ideas and plots from my favourite authors since I was knee high to a grasshopper. We all do it and it's been that way since Shakespeare and his contemporaries did it hundreds of years ago.

'Besides, it's the highest form of flattery!'

The arrival one day of a large envelope from her publisher Geoff Wright took Shirley by surprise. Initially its contents had baffled her. But when a cheque fell out of the enclosed pile of health industry magazines, her bemusement turned to gratitude.

Ever the entrepreneur, Geoff had been busy doing rights deals, licensing content from his authors' books to complementary businesses so they could reproduce it in their marketing collateral. He'd sold excerpts from Shirley's first non-fiction title, *Appointing People,* to a cross section of medical, dental, physio and ancillary associations.

She opened the Australian Dental Association (ADA) magazine first and read the excerpt from her book. The sole reason she then flicked to the classifieds section was her discovery earlier that morning of a list she'd made of London dentists the day after she'd left Nick Bond. She'd stood in a phone box at Kings Cross Station and scribbled down names and addresses from the phone book. At the memory, she'd fancied she felt a tingle in her upper right incisor. It persisted as she skimmed through the rest of the contents of a box she'd unearthed during a clean-out of keepsakes from 30 years of overseas travels.

'What if?' she dared to wonder now, peering at the advertisements for Adelaide dentists.

It was July 1997, and if her memory served her correctly, the nerve in that incisor was removed in July 1973. What were the chances? What if this turns out to be the third time lucky?

While she was sketchy on a few details, she remembered he was an 'old boy' from St Peter's College and had been one of few Australians accepted into the master's degree at the Eastman Dental Hospital.

She also knew his name started with a 'J'.

In a strange parody of sending her first manuscript off in the hope of having it published, she wrote and submitted an inspired advertisement, then settled in to wait.

Would anybody call?

A week later someone did indeed call about the ad and she was momentarily struck dumb.

'Dr Jeff Mount here, calling from Adelaide,' came the voice through the receiver. 'I'm calling in response to your advertisement in the ADA magazine this month.'

'Oh!' she said, not quite sure what to say in the face of apparent success.

Jeff put two and two together. 'I hasten to add, I'm not the man you're looking for!'

Shirley felt a wave of relief as he explained that the ad had caught his eye because London University was also his post-grad alma mater.

'I figured I could probably help you find him,' he said.

Not for one moment had it occurred to either Jeff or Shirley that it would take more than a couple of calls to identify her ever-elusive dentist. Nor could she have predicted that the search itself would eventually pale in significance to the friendship she would foster with Dr Jeff Mount.

Good days, bad days

Between 1998 and the end of 1999, Shirley's life continued in all the usual *unusual* ways, yet it seemed to be almost normal to her. She was settled in Avoca and enjoying the stimulation of her freelance work and ongoing tutoring for Stott's.

Agent Shelley continued to keep in touch, mainly to hassle her about the second novel: 'Where is it?' She'd recovered from her cancer and broken marriage, had moved to Paris and wrote that she was being hassled by the publisher for Shirley to get a move on. 'I'd promised you were writing another Australian story and they want it on the shelves before next Christmas!' When Shirley had recovered from Shelley's imagined, deceitful promise and the backhanded compliment, she replied with an honest promise that she would be the first to know if and when she decided to get back into the game.

Her journeys home to Melbourne took longer now, but were always rewarding.

Rob was Head of the local Primary School in Glen Waverley, Bev was as busy as ever with her choir, local church, community services and ever increasing duties in the care of Alan.

Steven had completed his marketing degree, was working in marketing in Melbourne and busy socialising and playing sport in his spare time. Dale had completed his science degree and had met the love of his life during an 18 month working holiday in the UK and Scotland. He'd moved to Sydney to be with her. Shirley had met the beautiful Camille before any of the family when they'd visited her in Ultimo. She'd reported to Alan and Bev that Dale's hands didn't leave her body at any time, reminding them of one of Margery's old sayings: *Aint love gland!*

She needed the breathing space Avoca afforded her and visited her friends in Sydney regularly.

Gaby and Chris in Beecroft often invited her to lunches and dinners, and Gaby was with her when her next car accident occurred.

She was stationery behind half a dozen cars at traffic lights on a busy Sydney road, and the driver this time was also a young man in his father's car. He bashed into her at speed, ramming her into the stationery car in front of her. This created a ricocheting effect, to varying degrees crashing everyone forward and back. The worst of it was that Gaby was with her, they'd copped a serious hit and Gaby had also suffered whiplash.

When the police arrived, Shirley was sitting on the edge of the gutter with her head between her knees, and Gaby was leaning against the car, watching over her.

The father's insurance paid for repairs and open-ended medical treatment. Gaby sought medical help and recovered relatively quickly. Following months of physiotherapy, Shirley tired of being in a holding pattern – not going back, but not going forward either. She took matters into her own hands and went to a gym. The owner worked out a program and supervised the implementation three days a week. On alternate days she swam for 40 minutes in a nearby public swimming pool. Three months later, she was cured!

Predictably, she ignored the usual advice about seeking a lawyer, called the insurance company direct and accepted a payout for expenses and lost income she could validate, and that was that.

With her health restored, Shirley moved into the downstairs apartment in Avoca that had been added by a local builder earlier in the year, and leased her upstairs two-bedroom house to a stunning woman named Marie vanSteyne.

Marie was a New Zealander with the Maori maiden name of Wehipeihana. She was also a writer and the same age as Shirley. Divorced with two daughters, she'd left home early, struggled with her identity under the weight of prejudice, travelled the world and lived a demanding, exotic, ever-changing life that was arguably more complex and eclectic than even her landlord's.

Her favourite aphorism explains the core of her life's journey and is credited to a NZ Maori elder. 'When you know where you come from you will understand who you are.'

They formed a friendship that was special to them both, and still is.

Shirley met Malcolm, the man with whom she'd had her one serious relationship during the four years she was on the Central Coast. They met at rock 'n roll dance classes.

When she vowed she'd never fall for an older man again, she hadn't planned on a much younger one who came with two children. He was a baby boomer 13 years her junior and his adorable daughters became part of the bond they developed as a couple. That the girls loved Shirley was a positive for him, and it allowed Shirley to experience something she'd yearned for since losing the opportunity to have children of her own.

It was an affair that ended with the same intensity with which it had begun. After a violent altercation between them that left her with broken ribs, Shirley called it quits. She farewelled him and his daughters at his front door before driving home with a conflicted heart. She'd lost the chance to realise a dream from half a lifetime ago, but had withstood the wrench of it because of the wisdom and strength she'd developed. She knew that Malcolm's behaviour had been a bridge too far and he wouldn't be able to change.

After the relationship had ended she'd travelled both overseas and domestically on holidays with Beris. At the end of each journey, she felt in increasing increments the lure of returning home – to the Mornington Peninsula. Whilst Sydney was still her favourite city, she was glad to be out of the big smoke now, at home in country environments where she didn't have to battle the pace of city life.

When Alan's mental health had seriously deteriorated and he'd been moved into the nursing home attached to his retirement village, it seemed that fate had yet again intervened.

She drove to Melbourne, collected Bev and together they made the familiar trek to the scene of their childhood holidays at Grandma's. A house they inspected in Mount Martha was in many ways similar to her Avoca property before she'd extended it.

'You could do the same here,' Bev suggested.

And so it was decided. She sold Avoca Beach, purchased herself a red Toyota Corolla and drove home to Victoria in style. With air conditioning, mag wheels and a sunroof, it was the classiest car she'd ever had.

Life ends, and life begins again

On the eve of a new century, back home where her first memories took hold, Shirley settled quickly into the seaside hamlet of Mt Martha. Now she lived within an hour's drive of family and many old friends and her home boasted sweeping views of the peninsula and Bass Straight.

Her Stott's commitments and freelance writing continued, the rewards of which were much greater than the money they delivered. Four of her long-term students had written manuscripts that she'd critiqued and edited, and they'd since gone on to secure publishing deals.

She made friends with the locals, sold some shares, briefed a draftsman and three months later had a builder constructing a downstairs apartment in her new house. The world was older now, but on most days she considered it her oyster.

It was good to be home, which for her was a contradiction in terms if ever there was one. In the 25 years since she'd entered the property market she'd undertaken 14 renovations and made a home for herself in 11 of them.

Since the day 53 years ago that she had come into the world, she'd lived at 45 different residences, with addresses in Australia, Hong Kong, America and the UK. Whilst she'd be happy if she never received another bouquet of red roses in her life, she figured that surely it was time to stop and smell the ones she always planted after the renovations were done.

During her weekly visit with Alan, he'd admitted that for many years he'd blamed himself for her nomadic tendencies. After all, she had spent her childhood moving from town to town for his numerous promotions. But he'd decided recently that her restlessness was a by-product of a continuing search for her soul mate.

'I think he'll find you now that you're home again,' he told her with a beautiful smile.

As it turned out, it was the last conversation father and younger daughter would have. Alan suffered a stroke on 7th February and passed away in hospital seven days later.

Curiously, he'd been predicting his imminent demise since mid-December, when Shirley had just moved back to Victoria. The day she'd accompanied him to Christmas lunch at the nursing home, he'd told her how happy he was that she'd come home 'just in time'. There'd been nothing morose about his proclamation, which he'd subsequently reaffirmed every other week. Whilst his memory and conversational skills had slowed and he relied on a walking frame to get around, he was cheerful – essentially a quieter, more philosophical version of his old self.

What struck Shirley more than anything was how resolute he was about the timing of the event: 'I've been single for 29 years, married for 29 years, and widowed for nearly 29 years. I'm going soon, Shirley,' he'd said. 'Before my 88th birthday.'

Throughout Alan's final days both daughters remained by his bed. He hadn't been able to speak but, like little pixie Craig all those years ago, he continued to smile at his beloved girls until the end.

He slipped away at 3am, a couple of hours after his daughters had left for the night.

It had been the first chance he'd had to exit the stage unaccompanied. And fittingly, it was St Valentine's Day – the perfect date for a sentimental bloke to end his season.

Age Five

In quiet moments of emptiness, Shirley shed tears, lamenting the absence of her father's love and company.

Alan's death had also started her wondering if she'd ever again encounter a man who wouldn't let her down. And whilst former flames continued to contribute to her social life, none of these interactions made a meaningful impact on her heart.

Darren McKay had resurfaced from the UK. Life had been tough for him since their last catch up. His second marriage had broken down 12 months after his 18 year-old son had died in a car crash 100 metres from home.

He'd resigned from his position as CEO of a major toy company in London and he had 'happened' to acquire a cabin in Portsea, not 15 minutes from Shirley's house. The latter, of course, may not have been a matter of fate or coincidence – Darren had been tracking her down from all corners of the world since her early television days. She'd accompanied him to his daughter's wedding and they'd enjoyed time together in Portsea and Mt Martha, but she'd followed her instinct to keep it light and cheerful.

Another old lover from Sydney, Ian, took her for a holiday in Tasmania on the back of his motorbike. They'd had a great time on the Apple Isle but as he was leaving her house the next morning to return to Sydney, he'd accidentally hit a neighbour's dog. He had ferried the dog and neighbour to the nearest vet, but it was curtains for the pet and its mistress was broken hearted.

Shirley had known nothing of it until the woman dropped in a few days later to introduce herself and give her the bad, and good news.

Her 'handsome old friend, Ian' had been 'very kind' after what had happened to Fido. He'd even stayed over to console her!

The theme continued with Mick, the builder (who'd built the apartment downstairs). He'd attempted to consummate their commercial transaction, to no avail.

It would be an understatement to say that she was fed up with men. The exception was yet another 'John', whom she'd met through Di Tiffin. He was a widower who'd retired to the peninsula and had no agenda other than enjoying their friendship. He'd taken her to hospital when she'd required bi-lateral surgery for carpel tunnel syndrome, drove her home and made sure she was okay before heading back to his lonely cottage. Shirley had been the catalyst that led him to his new partner, which he'd said was a wonderful gift. He'd thought he'd never experience romance again after his wife had died.

But even that – her interminable typecasting as the loyal friend, dedicated employee, employer, lover, facilitator, counsellor, tutor, host and general factotum – was wearing thin.

Everyone around her went on living their lives, for better and worse. She, however, remained in a limbo comprising the 'three Rs' – reading, 'riting and renovating. She was just an observer. Growing older with no one to share the joy and the pain wasn't fair.

Shirley wanted a fourth R in the equation: real love.

5th Intermission

Dale, Rob, Steve, Bev & Gareth at Steve's 21st – 5/09/1988

With Denise & Lyn at Camberwell High School Golden Jubilee Dinner, 1991

Ken & Elaine Moon
The University of New England

AGE SIX (2001 – 2016)

The sixth age shifts into lean and sensible slacks
With spectacles on nose, and pouch on side;
Her youthful hose well saved, in a world almost too wide
For her slim shanks; and her strong voice,
Turning towards a subtler tone,
A contented, gladder woman in heart, and sound.

Shirley had decided long ago that she'd never say yes to a man again unless he came complete with excellent people skills, unquestionable ethics, consideration for others, a sense of humour and, of course, a deep love for her.

It was Jeff's kindness that had first caught her attention. His initiative to help her find the London dentist who'd saved her from disaster all those years ago was special. He'd also had a similar upbringing to hers. His mum and dad were old school and very similar to Margery and Alan. But what had really got her hooked was his wicked sense of humour. It never failed to make her laugh.

When they'd first got together and people asked them how they met, he'd reply: 'I answered an advertisement in the ADA magazine for a handsome, intelligent, sexy man in the prime of his life and felt it my duty to reply.'

They'd developed a friendship on the phone, and by mail. Jeff was a book lover and wanted to read everything she'd ever written. When he'd finished the lot, and 'the dentist' had not yet been identified, Shirley decided to give herself a brief holiday for her 50th birthday and jumped onto a plane to Adelaide, ostensibly to simplify the search.

Jeff told her that he was married two days before she left for Adelaide. Thankfully she'd also committed to a four day 'underground' research assignment in Cooper Pedy's opal mining fields en route home from South Australia so was able to keep her disappointment to herself.

She kept her birthday to herself, too.

The chance of it all

Unsurprisingly, Shirley and Jeff got on famously and he and his wife threw a dinner party in her honour. She also met his parents. Graham, his unrivalled father in the dental fraternity added energy and depth to the search. He'd retired but he knew everyone and was keen to help.

Months later, Jeff confirmed the dentist's name, and somewhat more than that. Jack Cavander had left his wife and three children in Adelaide years ago, closely pursued by his father-in-law with a 12 gauge shotgun. Last known, he was working in a dental hospital in Saudi Arabia.

Undeterred – it was more than unfinished business now – Shirley called her foreign affairs friend, now in Canberra, who introduced her by mail to the current consul in Australia's embassy in Dubai. He responded promptly to her letter that concluded: 'Unfortunately, Dr Cavander left Dubai a few years ago…' and she immediately interpreted the consul's formal regrets with a line from Banjo's Clancy of the Overflow: '…*and we don't know where he are!*'

A long-distance, four-year friendship had begun, and in early 2000 Jeff wrote Shirley a letter that was unlike any letter she'd ever received from a man. He was replying to hers telling him of the death of her father, and also that she'd ended her relationship with Malcolm before she left Avoca Beach.

He was sad to learn of her father's death, and very glad she'd moved to the peninsula. He wrote of her love for Malcolm's children, the loss of her dream of becoming a step-mother, and her strength of character to refuse to be treated with less than total respect. He'd been lecturing and attending meetings semi-regularly in Melbourne for years, but it was the first time he'd mentioned visiting her. She couldn't help wondering if his life was not going according to plan.

Age Six

When he called from Adelaide to invite her to his 50th birthday in January 2001, she'd almost given up on him. He'd had a busy year with staff changes and various issues and was sorry he hadn't made it to Melbourne in 2000.

Shirley promptly phoned Marie vanSteyne, who'd decided to follow her from Avoca Beach with partner Robin and was moving to Mt Martha before Christmas, providing they'd found suitable accommodation by then. Marie was always up for an adventure and would love to join her. Then Shirley had a serious talk to herself and decided she was chasing rainbows. Jeff's party was being held at his home in the Adelaide Hills. There was only frustration and potential trouble to be had by going alone. If his marriage was in trouble, he would have told her.

She spent Christmas with the Gosbells, took a holiday with Beris and arrived home shortly after Marie and Robin had landed. It was wonderful to have Marie's company again, and remarkably opportune although they didn't know it at the time.

Jeff called after the party to tell her he was coming to Melbourne soon and would let her know the moment he had a firm date. They spent most of the call laughing, as they always did, concluding with his disappointment that she hadn't made it to the party because she was sorely missed…but it was high time he visited her!

She heartily agreed and they hung up laughing. Beris always said that the best, most steadfast friendships are the ones that begin with laughter. All was not lost.

Shirley had been working part-time for Centro Properties in Melbourne, writing and re-jigging their diverse brochures and general marketing profile, and had nearly completed everything she'd been engaged to do. The boredom was beginning to tell when she stumbled upon an opportunity close to home that would give her purpose and a sense of belonging in the local community.

When she'd completed the last assignments, she gave the boss notice. He was shocked and alarmed! The top guns were negotiating major expansions and changes to their entire operation. It was confidential, but they were hoping she'd join their full-time executive staff.

Fuck! She'd give it some thought and phone him tomorrow.

By the time she hit the freeway home she had a solution and drove straight to Marie's. She'd be perfect for the job, had the right personality, mix of experience and writing skills, not to mention her partner Robin's expertise in big business and exceptional know-how on the international stock market! The boss was disappointed and hesitant but told Shirley he only had her recommendation to go by so 'I guess I'll have to give her a go.' Marie settled in fast and was highly regarded at Centro for several years thereafter.

Shirley's new enterprise was in full swing when Jeff finally arrived. He'd locked in the 13th July, with dinner confirmed for his first night in town, continuing to phone every couple of weeks for the two months leading up to it.

'It's in the diary, Jeff!' she'd say every time and they'd laugh together.

She had been accepted by the Mornington Adult Education Committee to become an evening tutor at Mornington High School, commencing with three of the most popular courses she'd written and tutored for Stott's Off Campus College. She'd re-written the correspondence courses for 'live' teaching, designed and written the advertisements for the programs, and finished up re-writing half the tutors' promotional blurbs. No surprises there.

They were going to press that very week in July. The courses would commence in September.

Early afternoon of the 13th July, 2001, Shirley drove to Bev and Rob's in Mount Waverley (they'd moved to their second-ever home by then) with her outfit for the evening on coat hangers and her wet-pack, makeup and a few unrelated items for Bev in a plastic bag.

Bev remembered her sister mentioning an Adelaide friend who'd invited her to his 50th birthday last year, but had no details. Shirley didn't elaborate. Knowing how her sister loved telling stories, Bev instantly twigged that this was not just another man-friend on the make. He was different, and she needed to know why.

Shirley expanded on their four-year friendship without answering her question.

According to Rob who was present at the time, her face was a picture when Bev retaliated.

'Why aren't you telling me why you've opted for a bath in our spa? Why are you dressing up for another mind-bogglingly boring dinner date because a girl has to eat? And why are you driving into the traffic logged city of Melbourne to meet a man you've only met once?' she demanded, surprising herself with her wit and candour.

Age Six

'You've got a fabulous life, Shirl, best of both worlds! Why on earth would you want a full-time man now?'

Shirley was obviously gobsmacked and laughed hysterically.

'Bev,' she finally managed with a stern voice and mock-serious face. 'He's a dentist.'

'Oh. For heaven's sake,' Bev replied with a frown and a sigh of relief. 'Why didn't you say so in the first place? That changes everything!'

Shirley had been sitting in reception for 20 minutes when she realised something was wrong. Jeff would have to be here by now.

'Is there another reception in this hotel?' she asked an impatient man with a beard down to his waist.

'Fucked if I know,' he'd replied.

'Come with me,' a staff member intercepted and escorted her down a long corridor to the other end of the building.

Jeff saw her coming, leapt out of his lounge chair as if the heavens had opened up, leaving five male dentists open-mouthed in their chairs as he rushed towards her, embraced her and kissed her on the lips.

She shook hands with everyone and joined them for a drink, side-stepping unsubtle questions until the cab arrived to take them to Lynch's Restaurant where Jeff had booked a table for two. It was a shock to both of them when two cabs arrived. All five men had decided to join them for dinner!

In the avant-garde Melbourne clique, Jeff's unexpected and immediately imagined clandestine lover showing up unannounced was altogether too interesting to pass up.

Shortly after everyone had finished their entrées, Shirley excused herself to go to the Ladies. When she exited, Jeff was waiting for her near the kitchen door. He grabbed her hand, walked her a few steps back to the wall between the Ladies and Gents and kissed her passionately. It took a while and the waiters had delivered plates of food and returned with empty plates before they'd stopped kissing and started talking.

As one of the best restaurants in Melbourne, the head waiter advised the chef to hold the main course for Table 23. Two of the customers were embraced in deep discussion in the passage, and three of the remaining party had adjourned to the bar and were smoking Cuban cigars that would take at least 20 minutes.

Jeff explained that he'd offered his services to Prof Derrick Setchell, long-term friend and Head of Eastman Dental Hospital at London University, to teach the new intake of Masters' students. It had taken Derrick eight months to secure approval because it was a new initiative. Jeff's 12 month contract would begin mid-September, and would she please come with him.

He'd thought of her every day for the last four years. He couldn't promise anything, didn't know how things would turn out, but he was taking a 12 month sabbatical from his marriage and practice and dared to dream she would take the chance with him.

Shirley drove home to Mt Martha as the sun was coming up. She had no choice because she was expecting Marie and Robin and two family visitors of theirs for lunch. Marie rang her at 10 o'clock, desperate to know how last night's date had gone and turned up 10 minutes later.

'Are you going to go?' she finally pressed whilst helping out in the kitchen.

'I don't know,' Shirley replied. 'I'm going to have to think about it.'

Two days later she received an air-express envelope from Jeff containing a short letter and a weighty paperback novel, *On Green Dolphin Street* by Sebastian Faulks. He wrote that the story, and the protagonist in the novel expressed many of the feelings and thoughts he'd been having for a long time. It had helped him make a decision and hoped it would do the same for her.

She took the phone off the hook, shut her study door and sat in Alan's leather chair in the lounge to read it. It took eight hours and she knew before she'd finished it that she was going to London.

Lucky 13, and a bedsit in Chelsea

Shirley employed Steven to manage the downstairs tenancy and oversee her financial affairs whilst she was gone. She gave personal notice to Phil Witherton at Stott's over lunch in the city and handled the unenviable task of resigning directly to the head of the Mornington education program. Bookings were already coming in. Unfortunately she knew no one to replace her, and neither did they.

She stored her Toyota at a local self-storage garage, said farewell to her downstairs 'jockey' tenant and his dog, locked her house upstairs for the duration and caught the bus in Frankston to Tullamarine Airport.

Age Six

Jeff left for London a week after 9/11 had rocked America and the world. It was not an easy or comfortable time to travel overseas but he arrived safely and settled into the Sloane Avenue bedsit in Chelsea that he'd secured from a patient in Adelaide.

Shirley arrived early one morning in October, Jeff met her at Heathrow, took her to the bedsit, ran her a bath and promptly took her to bed prior to taking the tube to Russell Square for a day's work training qualified dentists from all corners of the globe in the intricate skills of operative dentistry.

From a long, platonic friendship to a full-on relationship in a tiny apartment, it was amazing how quickly they adjusted to living together. Whilst maximising their time alone, they became part of the dental fraternity social scene, escaped for romantic weekends in England, Scotland and Ireland, travelled extensively throughout central Europe for Jeff's lecturing commitments, and even managed to entertain at home.

The kitchen in the bedsit was an alcove in the living/dining room but Shirley could cook a banquet in a broom cupboard as long as there was an oven and a sink. Derrick and wife Christine, also a dentist, were their first guests. They'd dined with Jeff and his wife many times down the years and their curiosity about Jeff's sudden 'live-in' companion had triggered the invitation.

'Are you really a cousin of Jeff's?' Derrick asked at the first opportunity.

Shirley laughed unreservedly, appreciating at once that her quick-witted man had set this up.

'Well, we could be…' she returned. 'We were brought up the same way, and both our mothers were 'Jones' girls – Margery and Margaret no less!'

From that moment on, Derrick and Chris welcomed her into their lives like an old friend. They hadn't seen Jeff so relaxed and happy for a long time, but worried about the trouble ahead when the shit hit the fan.

'Let's hope their love is strong enough,' Chris sighed heavily.

They'd recently returned from a few days in Chicago, thanks to Jeff's commitment to present at a bi-annual dental conference, and had dined with George and Ann Holmes. The African-American surgeon Shirley had met on a bus in the Northern Territory immediately struck common ground with Jeff, and Ann and Shirley got on like a house on fire.

This was followed by an equally wonderful, brief holiday visiting Shirley's old foreign affairs friend, Fred, now Australia's Ambassador in Barbados with new partner Wendy.

They were reminiscing in a bar one Saturday afternoon in March 2002, when Jeff suddenly became strangely withdrawn. Eventually he found the courage to tell Shirley that his guilt and regret about his wife had caught up with him, she'd decided to take six weeks' leave to visit him and had booked her flights, arriving early May.

In short, he'd decided he needed to give his marriage a second chance.

Shirley booked her flight home and left Chelsea a week later in a cab to Heathrow. It was an unforgettably bizarre day into night, in the first instance because she'd spent it teaching Jeff how to survive alone.

She saw much more than the big picture of Jeff's life now and would always be grateful she'd met her soul mate and had six beautiful months with him. She knew she would love him without judgement and miss him for the rest of her life.

Jeff's feelings for her were also undeniable, but deeply confused. Equally aware of Shirley's life now, he acknowledged she knew more than he could have imagined about guilt ridden husbands and controlling wives.

Notwithstanding, the very few people 'in the know' at the time expressed similar concerns to Shirley and the consensus was that he was damned if he did, and damned if he didn't.

The second unprecedented experience that Saturday was waiting for her at the airport.

She went through security, bought a glass of wine in a bar and joined a man at a table because it was the only empty seat. He introduced himself, she extended her hand and he offered her a cigarette – her first in six months, although she'd had a few cigars with Jeff and Derrick.

He was a quietly spoken, middle-aged psychiatrist on his way to Tel Aviv to attend the funeral of his brother who was sitting at the table in the restaurant that was destroyed a few days earlier by Osama Bin Laden's suicide bombers.

Shirley expressed her sympathy and they chatted about his beloved brother for a while, but he'd noted her sadness when she'd joined him and redirected the conversation.

'You're carrying some pain too,' he commented gently. 'Please tell me about it.'

She smiled and gave him a potted version of events and why she was heading home.

'What does Jeff do for a living, Shirley?' was his first and only question.

'He's a dentist – specialises in crown and bridge and implants – in Adelaide,' she replied.

'Ah,' he murmured, lit another cigarette and repositioned himself at the table. 'I know quite a bit about dentists and their wives – and Adelaide too,' he surprised.

'Your Jeff is obviously one of those ethical, intelligent, rugged individualist types; sharp-witted, generous to a fault and bloody good company. He's successful, constantly updates his specialist skills, likes strong women, has some depression in his makeup and is dedicated to helping people. A significant number of dentists fit this description. How am I doing?'

Shirley smiled openly for the first time, nodded self-consciously but said nothing. She was speechless.

'Dentistry is like no other calling, Shirley. People who become dentists have chosen to sell the most reluctant product of all – nobody wants to go to them! We purchase their product because we have to and turn up nervous, in pain and/or stressed out about what has to be done and how much it's going to cost. Your Jeff is a complex man who has to overcome the objection every day whilst his brain and steady hands do the work in the confines of people's supersensitive mouths. It's a high-stress job that doesn't get any easier.'

He paused for a moment, but Shirley remained silent. She'd never imagined herself needing to be counselled by a psychiatrist.

'It's an interesting case. Your Jeff must have done a lot of soul searching to do what he did…go to so much trouble to justifiably leave the country for 12 months. Of course, a man of principles, extricating himself from the decorous, conservative, elitist Adelaide to seek a better life, and/or wife, would have no choice. If he'd tried to make the break at home, he probably wouldn't have got out of it alive.

'The statistics aren't encouraging,' he continued as if he was talking to himself. 'Dentists commit suicide more than any other health professional. I've got more dentists' wives on my patient list than any of the others too. The reason the wives don't take their lives as often is because they turn up for counselling.'

Shirley's flight was called, she thanked him and wished him 'all the best'.

'My best advice to you,' he said directly, 'is to go home and make a new start. I'm sorry for both of you, but this might be a lucky break. Look forward, not back,' were his final words.

She'd been home several weeks before she started thinking about the psychiatrist's acuity and woke up in shock one morning, realising she'd let Jeff and herself down in their final hours.

Thanks to her 'ladylike' upbringing, she'd been courteous but said little, bottling up her feelings and teaching him how to do the laundry and iron his shirts! Why didn't she help him talk about his guilt, and perhaps come to terms with it?

She penned a letter to him and slept on it before she posted it. They'd been communicating by email every other week, as if somehow their friendship could be maintained, but sending a letter seemed more personal.

Three months after Shirley had left London the phone rang late at night. Jeff was in his office at the hospital and he talked for an hour, mostly in tears.

He told her how shattered he was when she left, how distraught he was the day his wife arrived and he realised he'd made a terrible mistake. It was taking all of his strength and resources to maintain a respectful, responsible relationship with Cassandra. She'd refused to go home until her set date in a couple of weeks and was accompanying him to business and social events, despite having ended the marriage the week she arrived.

He'd planned to call her the day Cassandra left, but couldn't wait any longer. What if she was selling up again and leaving town? Was it possible for her to trust him now, and come back to London?

She said yes to both questions and was seriously tested to get her affairs in order and jump onto a plane before the end of the month. But of course she did.

Predictably, she had put her house on the market and the agent had just secured an investment purchaser. It was a 30 day contract and she'd planned to board with Beris or Marie whilst deciding what to do with the rest of her life. But the timing was fated. She'd be needing time to pack up and move to Adelaide when she returned in September so she negotiated with the new owners to rent back on a month to month basis.

Once again she locked up the house, said goodbye to her tenant and his dog, and took a bus to the airport for the long trip back to London.

Age Six

At first opportunity they sat down purposefully to discuss imminent and future plans. It was not going to be easy for Jeff returning to Adelaide. It was not going to be easy for 'the other woman' either.

Jeff was a dental officer in the Royal Australian Navy when he and Cassandra met. He'd been called up to go to Vietnam but was redirected to Darwin when Cyclone Tracey hit. Cassandra was an intelligence officer for the Australian government and was apparently well suited to the work. She kept to herself, preferred her own company and needed to be in control.

All of Jeff's family and close friends had been shocked when he brought his wife-to-be home from Darwin 25 years ago. They'd expected him to marry a local girl – one of the beautiful string of girls he'd dated during his university years. But they'd eventually accepted her and no doubt the same family and friends would be equally shocked again.

He'd decided to move in with Graham and Marg when he returned. They'd met Shirley when she visited in 1997 and enjoyed the meeting very much. He was confident it wouldn't take long for them to see how happy he was. The fact that they'd been through many highs and lows with their other three children would surely be a leveller. One of Jeff's brothers had also left a wife, and two children, remarried and had another three and they'd adjusted to that. His sister's marriage had had its moments, particularly with regard to Tom, the first born of their three sons. But Tom had turned out to be a terrific young man and everything had been good for a long time now. All families have their problems, don't they? Fifty per cent of marriages had been breaking up since statistics were kept at the turn of the last century and this had to be known to GJ and Marg.

Then again, Jeff was the first born and the expectations ran high. Whilst he'd had no children and his marriage had forever surprised them, he'd followed in his father's footsteps and everything he did reflected back to Graham. The fate of the number one son of a traditional, successful great generation father was written and change wasn't welcome.

Shirley had an idea.

'Let's make a pact,' she said brightly, changing the mood with her enthusiasm.

'You've kept your doubts and fears to yourself all your life, Jeff, as if it's a weakness to acknowledge them. It's a man thing, I know, but you've done it to live up to your father's, and everybody else's expectations. We've got so much going for us but we have to talk through our troubles together to survive what's coming. I don't want to control you. I couldn't anyway. I love you as you are and want to share equally our trials and tribulations, not just our joys and achievements. We can learn from each other and arrive at good decisions that will make us stronger, wiser and more resilient.

'I want us still to be as happy as young lovers when we're old…laughing all the way to our graves! I love you, Jeffrey Douglas Mount.'

'I adore you, Shirley Joy McLaughlin,' he returned. 'We'll do it!'

When the going gets tough...

For supposed soul mates, their reunion back home in Australia had been decidedly unspectacular.

Whilst they'd left London together they'd parted ways in Singapore, with Shirley flying to Melbourne and Jeff to Adelaide.

The ensuing sense of estrangement between them persisted when she joined him for a weekend in Adelaide a few weeks later. She'd been relegated to a hotel near Jeff's parents' house in North Adelaide where he was boarding. He'd been distracted with the practice demanding all he had to give, particularly in light of Cassandra's continued presence there.

When Jeff flew to Melbourne to attend Shirley's farewell party in Mt Martha, she was greatly relieved that he'd begun laying foundations for their future together. He'd rented them a house in a suburb close to the city, and on the day she arrived two weeks later she'd run into his lawyer who'd been dropping off legal separation documents.

Jeff practised on for their first year together, whilst Shirley bought a heritage-listed terrace house in Kent Town and spent the week days supervising its restoration. By the time they moved in, she'd transformed the two-storey property (plus a basement) into a luxury inner-city villa and they'd decided to celebrate by throwing a Christmas party for friends and family.

Most of the party goers had a good time and Shirley didn't fan the flames. Even after a frightening incident where a member of the family had threatened her with violence, she didn't solicit support from the concerned witnesses, most of whom were close friends of Jeff's. Her stoicism made for a lonely re-introduction to Adelaide, but she'd known from the start that her acceptance into the long-established clan would take time.

Gradually she made local friends who supported her and Jeff, and most members of his immediate family and close friends were warm and welcoming. It was hard to understand the mixed messages she was receiving, but she kept her counsel for a long time. She hadn't forgotten that Jeff's first wife didn't receive a magnanimous welcome when he brought her home either.

Cassandra had considered herself a leader and controller throughout her life, yet became a support staff member in Jeff's practice the moment they married. Commencing as a dental nurse, she eventually took on the independent role of practice manager and was happy alone in the back room with control of the staff and the finances.

When she later attempted suicide, she was found by their long-serving couple who'd cleaned the house on Tuesday mornings for years. Apparently she'd been threatening for nearly 12 months, repeatedly telling the staff over Friday night drinks that if Jeff didn't leave Shirley, she'd kill herself.

The pain of learning after the event that trained health professionals were aware from the start was hard to reconcile. Why didn't somebody, anybody present when Cassandra's threats began, insist on getting her some help? Perhaps they did, and she rejected them.

Jeff and Shirley arrived as the ambulance was pulling into the Adelaide Hospital driveway. She was recovering consciousness when they wheeled her into Emergency. The matron took them into her office to explain the situation and forward plans.

'You can visit her shortly in her room, Jeff,' she said, 'but she'll be at her most controlling self when you arrive so please be prepared.'

They went to the room together. Shirley remained outside. Cassandra was still heavily drugged but smiled when Jeff approached. It was one of the saddest moments Jeff could remember and they cried tears of pity walking back to the car.

With her history, Shirley knew as much as the matron about the covert, tacit depression that leads to successful suicides. Deeply conscious of Jeff's sense of guilt and hopelessness, she waited to expand on the matron's words of advice.

People who kill themselves don't speak of it in advance. They tell no one of their plans because they've already decided that everyone who knows and loves them would be better off without them. For the first time in their life they find the extraordinary courage to take control, and end it. With few exceptions, it comes as a total shock to family and friends.

Jeff absorbed some of this immediately, and all of it a week later. Cassandra recovered physically in a few days, was moved to a rehab hospice for a couple of weeks and had agreed to psychiatric counselling.

Jeff's lawyer, Diane, an old friend of theirs who knew Jeff would give Cassandra whatever she wanted which would be everything, had the knowledge and professional and personal valour to ring Shirley at home to offer some confidential advice. Whilst Cassandra was in care, Jeff should go to the family home and remove his cherished belongings. This was likely to be the only opportunity he would get. The chance of him getting anything else in the final settlement was zilch, Diane advised.

Jeff was philosophic about whatever financial loss he had to bear and saddened by the veracity of Di's judgment, but acknowledged her mindful advice.

Shirley went with him to help. The weekend was nasty and everyone involved had reason to be remorseful. Jeff did the best he could with the unexpected visitors, but lifelong friends were involved and for him it was heartbreaking.

Shirley was shocked and felt desperately vulnerable. She was unable to do more than support her man, keep calm and try not to burst into tears.

On the Saturday morning, a neighbour who said she'd seen Jeff's car in the driveway dropped in and marched down the passage to find Shirley, who was re-making their twin beds in the guest room at the time.

'You've been sleeping in the matrimonial bed since you got here, and that's disrespectful and disgusting!' she spat.

That was immediately followed by possibly the worst of the lies that had circulated around Adelaide and developed a life of their own.

'You stayed in London when Cassandra visited Jeff! You rented a bedsit nearby and kept in constant contact with him, saw him regularly at the uni and made it impossible for him to forget you and reignite his marriage. You left him the day before Cassandra arrived and moved back in the day she left!'

Late that afternoon, three of Jeff and Cassandra's long-standing friends drove up to the front door with a police escort, demanding to enter the house. Fuck! Had Jeff's arrival at the property been announced on the South Australian evening news bulletins?

The three assailants looked ready to shoot him, a man whose loyalty and personal contribution to each one of them in dental care alone was seriously beyond any price they had never had to pay!

Jeff had happened to see the private vehicle and police car coming down the long driveway and grasped immediately that they'd entered the locked gate illegally. When they pulled up at the front door, his mind had already cut to the chase. He walked out the front door, acknowledged his friends and told the policeman he would be back in a few minutes.

'Wait here,' he instructed firmly.

Re-entering the house he locked the front door, told Shirley to stay inside and took the three minute brisk walk to the gate. And yes, the lock had definitely been picked.

He walked back to the group of four and informed the policeman that he was responsible for breaking his lock, and the law.

'I am still the owner of this property and as long as I am, you are trespassing. I suggest you all leave immediately or I will have no recourse but to call triple 000 and report an attempted burglary.'

When they'd left the property, Jeff suggested that they have a glass of champagne.

They sat down together and discussed human nature, trying to understand why so many people had reacted personally and aggressively to Jeff's change of life.

Was it his new partner's persona, so different from the old? Was it Jeff's life and successes whilst fixed in a controlled, emotionally challenged marriage that had kept him immune to men and women's jealousies? Was he copping it now because he suddenly seemed to have it all?

Or was it boredom and discontent with their own lives? They couldn't make the break themselves, but he'd given them something risqué to talk about and retaliate against?

Ironically, it was the deplorable indictment on Jeff's known character that unexpectedly gave them some closure.

Cassandra's grip on the life Shirley and Jeff were building together was slowly but surely loosened. She ceased to work at the practice, received a handsome severance package, and had her bills at the property paid for by Jeff.

Yet whilst it seemed reasonable to believe that a divorce settlement would soon be in the works, any relief at the de-escalating drama was undermined when Jeff discovered that not one of his eight staff knew how to perform the critical administrative tasks that had previously been Cassandra's domain.

Shirley didn't attempt to grasp her modus operandi, not because she wasn't literate in the MYOB system, but because there wasn't time to learn it. Simply, if she didn't act quickly, nobody would be getting paid that week!

She topped-up the cheque account, recruited a new, computer-savvy practice manager and opted to pay everyone early on Fridays so they could deposit or cash their cheques at lunch time.

After she'd done a handover to the new practice manager, she told Jeff: 'Wives in professional practices don't work! I will interview applicants in your office and attend meetings as required, but I will never work in your practice again.'

Thereafter, until he retired, Shirley worked part-time for him – from home.

It was three tried and severely tested years that precipitated Shirley and Jeff's marriage.

The *real* third time lucky

Apparently Aussie blokes have always been backward in coming forward about matters of the heart. She'd learned as much from a lifetime of intimate discussions with girlfriends. Despite, or perhaps because of, her experiences with men of other nationalities she conceded the evidence.

But it was a verse from Shakespeare's *Julius Caesar* that motivated her to make the first move towards matrimony:

> *There is a tide in the affairs of men,*
> *Which, taken at the flood, leads on to fortune;*
> *Omitted, all the voyage of their life*
> *Is bound in shallows and in miseries.*

On an ordinary evening in November, 2004, she read her proposal to Jeff from behind the kitchen bar. The *decree nisi* was final and even though Jeff's settlement remained anything but, Shirley had realised she'd be waiting forever if everything had to be perfect.

Age Six

She opened the wedding greeting card she'd made to the first of two inserted pages on which she had typed her offer of her hand in marriage.

It was surprisingly condensed for a girl with a reputation for effusiveness.

My darling Jeffrey,

You are invited to a wedding on Easter Saturday afternoon, 26th March 2005 at Chloe's Restaurant, followed by a cocktail party, followed by a business class honeymoon to Cologne, Ferrara, Venice, Florence and Paris, departing Adelaide on Friday 1st April, 2005.

RSVP Shirley ASAP.

I'M just an old-fashioned girl who decided earlier this year that I want to marry you.

IF you could walk a mile in my shoes (with my feet), you'd know how it feels to be in love with you without the commitment of marriage, still with the titles of 'other woman' or 'de facto'.

IT is time for settlement in my life, and time to feel settled in yours. How about you? Will you marry me? Will you take me and make me the happiest woman in the world?

IF you say Yes, I will make you the happiest man in the world. I will honour you always; I will make you a home, wherever we are; I will make love to you whenever you want, and some; I will help you in your business, whatever you do; I will travel with you, wherever you want to go (but you'll always be free to plan boys' adventures); I will cook and clean for you, and love doing it; I will entertain your family, friends and colleagues, amuse you and never be boring.

IF you say yes, I will always be a little unpredictable, but totally reliable…I will go through the hard times with you and try not to complain; I will support your extra curricula activities in any way I can; I will comfort you when you're sad and look after you when you're sick, old or infirmed; I will laugh at your jokes, even when I've heard them before and actually remember them (thankfully not often); I will love you, fluffy, piggy and any other little creatures you bring into our home.

All this and more will I do if you say Yes.

Two days later, Jeff arrived home from work at the usual time. With a kiss and barely a word, he went upstairs to change into casual clothes, then descended to the cellar.

When he reappeared he held a bottle of champagne he'd been storing for years. With two glasses poured, he took a diamond-studded engagement ring out of his pocket and slid it across the kitchen bench to Shirley, just as she'd slid her proposal across to him two days earlier.

The weeks leading up to the wedding were excitingly different, although no more action-packed than usual. When they started to feel the pressure Shirley augmented Shakespeare's words. 'You're talented, young' *enough*, 'healthy and wealthy,' *well… as long as we remain healthy and can work for another decade, we should be able to support ourselves in retirement, and* 'the world's your oyster!'

Derrick and Chris arrived from London several weeks in advance of the wedding, Jeff took a week off and they escaped in the Range Rover with their English friends for an adventure to Alice Springs. A week later the Setchells continued their holiday and the bride and groom-to-be drove home to prepare for the influx of visitors from around Australia. They threw a buffet at home for 30 people on Easter Thursday, by which time Derrick and Chris had returned and were happily ensconced in the guest quarters.

The Gosbell family arrived from Melbourne and Sydney respectively. Bev and Rob were slightly ahead of Steven and Robyn, Dale, Camille and new baby Madi, first granddaughter for Bev and Rob. They were booked into a nearby hotel, as were Beris and Di who'd landed from Melbourne, Susie and Carl from Sydney and Jenny all the way from Perth.

On Good Friday Ken and Elaine Moon arrived from Sydney and joined their hosts and English house guests for dinner. Marie vanSteyne, who was reading a poem during the wedding service, arrived on the day.

On Saturday morning Bev and Rob arrived dressed and ready from their hotel the moment Shirley got home from the hairdresser; Bev was helping Shirley and she and Rob were giving the bride away.

Life-long friend of Jeff's, dentist/lawyer Tom Boland arrived on the doorstep from Sydney just as Jeff and Derrick were arriving home with the bouquet and pizzas for lunch. Tom was staying over and sleeping in their bed whilst the bride and groom adjourned to the

Age Six

Hotel Chancellor for the wedding night, and old Adelaide friend of Shirley's, Helen Wearing-Smith, now Roberts, with hubby Phil, had volunteered to linger at the function door of Chloe's for 15 minutes prior to the service in case Cassandra turned up.

Was there anything important they'd forgotten?

The wedding itself, and the cocktail reception that followed, reflected the protagonists' personalities to a T and, perhaps predictably, the four generations of guests' dispositions reflected the circumstances leading up to it. Everyone was so relieved and happy, it could have been the first wedding of a much younger couple whose family and friends never thought it would happen.

Just for starters, the bride was so early the driver took them around the block twice before pulling into Chloe's drive. The bride entered with right arm tucked in Rob's and left hand holding Bev's and the bouquet, and had started walking down 'the aisle' when Jeff, who was waiting with the celebrant heard a knock on the door behind him, turned to open it and walked out to look around. But there was no one there and as he walked back in he called to Shirley half way up the aisle, 'You didn't think I was fleeing, did you?' and she shrieked in accord with the hysterical crowd.

The laughter was easing and they were just beginning to absorb the bride's magnificent gown when new babe Madi started to cry.

The long, flowing greyish-blue silk gown with scattered pink and green posies studded with sparkles had been purchased at Fleur de Paris in Royal Street, New Orleans in early February, en route home from the annual Chicago Dental Conference.

Jeff had been seated in the Grand Salon in a magnificent armchair whilst the staff supervised the fashion parade, dressing and undressing Shirley until they got to this one. It was slightly big at the waist, had no sleeves and was too long, but the modifications wouldn't take long and she could make small 'arm' sleeves from left-over hem.

The manager had then led them to the millinery room and straight to a handmade European headpiece crafted with matching flowers and feathers from Switzerland and France that dated back to the turn of the previous century. One of the Fleur de Paris dressmakers had made the gown to match it and management had agreed that whoever bought the dress would be offered the antique headpiece at cost.

For the first time in her life Shirley didn't ask the prices until she produced her credit card. Nearly US$3k! Phew, but never mind. It depends on how you look at it. 'It's the last wedding I'm ever going to have, I can wear the gown to formal events for as long as we're invited, and I'll get the headpiece framed. At roughly $150 for every year of my single life, it's a bargain!'

The wedding ceremony was beautiful, despite the celebrant repeating some lines and losing her place with nervous hands halfway through the service Shirley had written and adeptly typed for ease of reading. They didn't know it then, but it was her first marriage booking. She'd come highly recommended, but perhaps for funerals? Marie read a three verse Apache Wedding Prayer and a member of the Bravura Harp Ensemble played 'The Rose' from Gypsy whilst the bride and groom signed the Registry.

The Ensemble entertained everyone during the reception and between the dancing, finger foods, drinks, speeches and finally the cutting of the cake, the guests barely drew breath. Jeff began the speeches, Shirley thanked friends individually who'd travelled far to be with them, and half a dozen guests spontaneously stepped up to say a few words. Bev surprised no one who knew her when she spoke quietly of how Shirley and Jeff had been seriously tested and how happy she and Rob and the family were to be here to celebrate this wonderful day.

Age Six

Old Adelaide boy offers cougar bride new start

The honeymoon was fantastic, the best European holiday or honeymoon for that matter they'd ever had.

They arrived in Adelaide like a couple of teenagers coming home from their first ball and spent the evening going through the wedding photos their photographer had kindly slipped under the front door.

'It feels like a new start, darling,' Shirley said.

'We'll make it one, baby!' Jeff replied.

As expected, two bundles of mail were delivered the next day, including a letter to Dr Mount advising the settlement was moving forward and the ex-wife wanted to proceed now. A separate letter addressed to Mrs Mount from Jeff's lawyer included a demand from Cassandra's lawyer for copies of her entire financial status, including all personal assets and bank statements of every account in her name for the last five years.

Welcome home to the Mounts, Shirley thought dryly.

They'd maintained separate financial affairs from the start. Shirley had been operating with a registered business name and ABN number since she purchased the entertainment agency in 1974. She'd maintained her own bookkeeping ever since and an accountant completed her annual tax returns. It was going to be a galling waste of her time to put the paperwork together for the purchase of their home and the major restorations that followed, along with the Mile End investment property and three years' worth of rental returns since, but so be it.

What troubled her most was the impact it was having on Jeff. His integrity, reputation and complex nature were at stake, and he would take this latest incursion personally. She'd seen him through several downers now and there had to be an end to this nightmare.

'We've learned to solve problems together and right now we need to get this settlement done, darling.' It was item 1 on her list.

'We do,' he agreed. 'How are you going with the paperwork for the lawyers?'

'Nearly there,' she smiled and went through her notes. She told him he was the most sensitive and honourable man she'd ever known and Cassandra would say the same.

'She's continuing her demands because it's the only way she knows how to keep you responding,' she sighed. 'We've all got hang-ups that keep psychoanalysts in business but the psych she's still seeing probably has a case study ready to publish,' she added glumly and expanded on the theme.

When children lock themselves in their bedrooms and scream until their parents cave in and give them what they want, this isn't an upbringing. Cassandra was inexcusably dragged up, kicking and screaming all the way into the adult world. Jeff concurred. There'll never be enough when you've grown up with no expectations of getting what you want, short of being in total control over the giver.

'Her psychiatrist would have quickly picked up on this, along with her innate intelligence that's always been a blessing and a curse,' Shirley concluded and moved to item 2.

'I'm sure she believed she was in love when you asked her to marry you, and probably felt she had everything she'd ever wanted. For a while, she did. You exercised her brain, trained her to become a nurse and promoted her to practice manager where she learned a new set of skills that enabled her to run the shop. Is that a reasonable assessment?'

Jeff pondered his answer. 'Taking on the practice management role may have been the beginning of the end of our relationship. She'd broken contact with her parents and siblings, probably never quite trusted me either, and more or less proved it when she gave me the MG for my 40th birthday and said I'd probably enjoy it more when I left her. There were other things years before that, of course, but it struck a chord and I still remember that day very clearly.'

'You employed her for 25 years and gave her a wonderful life and everything she wanted,' Shirley responded quietly, 'but you finally left her, as she said you would. Her efforts to stop you weren't working this time so she had to do something to get what she wanted. Totally out of character, she made a callous, dumb mistake when she set up the old cleaning couple to find her. Without their guaranteed arrival early next morning, she'd be the only one who'd ever know she'd taken just enough drugs to pass out for 10 or 12 hours. Pride before the fall…underestimating everyone, from the Matron down.

'It's terribly sad but you can't change or help Cassandra, any more than she can, Jeff. You were right when you told me that her parents dragged her up without discipline or any practical lessons about give and take, let alone compromise. Right now she's left her office and is literally back in her childhood bedroom, screaming to get everything you own, plus a slice of mine. It's all she knows, and that's all I've written down…can we talk about the settlement now?'

'I wish you would, baby,' he groaned and was rewarded with a throaty shriek.

'You've agreed to give Cassandra the house and the property, half your super and all of hers, which she doubled whilst you were in London. Then there's a sizeable fixed deposit, all assets in the house and equipment in the garage, and the 132 original paintings valued at well over a million dollars that you left behind when we took 33 of your favourites two years ago. That sounds fair, doesn't it?'

'What more could she want?'

Shirley smiled, asked if that was a joke and should she pour him a Scotch. They were finally getting to the point.

'You know more about settling difficult, stressful cases than anybody else I know, Jeffrey Mount. I don't have the answer, but you do. You deal with referred patients every day of the week who've been stuffed around by so called experts. You take control and put them out of their misery, freeing them from pain and restoring their ability to eat and sleep again!

'You've been so busy caring for your patients, pacifying Cassandra and the family and daring to get married and take a honeymoon in the meantime, that you haven't had time to stop and write yourself a treatment plan! You're the patient ex-husband who's tried everything to do the right thing for everyone, but it hasn't worked. You've been fucked around for years by mainly well-meaning family and friends, and lawyers who'll string this out for as long you continue to pay them. Cassandra is the tragic ex-patient/ex-wife who never learned to negotiate and is stuck with mere intelligence and a controlling disposition that she's applied to everyone involved in helping her destroy you. Are you getting it now? You need a treatment plan that will put everyone out of their miseries, especially Cassandra.'

'Tell it to the Judge, I s'pose,' he smiled cheekily. 'Call Diane tomorrow and tell her I'm through with fucking negotiations, book a court and leave it to the umpire to end the game.

'It'd be nice if he'd call it a draw, especially since there's no children involved, but I'm assuming from your knowledge of this business that it's far too late for that.'

Overwhelmed with relief, it was Shirley's turn to be cheeky.

'And to think I'd married a sailor, followed by a fucking bigamist before you'd even finished uni! Your marriage to one woman for 25 years is commendable, I think…but we all make mistakes, especially when we're young, and most of us have to lose on and off all of our lives.'

'So I give away 80 per cent of everything I've earned for the last 29 years of my life, four of which you've greatly contributed to, and we start again to build a nest egg for our old age?'

'It's only money. And we can do it. The sexiest thing that's ever happened to me was becoming a cougar in my 50s. Just keep calling me baby and we'll be fine, darling.'

2005 was rushing by. The settlement was done and all was well in their world when Jeff asked Shirley to drop everything because they needed to talk. Wow. What could it possibly be?

'I've been thinking…' he began hesitantly, 'that it might be a good idea to sell up and make a new start.'

'What…where…you mean sell the house and move out of town to the Hills? Darling, nobody will buy your practice without restrictions. You wouldn't be able to work inside 50 miles of the CBD! How could you do implant surgery without access to operating theatres in the city hospitals?'

'No, no! I don't mean stay in Adelaide! Somehow it's lost a lot of its appeal to me. I mean go somewhere new and start our lives afresh?'

'Oh!'

'If you could choose anywhere in Australia, where would you like to go, baby?'

They looked at one another for a few moments and their expressions were identical, both open mouthed with the beginning of wondrous smiles as they whispered one word together: 'Tasmania!'

'Tassie! Tassie! Oh Jeffrey, I'm speechless.'

'That's good because I haven't finished. Let's keep it to ourselves and go across on the Spirit for a caravan holiday over Christmas and New Year. We can look at property, see if there's anything that appeals? Hobart's the place,

I could work solo or buy into a practice, and Tassie desperately needs a study club for continuing education. Our money will go a lot further on the island than here and if we find something suitable, we could tenant it for 12 months and come home and sell up. What do you think?'

'I love you very much.'

'Is that a yes?'

'I can hardly wait!' she replied, and promptly dropped a 'confidential' letter to the Gosbells. Bev thought it was inspired; a new life of their own making, free and unencumbered.

'Good luck, Shirley & Jeff,' she wrote back on behalf of the Gosbells. 'We'll be your first visitors, as usual.'

It had taken 40 years but Shirley was truly happy and finally secure, reminding her nephews of the days when they were growing up and she would tell them wicked and wonderful things. Stuff like *Good girls go to heaven, bad girls go everywhere,* and *If I ever get over this, I'll never have another!* They used to giggle and talk behind their hands because she treated them like grownups.

The world had changed dramatically since their childhood days, but somehow Shirley hadn't. And now she was going to Tassie! It had to be the only place in Australia that she hadn't yet lived.

The Apple Isle

They bought a property in the southern Hobart suburb of Tinderbox. Tenants were quickly installed by the agent, and Shirley and Jeff returned to Adelaide with a 12 month deadline to sell up the practice, and two properties.

It was a close call on all counts, but they did it.

When they put the Adelaide practice on the market, several of Jeff's lifelong friends confidentially approached Shirley to try and change *her* mind!

They understood why she might want to leave town, but Jeff? Never.

Those who'd caused much pain and stress (even after they were married) were informed in no uncertain terms that it was Jeff's idea, but bullies don't change so they probably never believed it. Shirley remembers feeling strangely relieved to discover their total lack of insight or understanding of Jeff, a man they'd known all their lives yet never known beyond their own prejudices.

Before they left Adelaide, they made an appointment with the Public Trustee to update their affairs. From this day forward everything would be 50/50, an equal partnership in every way. They re-wrote their original Wills, registered to be organ donors and appointed each other their Powers of Attorney. Finally they sat down at the dining room table and handwrote individual 'Living Wills', as required by Law.

After reading the examples of every conceivable request in the event of brain damage through to needing life support, Jeff remarked that before he got that bad he was going down to the back paddock in Tinderbox with his favourite gun.

Predictably Shirley responded briskly. 'How selfish is that! I've got to walk around the property to find you first, clean up all the blood, call the police and the ambulance and try to rescue the vegetables!'

Jeff retaliated in usual form. 'If you're still alive you'll be off with the plumber in a flash, or totally forget that I usually come home for dinner anyway. Don't worry. I'll decompose happily enough in the vegie patch thanks. How do you want to go?'

'When you retire I insist you bring home one of those cute little prescription pads. If I get bad first, I know you'll be able to convince any old pharmacist that you're still registered and get him to dispense some seriously fatal drugs. If you do happen to go first, unlikely because you're my toy boy and *so* much younger (3½ years), I'll go a week later from a broken heart.'

They moved to Tassie in January 2007 and settled quickly after the renovations, of course. With five acres, water and mountain views, dams and rose gardens, birds and ducks and wallabies plus three resident kookaburras, it was heaven on a stick.

Jeff's experience and reputation had naturally preceded him, his restorative practice grew and a couple of years later he appointed an associate, extending the specialisation to include general practice dentistry. (Jeff's first wife Cassandra settled back into the family home in the Adelaide hills where she lives happily with her beloved dog to this day. A part-time gardener helps her maintain the property in pristine condition and she has recently discovered travelling on package tours to all corners of the globe.)

Shirley continued to work for Jeff part-time from home, did some freelance writing and began a girls' lunch group (ages 45 – 86) that became a baker's dozen and created a terrific network of friends. The girls' men became friends too and shared semi-regular lunches, parties and dinners with their wives.

Jeff set up the inaugural Tassie Dental Study Club for continuing education for local dentists and organised, ran and led the educational lectures bi-monthly and engaged countless guest lecturers from the mainland and the world, many of whom stayed with 'the Mounts'. Run as a non-profit club, Shirley was the bag lady, bookkeeper and caterer, and always the only non-dental woman at the dinners following the bi-monthly meetings.

There was one annual holiday locked into their diaries in October or November every year that they certainly earned. It was fishing! A born hunter gatherer and fisherman, Jeff had become hooked on big game fishing in his 20s. By the time Shirley joined him on the Great Barrier Reef in 2002, he'd already caught 65 black marlin, ranging in weight from 500 pounds to over 1,000. Watching those magnificent, prehistoric creatures rising out of the ocean was incomparable to anything Shirley had ever witnessed before and she still misses the five day hunts at sea. She accompanied Jeff for their first eight years together but had to stop because of back and hip troubles. She still goes with him, but stays in a hotel on The Esplanade and enjoys the ambiance and unique ethnicity of Cairns.

During their years in Hobart, they also established some friendships through chance and circumstance. Jeff Hadley, Manager of Wilkins Airbase in Antarctica, lived over the road and had become a close, but lonely friend. They introduced him to another friend, Jane McMullen, whose husband had died from cancer. Jeff and Jane fell in love chatting by the fire in the family room while Shirley was stacking the dishwasher, and married three years later.

The Goodman clan led by Stan, the 82 year old father of the family who'd recently lost his wife Shirley, was a patient of Jeff's. Stan's two sons Scotty and Matthew were both in their 50s, and Matthew's legal firm had done the conveyancing work for Tinderbox. Matthew's son, Neddy, was 14 years at the time when the six of them travelled together to London, with the Goodwood Festival of Speed their POV. Five males from three generations, plus lady Shirl sounded like a challenge, but they all had a blissful holiday. The Goodman men were fabulous company, despite two of them needing wheel chairs during their travels.

Family and old friends from Oz and around the world (many of whom had 'always wanted to come to Tasmania!') visited semi-regularly and the years rushed by with the usual business trips, constant entertaining at home, fishing adventures and romantic escapes to foreign domains, interspersed with an increasing number of anticipated and unexpected, heartfelt losses of family and friends.

Suddenly, ostensibly without warning, they found themselves discussing retirement!

How could this be? It seemed such a short time since they'd re-created their lives and moved to the beautiful Apple Isle.

The changing times

Right from the start, Tasmania had begun the best chapter of Shirley's life. She'd settled in effortlessly and it had quickly become her home.

The years had rushed by and the transition from her 50s into her 60s had been relatively painless. The few health issues that come with genes and age served only as a reminder to 'make the most of everything' and she and Jeff continued to work hard and travel regularly.

But despite her ongoing rigour, Shirley had started to find that the intrepid journeys she'd been embarking on since she was 16 years-old weren't as much fun as they used to be. Airport security was vexing and the long hauls more tiring. The news of the world beyond Tasmania was increasingly precarious and she counted her blessings that she was living on the safest, most beautiful island on the planet.

Throughout history, every generation had believed the world was coming to an end at some point in their lives, particularly as they aged.

When he'd turned 60, Alan had developed a habit of proclaiming that he'd lived through the Golden Age and that the world would continue to decline in its wake. He'd feared for Steven and Dale, and couldn't imagine any future at all for his great grandchildren. Anyone from the great generation would undoubtedly agree.

Most had experienced economic hardship, participated in a war and returned home to raise families in a practising Christian culture. That it had been rampant with sexism, racism and homophobia hadn't stopped them from surviving and carrying on. The baby boomers' contributions to the 70s and 80s were mainly good, yet the emergence of a 24/7 news cycle in the

90s meant being privy to what seemed like every incidence of murder and mayhem at home and abroad. We saw images depicting conflicts and wars near and far, and the beginning of terrorist attacks that terrified us all.

In his final role as a district inspector for schools, Alan was dismayed by the lacklustre teachers, and the way in which governments endemically continued to waste tax payers' money by employing underperforming public servants. Ahead of his time, and as a man who no longer believed in God, he saw a connection between the decline in Christian faith (as a benchmark for integrity and generosity of spirit), and a declining relationship between the political system and the people.

And 30 years later, as Shirley read her *Weekend Australian*, she'd find supporting evidence of same on every page.

Politicians' refusal to face the facts on climate change was appalling (and greedy, too, considering they only do it to avoid putting their corporate mates out of work!) and economically irresponsible, and hitting the poorest people most. One of Shirley's favourite journos wrote that we're entering the 'realm of third world countries' with residential power disconnections rising by as much as 140 per cent and the average household paying more than double to keep the lights on than it did a decade ago. Global powers had already spent a trillion dollars subsidising wind and solar power, but they haven't achieved one per cent of world energy provision, and global emissions over the past 20 years have been reduced by less than one per cent!

'So much for inspiration,' she thought, fast losing the will to keep turning the pages.

Who would have believed there'd be a rise in religious fanaticism so long after the Iranian revolution in 1979? Another misjudgement in Western policy? The last religious wars were in the 17th century and the progress of science and technology had reduced religious belief since then, so why did this Middle Eastern rage begin? The economic despair of people toiling in backward economies? The sexual frustration of young men living under a regime that prohibits sex before marriage? Shirley decided not to go there. An article featuring the Vatican's third most senior official headed the next page and she'd read enough of the Royal Commission into Institutional Responses to Child Sexual Abuse, not to mention her long ago acquaintance with Cardinal George Pell.

The ancient Greeks had believed for centuries that the world was going to end and became quite pragmatic about the dissolution of civilisation.

She binned the paper and went to make herself a coffee. Pragmatism wasn't going to be easy. This, after all, was her *life*.

A handful of friends

Looking back could be equally as confronting as reading the paper, but she was resolved.

'Where should I begin though?' she asked aloud. The cover of *Great Expectations* by Charles Dickens caught her eye from its home on her bookshelf.

'At the beginning,' she imagined the writer himself replying wearily.

One of her mother's favourite pieces of advice gave her some perspective. 'If you can count your friends on one hand by the time you're my age, you'll be doing exceptionally well.'

Shirley had already lived 12 years more than her mother and could still count her true friends on one hand, but it was only a POV. Over the course of her life there had been many people who'd been or still were major influences. They'd made significant contributions to each of her seven ages.

First Age? Okay. Full of learning, 'starring,' moving on and settling in again, and growing up fast in a loving environment with exceptional parents and a very special sister.

Lingering memories of bullies and sexual harassers, including her friend Lyn's father, were long since put away. Lyn Abels, nee Armstrong, whom she met at Camberwell High in 1958 recouped together from her father's abuse and never discussed it again.

> **Lyn Armstrong** married a New Zealander, gave birth to a daughter, left the marriage a year later and returned home to Melbourne where she met John Abels, sole parent of a daughter of the same age. They married, brought up their girls as sisters, and are now proud grandparents. Lyn and John live on the

Mornington Peninsula and were close neighbours until Shirley sold up in 2002.

Lyn's daughter, Leilani, is a successful business woman, her partner is 12 years younger and the love of her life and they have a two year-old son.

John's first wife died from complications of multiple sclerosis and his daughter Amanda was diagnosed with MS aged 24. Now also 43, she's stable but struggles sometimes and only her husband and parents know. 'I have it, it doesn't have me,' she says.

Second Age? Long-awaited freedom! Her most coveted was that of her 'first time'; the setting on board the *Castel Felice* was flawless, as was the lover. How lucky she'd been to meet Andreas, who'd given her a literary introduction to sex and facilitated her safe journey to Hong Kong. Her subsequent employment as secretary to the inimitable Gertrude Johnson at The Princess Theatre was equally fortuitous and life-changing when Miss Johnson's mentoring inadvertently awakened her to the fact that she wasn't cut out to be an actress.

She'd been a happy, ambitious 20 year-old when she married her first husband, an ordinary, gentle, likeable young man. The loss of the twins, Allan's departure overseas and the death of her mother inside five months were the catalysts for their parting, but it had been a mistake from the start. They had little in common beyond the desire to be loved.

Allan Uebergang later remarried and had children. The aunty who'd hosted their honeymoon on a farm in Lutheran country, central Victoria in 1967, tracked Shirley down in 1995 and called to congratulate her on her latest book. Allan was still in the police force but had contracted a rare and debilitating disease that saw him confined to a wheel chair for many years. The marriage didn't survive but he'd miraculously recovered and was in charge of a police station in or near Warrnambool, the place of his birth.

Her Third Age took off in an American whirlwind, with high hopes for a fabulous future. During those 12 months, flatmate Vickie and her Wallington Brother employers respectively made and marred her, for life. Well, for a while anyway.

Unlike most of the men in Shirley's life, none of the Yanks resurfaced.

> **Pete and Mick Wallington** had orchestrated her deportation, she'd kept her counsel and they kept their promise. She'd lied to avoid meeting **Sinatra** on the first setup, and declined a second when Frankie visited for the next thousand-dollars-a-set tennis match in OKC. A potential affair with a man called **Jones** might have been cool, but Tom was last seen exiting the Grand Ole Opry car park in 1972.
>
> Just for the record, Mick's still alive and lives in Florida; 96 and still wheeling and dealing!

She'd never quite get over the Golden Eagle plane crash that killed the woman who'd taken her place, or the distressing news that Vickie Morris had been interned in a mental home in Washington State two years after Shirley's 1993 follow-up visit to the States.

But the lessons learned in America far outweighed the downsides they had wrought. Being rescued by her father and travelling the world with him had renewed her soul and strengthened her resolve to 'make the most of everything'. Likewise, the trials and tribulations of her television career that followed, including her bullied exit, merged into one amazing experience. She knew Margery would be proud she'd maintained her standards to the end.

She'd made a lifelong friend in Helen Keightley, and launched a promising career at the South Australian Film Corporation in Adelaide, but concluded the Third Age with another ill-chosen husband. How little she'd learned by the age of 25!

> **Nick Bond, a.k.a. James** continued to visit friends they'd made together in 1973 in London, and years later Shirley received a letter from one of those friends whose husband had finally told

Nick to fuck off. The letter served as an apology for misjudging her when she left him so early in the marriage. Nick had been visiting them unannounced for years, always following another breakthrough (read breakdown) with one enterprise or another, but they caught him stealing some cash from her wallet and finally grasped what a 'rotten, lying, two-faced bastard' he was. He'd be dead now, and probably not from natural causes.

When the Fourth Age dawned, Tim Black had become a major client, as had Darren McKay. She was running her entertainment agency, living with Allan Eaton, and could count on one hand the friends she'd made during those five, frenetic years.

There was Beris – and Susie Coles, Col Elliott, Geraldine Doyle and Horizontal Paddy. She'd lost her beloved Miss B, but Susie and husband Carl, Col and wife Kaz, and Gerro and Paddy remain in touch.

> **Markeeta Little Wolf** secured a new manager in Australia and continued to perform for several years but returned to America with her mother in the early 80s and went into real estate. She married an American and was the Mayor of Waitsburg, Washington for some years. In 2011, 25 years after quitting showbiz, she returned to the stage for a one-off performance.
>
> **Omar Sharif** stopped sending postcards and didn't bother to contact her when he returned to Australia for a season at the Princess Theatre.

Another five years in the people business followed with Chandler and McLeod, where she learned a great deal about the human condition and established lifelong bonds with Robyn Williams, Diane Tiffin, Jenny Casson and Lois Wood.

Shirley's special friendship with Barry Ewen had all but ended when a chance meeting in Sydney led to four years of freelance consulting, 'Shirley's Place' in Balmain, and the development of several enduring friendships.

Kristina Rixon ('Boppy') returned to Albury, married Andrew White and had four children, who are now grown up. Boppy and Shirley have continued to visit each other down the years, especially on important birthdays, and Boppy will visit the Mounts in 2017 to celebrate her 50th and Shirley's 70th. (Jeff says, 'House guests are like fish, they go off after three days,' but it's never been a problem with Kristina!)

Gaby Dongés and **Aviator John** continue to live in the homes in which Shirley first met them in Sydney. Gaby and her children and grandchildren are doing well but her wonderful partner, Chris Fletcher, passed away recently following a short illness.

Jan Bray, who has just turned 60, is a lifetime fund raiser for the National Breast Cancer Foundation, lives on the Sunshine Coast at Pacific Paradise and has been the Community Development Manager for the Mother's Day Classic for the last five years. Her husband Graeme's memory has gone and she visits him most days in a nursing home nearby.

Alessia Bighi and her brother have continued to run the 'Marfy' empire in Ferrara, Italy. Whilst Alessia is happily divorced, the ever-increasing intake of refugees and Italy's near bankrupt economy motivated her to work through a maze of rules and regulations to enrol her teenage children, Aurora and Gabriele, in Australian schools. Finally visas have been issued, they are due to arrive in Sydney in late November 2017, and hope to be able to settle here permanently.

These friendships sustained her through some difficult years. The world had once again become her oyster when she returned to Hawthorn and opened **gourmet away**. When she sold up two years later, she rented her house to the Hawthorn Football Club and took Jenny on a 12 month working holiday to England, via the world.

Age Six

The penultimate Fifth Age was a medley of triumph, trouble and tragedy. At times, she'd wondered if it would be her last!

But it had also been when she achieved her dream to write what she wanted to write – and make a living at it! Well, with the help of Stott's freelance income, support from dear friends Geoff and Lesley Beaumont, nee Wright, and a lot of hard work at the desk and on the road.

She smiled at her published books, casually stacked and looking a bit tired on the bottom shelf of her bookcase. 'I'm sorry it took me so long to create you,' she said, reflecting then that half of them wouldn't be there without the abilities, and stick-ability of her volatile literary agent, Shelley Power, who lived in Paris.

In 2004, Beris sent Shirley eight pages of outrageous headline stories (with photos of everyone involved) from London's tabloid press that shed new light on Shelley, literary agents in general and the publishing business at large.

Divorcee, 61, dating murderer Bamber

MURDERER Jeremy Bamber is dating from behind bars a divorcee 20 years his senior and has planned their first night together if he wins his bid for freedom. Shelley Power met Bamber, 41, as she worked with him on a book about the events of the night when five of his family were shot dead.

He is serving five life sentences for killing his adoptive parents Nevill and June Bamber, half-sister Sheila Caffell and her two sons 17 years ago. He is awaiting the result of an appeal against his conviction for the massacre at his family's Essex farm house. If it is successful, he could walk free within days…

The woman he has promised to spend his first taste of freedom with is 61-year-old Mrs Power, a literary agent who has attended his 12-day Appeal Court hearing daily…

There were several unexpected life-of-the-book friendships that evolved during the exhausting book tours and research assignments, but one special friend endured – and continues to grow to this day.

Dr George B. Holmes, Jr. whom Shirley first met on a bus from Alice Springs to Uluru (Ayres Rock) in 1993 whilst researching her novel *Billy Batchelor*, became a lifelong friend. An internationally renowned professor of orthopaedic surgery, George is heading towards retirement and he and wife Ann are enjoying more time with their children and grandchildren, and overseas friends.

Shirley and Jeff continue to visit them at home in Chicago, and holiday in their 'second home' in New Zealand. George and Ann reciprocate in Tasmania.

Her Fifth Age had been many things but 'boring' wasn't one of them.
She'd arrived home in time to spend many happy days with her father during his last precious months on earth and that was a blessing beyond words.

Making the most of everything

In early 2014 Shirley and Jeff decided it was time to set a plan for retirement. Their friendships in Hobart were solid and would hopefully not be affected by a change of address.

Firstly, sell Tinderbox. They'd had seven wonderful years living there, but it was beyond their needs now. Secondly, sell the practice. Jeff would continue some pro bono activities post retirement but 43 years of dentistry, the last 30 performing daily surgical procedures in the confines of people's mouths had taken its toll on his right hand. He'd loved it, but it was time to stop.

The third decision they needed to make was unresolved. Where did they want to live? Hobart, or Launceston, the state's 'Northern capital' that has been described as an easy place to live with big city benefits? Whilst Jeff worked hard finding a buyer for his practice, Shirley jumped back into real estate duties.

Tinderbox sold quickly. Shirley secured a rental for 12 months close to the city and began inspecting properties in Hobart. The only houses on the

Age Six

market at the time that met their short list of essentials were beyond their expectations, in size and price. The interest in Launceston was increasing.

Several times a year they'd rented a friend's shack in Miena during the fishing season and had made a coterie of like-minded friends, many of whom lived in Launy (pronounced 'Lonny'). Jeff had finally found a perfect *fishing cabin* to buy. Actually, it was a new house with wonderful views overlooking the Great Lake in central Tassie. A couple of months later, they found a perfect property in Launceston – an old house this time, in need of some renovations, with equally wonderful views overlooking the city and the mountains beyond.

They moved to Prospect in Launy on the 1st September 2015. Jeff commuted to Hobart three days a week until settlement of the practice in December.

Shirley was supervising the ongoing renovations when she discovered that her very first boyfriend, David Streeter, lived five minutes away! Talk about coming full circle. He was a neighbour again! She couldn't explain it if she tried, but he didn't seem to have changed at all. He was simply a 72 year old version of himself.

David had married Mal 47 years ago and they have two daughters and three grandchildren, who live on the mainland. They ran their own businesses for most of their lives and had recently retired. A teenage romance 57 years ago had suddenly blossomed into a close friendship between four retired seniors.

It hadn't been mentioned, but in the early days the repartee at dinner parties was becoming tedious when Shirley would answer the persistent question of 'how did you guys meet?'

Shirley would begin: 'We were at Warracknabeal High School together. I was 13 and David was 15,' she'd smile, and pause.

'David was my very first boyfriend!' she'd exclaim. 'He taught me to kiss in the back lane after school!'

David would sometimes get a chance to say, 'and Shirley was my first girlfriend!'

Mal must have decided there and then that she'd heard this story once too often and spoke up authoritatively.

'Excuse me please, but it was *Shirley* who taught David to kiss!'

Looking forward – with love

> *To you I give myself, for I am yours*
> Rosalind and Orlando, As You Like It

Shirley's 60s were nearly over when Jeff began planning a stunning surprise holiday to Aitutaki in the Cook Islands for her 70th birthday.

A thousand memories of an exciting, hazardous, sad and joyous life rushed in and despite, or probably because of her seventh age looming fast, she began to reflect on the most wondrous of all human experience: love.

She'd had more than her share from the day she was born, yet to meet her soul mate in her 50s had been the biggest surprise and the greatest gift of all. The evolution of the love she shared with Jeff had initiated true self-discovery, profound generosity, trust and surrender.

'Giving and receiving is all that we have and everything that we are,' she said to her old nemesis, the kitchen clock. 'How lucky was I to be born with flawed teeth!'

She thought of the loves of her life that whilst no longer of the mortal realm remained larger than life in her memories. She took up her mother's faded, hard-back copy of *Shakespeare's Complete Works* and some special diaries and folders and gave herself over to nostalgia for a few minutes.

Her biggest loss had been Margery. When she opened *Macbeth* she remembered that Shakespeare tended to resort to the natural world in search of metaphors for mothers. His Lady Macduff said it all, bringing tears to her eyes.

'The poor wren, the most diminutive of birds, will fight,
Her young ones in her nest, against the owl.'

Poor Margery, skeletal and weak, fought for her little girls, kept them close and taught them to be strong, no matter what came their way.

She searched for a verse to describe her love for Alan and was overwhelmed with abundant examples of dearly loved fathers. In *King Lear*, Goneril delivered the mother of all father speeches:

'Sir, I love you more than words can wield the matter;
Dearer than eye-sight, space, and liberty…
A love that makes breath poor, and speech unable;
Beyond all manner of so much I love you.'

It was a bit over the top, but every word rang true for the deep respect and love she had for her father.

The loss of the little pixie, Craig, still defied words. But in the face of it his parents had displayed valour that had been an example to all. They'd then transcended their own paradigm when their darling Gareth failed to wake one morning. Bev and Rob's courage had never failed; they'd got on with the living when life itself was more painful than death.

The Bard's pithy lines from *Macbeth* summed it up best:
'But screw your courage to the sticking-place,
And we'll not fail.'

Of many other losses, the person Shirley missed most was her dearest, oldest friend, who died on her 73rd birthday on 23rd October, 2008.

Beris had retired to Sydney several years earlier and was in good form when she visited Shirley and Jeff in Hobart, just a few months prior to undergoing the life-threatening surgery that ultimately killed her. Her son, Jason, flew to Sydney to be by her side and phoned Shirley with tearful updates during the longest week of his life. The first operation led to a second, requiring an emergency dash to another hospital and another surgical team. She stopped breathing on the fourth day and the coroner confirmed the cause of death was surgical complications following the removal of an aneurism.

Fortunately she never regained consciousness.

Shirley and Jeff visit Jason and his wife Jackie whenever they can when in Melbourne and they all talk about Beris as if she's still there.

She opened to the final pages of a folder containing the death verification of Jeff's wonderful father.

GJ had suffered long enough and died, thankfully in his sleep, aged 91.

At his funeral, the venue had overflowed with extended family and a lifetime of his friends and colleagues. Jeff's mother Marg had been confused and unsettled during the beautiful service. When she reached out to touch the coffin as her six strong grandsons carried it out to the hearse, there hadn't been a dry eye left in the house. She'd chatted to everyone in her inimitable style at the wake and eventually fell asleep on the couch. Although she seemed happy enough in the nursing home she'd been settled in near daughter Marianne, from time to time she would still ask when Graham would be coming home.

The last page in the folder had been inserted recently and her thoughts turned to Ken Moon, her former uni tutor and close friend, who'd died recently following several years in a nursing home suffering Alzheimer's. As her eyes welled up, Shirley reflected on Ken's friendship and mentoring that had made a difference to her life, professionally and personally.

Slowly she put Shakespeare and the 'deceased' files back on the shelves. The inevitability of death hung heavily in the air and she was reminded of just how quickly her sixth age was rushing by.

But this awareness didn't strike fear or sadness in her heart; rather, it was a cue that for her and her beloved Jeff there wasn't a moment to lose. Whatever their allotted time on earth might be, the time was now to enjoy the fruits of their labours. Retiring with no obligations beyond each other, family and friends was a big ask for both of them, and their decision to ease into an unknown world by fulfilling some dreams on their individual and joint bucket lists had been working a treat.

Whilst for both of them the unpredictability of the future had escalated with age, after 17 years together they'd never broken their wedding vows. They continued to make each other laugh many more times than the stipulated 'once a day'.

Shirley had grown to realise that without her loving upbringing, and the example of true courage and altruism provided her by Bev and Rob, she would never have truly come to know herself and in doing so find her soul mate.

> The **Gosbell** family continues to live life to the full.
>
> Following **Bev** and **Rob's** 50th wedding anniversary on 28 August 2015 they sold the family home and purchased an apartment in Rylands in Hawthorn. They haven't retired yet; both continue to work for charities, Bev still sings with the Monash Chorale and both play instruments in the Oakleigh Brass Band. Most of their precious free time is spent with their sons and grandchildren.
>
> **Steven and Dale** are in their late 40s. Steven and wife Robyn live in Melbourne and continue to run busy careers whilst bringing up Brooke (12) and Jade (10). Dale and wife Camille live in Sydney and are likewise committed to their respective careers whilst bringing up Madi (11) and Bailey (9).

Shirley had also worked out that at least half of her success, and probably most of her mistakes involved men. (When Jeff had said as much to her over the course of conversation, she'd pointed out that if he'd come along early he might have saved her – and a number of the men – a lot of pain.)

Her family had always said she was 'different'. Last year Bev had sent her a card with the message: 'You celebrate your birthday once a year? Ugh. How mainstream!' Inside, she'd written: 'Dear Shirl, You have never been mainstream!'

Shirley loved the card, recalling one similar she'd been given by her mother when she was young, yet she'd never understood exactly how she was unusual.

She'd gone through life assuming that the men who'd pursued for 40 years, most of whom were pre boomers, were chasing the 'free love' and 'rock 'n roll' of baby boomers, who'd likely seemed to be having much more fun.

It hadn't occurred to her that it was her independence and persona, and all that went with it that had attracted them. Whilst acknowledging some mistakes along the way, she'd put the lion's share of the blame down to the men, having guessed that all women of her age and single status were copping the same. She'd known for sure that Robyn did!

This logic, based on a statistic of two, made it easy to sidestep responsibility for her part in the game. With subjective judgment and a closed mind, what was there to question?

Four of her long-time men friends, with whom she was involved at one time or another, had eventually gone back to their first, second or third wives. Although four examples could only be viewed as anecdotal, she learned of all four because each man called to tell her – and they remarried their ex-wives, too!

She kind of 'got it' that she'd rejected them and they needed to tell her they'd been accepted again by a woman who'd never stopped loving them, but there was one man in the mix who should have opened her mind on two counts.

When Darren McKay tracked her down in Hobart, it suddenly became clear that she had totally misjudged at least his intentions.

Perhaps it was because she was different that all four had been deeply affected by her rejection? She'd lived a fabulous life of extremes, and felt so much at both ends of the spectrum… There was never a dull moment. The world was her oyster. And they'd wanted to share it.

During a long catch-up phone call, Darren had grilled her about her marriage. 'Are you happy?' and 'Is this the man you've been looking for all your life? What's he got that makes him The One?'

Before they'd eventually hung up, he'd said: 'The biggest regret of my life is Shirley McLaughlin.'

They put each other on their respective Christmas lists, he called from time to time and 12 months later rang to tell her he was re-marrying his second wife. It was his last contact and rightly so, but she would always regret how casually she had treated his reappearances over half a lifetime.

'Darren was a loyal friend and deserved better,' she summarised to Jeff at the end of a long conversation that had brought her full circle. 'You were a loyal friend for years, too,' she said, 'before we acknowledged our love and got together.'

'Does that mean I got better than I deserved?' he retorted, not missing a beat.

In Shirley's younger years, the three 'big ones' had been death, divorce and moving. In her sixth age, she'd acquired a different POV.

After waiting months for a diagnostic appointment, Shirley took Jeff with her to see a neurologist following the results of an MRI brain scan. They emerged an hour and a half later, palpably relieved.

The discovery of temporal lobe atrophy led to a diagnosis of a Mild Cognitive Impairment (MCI) that may well have begun with her premature birth and/or contraction of encephalitis at 18 months. Neurologist Emma confirmed that short of being hit by a bus, Shirley was going to make the Biblical three score years and 10 on the 13th May, 'and could well live sanely enough for another decade or more.'

She then advised that all her patient had to do was to accept that she was no longer exceptional.

'You're running about average,' she smiled warmly. 'Join the rest of us!'

Shirley said that she'd had an extraordinary life and had never been going to get out of here alive anyway.

The second event was entirely unexpected and remains a mystery.

During a visit to Adelaide, Jeff discovered via a former colleague that Dr Jack Cavander was alive and well and living alone in his recently deceased parent's home just out of town. Once in possession of Jack's mobile number,

Age Six

Shirley had wasted no time in contacting the man who'd indirectly led to her finding her soul mate.

By then in his early 70s, Jack had acknowledged that he had worked in the London surgery in July 1973, and that he'd worked in a surgery in inner Melbourne in 1978. He admitted to frequenting Carlton pubs and eating houses around that time and could recall the name and street number of the hotel in question. He'd also worked in Saudi Arabia from the late 80s through to 1997.

Everything had matched up until Shirley broached the topic of his family. He'd not only denied leaving a wife and three children behind in Adelaide, he'd also refuted having ever been married or having had children.

Sensing his defensiveness, Shirley reassured him that the details had probably been fabricated by rumourmongers or perhaps were the misguided product of Chinese whispers. But Jack's voice and demeanour towards her had changed by the time he replied.

He had no recollection of fixing her upper central incisor on that fateful afternoon in London. Similarly, he claimed he couldn't recall taking her to dinner, kissing her and asking her to stay in contact and phone his parents when she got home.

He stammered and coughed a little when the conversation had turned to their chance encounter in Carlton and eventually he'd concluded that he'd had lots of girlfriends. Along with a reiteration that he's never married, he asserted he was definitely not the dentist she was looking for. He'd even gone as far as to volunteer the name of another dentist he was 'pretty sure' *could* have been the one.

Jeff, however, had known the other man well and confirmed Shirley's suspicions when he told her he didn't fit the brief at all.

So ends the story of how Shirley met Jeff.

Facing the seventh age was looking like she'd have to accept three new big ones.

Death and taxes were definitely right, but she couldn't remember the third. She tried to think of a word to sum up Emma's diagnosis and suddenly got it: Taxes, dementia and death.

'Bugger,' she shrugged to the flashing modem on her desk. 'Everything but love goes away in the end.'

6th Intermission

Easter Saturday,
25th March, 2005

Derrick & Chris Setchell, UK
Tom Boland, Sydney

Dr & Mrs Jeff Mount

Rob & Bev

The girls from around Australia

With Alessia in Ferrara

Say it and Smile!

Dr Jeffrey D Mount
B.D.S. (Adel.), M.Sc.(Lond.), F.R.A.C.D.S., F.A.D.I.
Restorative Dentistry

Dr Jeffrey D Mount & Associates
Dr Peter Alldritt
Dr Alister Dickson

Dental Surgeons
25 King William Street
Adelaide SA 5000 Australia

The Incisor
SOUTH AUSTRALIAN FOUNDATION FOR DENTAL EDUCATION AND RESEARCH INC.

Issue 3
May 2004

Board of Management

Patron
Prof. W R Hume

President and Chair
Dr J D Mount

Vice-President
Dr I McI Smylie

Secretary/Treasurer
Mr R S Powers

Trustee Members
Dr J K Denton
Mr M J Williams

Members
Dr B Kardachi
Dr N Paniyaris
Dr B W Phillips
Dr D Wilson

ADA Representative
Dr C Pazios

University Appointments
Prof Neville Marsh
    Deputy Vice Chancellor
Prof D B Frewin
    Executive Dean
    Faculty of Health Sciences
Assoc Prof V B Burgess
    Dean of the Dental School

Honorary Executive
Officer & Secretary:
Mr R S Powers
Ms H Lewis

Advertising, letters/articles,
editing and production
inquiries
The Incisor
Shirley McLaughlin
Phone 08 8363 5877
Fax 08 8363 2177
Mobile 0417 253589

Dental nurse, Sue, Accountant, Trina in Adelaide

Dr Jeff Mount says: 'One of my greatest pleasures is reviewing patients who've been seeing the hygienist for many years and being able to look back over their treatment cards and see notations "Nothing to be done" year after year. This tells me we have a Preventive Care Program that works.'

Keep your teeth healthy and white
Visit your Hygienist every six months

Steven and Dale Gosbell

Ann & George Holmes, Chicago

Rick & Julie Roblee, Fayetteville AR

Jeff's 2nd best catch

The Hobart Girls' Lunch Group

Tinderbox, Hobart, Tasmania

Geoff & Lesley Wright (Williams)

Marie vanSteyne

Scotty, Matthew & Ned and Stan Goodman

Mal & David Streeter

Camille & Dale

Steven & Robyn

Jane & Jeff Hadley

The Gosbell Family - 50th Wedding Anniversary 28/08/2015

Graham Mount
19th December 1924 ~ 26th May 2016

Diane & Beris

The World's Your Oyster!

AGE SEVEN (2017 –   )

Last scene of all
That ends this strange eventful history,
Is second childishness, and mere oblivion:
Lovely teeth, but sans eyes, sans taste, sans everything.

So many photos, all taken with love and remembrance of the best days of her life. What would Shirley have done without them, or the countless written records she'd kept to refresh her memories of the life she has lived and the people she has loved?

Most telling, would she have conceived the idea of summonsing her beloved nephews as narrators of the memoir she was never going to write, but for the encouragement and support of her inimitable soul mate, Jeff? It has taken two years, and he's been with her all the way.

Getting to 70 has certainly been one hell of a ride, and it isn't over yet. The last 25 years are supposed to rush by like 10, so if she should live beyond 75 she'll be at a crossroad with no sign posts. That will of course be perfect for her; she's been navigating unchartered territory since she got out of nappies.

According to early reviewers of the Bard's plays, the only weakness of *As You Like It* was its hasty close. Shirley, however, is comfortable with the idea of a quick end…as long as there is plenty of rich Shakespearean drama until the curtain falls.

To her mind, protagonist Rosalind's 'Epilogue' doesn't flag or lose interest, its wit doesn't fail and it is faithful to life to the end. What more could you want?

EPILOGUE

It is not the fashion to see the lady the Epilogue; but it is no more unhandsome than to see the lord the Prologue.

If it be true that good wine needs no bush, tis true that a good play needs no epilogue; yet to good wine they do use good bushes, and good plays prove the better by the help of good epilogues. What a case am I in then, that am neither a good epilogue nor cannot insinuate with you in the behalf of a good play! I am not furnished like a beggar, therefore to beg will not become me: my way is to conjure you, and I'll begin with the women.

I charge you, O women, for the love you bear to men, to like as much of this play as please you; and I charge you, O men, for the love you bear to women (as I perceive by your simpering, none of you hates them), that between you and the women the play may please. *As I am a woman*, I would kiss as many of you as had beards that pleased me, complexions that liked me, and breaths that I defied not; and, I am sure, as many as have good beards or good faces or sweet breaths will, for my kind offer, when I make curtsey, bid me farewell.

www.ingramcontent.com/pod-product-compliance
Lightning Source LLC
Chambersburg PA
CBHW080344300426
44110CB00019B/2503